Advances in Fractional Order Derivatives and Their Applications

Advances in Fractional Order Derivatives and Their Applications

Editor

Sameerah Jamal

 Basel • Beijing • Wuhan • Barcelona • Belgrade • Novi Sad • Cluj • Manchester

Editor
Sameerah Jamal
School of Mathematics
University of the Witwatersrand
Johannesburg
South Africa

Editorial Office
MDPI
St. Alban-Anlage 66
4052 Basel, Switzerland

This is a reprint of articles from the Special Issue published online in the open access journal *Fractal and Fractional* (ISSN 2504-3110) (available at: www.mdpi.com/journal/fractalfract/special_issues/fractional_derivative).

For citation purposes, cite each article independently as indicated on the article page online and as indicated below:

Lastname, A.A.; Lastname, B.B. Article Title. *Journal Name* **Year**, *Volume Number*, Page Range.

ISBN 978-3-0365-8699-1 (Hbk)
ISBN 978-3-0365-8698-4 (PDF)
doi.org/10.3390/books978-3-0365-8698-4

© 2023 by the authors. Articles in this book are Open Access and distributed under the Creative Commons Attribution (CC BY) license. The book as a whole is distributed by MDPI under the terms and conditions of the Creative Commons Attribution-NonCommercial-NoDerivs (CC BY-NC-ND) license.

Contents

About the Editor vii

Preface ix

Reginald Champala, Sameerah Jamal and Suhail Khan
Fractional Pricing Models: Transformations to a Heat Equation and Lie Symmetries
Reprinted from: *Fractal Fract.* 2023, 7, 632, doi:10.3390/fractalfract7080632 1

Wenjuan Yao, Yi Huang, Boying Wu and Zhongxiang Zhou
Image Enhancement Model Based on Fractional Time-Delay and Diffusion Tensor
Reprinted from: *Fractal Fract.* 2023, 7, 569, doi:10.3390/fractalfract7080569 13

Emad Awad, Sharifah E. Alhazmi, Mohamed A. Abdou and Mohsen Fayik
Anomalous Thermally Induced Deformation in Kelvin–Voigt Plate with Ultrafast Double-Strip Surface Heating
Reprinted from: *Fractal Fract.* 2023, 7, 563, doi:10.3390/fractalfract7070563 47

Oscar Herrera-Alcántara and Josué R. Castelán-Aguilar
Fractional Gradient Optimizers for PyTorch: Enhancing GAN and BERT
Reprinted from: *Fractal Fract.* 2023, 7, 500, doi:10.3390/fractalfract7070500 70

Aatef Hobiny and Ibrahim Abbas
The Effect of Fractional Derivatives on Thermo-Mechanical Interaction in Biological Tissues during Hyperthermia Treatment Using Eigenvalues Approach
Reprinted from: *Fractal Fract.* 2023, 7, 432, doi:10.3390/fractalfract7060432 83

McSylvester Ejighikeme Omaba, Hamdan Al Sulaimani, Soh Edwin Mukiawa, Cyril Dennis Enyi and Tijani Abdul-Aziz Apalara
Combined Liouville–Caputo Fractional Differential Equation
Reprinted from: *Fractal Fract.* 2023, 7, 366, doi:10.3390/fractalfract7050366 98

Jollet Truth Kubayi and Sameerah Jamal
Lie Symmetries and Third- and Fifth-Order Time-Fractional Polynomial Evolution Equations
Reprinted from: *Fractal Fract.* 2023, 7, 125, doi:10.3390/fractalfract7020125 113

Abdelkader Moumen, Hamid Boulares, Jehad Alzabut, Fathi Khelifi and Moheddine Imsatfia
New Results for Homoclinic Fractional Hamiltonian Systems of Order $\alpha \in (1/2, 1]$
Reprinted from: *Fractal Fract.* 2022, 7, 39, doi:10.3390/fractalfract7010039 128

Xiaoming Wang, Ghazala Akram, Maasoomah Sadaf, Hajra Mariyam and Muhammad Abbas
Soliton Solution of the Peyrard–Bishop–Dauxois Model of DNA Dynamics with M-Truncated and β-Fractional Derivatives Using Kudryashov's R Function Method
Reprinted from: *Fractal Fract.* 2022, 6, 616, doi:10.3390/fractalfract6100616 140

Wen Cao and Yufeng Xu
Collocation Method for Optimal Control of a Fractional Distributed System
Reprinted from: *Fractal Fract.* 2022, 6, 594, doi:10.3390/fractalfract6100594 154

Minghao Wang, Enli Chen, Ruilan Tian and Cuiyan Wang
The Nonlinear Dynamics Characteristics and Snap-Through of an SD Oscillator with Nonlinear Fractional Damping
Reprinted from: *Fractal Fract.* 2022, 6, 493, doi:10.3390/fractalfract6090493 167

Gangwei Wang, Bo Shen, Mengyue He, Fei Guan and Lihua Zhang
Symmetry Analysis and PT-Symmetric Extension of the Fifth-Order Korteweg-de Vries-LikeEquation
Reprinted from: *Fractal Fract.* **2022**, *6*, 468, doi:10.3390/fractalfract6090468 . . . . **191**

Kang-Jia Wang and Feng Shi
A New Perspective on the Exact Solutions of the Local Fractional Modified Benjamin–Bona–Mahony Equation on Cantor Sets
Reprinted from: *Fractal Fract.* **2023**, *7*, 72, doi:10.3390/fractalfract7010072 . . . . **200**

About the Editor

Sameerah Jamal

Sameerah Jamal received her Ph.D in 2013 from the School of Mathematics, Faculty of Science, University of the Witwatersrand, Johannesburg, South Africa. At present, she is an Associate Professor in the same department. Her research interests are exact solutions and symmetries of differential equations, and she has published more than 60 articles in peer-reviewed journals.

Preface

This reprint is a compilation of advanced applications in fractional calculus. The subject of fractional order differential equations has eclipsed modern day scientific research in a profound way. There are now an uncountable number of techniques, both analytical and numerical, aimed at developing a deep understanding of such equations. The various theories and types of derivatives continue to evolve and enrich the known literature. In this reprint, in a series of articles, we delve into some of the exciting and multi-faceted implementations of fractional order derivatives.

Sameerah Jamal
Editor

Article

Fractional Pricing Models: Transformations to a Heat Equation and Lie Symmetries

Reginald Champala [1], Sameerah Jamal [1,2,*] and Suhail Khan [3]

1. School of Mathematics, University of the Witwatersrand, Johannesburg 2001, South Africa; 1114409@students.wits.ac.za
2. DSI-NRF Centre of Excellence in Mathematical and Statistical Sciences (CoE-MaSS), Johannesburg 2001, South Africa
3. Department of Mathematics, University of Peshawar, Peshawar 25120, Khyber Pakhtoonkhwa, Pakistan; suhail@uop.edu.pk
* Correspondence: sameerah.jamal@wits.ac.za

Abstract: The study of fractional partial differential equations is often plagued with complicated models and solution processes. In this paper, we tackle how to simplify a specific parabolic model to facilitate its analysis and solution process. That is, we investigate a general time-fractional pricing equation, and propose new transformations to reduce the underlying model to a different but equivalent problem that is less challenging. Our procedure leads to a conversion of the model to a fractional 1 + 1 heat transfer equation, and more importantly, all the transformations are invertible. A significant result which emerges is that we prove such transformations yield solutions under the Riemann–Liouville and Caputo derivatives. Furthermore, Lie point symmetries are necessary to construct solutions to the model that incorporate the behaviour of the underlying financial assets. In addition, various graphical explorations exemplify our results.

Keywords: bond option pricing; Black–Scholes model; Riemann–Liouville; heat equation

1. Introduction

In recent times, fractional-based models are at the forefront in financial modelling. Such models display two very important properties: self-similarity and long-range dependence [1–3]. In [4], it was further posed that stock price volatility is well described by fractional Brownian motion since it has random-like features to portray uneven fluctuations in stock price. This is one of the many reasons why fractional derivatives are preferred in many spheres. Moreover, based on the collective arguments in the literature, such as [5–8], the time-fractional Black–Scholes equation is consistent with the integer-order Black–Scholes model in the limit as the order of the fractional derivative tends to one. In [9], the fractional Black–Scholes equation was solved by using the Green's function.

Taking into account the above discussion, we consider the general fractional bond pricing equation

$$\frac{\partial^\alpha V}{\partial t^\alpha} + \frac{1}{2}\rho^2 S^{2\gamma}\frac{\partial^2 V}{\partial S^2} + (\kappa - \lambda\rho S^\gamma + \beta S)\frac{\partial V}{\partial S} - SV = 0, \quad V(S,t), \tag{1}$$

where $\kappa, \beta, \rho, \lambda$ (the market price of risk) and γ are constants, t is time, S is the stock price or instantaneous short-term interest rate at current time t and $V(S,t)$ is the current value of the bond. As expected, α ($0 < \alpha < 1$) is the order of the fractional derivative, and an integer order model is obtained for $\alpha = 1$.

Equation (1) is a parabolic partial differential equation (PDE) with various versions, for example, the Vasicek $\gamma = 0$, Dothan $\kappa = \beta = 0, \gamma = 1$ and Cox–Ingersoll model $\gamma = 1/2, \lambda = 0$ [10–13]. In [14], the above model was considered subject to classical derivatives and a boundary condition.

Transformations are a fascinating subject, and have been the central driving force of mathematics for more than a century. In the 19th century in particular, the concept of transformations and permutations led to groundbreaking mathematical advancements, i.e., the discovery of new geometries and algebraic instruments. Since then, the study of transformations has grown in leaps and bounds. As an instrument in the study of all possible types of differential equations, transformations are the heart and soul of analytical solution techniques. Furthermore, transformative methods may sometimes be used in conjunction with numerical approaches. Explicitly, transformations simplify the equation, either by creating an easier form of the equation, or through combining variables, and thereby decreasing the number of variables. The only challenge, of course, is the calculation of such transformations.

In this paper, we construct several transformations that are crucial in simplifying the above model. We also apply another type of transformation later on in the study, this time calculated from symmetry methods [15]. In a profound and unique way, a symmetry of a differential equation is a transformation (or mapping) of its solution manifold into itself.

The aim of this paper is twofold: firstly, to construct equivalence formulae that transforms the given fractional equation into a fractional heat transfer equation. This process is, to the best of our knowledge, the first of its kind for this model. Secondly, through rigorous mathematical proofs, we provide symmetry invariant solutions to the original equation. To support these theoretical observations, graphical examples are presented under the proposed fractional framework. Results indicate that such a study is highly effective in financial modelling.

The plan of the paper is as follows. In Section 2, we note the fractional derivatives to be applied in the theory below. Section 3 is the main section, where we introduce the parameters and transformations required to manipulate the fractional model (1) into the fractional heat equation. We further define some elementary properties of the heat equation followed by novel symmetry-generated solutions of the pricing model (1). Finally, in Section 4, we end with a meaningful discussion of the obtained solutions.

2. Preliminaries

We define the two fractional derivatives used in this paper, more detailed properties of these derivatives are well-known and can be found in the literature cited here. We note that many other fractional derivates exist, but we limit ourselves to two of the most popular ones. A wealth of knowledge on fractional calculus can be found in the texts [16,17] to establish a comprehensive grasp of the subject material. Let α be any positive real number and n be a natural number such that $n - 1 \leq \alpha < n$.

The Riemann–Liouville derivative of order α is defined as [18]:

$$D_t^\alpha u(t,x) = \frac{1}{\Gamma(n-\alpha)} \frac{\partial^n}{\partial t^n} \int_0^t (t-\tilde{\tau})^{n-\alpha-1} u(\tilde{\tau},x) d\tilde{\tau}. \qquad (2)$$

Similarly, the Caputo derivative of order α is defined as [18]:

$$D_t^\alpha u(t,x) = \frac{1}{\Gamma(n-\alpha)} \int_0^t (t-\tilde{\tau})^{n-\alpha-1} \frac{\partial^n}{\partial t^n} u(\tilde{\tau},x) d\tilde{\tau}. \qquad (3)$$

The methods used involve symmetries of differential equations, which have been extended to FDEs by the works [19–22], both in the Riemann–Liouville and Caputo sense, with interesting discussions in the publications [23–25].

First, we recall the basic theory for finding symmetries under a Riemann–Liouville time-fractional derivative. Consider the equation

$$\frac{\partial^\alpha u}{\partial t^\alpha} = M(x,t,u,u_x,u_{xx}), \qquad (4)$$

where $0 < \alpha < 1$ is the parameter describing the order of the fractional time derivative.

Suppose that (4) is invariant under the one-parameter Lie group of point transformations:

$$
\begin{aligned}
\bar{t} &= t + \epsilon\tau(x,t,u) + O(\epsilon^2),\\
\bar{x} &= x + \epsilon\xi(x,t,u) + O(\epsilon^2),\\
\bar{u} &= u + \epsilon\eta(x,t,u) + O(\epsilon^2),\\
\frac{\partial^\alpha \bar{u}}{\partial \bar{t}^\alpha} &= \frac{\partial^\alpha u}{\partial t^\alpha} + \epsilon\eta_\alpha^0(x,t,u) + O(\epsilon^2),\\
\frac{\partial \bar{u}}{\partial \bar{x}} &= \frac{\partial u}{\partial x} + \epsilon\eta^x(x,t,u) + O(\epsilon^2),\\
\frac{\partial^2 \bar{u}}{\partial \bar{x}^2} &= \frac{\partial^2 u}{\partial x^2} + \epsilon\eta^{xx}(x,t,u) + O(\epsilon^2),
\end{aligned}
\qquad (5)
$$

where ϵ is an infinitesimal parameter, and the standard prolongation formulae are:

$$
\begin{aligned}
\eta^x &= \eta_x + \eta_u u_x - (\xi_x + \xi_u u_x)u_x - (\tau_x + \tau_u u_x)u_t,\\
\eta^{xx} &= \eta_{xx} + 2\eta_{xu}u_x - 2\xi_{xu}u_x^2 - \xi_{xx}u_x - 2\tau_{ux}u_t u_x - \tau_{xx}u_t - \xi_{uu}u_x^3\\
&\quad - \tau_{uu}u_x^2 u_t + \eta_{uu}u_x^2 - 3\xi_u u_x u_{xx} - \tau_u u_t u_{xx} + \eta_u u_{xx} - 2\xi_x u_{xx}\\
&\quad - 2\tau_u u_x u_{tx} - 2\tau_x u_{tx}.
\end{aligned}
\qquad (6)
$$

By the generalised Leibniz rule and a generalisation of the chain rule, the prolongation formula under the Riemann–Liouville formulation is also [20]

$$
\begin{aligned}
\eta_\alpha^0 &= \frac{\partial^\alpha \eta}{\partial t^\alpha} + (\eta - \alpha D_t(\tau))\frac{\partial^\alpha u}{\partial t^\alpha} - u\frac{\partial^\alpha \eta_u}{\partial t^\alpha} + \mu + \sum_{n=1}^{\infty}\binom{\alpha}{n}D_t^n(\xi)D_t^{\alpha-n}(u_x)\\
&\quad + \sum_{n=1}^{\infty}\left[\binom{\alpha}{n}\frac{\partial^n}{\partial t^n}\eta_u - \binom{\alpha}{n+1}D_t^{n+1}(\tau)\right]D_t^{\alpha-n},
\end{aligned}
\qquad (7)
$$

and

$$
\begin{aligned}
\mu &= \sum_{n=2}^{\infty}\sum_{m=2}^{n}\sum_{k=2}^{m}\sum_{r=0}^{k-1}\binom{\alpha}{n}\binom{n}{m}\binom{k}{r}\frac{1}{k!}\frac{t^{n-\alpha}}{\Gamma(n+1-\alpha)}\\
&\quad \times (-u)^r\frac{\partial^m}{\partial t^m}\left(u^{k-r}\right)\frac{\partial^{n-m+k}\eta}{\partial t^{n-m}\partial u^k}.
\end{aligned}
\qquad (8)
$$

By convention, $\eta(x,t,u)$ is assumed to be linear in the variable u, so that μ vanishes. Let the symmetry generator

$$
X = \tau(x,t,u)\frac{\partial}{\partial t} + \xi(x,t,u)\frac{\partial}{\partial x} + \eta(x,t,u)\frac{\partial}{\partial u} \qquad (9)
$$

span the associated Lie algebra, and

$$
\tau(x,t,u) = \frac{dt^*}{d\epsilon}\bigg|_{\epsilon=0}, \quad \xi(x,t,u) = \frac{dx^*}{d\epsilon}\bigg|_{\epsilon=0}, \quad \eta(x,t,u) = \frac{du^*}{d\epsilon}\bigg|_{\epsilon=0}.
$$

Let $H = \frac{\partial^\alpha u}{\partial t^\alpha} - M(x,t,u,u_x,u_{xx})$; then, the infinitesimal criterion for invariance to determine symmetries is expressed as $XH = 0$, when $H = 0$, and where X is extended to all derivatives appearing in the equation through the appropriate prolongation. Moreover, the transformation (5) leaves invariant the lower limit of the fractional derivative $\frac{\partial^\alpha u}{\partial t^\alpha}$, i.e., we have the additional constraint:

$$
\tau(x,t,u)\bigg|_{t=0} = 0. \qquad (10)
$$

This procedure is algorithmic and yields the symmetries of a time-fractional equation.

The method outlined above is similar if the fractional derivative is Caputo, but with different general prolongation formulae—see [22] for full details. However, the most important notion is that both of these derivatives produce the same Lie point symmetries, so that symmetry calculations using just one of the derivatives is sufficient.

3. Main Results—New Transformations

This section has three parts to it: firstly, we establish the required transformations to change the above model into the 1 + 1 time-fractional heat transfer equation; secondly, we list the Lie group details that are relevant for our version of the fractional and classical heat equation in order to take our study further. Finally, we prove several theorems on the resulting solutions of Equation (1).

3.1. Transformation of Equation (1)

In this section, we establish successive transformations that convert Equation (1) to a version of the heat equation. The change of variables is necessary to apply some interesting symmetry results to the model (1). It turns out that (1) is transformable under certain forms of its arbitrary parameters. Hence, we prove the following result.

Theorem 1. *The fractional pricing model Equation (1) is reducible to the fractional heat equation*

$$\frac{\partial^\alpha \omega}{\partial \hat{t}^\alpha} - \frac{1}{\Gamma(\alpha+1)} \frac{\partial^2 \omega}{\partial y^2} = 0, \quad \omega \equiv \omega(y, \hat{t}), \tag{11}$$

under the specific parameter settings, viz. $\gamma = 2, \kappa = \beta = 0, \lambda = -\frac{1}{\rho}$, *and ρ is arbitrary. The transformations are*

$$\hat{t} = -t^\alpha, \tag{12}$$

$$y = -\frac{\sqrt{2}}{S\rho}. \tag{13}$$

Proof. A transformation of the independent variables of the form y and $\hat{t}$ reduces Equation (1) to

$$a(y)\frac{\partial V}{\partial y} + c(y)V + \Gamma(\alpha+1)\frac{\partial^\alpha V}{\partial \hat{t}^\alpha} - \frac{\partial^2 V}{\partial y^2} = 0, \tag{14}$$

where $V(y, \hat{t})$,

$$a(y) = y\left(-\frac{2}{y^2} - \frac{\sqrt{2}}{y\rho}\right),$$

and

$$c(y) = -\frac{\sqrt{2}}{y\rho}.$$

Thereafter, we let

$$V(y, \hat{t}) = \omega(y, \hat{t}) \cdot e^{-\phi(y,\hat{t})},$$

where

$$\phi(y, \hat{t}) = \frac{y}{\sqrt{2}\rho} + \log(y) + \frac{\hat{t}^\alpha}{2\rho^2 \alpha \Gamma(\alpha)\Gamma(\alpha+1)}, \tag{15}$$

and the result follows that Equation (1) is converted to the fractional heat Equation (11). □

3.2. The Heat Equation

The classical heat equation has appeared in many studies [26,27], and a fourth-order nonlocal heat model was recently explored in [28]. Indeed, we showcase here that the heat equation is of the most useful of PDEs. Equation (11) shares some group properties with the classical integer-order heat equation.

The Lie point symmetries of (11) are well known for $\alpha = 1$; they are:

$$Z_1 = \frac{\partial}{\partial y}, \quad Z_2 = \frac{\partial}{\partial \hat{t}}, \quad Z_3 = \omega \frac{\partial}{\partial \omega},$$

$$Z_4 = y\frac{\partial}{\partial y} + 2\hat{t}\frac{\partial}{\partial \hat{t}},$$

$$Z_5 = 2\hat{t}\frac{\partial}{\partial y} - y\omega\frac{\partial}{\partial \omega},$$

$$Z_6 = 4\hat{t}y\frac{\partial}{\partial y} + 4\hat{t}^2\frac{\partial}{\partial \hat{t}} - (y^2 + 2\hat{t})\omega\frac{\partial}{\partial \omega},$$

$$Z_\theta = \theta(y,\hat{t})\frac{\partial}{\partial \omega}, \tag{16}$$

where θ is an arbitrary solution of the heat equation, i.e., $\theta_{\hat{t}} = \theta_{yy}$. The first six symmetries form a six-dimensional Lie algebra with the last symmetry spanning an infinite-dimensional sub-algebra. The commutator relations are presented in Table 1.

Table 1. Lie commutator table for the symmetries of (11) when $\alpha = 1$.

(,)	Z_1	Z_2	Z_3	Z_4	Z_5	Z_6
Z_1	0	0	0	Z_1	$-Z_3$	$2Z_5$
Z_2	0	0	0	$2Z_2$	$2Z_1$	$4Z_4 - 2Z_3$
Z_3	0	0	0	0	0	0
Z_4	$-Z_1$	$-2Z_2$	0	0	Z_5	$2Z_6$
Z_5	Z_3	$-2Z_1$	0	$-Z_5$	0	0
Z_6	$-Z_5$	$2Z_3 - 4Z_4$	0	$-2Z_6$	0	0

For $0 < \alpha < 1$, following the procedure from Section 2, the Lie point symmetries of (11) are:

$$Z_1, \quad Z_3, \quad Z_7 = 2\hat{t}\frac{\partial}{\partial \hat{t}} + \alpha y\frac{\partial}{\partial y}, \quad Z_\theta. \tag{17}$$

The first 3 symmetries form a 3-dimensional Lie algebra with the last symmetry spanning an infinite-dimensional sub-algebra. The commutator relations are in Table 2.

Table 2. Lie commutator table for the symmetries of (11) when $0 < \alpha < 1$.

[,]	Z_1	Z_7	Z_3
Z_1	0	αZ_1	0
Z_7	$-\alpha Z_1$	0	0
Z_3	0	0	0

3.3. Invariant and Mittag-Leffler Solutions

Next, we consider a linear combination of symmetries $Z = Z_1 + bZ_3$ (b is an arbitrary constant), and the method of invariants yields the transformation

$$\omega(y,\hat{t}) = \psi(\hat{t})e^{by}, \tag{18}$$

so that Equation (11) becomes the fractional ordinary differential equation (FODE):

$$D_{\hat{t}}^\alpha \psi(\hat{t}) - \frac{b^2}{\Gamma(\alpha+1)}\psi(\hat{t}) = 0. \tag{19}$$

Theorem 2. *A solution $V(S,t)$ for the general pricing Equation (1) for $\alpha = 1$, and under the parameters $\gamma = 2, \kappa = \beta = 0, \lambda = -\frac{1}{\rho}, C$, and ρ are arbitrary, is the invariant solution:*

$$V(S,t) = -\frac{C\rho S}{\sqrt{2}} \exp\left(-b^2 t - \frac{\sqrt{2}b}{\rho S} + \frac{1}{\rho^2 S} + \frac{t}{2\rho^2}\right). \tag{20}$$

Proof. Since the symmetry generators Z_1 and Z_3 occur for integer-order derivatives, the combination $Z = Z_1 + bZ_3$ can be used to reduce the classical heat equation:

$$\omega_{\hat{t}} - \omega_{yy} = 0.$$

In this case, the reduction procedure leads to Equation (19) with $\alpha = 1$, and hence, the solution becomes:

$$\psi(\hat{t}) = C \exp\left(b^2 \hat{t}\right),$$

and Equation (18) presents that the classical heat equation has a solution of the form

$$\omega(y,\hat{t}) = C \exp\left(b^2 \hat{t} + by\right). \tag{21}$$

By Theorem 1, we reverse all transformations, and the result follows. □

An analogous result may be found for fractional-order derivatives. When $0 < \alpha < 1$, the solution of Equation (19) depends on the type of fractional derivative. Thus, we establish the following theorems and we note that as $\alpha \to 1$ in the theory below, we recover Theorem 2.

Theorem 3. *The general fractional pricing Equation (1), under a Riemann–Liouville fractional derivative with $0 < \alpha < 1$, and parameters $\gamma = 2, \kappa = \beta = 0, \lambda = -\frac{1}{\rho}$, and ρ arbitrary, admits the invariant solution:*

$$V(S,t) = -\frac{C\rho S}{\sqrt{2}} (-t^\alpha)^{\alpha-1} E_{\alpha,\alpha}\left(\frac{b^2(-t^\alpha)^\alpha}{\Gamma(\alpha+1)}\right) \exp\left(-\frac{\sqrt{2}b}{\rho S} + \frac{1}{\rho^2 S} - \frac{(-t^\alpha)^\alpha}{2\alpha\rho^2 \Gamma(\alpha)\Gamma(\alpha+1)}\right). \tag{22}$$

Proof. Under the Riemann–Liouville derivative, the solution of the FODE (19) is given by Laplace transforms, as

$$\psi(\hat{t}) = C\hat{t}^{\alpha-1} E_{\alpha,\alpha}\left(\frac{b^2}{\Gamma(\alpha+1)} \hat{t}^\alpha\right), \tag{23}$$

where $C = D^{-(1-\alpha)}\psi(0)$ [29], and $E_{\alpha,\alpha}$ is the generalised Mittag-Leffler function defined as

$$E_{\alpha,\alpha}(z) = \sum_{k=0}^{\infty} \frac{z^k}{\Gamma(\alpha k + \alpha)}, \tag{24}$$

with $\alpha > 0$. From (18), the solution of the fractional heat Equation (11) becomes

$$\omega(y,\hat{t}) = C\hat{t}^{\alpha-1} E_{\alpha,\alpha}\left(\frac{b^2}{\Gamma(\alpha+1)} \hat{t}^\alpha\right) e^{by}. \tag{25}$$

Thereafter, the result follows upon the application of Theorem 1 and its invertible transformations. □

In Figures 1 and 2, we showcase various graphical solutions from Theorem 3.

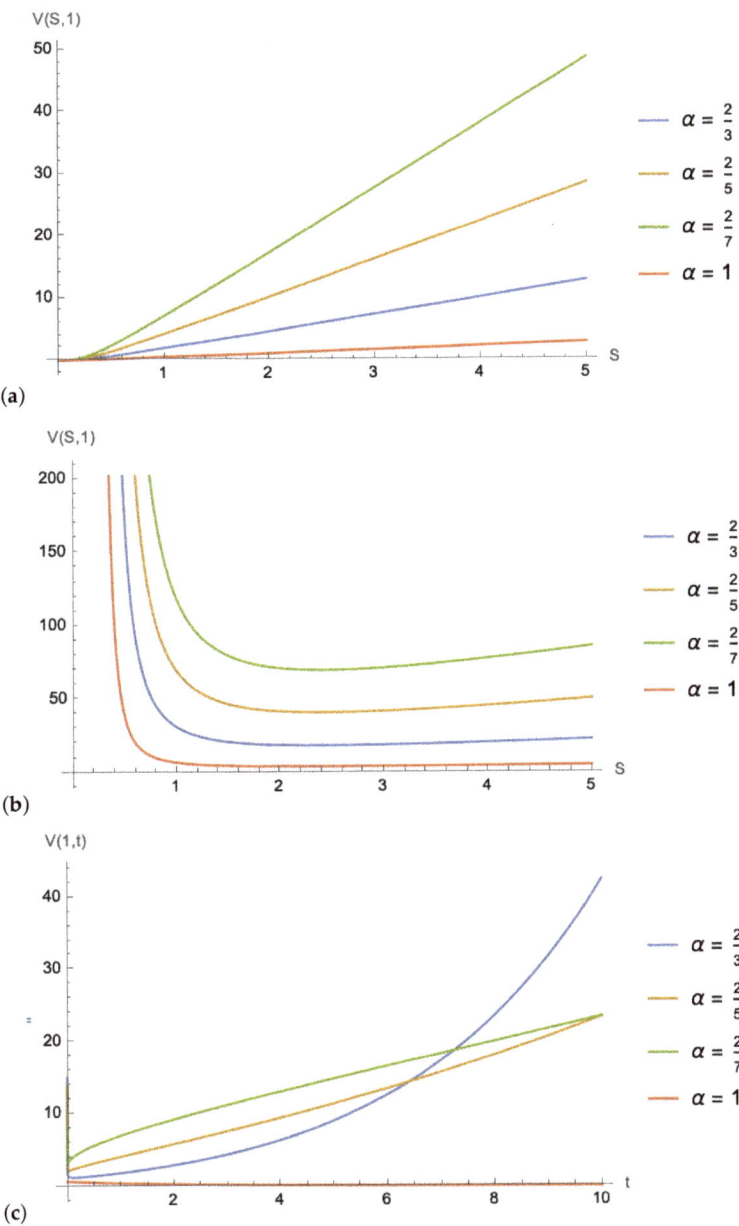

Figure 1. Graphical solutions of Equation (22) with various parameter selections. In (**a**), $b = (-1)^{\frac{\alpha}{2}}$, $C = \sqrt{2}, \rho = 1, t = 1$. In (**b**), $b = (-1)^{\frac{\alpha}{2}+1}, C = \sqrt{2}, \rho = 1, t = 1$. In (**c**), $b = (-1)^{\frac{\alpha}{2}}, C = \sqrt{2}$, $\rho = 1, S = 1$.

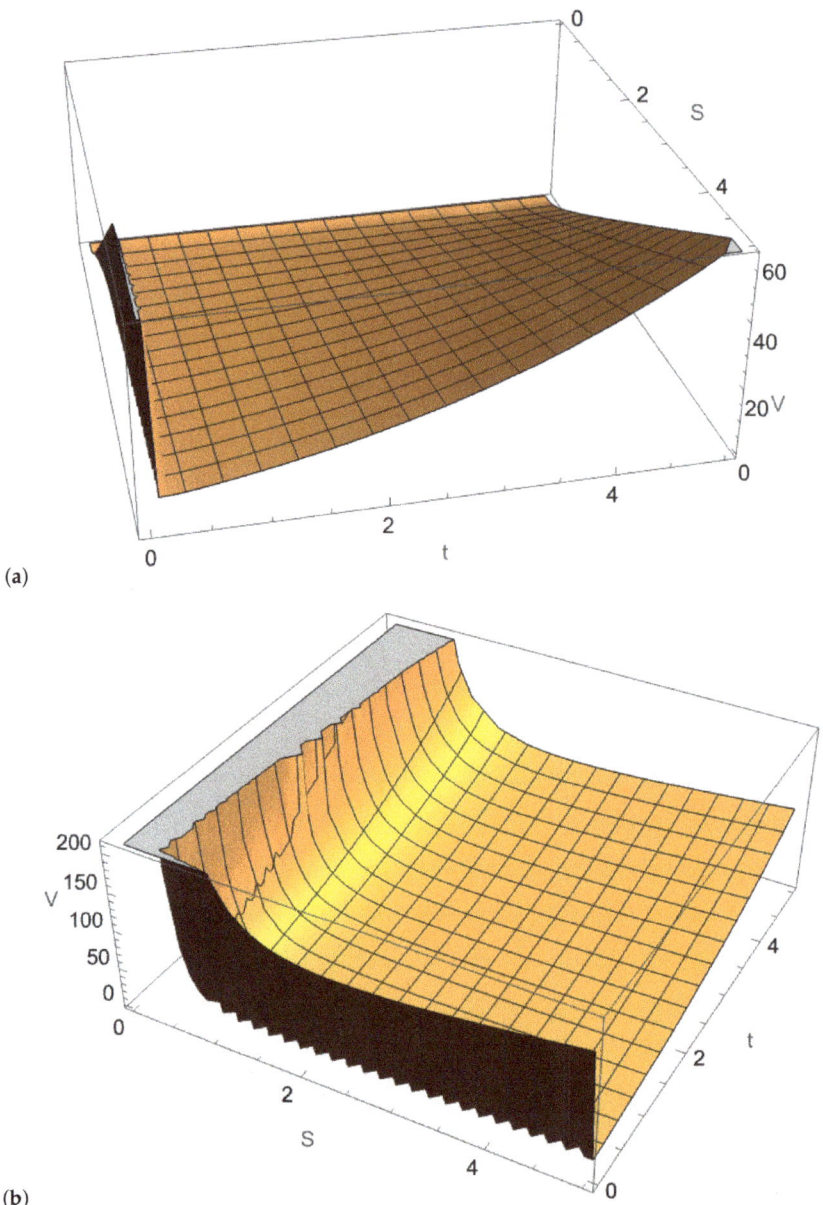

Figure 2. Graphical solutions of Equation (22) with various parameter selections. In (**a**), the 3D plots when $b = 1, C = \sqrt{2}, \rho = 1, \alpha = \frac{2}{3}$. Lastly, in (**b**), the 3D plots when $b = -1, C = \sqrt{2}, \rho = 1, \alpha = \frac{2}{3}$.

On the other hand, if we invoke the Caputo derivative of order α, the solution of the general fractional pricing equation is given by the next theorem.

Theorem 4. *The general fractional pricing Equation (1), under a Caputo fractional derivative with $0 < \alpha < 1$, and parameters $\gamma = 2, \kappa = \beta = 0, \lambda = -\frac{1}{\rho}$, and ρ arbitrary, admits the invariant solution:*

$$V(S,t) = -\frac{C\rho S}{\sqrt{2}} E_\alpha\left(\frac{b^2(-t^\alpha)^\alpha}{\Gamma(\alpha+1)}\right) \exp\left(-\frac{\sqrt{2}b}{\rho S} + \frac{1}{\rho^2 S} - \frac{(-t^\alpha)^\alpha}{2\alpha\rho^2\Gamma(\alpha)\Gamma(\alpha+1)}\right). \quad (26)$$

Proof. The proof is similar to that of Theorem 3; however, under the Caputo derivative of order α, the solution of (19) is given by

$$\psi(\hat{t}) = CE_\alpha\left(\frac{b^2}{\Gamma(\alpha+1)}\hat{t}^\alpha\right), \quad (27)$$

where E_α is the classic Mittag-Leffler function defined as

$$E_\alpha(z) = \sum_{k=0}^\infty \frac{z^k}{\Gamma(\alpha k+1)}, \quad (28)$$

with $\alpha > 0$. Therefore, from (18), we have

$$\omega(y,\hat{t}) = E_\alpha\left(\frac{b^2}{\Gamma(\alpha+1)}\hat{t}^\alpha\right)e^{by}, \quad (29)$$

which also solves Equation (11), and to obtain the solution $V(S,t)$ for the general bond pricing equation, we invoke the transformations from Theorem 1. □

In Figures 3 and 4, we showcase various graphical solutions from Theorem 4.

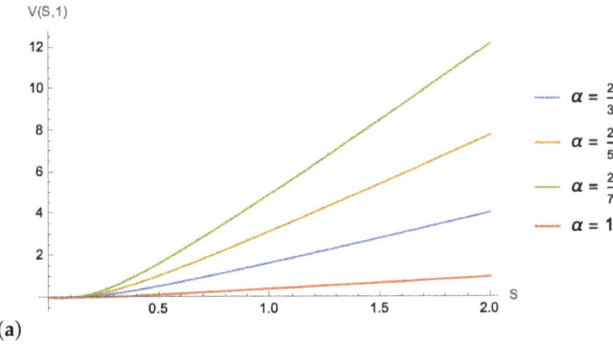

(a)

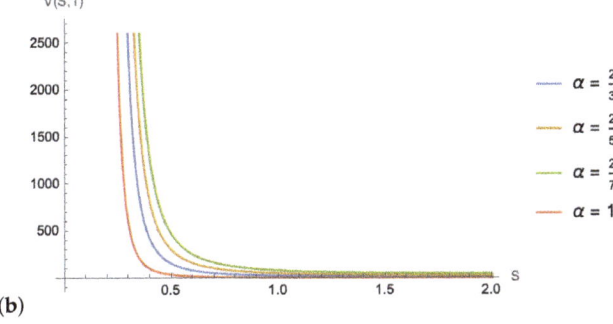

(b)

Figure 3. *Cont.*

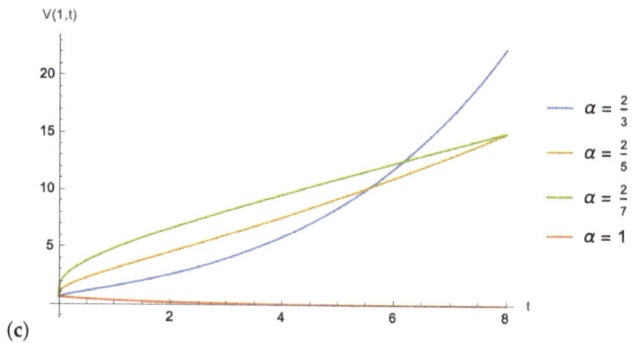

(c)

Figure 3. Graphical solutions of Equation (26) with various parameter selections. In (**a**), $b = (-1)^{\frac{\alpha}{2}}$, $C = -\sqrt{2}, \rho = 1, t = 1$. In (**b**), $b = -(-1)^{\frac{\alpha}{2}}, C = -\sqrt{2}, \rho = 1, t = 1$. In (**c**), $b = (-1)^{\frac{\alpha}{2}}, C = -\sqrt{2}$, $\rho = 1, S = 1$.

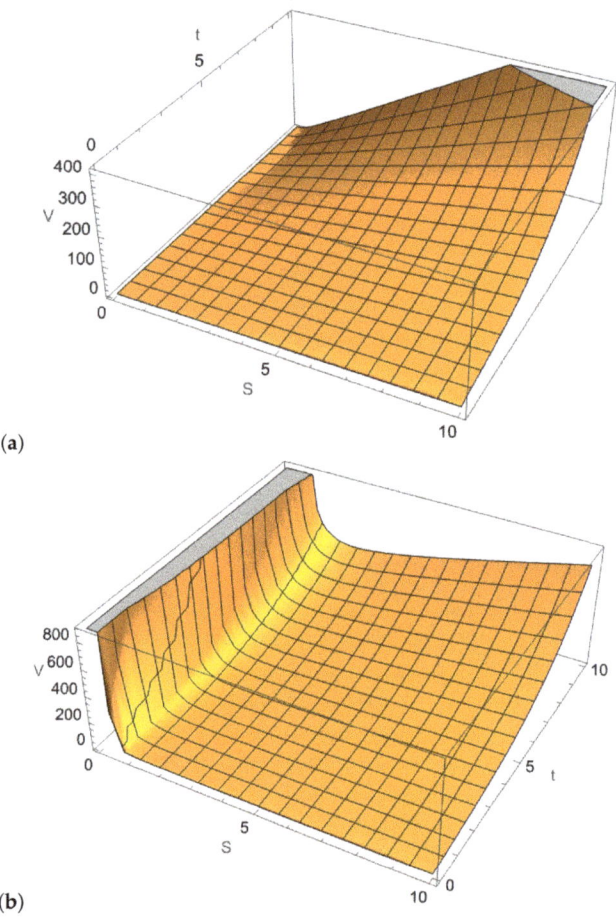

(a)

(b)

Figure 4. Graphical solutions of Equation (26) with various parameter selections. In (**a**), 3D plot when $b = 1, C = -\sqrt{2}, \rho = 1, \alpha = \frac{2}{3}$. In (**b**), 3D plot when $b = -1, C = -\sqrt{2}, \rho = 1, \alpha = \frac{2}{3}$.

4. Results and Conclusions

The general pricing equation under study has had a major impact on the field of mathematical finance and the interpretation of financial instruments by serving as a foundation for a myriad of well-known models. These models arise from altering the market price of risk and other constant parameters, as such, there are more opportunities to develop and gain more insight through further experimentation. In this paper, we presented one such model and presented a way of arriving at solutions by leveraging the heat equation's well-known symmetries and exploring the various definitions of fractional derivatives that the literature has to offer.

A study of Equation (1) resulted in two kinds of solutions for each fractional case, in addition to the standard integer derivative case. These solutions arise from the definition chosen to interpret the fractional derivative. The first is the Riemann–Liouville definition and the second is the Caputo fractional derivative. These derivatives are widely used in fractional calculus for various purposes and we have explored both for the potential solutions that they present. All of our results were collected via theorems and proofs.

Numerically, we note that the solutions via the Riemann–Liouville fractional derivative versus the Caputo fractional derivative are generally not the same. However, under both derivatives, the solutions behave similarly for $0 < \alpha < 1$ and $\alpha \to 1$. We observe a higher bond value, for variable time and fixed stock price, and a fractional derivative $0 < \alpha < 1$. That is, for $\alpha \to 1$ under those same conditions, we find lower bond values. Graphically, we also discover that the parameter b has a strong influence on the value of the bond, given a fixed time and variable stock price, with $b > 0$ producing rapidly decaying values. This occurs due to the dominance of the time variable in the exponent's argument. Overall, for sufficiently large values for the variables S and t, the solution $V(S, t)$ exhibits a similar behaviour of growth with the evolution of the variables and $b < 0$. This model depicts a situation where the current value of the financial instrument is capable of growing over time. More importantly, given the restrictions on b, the dynamic of having the fractional derivative in the model implies improved bond values.

Mathematically, it is almost impossible to solve differential equations, especially those highly nonlinear and that possess higher-order derivatives, without the addition of a transformation—the branch of fractional equations is no different. Moreover, the goal of most transformations is to provide simpler versions of an original equation, such that tools from advanced calculus readily apply towards finding solutions. The transformation is a highly effective approach, and the only challenging element is to construct such transformations.

Our framework described above shows how important transformations are in fractional calculus. The above study further emphasises the compatibility of symmetry methods with fractional derivative models, especially for parameter selection in modelling scenarios.

Author Contributions: Conceptualization, S.J.; formal analysis, R.C.; writing-original draft preparation, S.J.; writing-review and editing, S.K.; visualization, R.C. All authors have read and agreed to the published version of the manuscript.

Funding: This research received no external funding.

Data Availability Statement: Not applicable.

Acknowledgments: S.J. acknowledges the DSI-NRF Centre of Excellence in Mathematical and Statistical Sciences (CoE-MaSS), South Africa. Opinions expressed and conclusions arrived at are those of the authors and are not necessarily to be attributed to the CoE-MaSS.

Conflicts of Interest: The authors declare no conflict of interest.

References

1. Zhang, W.-G.; Xiao, W.-L.; He, C.-X. Equity warrants pricing model under fractional Brownian motion and an empirical study. *Expert Syst. Appl.* **2009**, *36*, 3056–3065. [CrossRef]
2. Garzarelli, F.; Cristelli, M.; Pompa, G.; Zaccaria, A.; Pietronero, L. Memory effects in stock price dynamics: Evidences of technical trading. *Sci. Rep.* **2014**, *4*, 4487. [CrossRef] [PubMed]
3. Panas, E. Long memory and chaotic models of prices on the London metal exchange. *Resour. Policy* **2001**, *4*, 485–490. [CrossRef]
4. Jumarie, G. Derivation and solutions of some fractional Black–Scholes equations in coarse-grained space and time. Application to Merton's optimal portfolio. *Comput. Math. Appl.* **2010**, *59*, 1142–1164. [CrossRef]
5. Liang, J.R.; Wang, J.; Zhang, W.J.; Qiu, W.Y.; Ren, F.Y. The solutions to a bi-fractional Black-Scholes-Merton differential equation. *Int. J. Pure Appl. Math.* **2010**, *128*, 99–112.
6. Fall, A.N.; Ndiaye, S.N.; Sene, N. Black-Scholes option pricing equations described by the Caputo generalized fractional derivative. *Chaos Solitons Fractals* **2019**, *125*, 108–118. [CrossRef]
7. Giona, M.; Roman, H.E. Fractional diffusion equation on fractals: One-dimensional case and asymptotic behaviour. *J. Phys. A-Math. Gen.* **1999**, *25*, 2093. [CrossRef]
8. Yavuz, M.; Özdemir, N. European vanilla option pricing model of fractional order without singular kernel. *Fractal Fract.* **2018**, *2*, 3. [CrossRef]
9. Wyss, W. The fractional Black-Scholes equation. *Fract. Calc. Appl. Anal.* **2000**, *3*, 51–61.
10. Vasicek, O. An equilibrium characterization of the term structure. *J. Financ. Econ.* **1977**, *5*, 177–188. [CrossRef]
11. Dothan, L. On the term structure of interest rates. *J. Financ. Econ.* **1978**, *6*, 59–69. [CrossRef]
12. Cox, J.C.; Ingersoll, J.E.; Ross, S.A. An intertemporal general equilibrium model of asset prices. *Econometrica* **1985**, *53*, 363–384. [CrossRef]
13. Brennan, M.J.; Schwartz, E.S. Analyzing convertible bonds. *J. Financ. Quant. Anal.* **1980**, *15*, 907–929. [CrossRef]
14. Maphanga, R.; Jamal, S. A Terminal Condition in Linear Bond-Pricing under Symmetry Invariance. *J. Nonlinear Math. Phys.* **2023**, 1–10. [CrossRef]
15. Lie, S. Theorie der Transformationsgruppen I. *Math. Ann.* **1880**, *16*, 441–528. [CrossRef]
16. Miller, K.S.; Ross, B. *An Introduction to the Fractional Calculus and Fractional Differential Equations*; Wiley: New York, NY, USA, 1993.
17. Kiryakova, V. *Generalised Fractional Calculus and Applications*; Pitman Research Notes in Mathematics; Longman: London, UK, 1994; Volume 301.
18. Podlubny, I. *Fractional Differential Equations: An Introduction to Fractional Derivatives, Fractional Differential Equations, to Methods of Their Solution and Some of Their Applications*; Academic Press: New York, NY, USA, 1998.
19. Buckwar, E.; Luchko, Y. Invariance of a partial differential equation of fractional order under the Lie group of scaling transformations. *J. Math. Anal. Appl.* **1998**, *227*, 81–97. [CrossRef]
20. Gazizov, R.K.; Kasatkin, A.A.; Lukashchuk, S.Y. Symmetry properties of fractional diffusion equations. *Phys. Scr.* **2009**, *T136*, 014016. [CrossRef]
21. Gazizov, R.K.; Kasatkin, A.A.; Lukashchuk, S.Y. Continuous transformation groups of fractional differential equations. *Vestn. USATU* **2007**, *9* 125–135.
22. Bakkyaraj, T. Lie symmetry analysis of system of nonlinear fractional partial differential equations with Caputo fractional derivative. *Eur. Phys. J. Plus* **2020**, *135*, 126. [CrossRef]
23. Leo, R.A.; Sicuro, G.; Tempesta, P. A theorem on the existence of symmetries of fractional PDEs. *C. R. Acad. Sci. Paris Ser. I* **2014**, *352*, 219–222. [CrossRef]
24. Sahadevan, R.; Bakkyaraj, T. Invariant analysis of time fractional generalized Burgers and Korteweg-de Vries equations. *J. Math. Anal. Appl.* **2012**, *393*, 341–347. [CrossRef]
25. Kubayi J.T.; Jamal, S. Lie Symmetries and Third- and Fifth-Order Time-Fractional Polynomial Evolution Equations. *Fractal Fract.* **2023**, *7*, 125. [CrossRef]
26. Jamal, S. Imaging Noise Suppression: Fourth-Order Partial Differential Equations and Travelling Wave Solutions. *Mathematics* **2020**, *8*, 2019. [CrossRef]
27. Obaidullah, U.; Jamal, S. A computational procedure for exact solutions of Burgers' hierarchy of nonlinear partial differential equations. *J. Appl. Math. Comput.* **2020**, *65*, 541. [CrossRef]
28. Yang, X.; Wu, L.; Zhang, H. A space-time spectral order sinc-collocation method for the fourth-order nonlocal heat model arising in viscoelasticity. *Appl. Math. Comput.* **2023**, *457* 128192. [CrossRef]
29. Kimeu, J.M. Fractional Calculus: Definition and Applications. Master's Thesis, Western Kentucky University, Bowling Green, KY, USA, 2009.

Disclaimer/Publisher's Note: The statements, opinions and data contained in all publications are solely those of the individual author(s) and contributor(s) and not of MDPI and/or the editor(s). MDPI and/or the editor(s) disclaim responsibility for any injury to people or property resulting from any ideas, methods, instructions or products referred to in the content.

fractal and fractional

Article

Image Enhancement Model Based on Fractional Time-Delay and Diffusion Tensor

Wenjuan Yao [1], Yi Huang [1,*], Boying Wu [1] and Zhongxiang Zhou [2]

1. School of Mathematics, Harbin Institute of Technology, Harbin 150001, China; mathywj@hit.edu.cn (W.Y.); mathwby@hit.edu.cn (B.W.)
2. School of Physics, Harbin Institute of Technology, Harbin 150001, China; zhouzx@hit.edu.cn
* Correspondence: 21s012036@stu.hit.edu.cn

Abstract: Image enhancement is one of the bases of image processing technology, which can enhance useful features and suppress useless information of images according to the specified task. In order to ensure coherent enhancement for images with oriented flow-like structures, we propose a nonlinear diffusion system model based on time-fractional delay. By combining the nonlinear isotropic diffusion equation with fractional time-delay regularization, we construct a structure tensor. Meanwhile, the introduction of source terms enhances the contrast of the image, making it effective for denoising images with high-level noise. Based on compactness principles, the existence of weak solutions for the model is proved by using the Galerkin method. In addition, various experimental results verify the enhancement ability of the proposed model.

Keywords: image enhancement; Caputo-fractional derivative; time-delay regularization; anisotropic diffusion model

Citation: Yao, W.; Huang, Y.; Wu, B.; Zhou, Z. Image Enhancement Model Based on Fractional Time-Delay and Diffusion Tensor. *Fractal Fract.* **2023**, *7*, 569. https://doi.org/10.3390/fractalfract7080569

Academic Editor: Sameerah Jamal

Received: 9 June 2023
Revised: 20 July 2023
Accepted: 21 July 2023
Published: 25 July 2023

Copyright: © 2023 by the authors. Licensee MDPI, Basel, Switzerland. This article is an open access article distributed under the terms and conditions of the Creative Commons Attribution (CC BY) license (https://creativecommons.org/licenses/by/4.0/).

1. Introduction

Image processing technology is widely used in fields such as medical image processing, text recognition and speech recognition, and unmanned driving. As an important part of image processing technology, image enhancement focuses on enhancing the useful information in the image and improving the clarity of the image. In recent years, many enhancement methods for digital images have been proposed, roughly divided into four categories: spatial domain-based methods [1,2], frequency domain-based methods [3,4], deep learning-based methods [5,6], and partial differential equations-based method. The spatial domain-based method has fast computation speed but cannot provide relevant information between pixels. The frequency domain-based method can provide detailed information but it requires a large amount of computation. The image enhancement algorithm based on deep learning can learn the complex transformation of an image, but its training time is long and it lacks interpretability. The method based on partial differential equations has always played a significant role in the field of image processing, which was firstly elaborated by Gabor [7] and Jain [8]. This method is based on strong mathematical theories. Its basic idea is to evolve the initial image through partial differential equations and obtain the enhanced image.

In this paper, we focus on the problem of image enhancement with oriented flow-like structures. These structures usually exist in the fields of fluid mechanics, geology and biology, texture analysis, computer vision and image processing. In the development of image processing using partial differential equations, the most classic model is the PM model proposed by Perona and Malik et al. [9]. Based on the PM model, the integer-order isotropic diffusion equation was developed rapidly, such as the viscoelastic equation and wave equation, which further stimulated the emergence of the anisotropic diffusion equation. Nitzberg [10] and Cottet et al. [11] pioneered the description and analysis of various anisotropic diffusion methods. Furthermore, Weickert's work about diffusion tensors greatly promoted the research on anisotropic diffusion methods in the field of image processing. They proposed a multi-scale method that successfully completes the connection of interruption lines and the enhancement of flow-like structures. In this model, operators of interest, such as second-order moment matrices and structural tensors, are used to control nonlinear diffusion filtering. Since then, many scholars have conducted extensive research about this method [12–18]. For examples, Nnolim et al. [17] described a fuzzy image contrast enhancement algorithm based on a modified partial differential equation. The algorithm utilizes multi-scale local global enhancement of logarithmic reflectance and illumination components. The model successfully avoids the numerous steps required by standard DCP based methods and produces good visual effects. Gu et al. [18] proposed a SAR image enhancement method combining the PM nonlinear equation and coherent enhancement partial differential equation. The mixture model not only avoids noise enhancement but also enhances image edges.

Along with the development of image processing for integer-order partial differential equations, fractional-order partial differential equations [19–22] have also been developed rapidly. For example, Bai et al. [19] proposed a new nonlinear fractional-order anisotropic diffusion equation using spatial fractional derivatives to obtain more natural images. Sharma et al. [20] proposed an image enhancement model based on fractional-order partial differential equations, which can reduce the impact of noise and enhance the contrast of images nonlinearly. Chandra et al. [21] proposed a new image enhancement method based on linear fractional-order meshless partial differential equations to improve the quality of tumor images. The model can maintain fine details of smooth regions while denoising, and can nonlinearly increase the high-frequency information of the image. Ben-loghfyry [23], based on anisotropic diffusion and the time-fractional derivative in the Caputo sense, proposed a new reaction–diffusion equation to restore texture images.

In order to obtain the proposed model in this paper, the four classic models involved are explained below. Weickert studied anisotropic diffusion filters and derived a coherence-enhancing diffusion (CED) equation [24]:

$$\begin{cases} \frac{\partial u}{\partial t} = \text{div}(D\nabla u), \ (x,t) \in \Omega \times (0,T] \\ u(x,0) = u_0(x), \ x \in \Omega \\ \frac{\partial u}{\partial \vec{n}} = 0, \ (x,t) \in \partial\Omega \times (0,T] \end{cases} \quad (1)$$

where $\vec{n}$ is the unit outer normal vector, u_0 is the observed image as the initial data for the diffusion equation, $D := g_1(J)$ is a diffusion tensor, g_1 is a nonlinear diffusion filter, J is a linear structure tensor obtained by the convolution of $\nabla u_\sigma \nabla u_\sigma^T$ and Gaussian kernel G_ρ, specifically, $J = G_\rho * (\nabla u_\sigma \nabla u_\sigma^T)$. The nonlinear diffusion filter of the CED model is controlled by a diffusion tensor, which can interrupt lines and enhance oriented flow-like structures. Wang et al. proposed coupled diffusion equations (CDEs) instead of the traditional linear method in image restoration [14]:

$$\begin{cases} \frac{\partial u}{\partial t} = \text{div}(g_1(J)\nabla u), \ (x,t) \in \Omega \times (0,T] \\ \frac{\partial J_{i,j}}{\partial t} = \text{div}(g_2(|\nabla u_\sigma|)\nabla J_{i,j}), \ (x,t) \in \Omega \times (0,T] \\ \frac{\partial u}{\partial \vec{n}} = 0, \ \frac{\partial J_{1,1}}{\partial \vec{n}} = \frac{\partial J_{2,2}}{\partial \vec{n}} = 0, \ (x,t) \in \partial\Omega \times (0,T] \\ u(x,0) = u_0(x), \ J_{i,j}(x,0) = (\nabla u_0 \nabla u_0^T)_{i,j}, \ i,j = 1,2, \ x \in \Omega \end{cases} \quad (2)$$

where $g_2(s) = \frac{1}{1+(s/K)^2}$. The CEDs combine image restoration with singularity detection and can gradually eliminate the sensitivity of parameters to the image. Diffusion-based image enhancement methods generally use a spatial regularization, while they cannot use enough historical information. To this end, Chen et al. introduced time-delay regularization and then proposed the following model [25]:

$$\begin{cases} \frac{\partial u}{\partial t} = \text{div}(L(v)\nabla u) - \lambda(u - u_0), \ (x,t) \in (0,T] \\ \tau \frac{\partial v}{\partial t} + v = \nabla u_\sigma, \ (x,t) \in \Omega \times (0,T] \\ u(x,0) = u_0, \ v(x,0) = 0, \ x \in \Omega \\ \frac{\partial u}{\partial \vec{n}} = 0, \ (x,t) \in \partial\Omega \times [0,T] \end{cases}$$

where $\tau > 0$, $\sigma \geq 0$. u_0 is the initial image, $L = \lambda_1 L_1 + \lambda_2 L_2$, $L_1 = vv^\mathsf{T}$, $L_2 = (v^\perp)(v^\perp)^\mathsf{T}$, $\lambda_1 = \frac{1}{1+k|v|^2}$, $\lambda_2 = \frac{\alpha|v|^2}{1+k|v|^2}$, $k > 0$, $\alpha > 0$, $v = \nabla \tilde{u}$, $\tilde{u}$ is the time-delay regularization of u. For images with high levels of noise, they perform the pre-smoothing by combining spatial regularization at a small scale with time-delay regularization, which is particularly important for preserving textures and edge structures. This method has successfully been applied to Cotte and Ayyadi models [26].

The traditional integer-order partial differential equations cannot describe complex phenomena. To this end, countless scholars have studies on fractional calculus [19–22,27–33], which is an extension of integer calculus and has advantages in modeling complex phenomena with memory and genetics. The image enhancement model based on fractional calculus has long-term memory and non-locality, which can fully utilize the past information of the image and describe more complex diffusion progress. For example, Ben-loghfyry et al. proposed a reaction–diffusion equation based on anisotropic diffusion and Caputo's time-fractional derivative to restore texture images [23]:

$$\begin{cases} \frac{\partial^\alpha u}{\partial t} = \text{div}(D\nabla u) - 2\lambda \omega, \ (x,t) \in \Omega \times (0,T) \\ \frac{\partial^\beta u}{\partial t} = \Delta \omega - (f(x) - u), \ (x,t) \in \Omega \times (0,T) \\ \langle D\nabla u, \vec{n} \rangle = \frac{\partial \omega}{\partial \vec{n}}(x,t) = 0, \ (x,t) \in \partial\Omega \times (0,T) \\ u(x,0) = f(x), \ \omega(x,0) = \omega_0(x), \ x \in \Omega \end{cases}$$

where $(\alpha, \beta) \in (0,1)^2$, $\Omega \subset \mathbb{R}^2$ is a bounded area, the boundary $\partial\Omega$ is Lipschitz continuous, $\vec{n}$ is the unit outer normal vector, $\lambda > 0$, $f \in L^2(\Omega)$, and $D := D(J_\rho(\nabla u_\sigma))$ is a diffusion matrix based on J_ρ. The memory potential of the two coupled time-fractional diffusion equations effectively guarantees the superiority of the model.

In this paper, we propose an image enhancement model coupling a nonlinear anisotropic diffusion equation, a nonlinear isotropic diffusion equation and a fractional time-delay equation. Specifically, the spatial direction of the structure tensor is regularized by nonlinear isotropic diffusion, and the temporal direction of the the structure tensor is regularized by a fractional time-delay equation. Then, the diffusion tensor of the CED is constructed by using the obtained structure tensor. Additionally, we also introduce a source term which changes the diffusion process. The proposed model can better enhance the coherence structure and contrast of images, especially in processing noisy images or low-contrast areas. It should be noted that due to the introduction of source terms, the proposed model is more suitable for handling white noise than other existing models. We prove the existence and uniqueness of weak solutions. The proposed system of image enhancement equations based on fractional time-delay and the diffusion tensor has the following characteristics:

- The nonlinear isotropic diffusion equation is applied to make use of the spatial information in the image. The fractional time-delay equation is applied to make use of the past information of the image. The diffusion tensor of CED is applied to complete interrupted lines and enhance flow-like structures.
- The introduced source term is used to make a contrast enhancement between the image and its background by changing the diffusion type and behavior. In addition, this term can also reduce the noise in the image.
- Based on the theory of partial differential equations and some properties of fractional calculus, we prove the existence and uniqueness of weak solutions.

- The comparative experimental results verify the superiority of the proposed method. It shows that this model can complete the connection of interrupted lines, enhance the contrast of images, and deepen the fluidity characteristics of various types of lines.

The paper is organized as follows. In Section 2, we establish an image enhancement model with fractional time-delay regularization and diffusion tensors, and provide a detailed explanation of the model. Section 2.3 deduces the theoretical part of the model, defines the Galerkin estimation of the model and the form of weak solutions, and proves the existence and uniqueness of weak solutions. Section 3 mainly designs a stable and efficient numerical format for the proposed model and conducts numerical experiments on different images. Section 4 summarizes the results.

2. The Proposed Model and Its Theoretical Analysis

2.1. Preliminary Knowledge

Definition 1 ([34,35]). *Assume that γ is a positive rational number, $\gamma \in \mathbb{R}^+$, $n-1 < \gamma \leq n$, and $n-1$ is a positive integer. $u(t)$ is an integrable function on the interval $(0,T)$, then the Caputo-type fractional derivative of u with order γ is*

$$D_c^\gamma u(t) = \frac{1}{\Gamma(n-\gamma)} \int_0^t \frac{u^{(n)}(s)}{(t-s)^{\gamma-n+1}} ds, \ t > 0$$

where $\Gamma(\cdot)$ is a gamma function. When $\gamma = n$, the Caputo-type fractional order of order γ is a common integer-order derivative of order n, $D_c^\gamma u(t) = u^{(n)}(t)$.

Generally, the sign of a Caputo-type fractional derivative contains information about the boundary point of the integral interval, but only the interval $(0,T)$ is involved in this paper, so the sign is simplified to $D_c^\gamma u(t)$, which represents the right limit of u at $t=0$, which is the derivative of $u(0+)$ when it exists.

Theorem 1 ([36]). *Assume that $\gamma \in (0,1)$, $\mathcal{H}$ is a Hilbert space and $\omega : [0,T] \to \mathcal{H}$ such that $\|\omega(t)\|_{\mathcal{H}}^2$ is absolutely continuous. Then*

$$D_c^\gamma \|\omega(t)\|_{\mathcal{H}}^2 \leq 2(\omega(t), D_c^\gamma \omega(t))_{\mathcal{H}}$$

for each a.e. $t \in (0,T]$.

Proposition 1 ([37]). *Suppose that $u(t)$ and $g(t)$ are integrable functions defined on the interval $(0,T)$, then*

$$\int_0^T g(t) D_c^\gamma u(t) dt = \int_0^T u(t) D_{(t,T)}^\gamma g(t) dt + \sum_{j=0}^{n-1} D_{(t,T)}^{\gamma+j-n} g(t) D^{n-1-j} u(t)|_0^T$$

where $D_{(t,T)}^\gamma g(t) = \frac{1}{\Gamma(n-\gamma)} (\frac{d}{dt})^n \int_t^T (t-s)^{n-\gamma-1} g(s) ds$ is a Riemann–Liouville fractional derivative.

2.2. The Proposed Model

In this subsection, we propose a new image enhancement model based on fractional time-delay regularization and diffusion tensor. Assuming that $\Omega \subset \mathbb{R}^n$ is a bounded region, $\partial \Omega$ is a Lipschitz continuous boundary, and the mapping $u : \Omega \to \mathbb{R}$ represents a positive real-valued function of the gray image $u(x)$, then we establish the following image enhancement model:

$$\begin{cases} \frac{\partial u}{\partial t} = \operatorname{div}(g_1(J)\nabla u) + \lambda(u - \widetilde{u}), \ (x,t) \in \Omega \times (0,T] \\ \tau D_c^\gamma J_{i,j} + J_{i,j} = v_{i,j}, \ (x,t) \in \Omega \times (0,T] \\ \frac{\partial v_{i,j}}{\partial t} = \operatorname{div}(g_2(|\nabla u_\sigma|)\nabla v_{i,j}), \ (x,t) \in \Omega \times (0,T] \\ \langle g_1(J)\nabla u, \vec{n} \rangle = 0, \ \frac{\partial v_{1,1}}{\partial \vec{n}} = \frac{\partial v_{2,2}}{\partial \vec{n}} = 0, \ \frac{\partial v_{1,2}}{\partial \vec{n}} = \frac{\partial v_{2,1}}{\partial \vec{n}} = 0, \ (x,t) \in \partial\Omega \times (0,T] \\ u(x,0) = u_0(x), \ J_{i,j}(x,0) = 0, \ v_{i,j}(x,0) = (\nabla u_0 \nabla u_0^\mathsf{T})_{i,j}, \ i,j = 1,2, \ x \in \Omega \end{cases} \quad (3)$$

where $\lambda > 0$ is an adaptive adjustment parameter, $\widetilde{u}$ is the average value of the image, $\tau > 0$ is the time-delay regularization parameter, $\gamma \in (0,1)$ is the fractional parameter, $u_\sigma = G_\sigma * u_0$ is the image with Gaussian convolution, $J = (J_{i,j})_{i,j=1,2}$ is the structural tensor, $\vec{n}$ is the unit outer normal vector of $\partial\Omega$, g_1 is the diffusion matrix, and g_2 is the diffusion function. D_c^γ is the Caputo time-fractional derivative, see Definition 1. In the model, the nonlinear isotropic diffusion equation is used to spatially regularize the structure tensor, the fractional time-delay equation is used to temporally regularize the structure tensor, and the coherent enhanced diffusion tensor based on the structure tensor is used to perform anisotropic diffusion.

The interpretation of the terms of our model is as follows:

- The first equation is an anisotropic diffusion equation, which can enhance flow-like structures and connect interrupted lines. Since the eigenvalues $\mu_i (i = 1,2)$ in J imply the coherent structure, we select $\kappa = (\mu_1 - \mu_2)^2$ as the measure of coherence. More related details can be found in reference [24]. Specifically, the eigenvectors of structural tensors provide optimal choices for local directions, while the corresponding eigenvalues represent local contrast along these directions. By constructing diffusion tensor D with the same eigenvector as J and selecting appropriate eigenvalues for smoothing, it can be ensured that the model can complete the connection of interrupted lines and enhance similar flow structures. The source term in the first equation is used to change the diffusion type and behavior so as to make a contrast enhancement between the target image and the background and enhance the texture structure; more details are referred to in [38].
- The second equation performs as a fractional time-delay regularization, which considers the past information of the image. Meanwhile, the long-range dependency of this equation can avoid excessive smoothing.
- The final equation is based on a structure tensor; this equation is an isotropic diffusion equation, which performs well when dealing with the discontinuity. Let $s = |\nabla u_\sigma|$, and choose the diffusion function $g_2(s) = \frac{1}{1+(s/K)^2}$, where K is a threshold value. Alternatively, we can choose the diffusion function as $g_2(s) = \frac{1}{\varepsilon + (s)^2}$, where ε is a smaller positive number. The diffusion coefficient changes with the local features of the image, thereby preserving the edge information of the image and avoiding texture and edge information to be blurred.

Comparing with the existing methods, the key points of the proposed model lie in the construction of the diffusion tensor, the introduction of the fractional-order time delay, and the instruction of the source term. Most existing models rely on the spatial regularization of structural tensor, but these methods cannot extract the past information of images during the diffusion process. Chen et al. [25] proposed the concept of time-delay regularization, which compensates for the shortcomings of spatial regularization, but its application is not widespread. To this end, the proposed model in this paper regularizes the structural tensor in space using nonlinear isotropic diffusion, and regularizes the structural tensor in time using the time-delay method. Moreover, the two diffusion methods can extract feature values and better enhance the coherence structure of the image. Furthermore, extending the model from the integer order to fractional order greatly enriches the theoretical research value and applicability of the model. In addition, introducing the source term into the model ensures that the image only has black color and white color, where the black color represents the flowing structure, and white color represents the background. It can only restore the original image and enhance the contrast loss of pure diffusion filters and is also suitable for processing white noise.

2.3. The Theoretical Analysis of the Proposed Model

Let

$$L_0 u = -\text{div}(g_1(J)\nabla u) - \lambda\, u$$
$$L_1 J_{i,j} = \frac{1}{\tau} J_{i,j},\ i,j = 1,2$$
$$L_2 v_{i,j} = -\text{div}(g_2(|\nabla u_\sigma|)\nabla v_{i,j}),\ i,j = 1,2$$

where L_0, L_1, and L_2 denote three operators and $\tau > 0$. Then we can convert the model (3) into the following form:

$$\begin{cases} \frac{\partial u}{\partial t} + L_0 u = \lambda(u - \widetilde{u}),\ (x,t) \in \Omega \times (0,T] \\ D_c^\gamma J_{i,j} + L_1 J_{i,j} = \frac{1}{\tau} v_{i,j},\ (x,t) \in \Omega \times (0,T] \\ \frac{\partial v_{i,j}}{\partial t} = L_2 v_{i,j},\ (x,t) \in \Omega \times (0,T] \\ \langle g_1(J)\nabla u, \vec{n} \rangle = 0,\ \frac{\partial v_{1,1}}{\partial \vec{n}} = \frac{\partial v_{2,2}}{\partial \vec{n}} = 0,\ \frac{\partial v_{1,2}}{\partial \vec{n}} = \frac{\partial v_{2,1}}{\partial \vec{n}} = 0,\ (x,t) \in \partial\Omega \times (0,T] \\ u(x,0) = u_0(x),\ J_{i,j}(x,0) = 0,\ v_{i,j}(x,0) = (\nabla u_0 \nabla u_0^\mathsf{T})_{i,j},\ i,j = 1,2,\ x \in \Omega \end{cases}$$

Assume $u_0 \in L^2(\Omega)$, $(\nabla u_0 \nabla u_0^\mathsf{T})_{i,j} \in L^2(\Omega)(i,j = 1,2)$; the function $g_1(J) \in C^\infty(\mathbb{R}^{2\times 2}, \mathbb{R}^{2\times 2})$ keeps the uniform positive definiteness and the symmetry of J

$$\|g_1(J_1) - g_2(J_2)\|_{L^\infty(\Omega)} \leq \|J_1 - J_2\|_{L^2(\Omega)}$$

Now, we give a definition in the following form:

$$\begin{cases} B_0[u, \phi; t] := \int_\Omega g_1(J)\nabla u \cdot \nabla\phi\, dx - \lambda \int_\Omega u\phi\, dx \\ B_1[J_{i,j}, \phi_{i,j}; t] := \int_\Omega J_{i,j}\phi_{i,j}\, dx \\ B_2[v_{i,j}, \psi_{i,j}; t] := \int_\Omega g_2(|\nabla u_\sigma|)\nabla v_{i,j} \nabla \psi_{i,j}\, dx \end{cases} \quad (4)$$

for $\phi, \phi_{i,j}, \psi_{i,j} \in H^1(\Omega)$, a.e. $t \in (0,T]$. For fixed time $t \in (0,T]$, the bilinear forms are $B_0[u, \phi; t]$, $B_1[J_{i,j}, \phi_{i,j}; t]$, $B_2[v_{i,j}, \psi_{i,j}; t]$. Define mappings

$$u : [0,T] \to H^1(\Omega),\ J_{i,j} : [0,T] \to H^1(\Omega),\ v_{i,j} : [0,T] \to H^1(\Omega),\ i,j = 1,2$$

by

$$[u(t)](x) := u(x,t)$$
$$[J_{i,j}(t)](x) := J_{i,j}(x,t),\ i,j = 1,2$$
$$[v_{i,j}(t)](x) := v_{i,j}(x,t),\ x \in \Omega,\ 0 \leq t \leq T$$

Denote $H^1(\Omega)'$ as the dual space of $H^1(\Omega)$. If $f \in H^1(\Omega)'$, which means that f is a bounded linear functional on $H^1(\Omega)$, the norm is

$$\|f\|_{(H^1(\Omega))'} := \left\{ \sup\langle f, u \rangle | u \in H^1(\Omega), \|u\|_{H^1(\Omega)} \leq 1 \right\}$$

where $\langle \cdot, \cdot \rangle$ stands for the dual product of $H^1(\Omega)'$ and $H^1(\Omega)$. $(\cdot, \cdot)$ stands for the inner product in $H^1(\Omega)$. According to [39], the space $H^1(\Omega)'$ satisfies the following properties:
(i) Suppose $f \in (H^1(\Omega))'$, there exists functions $f^0, f^1, \cdots, f^n \in L^2(\Omega)$ such that

$$\langle f, u \rangle = \int_\Omega f^0 v + \sum_{i=1}^n f^i v_{x_i} dx, \ v \in H^1(\Omega)$$

(ii) For $u \in H^1(\Omega), v \in L^2(\Omega) \subset (H^1(\Omega))'$, we have

$$(v, u)_{L^2(\Omega)} = \langle v, u \rangle$$

For simplicity, when (i) holds, we denote $f = f^0 - \sum_{i=1}^n f_{x_i}^i$. Therefore, the Galerkin estimate of the equation system is

$$\begin{cases} \langle u', \phi \rangle + B_0[u, \phi; t] = -\lambda(\widetilde{u}, \phi) \\ (D_c^\gamma J_{i,j}, \phi_{i,j}) + B_1[J_{i,j}, \phi_{i,j}; t] = \frac{1}{\tau}(v_{i,j}, \phi_{i,j}), \ i,j = 1,2 \\ \langle v'_{i,j}, \psi_{i,j} \rangle + B_2[v_{i,j}, \psi_{i,j}; t] = 0, \ i,j = 1,2 \end{cases}$$

where $\phi, \phi_{i,j}, \psi_{i,j} \in H^1(\Omega)$, $B_0[u, \phi; t], B_1[J_{i,j}, \phi_{i,j}; t], B_2[v_{i,j}, \psi_{i,j}; t]$ are the time-dependent bilinear forms.

2.4. The Existence of Weak Solutions

Definition 2. *Functions*

$$u \in L^2(0, T; H^1(\Omega)), \ u' \in L^2(0, T; (H^1(\Omega))')$$
$$v_{i,j} \in L^2(0, T; H^1(\Omega)), \ v'_{i,j} \in L^2(0, T; (H^1(\Omega))')$$
$$J_{i,j} \in L^\infty(0, T; H^1(\Omega)), \ D_c^\gamma J_{i,j} \in L^2(0, T; (H^1(\Omega))')$$

are named the weak solution of (3) if the following hold.
(i) Functions $u, v_{i,j}, J_{i,j}$ satisfy the following system:

$$\begin{cases} \langle u', \phi \rangle + B_0[u, \phi; t] = -\lambda(\widetilde{u}, \phi) \\ (D_c^\gamma J_{i,j}, \phi_{i,j}) + B_1[J_{i,j}, \phi_{i,j}; t] = \frac{1}{\tau}(v_{i,j}, \phi_{i,j}), \ i,j = 1,2 \\ \langle v'_{i,j}, \psi_{i,j} \rangle + B_2[v_{i,j}, \psi_{i,j}; t] = 0, \ i,j = 1,2 \end{cases}$$

for each $\phi, \phi_{i,j}, \psi_{i,j} \in H^1(\Omega)$, $(i, j = 1, 2)$, a.e. $t \in (0, T]$.
(ii) $u(x, 0) = u_0(x)$, $J_{i,j}(x, 0) = 0$, $v_{i,j}(x, 0) = (\nabla u_0 \nabla u_0^\top)_{i,j}$, $i, j = 1, 2$.

We select a suitable basic space and one of the standard orthogonal bases to construct a finite dimensional approximation solution.

Assume there are some smooth functions $\omega_k = \omega_k(x)$, $(k = 1, 2, \cdots)$, $\{\omega_k\}_{k=1}^\infty$ is the orthogonal basis of space $H^1(\Omega)$, and $\{\omega_k\}_{k=1}^\infty$ is a standard orthogonal basis of space $L^2(\Omega)$. ω_k is an eigenfunction of the Laplacian operator with zero Neumann boundary conditions in $H^1(\Omega)$, and the corresponding eigenvalues $\{\lambda_k\}$ are arranged in a non-decreasing sequence. That is

$$\begin{cases} -\Delta \omega_k = \lambda_k \omega_k, \ x \in \Omega \\ \frac{\partial \omega_k}{\partial \vec{n}} = 0, \ x \in \partial \Omega \end{cases}$$

$$(\omega_k, \omega_k) := \int_\Omega \omega_k^2 dx = 1, \ 0 < \lambda_1 \leq \lambda_2 \leq \cdots$$

Then the space span$\{\omega_k\}_{k=1}^{\infty}$ has density in $H^1(\Omega)$. We define $u^n(t,x) : [0,T] \to H^1(\Omega)$, $J_{i,j}^n(t,x) : [0,T] \to H^1(\Omega)$, $v_{i,j}^n(t,x) : [0,T] \to H^1(\Omega)$ by

$$u^n(t,x) := \sum_{k=1}^{n} d_k^n(t)\omega_k(x) \tag{5}$$

$$v_{i,j}^n(t,x) := \sum_{k=1}^{n} (c_{i,j})_k^n(t)\omega_k(x) \tag{6}$$

$$J_{i,j}^n(t,x) := \frac{1}{\Gamma(\gamma)}\int_0^t (t-s)^{\gamma-1}\frac{1}{\tau}(v_{i,j}^n - J_{i,j}^n)ds \tag{7}$$

where n is a positive integer, the coefficients $d_k^n(t)$, $(c_{i,j})_k^n(t)$, $(i,j=1,2)$, $(0 \le t \le T$, $k = 1,2,\cdots,n)$ need to satisfy

$$\begin{cases} d_k^n(0) = (u_0,\omega_k) \\ (c_{i,j})_k^n(0) = ((\nabla u_0 \nabla u_0^\top)_{i,j},\omega_k), (k=1,2,\cdots,n) \end{cases} \tag{8}$$

and

$$\begin{cases} \langle (u^n)',\phi \rangle + B_0[u^n,\phi;t] = -\lambda(\tilde{u},\phi) \\ (D_c^\gamma J_{i,j}^n,\phi_{i,j}) + B_1[J_{i,j}^n,\phi_{i,j};t] = \frac{1}{\tau}(v_{i,j},\phi_{i,j}), \; i,j=1,2 \\ \langle (v_{i,j}^n)',\psi_{i,j}\rangle + B_2[v_{i,j}^n,\psi_{i,j};t] = 0, \; i,j=1,2 \end{cases} \tag{9}$$

There is a huge difference when dealing with the Caputo fractional derivative instead of the classical one. In the proposed model, the most important issue is how to deal with the function $J_{i,j}^n$ involving the singular kernel $(t-s)^{\gamma-1}$. The following lemma and theorem are presented to answer this question.

Lemma 1. *For any positive integer n, there exist functions $u^n(t,x)$, $v_{i,j}^n(t,x)$, $J_{i,j}^n(t,x)$ in the form of (5)–(7), and these functions satisfy the initial value condition (8) and the system (9).*

Proof. Assuming that $u^n(t,x)$, $v_{i,j}^n(t,x)$, $J_{i,j}^n(t,x)$ can be represented as (5)–(7), $\{\omega_k\}_{k=1}^{\infty}$ is the standard orthogonal basis of spatial $L^2(\Omega)$, it can be obtained that

$$((u^n(t))',\omega_k) = (d_k^n(t))'$$
$$\left((v_{i,j}^n(t))',\omega_k\right) = ((c_{i,j})_k^n(t))'$$

furthermore,

$$B_0[u,\omega_k;t] = \sum_{l=1}^{n} B_0[\omega_l,\omega_k;t]d_k^n(t), \; (k=1,2,\cdots,n)$$

$$B_2[v_{i,j},\omega_k;t] = \sum_{l=1}^{n} B_2[\omega_l,\omega_k;t](c_{i,j})_k^n(t), \; (k=1,2,\cdots,n)$$

Let $f^k(t) := -\lambda(\tilde{u},\omega_k)$, then (9) can be transformed into

$$\begin{cases} \frac{\partial d_k^n(t)}{\partial t} + \sum_{l=1}^{n} B_0[\omega_l,\omega_k;t]d_k^n = f^k(t) \\ \frac{\partial (c_{i,j})_k^n(t)}{\partial t} + \sum_{l=1}^{n} B_2[\omega_l,\omega_k;t](c_{i,j})_k^n = 0 \\ d_k^n(0) = (u_0,\omega_k), \; k=1,2,\cdots,n \\ (c_{i,j})_k^n(0) = ((\nabla u_0 \nabla u_0^\top)_{i,j},\omega_k), \; k=1,2,\cdots,n \end{cases}$$

further simplify

$$F_k(t, d_1^n(t), \cdots, d_n^n(t), (c_{i,j})_1^n(t), \cdots, (c_{i,j})_n^n(t)) := f^k(t) - \sum_{l=1}^n B_0[\omega_l, \omega_k; t] d_k^n$$

$$F_{n+k}(t, d_1^n(t), \cdots, d_n^n(t), (c_{i,j})_1^n(t), \cdots, (c_{i,j})_n^n(t)) := \sum_{l=1}^n B_2[\omega_l, \omega_k; t] (c_{i,j})_k^n$$

then, (9) can be transformed into an ordinary differential equation with the coefficients $d_k^n(t)$ and $(c_{i,j})_k^n(t)$:

$$\begin{cases} \frac{\partial d_k^n(t)}{\partial t} = F_k(t, d_1^n(t), \cdots, d_n^n(t), (c_{i,j})_1^n(t), \cdots, (c_{i,j})_n^n(t)) \\ \frac{\partial (c_{i,j})_k^n(t)}{\partial t} = F_{n+k}(t, d_1^n(t), \cdots, d_n^n(t), (c_{i,j})_1^n(t), \cdots, (c_{i,j})_n^n(t)) \\ d_k^n(0) = (u_0, \omega_k) \\ (c_{i,j})_k^n(0) = ((\nabla u_0 \nabla u_0^\top)_{i,j}, \omega_k) \end{cases} \quad (10)$$

where $i, j = 1, 2$, $k = 1, 2, \cdots, n$. Since g_1 and g_2 are both continuous, we can deduce that the functions F_k are continuous. Peano's theorem implies that for any n, the (10) has a solution $\{d_k^n(t), (c_{i,j})_k^n(t)\}_{k=1}^n$.

Therefore, there exist functions $u^n(t,x)$, $v_{i,j}^n(t,x)$, $J_{i,j}^n(t,x)$ in the form of (5)–(7), and these functions satisfy the initial value condition (8) and the system (9) for a.e. $t \in (0, T]$. □

Lemma 2 (Consistent Estimation Inequality). *There exists a constant C, only depending on Ω, T, g_1, g_2 and G_σ such that*

$$\max_{0 \le t \le T} \|u^n\|_{L^2(\Omega)} + \max_{0 \le t \le T} \left\| J_{i,j}^n \right\|_{H^1(\Omega)} + \max_{0 \le t \le T} \left\| v_{i,j}^n \right\|_{L^2(\Omega)}$$
$$+ \|u^n\|_{L^2(0,T;H^1(\Omega))} + \|v_{i,j}\|_{L^2(0,T;H^1(\Omega))}$$
$$+ \|(u^n)'\|_{L^2(0,T;(H^1(\Omega))')} + \left\|(v_{i,j}^n)'\right\|_{L^2(0,T;(H^1(\Omega))')}$$
$$\le C \left(\|u_0\|_{L^2(\Omega)} + \left\|(\nabla u_0 \nabla u_0^\top)_{i,j}\right\|_{L^2(\Omega)} + \|\tilde{u}\|_{L^2(0,T;L^2(\Omega))} \right)$$

Proof. (i) $\max_{0 \le t \le T} \|u^n\|_{L^2(\Omega)}$ estimation. Multiply the first equation of (9) by $(d_{i,j})_k^n(t)$, sum for $k = 1, 2 \cdots, n$. By virtue of (5), we can obtain the following equation:

$$((u^n)', u^n) + B_0[u^n, \phi^n; t] = -\lambda(\tilde{u}, u^n), \quad a.e.\ 0 < t \le T \quad (11)$$

Because $g_1(J^n) \in C^\infty(\mathbb{R}^{2 \times 2, 2 \times 2})$ keeps the uniform positive definiteness and the symmetry of J, we can obtain

$$\beta \|u_n\|_{H^1(\Omega)}^2 \le B_0[u^n, u^n; t] + \gamma \|u_n\|_{L^2(\Omega)}^2$$

where $\beta > 0$, $\gamma \ge 0$. Then (11) can be formulated as

$$\frac{d}{dt}\left(\|u^n\|_{L^2(\Omega)}^2\right) + 2\beta \|u^n\|_{H^1(\Omega)}^2 \le (\lambda + 2\gamma)\|u^n\|_{L^2(\Omega)}^2 + \lambda \|\tilde{u}\|_{L^2(\Omega)}^2 \quad (12)$$

for a.e. $t \in (0, T]$. Applying the Gronwall inequality yields the following estimation:

$$\max_{0 \le t \le T} \|u^n\|_{L^2(\Omega)}^2 \le C\left(\|u_0\|_{L^2(\Omega)}^2 + \|\tilde{u}\|_{L^2(0,T;L^2(\Omega))}^2\right) \quad (13)$$

(ii) $\max_{0\leq t\leq T}\left\|v_{i,j}^n\right\|_{L^2(\Omega)}$ estimation. Multiply the first equation of (9) by $(c_{i,j})_k^n(t)$ and sum for $k = 1, 2 \cdots, n$. According to (6), we obtain the following equation:

$$((v_{i,j}^n)', v_{i,j}^n) + B_2[v_{i,j}^n, v_{i,j}^n; t] = 0, \quad i,j = 1,2, \quad \text{a.e. } 0 < t \leq T \tag{14}$$

Since

$$((v_{i,j}^n)', v_{i,j}^n) = \frac{d}{dt}\left(\frac{1}{2}\| v_{i,j}^n \|_{L^2(\Omega)}^2\right) \quad \text{a.e. } 0 < t \leq T \tag{15}$$

bring (15) into (14) and integrate from 0 to t, and we obtain

$$\frac{1}{2}\left\|v_{i,j}^n\right\|_{L^2(\Omega)}^2 - \frac{1}{2}\left\|v_{i,j}^n(0)\right\|_{L^2(\Omega)}^2 + \int_0^T B_2[v_{i,j}^n, v_{i,j}^n; t]dx = 0 \tag{16}$$

Let $u^n \in L^2(0, T; L^2(\Omega)) \cap L^\infty(0, T; L^2(\Omega))$ such that

$$\|u^n\|_{L^\infty(0,T;L^2(\Omega))} \leq \|u_0\|_{L^2(\Omega)}$$

Due to g_2, $G_\sigma \in C^\infty$, we can gain that $g_2(|\nabla G_\sigma * u^n|) \in L^\infty(0, T; C^\infty(\Omega))$. Since g_2 is monotonically decreasing and greater than zero, then we have $g_2(|\nabla u_\sigma^n|) = g_2(|\nabla G_\sigma * u^n|) \geq z_0 \geq 0$. Therefore, we have $B_2[v_{i,j}^n, v_{i,j}^n; t] \geq z_0 \geq 0$. Based on (16), there holds

$$\left\|v_{i,j}^n\right\|_{L^2(\Omega)}^2 \leq \left\|v_{i,j}^n(0)\right\|_{L^2(\Omega)}$$

Thus, we have

$$\max_{0\leq t\leq T}\left\|v_{i,j}^n\right\|_{L^2(\Omega)}^2 \leq \|(\nabla u_0 \nabla u_0^\top)_{i,j}\|_{L^2(\Omega)}^2 \tag{17}$$

(iii) $\|v_{i,j}\|_{L^2(0,T;H^1(\Omega))}$ estimation. By (ii), we know that

$$\frac{d}{dt}\left(\| v_{i,j}^n \|_{L^2(\Omega)}^2\right) + 2 z_1 \|v_{i,j}\|_{H^1(\Omega)}^2 \leq 2 z_1 \|v_{i,j}\|_{L^2(\Omega)}^2 \tag{18}$$

Integrating Equation (18) from 0 to T yields that

$$\left\|v_{i,j}^n\right\|_{L^2(\Omega)}^2\Big|_{t=T} + 2 z_1 \|v_{i,j}\|_{L^2(0,T;H^1(\Omega))}^2 \leq 2 z_1 \int_0^T \|v_{i,j}\|_{L^2(\Omega)}^2 ds + \left\|v_{i,j}^n(0)\right\|_{L^2(\Omega)}^2$$

According to the Gronwall inequality in the integral form, it can be deduced that

$$\left\|v_{i,j}^n\right\|_{L^2(\Omega)}^2\Big|_{t=T} \leq (1 + 2 z_0 T e^{2 z_0 T})\|(\nabla u_0 \nabla u_0^\top)_{i,j}\|_{L^2(\Omega)}^2 \tag{19}$$

Combining (18) and (19), it can be obtained that

$$\|v_{i,j}\|_{L^2(0,T;H^1(\Omega))}^2 \leq C\|(\nabla u_0 \nabla u_0^\top)_{i,j}\|_{L^2(\Omega)}^2, \quad i,j = 1,2 \tag{20}$$

(iv) $\left\|(v_{i,j}^n)'\right\|_{L^2(0,T;(H^1(\Omega))')}$ estimation. Based on the properties of g_2, it can be seen that there exists a constant α_0 such that

$$\int_\Omega g_2(|\nabla u_\sigma|)\nabla v_{i,j}^n \nabla \psi_{i,j} dx \leq \alpha_0 \left\|v_{i,j}^n\right\|_{H^1(\Omega)} \|\psi_{i,j}\|_{H^1(\Omega)}$$

Giving $\psi_{i,j} \in H^1(\Omega)$ and $\|\psi_{i,j}\|_{H^1(\Omega)} \leq 1$, we can represent it as $\psi_{i,j} = \psi_{i,j}^1 + \psi_{i,j}^2$, where $\psi_{i,j}^1 \in \text{span}\{\omega_k\}_{k=1}^n$ and $(\psi_{i,j}^2, \omega_k) = 0, k = 1, 2, \cdots, n$. Because $\{\omega_k\}_{k=1}^\infty$ is orthogonal in $H^1(\Omega)$, there is

$$\|\psi_{i,j}^1\|_{H^1(\Omega)} \leq \|\psi_{i,j}\|_{H^1(\Omega)} \leq 1$$

By (9), it can be obtained that

$$((v_{i,j}^n)', \psi_{i,j}^1) + B_2[v_{i,j}^n, \psi_{i,j}^1; t] = 0, \; i,j = 1,2$$

Since $\|\psi_{i,j}^1\|_{H^1(\Omega)} \leq 1$,

$$\langle (v_{i,j}^n)', \psi_{i,j} \rangle = ((v_{i,j}^n)', \psi_{i,j}) = ((v_{i,j}^n)', \psi_{i,j}^1) = -B_2[v_{i,j}^n, \psi_{i,j}^1; t] = 0$$

$$|\langle (v_{i,j}^n)', \psi_{i,j} \rangle| \leq |B_2[v_{i,j}^n, \psi_{i,j}^1; t]| \leq \alpha_0 \|v_{i,j}^n\|_{H^1(\Omega)} \|\psi_{i,j}\|_{H^1(\Omega)} \leq \alpha_0 \|v_{i,j}^n\|_{H^1(\Omega)}$$

Thus,

$$\|(v_{i,j}^n)'\|_{(H^1(\Omega))'} = \sup_{\psi_{i,j} \in H^1(\Omega),\, \|\psi_{i,j}\|_{H^1(\Omega)} \leq 1} |\langle (v_{i,j}^n)', \psi_{i,j} \rangle| \leq \alpha_0 \|v_{i,j}^n\|_{H^1(\Omega)}$$

$$\|(v_{i,j}^n)'\|_{L^2(0,T;(H^1(\Omega))')}^2 = \int_0^T \|(v_{i,j}^n)'\|_{(H^1(\Omega))'}^2 dt$$

$$\leq \alpha_0 \int_0^T \|v_{i,j}^n\|_{H^1(\Omega)}^2 dt$$

$$\leq \alpha_0 \|v_{i,j}^n\|_{L^2(0,T;H^1(\Omega))}$$

$$\leq C \|(\nabla u_0 \nabla u_0^\top)_{i,j}\|_{L^2(\Omega)}^2$$

Therefore,

$$\|(v_{i,j}^n)'\|_{L^2(0,T;(H^1(\Omega))')}^2 \leq C \|(\nabla u_0 \nabla u_0^\top)_{i,j}\|_{L^2(\Omega)}^2 \tag{21}$$

(v) $\max_{0 \leq t \leq T} \|J_{i,j}^n\|_{H^1(\Omega)}$ estimation. According to the following fractional time-delay ordinary differential equation

$$\tau D_c^\gamma J_{i,j} + J_{i,j} = v_{i,j}, \; (x,t) \in \Omega \times (0,T]$$
$$J_{i,j}(x,0) = 0, \; i,j = 1,2, \; x \in \Omega$$

It can be obtained that

$$J_{i,j}^n := \frac{1}{\Gamma(\gamma)} \int_0^t (t-s)^{\gamma-1} \frac{1}{\tau}(v_{i,j}^n - J_{i,j}^n) ds$$

To estimate the inequality, we divide the interval $(0,T]$ equally, the length between the divided cells is a, which is denoted as $(ka, (k+1)a]$, and the equation within the interval is

$$\tau D_c^\gamma J_{i,j} + J_{i,j} = v_{i,j}, \; t \in (ka, (k+1)a]$$
$$J_{i,j}(x,0) = J_{i,j}(ka), \; i,j = 1,2, \; x \in \Omega$$

The solution of the equation in the interval $(ka, (k+1)a]$ is

$$J_{i,j}^n(t) = J_{i,j}^n(ka) + \frac{1}{\Gamma(\gamma)} \int_{ka}^{(k+1)a} (t-s)^{\gamma-1} \frac{1}{\tau}(v_{i,j}^n - J_{i,j}^n) ds$$
$$= J_{i,j}^n(ka) + \frac{1}{\tau\Gamma(\gamma)} \int_{ka}^{(k+1)a} (t-s)^{\gamma-1} v_{i,j}^n(s) ds + \frac{1}{\tau\Gamma(\gamma)} \int_{ka}^{(k+1)a} (t-s)^{\gamma-1} J_{i,j}^n(s) ds$$

Estimating inequalities involves

$$\left\|J_{i,j}^n(t)\right\|_{H^1(\Omega)} = \left\|J_{i,j}^n(ka)\right\|_{H^1(\Omega)} + \frac{1}{\tau\Gamma(\gamma)} \int_{ka}^{(k+1)a} ((k+1)a - s)^{\gamma-1} \left\|v_{i,j}^n(s)\right\|_{H^1(\Omega)} ds$$
$$+ \frac{1}{\tau\Gamma(\gamma)} \int_{ka}^{(k+1)a} ((k+1)a - s)^{\gamma-1} \left\|J_{i,j}^n(s)\right\|_{H^1(\Omega)} ds$$
$$\leq \left\|J_{i,j}^n(ka)\right\|_{H^1(\Omega)} + \frac{1}{\tau\Gamma(\gamma)} \max_{0\leq t\leq T}\left\|v_{i,j}^n(t)\right\|_{H^1(\Omega)} \int_{ka}^{(k+1)a} ((k+1)a - s)^{\gamma-1} ds$$
$$+ \frac{1}{\tau\Gamma(\gamma)} \max_{0\leq t\leq T}\left\|J_{i,j}^n(t)\right\|_{H^1(\Omega)} \int_{ka}^{(k+1)a} ((k+1)a - s)^{\gamma-1} ds$$
$$= \left\|J_{i,j}^n(ka)\right\|_{H^1(\Omega)} + \frac{1}{\gamma\tau\Gamma(\gamma)} a^\gamma \left(\max_{0\leq t\leq T}\left\|v_{i,j}^n(t)\right\|_{H^1(\Omega)} + \max_{0\leq t\leq T}\left\|J_{i,j}^n(t)\right\|_{H^1(\Omega)}\right)$$

Taking the maximum value at both ends of the inequality simultaneously, it has

$$\left(1 - \frac{1}{\gamma\tau\Gamma(\gamma)} a^\gamma\right) \max_{0\leq t\leq T}\left\|J_{i,j}^n(t)\right\|_{H^1(\Omega)} \leq \left\|J_{i,j}^n(ka)\right\|_{H^1(\Omega)} + \frac{1}{\gamma\tau\Gamma(\gamma)} a^\gamma \max_{0\leq t\leq T}\left\|v_{i,j}^n(t)\right\|_{H^1(\Omega)}$$

We can choose a such that $1 - \frac{1}{\gamma\tau\Gamma(\gamma)} a^\gamma < 1$. Because $J_{i,j}^n(ka) = 0$ in the interval $(0, T]$ and

$$\max_{0\leq t\leq T}\left\|v_{i,j}^n\right\|_{H^1(\Omega)}^2 \leq C_1 \left\|(\nabla u_0 \nabla u_0^\mathsf{T})_{i,j}\right\|_{L^2(\Omega)}^2$$

we set

$$C = \frac{\frac{1}{\gamma\tau\Gamma(\gamma)} a^\gamma C_1}{1 - \frac{1}{\gamma\tau\Gamma(\gamma)} a^\gamma}$$

Therefore,

$$\max_{0\leq t\leq T}\left\|J_{i,j}^n\right\|_{H^1(\Omega)} \leq C \left\|(\nabla u_0 \nabla u_0^\mathsf{T})_{i,j}\right\|_{L^2(\Omega)}^2 \qquad (22)$$

(vi) $\|u^n\|_{L^2(0,T;H^1(\Omega))}$ estimation. By integrating Equation (14) from 0 to T, we have

$$\|u^n\|_{L^2(\Omega)}^2|_{t=T} + 2\beta\|u^n\|_{L^2(0,T;H^1(\Omega))}^2$$
$$\leq (\lambda + 2\gamma) \int_0^T \|u^n\|_{L^2(\Omega)}^2 dt + \lambda\|\tilde{u}\|_{L^2(0,T;L^2(\Omega))}^2 + \|u^n(0)\|_{L^2(\Omega)}^2$$

Therefore

$$\|u^n\|_{L^2(0,T;H^1(\Omega))}^2 \leq C\left(\|u_0\|_{L^2(\Omega)}^2 + \|\tilde{u}\|_{L^2(0,T;L^2(\Omega))}^2\right) \qquad (23)$$

(vii) $\|(u^n)'\|_{L^2(0,T;(H^1(\Omega))')}$ estimation. Giving $\phi \in H^1(\Omega)$ and $\|\phi\|_{H^1(\Omega)} \leq 1$, we can represent it as $\phi = \phi^1 + \phi^2$, where $\phi^1 \in \text{span}\{\omega_k\}_{k=1}^n$ and $(\phi^2, \omega_k) = 0$, $k = 1, 2, \cdots, n$. Because $\{\omega_k\}_{k=1}^\infty$ is orthogonal in $H^1(\Omega)$, then we have

$$\left\|\phi^1\right\|_{H^1(\Omega)} \leq \|\phi\|_{H^1(\Omega)} \leq 1$$

By (5), it can be obtained that

$$\begin{aligned}\|(u^n)'\|^2_{L^2(0,T;(H^1(\Omega))')} &= \int_0^T \|(u^n)'\|^2_{(H^1(\Omega))'} dt \\ &\leq C\int_0^T \|u^n\|^2_{H^1(\Omega)} + \|\widetilde{u}\|^2_{L^2(\Omega)} dt \\ &\leq C\left(\|u_0\|^2_{L^2(\Omega)} + \|\widetilde{u}\|^2_{L^2(0,T;L^2(\Omega))}\right)\end{aligned}$$

Therefore,

$$\|(u^n)'\|^2_{L^2(0,T;(H^1(\Omega))')} \leq C\left(\|u_0\|^2_{L^2(\Omega)} + \|\widetilde{u}\|^2_{L^2(0,T;L^2(\Omega))}\right) \quad (24)$$

Combining the inequalities estimated by (17), (20)–(22), (13), (23) and (24), we obtain a consistent estimation inequality. □

In order to prove the existence of weak solutions for (3), we need to analyze whether the sequence $J^n_{i,j}$ has a subsequence with weak/strong convergence property in the corresponding space.

Lemma 3. *Let $F(t) = \{J^n_{i,j}(t)\}_{n\in N}$, where N is the index set, $J^n_{i,j}: [0,T] \mapsto X \in L^2(\Omega)$, then $F(t)$ is a relatively compact set in $C(0,T;L^2(\Omega))$.*

Proof. (i) Prove that $\{J^n_{i,j} | n \in N, t \in [0,T]\}$ is relatively compact in $L^2(\Omega)$. According to step (v) of the consistent estimation inequality, we can obtain

$$\max_{0\leq t\leq T}\left\|J^n_{i,j}\right\|_{H^1(\Omega)} \leq C\|(\nabla u_0 \nabla u_0^\mathsf{T})_{i,j}\|^2_{L^2(\Omega)}$$

Because $F(t)$ is uniformly bounded in $L^2(\Omega)$,

$$\left\|J^n_{i,j}\right\|_{C([0,T];H^1(\Omega))} \leq C$$

It means that $F(t)$ is bounded in $H^1(\Omega)$. Therefore, $\{J^n_{i,j} | n \in N, t \in [0,T]\}$ is relatively compact in $L^2(\Omega)$.
(ii) Proof of the equicontinuity of $F(t)$. For $\forall \varepsilon > 0$, with t_1 as the initial value diffused to t_2, then

$$J^n_{i,j}(t_2) = J^n_{i,j}(t_1) + \frac{1}{\tau\Gamma(\gamma)}\int_{t_1}^{t_2}(t_2-s)^{\gamma-1}(v^n_{i,j}(s) - J^n_{i,j}(s))ds$$

then for $\forall \varepsilon > 0, \exists \delta = \frac{\|v^n_{i,j}(s)-J^n_{i,j}\|_{H^1(\Omega)}\varepsilon}{\tau\gamma\Gamma(\gamma)}$, when $|t_1 - t_2| < \delta$, we have

$$\begin{aligned}\left\|J^n_{i,j}(t_2) - J^n_{i,j}(t_1)\right\|_{H^1(\Omega)} &\leq \frac{1}{\Gamma\tau(\gamma)}\int_{t_1}^{t_2}(t_2-s)^{\gamma-1}\left\|v^n_{i,j}(s) - J^n_{i,j}(s)\right\|_{H^1(\Omega)} ds \\ &\leq \frac{1}{\tau\gamma\Gamma(\gamma)}\left\|v^n_{i,j} - J^n_{i,j}\right\|_{H^1(\Omega)} |t_2 - t_1| \\ &\leq \frac{1}{\tau\gamma\Gamma(\gamma)}\left\|v^n_{i,j} - J^n_{i,j}\right\|_{H^1(\Omega)} \cdot \frac{\tau\gamma\Gamma(\gamma)\delta}{\left\|v^n_{i,j} - J^n_{i,j}\right\|_{H^1(\Omega)}}\end{aligned}$$

Therefore $\left\| J_{i,j}^n(t_2) - J_{i,j}^n(t_1) \right\|_{H^1(\Omega)} < \varepsilon$, which means $F(t)$ is equicontinuous. Finally, combining (i)–(ii) and according to the Arela–Ascoli lemma, $F(t)$ is a relatively compact set in $C(0, T; L^2(\Omega))$. □

Theorem 2. *Under the assumption that $u_0 \in L^2(\Omega)$, $(\nabla u_0 \nabla u_0^\mathsf{T})_{i,j} \in L^2(\Omega)$, there exists a weak solution of* (3).

Proof. (i) According to the consistent estimation inequality, the sequences $\{u^n\}_{n=1}^\infty$, $\{v_{i,j}^n\}_{n=1}^\infty$ are bounded in $L^2(0, T; H^1(\Omega))$, $\{(u^n)'\}_{n=1}^\infty$, $\{(v_{i,j}^n)'\}_{n=1}^\infty$ are bounded in $L^2(0, T; (H^1(\Omega))')$ and $\{J_{i,j}^n\}_{n=1}^\infty$ are bounded in $L^\infty(0, T; H^1(\Omega))$.

According to the weak/strong sequence compactness in $L^p(\Omega)$ and the compact embedding theorem in Sobolev spaces, there exist subsequences $\{u^{n_k}\}_{k=1}^\infty \subset \{u^n\}_{n=1}^\infty$, $\{v_{i,j}^{n_k}\}_{k=1}^\infty \subset \{v_{i,j}^n\}_{k=1}^\infty$. According to lemma (3), there exist subsequences $\{J_{i,j}^{n_k}\}_{k=1}^\infty \subset \{J_{i,j}^n\}_{k=1}^\infty$ and functions

$$u \in L^2(0, T; H^1(\Omega)), u' \in L^2(0, T; H^1(\Omega)')$$
$$v_{i,j} \in L^2(0, T; H^1(\Omega)), v_{i,j}' \in L^2(0, T; (H^1(\Omega))')$$
$$J_{i,j} \in L^\infty(0, T; H^1(\Omega)), D_c^\gamma J_{i,j} \in L^2(0, T; (H^1(\Omega))')$$

such that

$$\begin{cases} u^{n_k} \rightharpoonup u & \text{in } L^2(0, T; H^1(\Omega)) \\ (u^{n_k})' \rightharpoonup u' & \text{in } L^2(0, T; (H^1(\Omega))') \\ v_{i,j}^{n_k} \rightharpoonup v_{i,j} & \text{in } L^2(0, T; H^1(\Omega)) \\ (v_{i,j}^{n_k})' \rightharpoonup v_{i,j}' & \text{in } L^2(0, T; (H^1(\Omega))') \\ J_{i,j}^{n_k} \to J_{i,j} & \text{in } C(0, T; H^1(\Omega)) \\ D_c^\gamma J_{i,j}^{n_k} \rightharpoonup D_c^\gamma J_{i,j} & \text{in } L^2(0, T; (H^1(\Omega))') \end{cases} \quad (25)$$

(ii) Fixing a positive integer N, choosing functions $\phi, \phi_{i,j}, \psi_{i,j} \in C^1([0, T]; H^1(\Omega))$ satisfies

$$\phi(t) = \sum_{l=1}^N \alpha^l(t) \omega_l(x)$$

$$\phi_{i,j}(t) = \sum_{l=1}^N \alpha_{i,j}^l(t) \omega_l(x)$$

$$\psi_{i,j}(t) = \sum_{l=1}^N \beta_{i,j}^l(t) \omega_l(x), \ i, j = 1, 2$$

where $\{\alpha^l\}_{l=1}^N$, $\{\alpha_{i,j}^l\}_{l=1}^N$, $\{\beta_{i,j}^l\}_{l=1}^N$ are the given smooth functions. Choose $n \geq N$, multiplying (9) by $\{\alpha^l\}_{l=1}^N$, $\{\alpha_{i,j}^l\}_{l=1}^N$, $\{\beta_{i,j}^l\}_{l=1}^N$, and taking the summation for $l = 1, 2, \cdots, N$, integrate from 0 to t

$$\begin{cases} \int_0^T [\langle (u^n)', \phi \rangle + B_0[u^n, \phi; t]] dt = -\int_0^T [\lambda(\widetilde{u}, \psi)] dt \\ \int_0^T [(D_c^\gamma J_{i,j}^n, \phi_{i,j}) + B_1[J_{i,j}^n, \phi_{i,j}, t]] dt = \frac{1}{\tau} \int_0^T [(v_{i,j}^n, \phi_{i,j})] dt, \ i, j = 1, 2 \\ \int_0^T [\langle (v_{i,j}^n)', \psi_{i,j} \rangle + B_2[v_{i,j}^n, \psi_{i,j}; t]] dt = 0, \ i, j = 1, 2 \end{cases} \quad (26)$$

Let $n = n_k$, and take the limit on both ends of (25),

$$\int_0^T [\langle u', \phi \rangle + B_0[u, \phi; t]] \mathrm{d}t = -\int_0^T \lambda(\tilde{u}, \psi) \mathrm{d}t \tag{27}$$

$$\int_0^T [(D_c^\gamma J_{ij}, \phi_{i,j}) + B_1[J_{i,j}, \phi_{i,j}; t]] \mathrm{d}t = \frac{1}{\tau} \int_0^T (v_{i,j}, \phi_{i,j}) \mathrm{d}t, \ i, j = 1, 2 \tag{28}$$

$$\int_0^T [\langle v'_{i,j}, \psi_{i,j} \rangle + B_2[v_{i,j}, \psi_{i,j}; t]] \mathrm{d}t = 0, \ i, j = 1, 2 \tag{29}$$

Since $\phi, \phi_{i,j}, \psi_{i,j}$ are dense in $H^1(\Omega)$, there holds $\phi, \phi_{i,j}, \psi_{i,j} \in L^2(0, T; H^1(\Omega))$. Hence,

$$\langle u', \phi \rangle + B_0[u, \phi; t] = -\lambda(\tilde{u}, \psi)$$

$$(D_c^\gamma J_{i,j}, \phi_{i,j}) + B_1[J_{i,j}, \phi_{i,j}; t] = \frac{1}{\tau}(v_{i,j}, \phi_{i,j}), \ i, j = 1, 2$$

$$\langle v'_{i,j}, \psi_{i,j} \rangle + B_2[v_{i,j}, \psi_{i,j}; t] = 0, \ i, j = 1, 2$$

for each $\phi, \phi_{i,j}, \psi_{i,j} \in H^1(\Omega)$, a.e. $t \in (0, T]$.

(iii) For $\phi, \phi_{i,j}, \psi_{i,j} \in C^1([0, T]; H^1(\Omega))$, we have $\phi(T) = 0$, $\phi_{i,j}(T) = 0$, $\psi_{i,j}(T) = 0$, $(i, j = 1, 2)$. With the partial integration of (27)–(29), we have

$$\begin{cases} \int_0^T [-\langle \phi', u \rangle + B_0[u, \phi; t]] \mathrm{d}t = -\int_0^T \lambda(\tilde{u}, \psi) \mathrm{d}t + \langle u(0), \phi(0) \rangle \\ \int_0^T [(D_c^\gamma J_{i,j}, \phi_{i,j}) + B_1[J_{i,j}, \phi_{i,j}; t]] \mathrm{d}t \\ = \frac{1}{\tau} \int_0^T (v_{i,j}, \phi_{i,j}) \mathrm{d}t + T \sum_{j=0}^{n-1} D_{(0,T)}^{\gamma+j-n} \phi_{i,j}(0) D^{n-i-j} J_{i,j}(0) \\ \int_0^T [-\langle \psi'_{i,j}, v_{i,j} \rangle + B_2[v_{i,j}, \psi_{i,j}; t]] \mathrm{d}t = \langle v_{i,j}(0), \psi_{i,j}(0) \rangle \ i, j = 1, 2 \end{cases} \tag{30}$$

where $D_{(0,T)}^{\gamma+j-n} \phi_{i,j} = \frac{1}{\Gamma(n-\gamma)} \left(-\frac{\mathrm{d}}{\mathrm{d}t}\right)^n \int_t^T (t-s)^{n-\gamma-1} \phi_{i,j} \mathrm{d}s$.

Similarly, integrating each equation of (26) by parts yields

$$\begin{cases} \int_0^T [-\langle \phi', u^n \rangle + B_0[u^n, \phi; t]] \mathrm{d}t = -\int_0^T \lambda(\tilde{u}, \psi) \mathrm{d}t + \langle u^n(0), \phi(0) \rangle \\ \int_0^T [(D_c^\gamma J_{i,j}^n, \phi_{i,j}) + B_1[J_{i,j}^n, \phi_{i,j}; t]] \mathrm{d}t \\ = \frac{1}{\tau} \int_0^T (v_{i,j}, \phi_{i,j}) \mathrm{d}t + T \sum_{j=0}^{n-1} D_{(0,T)}^{\gamma+j-n} \phi_{i,j}(0) D^{n-i-j} J_{i,j}^n(0) \\ \int_0^T [-\langle \psi'_{i,j}, v_{i,j}^n \rangle + B_2[v_{i,j}^n, \psi_{i,j}; t]] \mathrm{d}t = \langle v_{i,j}^n(0), \psi_{i,j}(0) \rangle, \ i, j = 1, 2 \end{cases} \tag{31}$$

Let $n = n_k$, $k \to +\infty$, and apply (25). There holds

$$\begin{cases} \int_0^T [-\langle \phi', u \rangle + B_0[u, \phi; t]] \mathrm{d}t = -\int_0^T \lambda(\tilde{u}, \psi) \mathrm{d}t + \langle u_0, \phi(0) \rangle \\ \int_0^T [(D_c^\gamma J_{i,j}, \phi_{i,j}) + B_1[J_{i,j}, \phi_{i,j}; t]] \mathrm{d}t \\ = \frac{1}{\tau} \int_0^T (v_{i,j}, \phi_{i,j}) \mathrm{d}t + T \sum_{j=0}^{n-1} D_{(0,T)}^{\gamma+j-n} \phi_{i,j}(0) \cdot 0 \\ \int_0^T [-\langle \psi'_{i,j}, v_{i,j} \rangle + B_2[v_{i,j}, \psi_{i,j}; t]] \mathrm{d}t = \langle (\nabla u_0 \nabla u_0^\top)_{i,j}, \psi_{i,j}(0) \rangle, \ i, j = 1, 2 \end{cases} \tag{32}$$

Since $\phi(0), \phi_{i,j}(0), \psi_{i,j}(0), (i, j = 1, 2)$ are arbitrary, according to (30) and (32), we deduce that $u(0) = u_0$, $J_{i,j}(0) = 0$, $v_{i,j}(0) = (\nabla u_0 \nabla u_0^\top)_{i,j}, i, j = 1, 2$. □

2.5. Uniqueness of Weak Solutions

This section studies the uniqueness of the weak solution of the model in the text, and provides a detailed proof as follows.

Theorem 3. *Under the assumption that $u_0 \in L^2(\Omega)$, $(\nabla u_0 \nabla u_0^\mathsf{T})_{i,j} \in L^2(\Omega)$, there exists a unique weak solution of* (3).

Proof. Assume that the system (3) has two solutions, respectively, i.e., $(\bar{u}, \bar{J}_{i,j}, \bar{v}_{i,j})$, $(\hat{u}, \hat{J}_{i,j}, \hat{v}_{i,j})$, $(i, j = 1, 2)$. Consider the definition of weak solutions

$$\begin{cases} \langle \bar{u}', \phi \rangle + B_0[\bar{u}, \phi; t] = -\lambda(\tilde{u}, \psi) \\ (D_c^\gamma \bar{J}_{i,j}, \phi_{i,j}) + B_1[\bar{J}_{i,j}, \phi_{i,j}; t] = \frac{1}{\tau}(\bar{v}_{i,j}, \phi_{i,j}), \ i, j = 1, 2 \\ \langle \bar{v}'_{i,j}, \psi_{i,j} \rangle + B_2[\bar{v}_{i,j}, \psi_{i,j}; t] = 0, \ i, j = 1, 2 \end{cases} \quad (33)$$

where $\forall \phi, \phi_{i,j}, \psi_{i,j} \in H^1(\Omega)(i, j = 1, 2)$, a.e. $t \in (0, T]$. Similarly, applying (33) to $(\hat{u}, \hat{J}_{i,j}, \hat{v}_{i,j})$, $(i, j = 1, 2)$ and subtracting the result of two equations, we have

$$\begin{cases} \langle (\bar{u} - \hat{u})', \phi \rangle + B_0[(\bar{u} - \hat{u}), \phi; t] = -\lambda(\tilde{u}, \psi) \\ (D_c^\gamma(\bar{J}_{i,j} - \hat{J}_{i,j}), \phi_{i,j}) + B_1[(\bar{J}_{i,j} - \hat{J}_{i,j}), \phi_{i,j}; t] = \frac{1}{\tau}((\bar{v}_{i,j} - \hat{v}_{i,j}), \phi_{i,j}), \ i, j = 1, 2 \\ \langle (\bar{v}_{i,j} - \hat{v}_{i,j})', \psi_{i,j} \rangle + B_2[(\bar{v}_{i,j} - \hat{v}_{i,j}), \psi_{i,j}; t] = 0, \ i, j = 1, 2 \end{cases}$$

Selecting $\phi = \bar{u} - \hat{u}$, $\phi_{i,j} = \bar{J}_{i,j} - \hat{J}_{i,j}$, $\psi_{i,j} = \bar{v}_{i,j} - \hat{v}_{i,j}$ and integrating in Ω,

$$\begin{cases} \frac{1}{2}\frac{d}{dt}\|\bar{u} - \hat{u}\|_{L^2}^2 + \int_\Omega g_1(\bar{J}) \nabla(\bar{u} - \hat{u}) \cdot \nabla(\bar{u} - \hat{u}) dx - \lambda\|\bar{u} - \hat{u}\|_{L^2}^2 \\ = -\int_\Omega (g_1(\bar{J}) - g_1(\hat{J})) \nabla \hat{u} \cdot \nabla(\bar{u} - \hat{u}) dx \\ \tau \int_\Omega D_c^\gamma(\bar{J}_{i,j} - \hat{J}_{i,j}) \cdot (\bar{J}_{i,j} - \hat{J}_{i,j}) dx + \|\bar{J}_{i,j} - \hat{J}_{i,j}\|_{L^2}^2 \\ = \int_\Omega (\bar{v}_{i,j} - \hat{v}_{i,j})(\bar{J}_{i,j} - \hat{J}_{i,j}) dx \\ \frac{1}{2}\frac{d}{dt}\|\bar{v}_{i,j} - \hat{v}_{i,j}\|_{L^2}^2 + \int_\Omega g_2(|\nabla \bar{u}_\sigma|) \nabla(\bar{v}_{i,j} - \hat{v}_{i,j}) \cdot \nabla(\bar{v}_{i,j} - \hat{v}_{i,j}) dx \\ = -\int_\Omega (g_2(|\nabla \bar{u}_\sigma|) - g_2(|\nabla \hat{u}_\sigma|)) \nabla \hat{v}_{i,j} \cdot \nabla(\bar{v}_{i,j} - \hat{v}_{i,j}) dx \end{cases} \quad (34)$$

For the first equation in (34), using the smoothness and positive definiteness of $g_1(J)$, the Cauchy inequality with ε, and the Schwarz inequality, it can be obtained that

$$\frac{1}{2}\frac{d}{dt}\|\bar{u} - \hat{u}\|_{L^2}^2 + z_1\|\nabla(\bar{u} - \hat{u})\|_{L^2}^2 - \lambda\|\bar{u} - \hat{u}\|_{L^2}^2$$

$$\leq \int_\Omega |(g_1(\bar{J}) - g_1(\hat{J})) \nabla(\hat{u})| \cdot |\nabla(\bar{u} - \hat{u})| dx$$

$$\leq \|\nabla(\bar{u} - \hat{u})\|_{L^2} \left(\int_\Omega |(g_1(\bar{J}) - g_1(\hat{J})) \nabla \hat{u}|^2 dx \right)^{\frac{1}{2}}$$

$$\leq \|\nabla(\bar{u} - \hat{u})\|_{L^2} \|\nabla \hat{u}\|_{L^2} \sum_{i,j=1}^{2} \|(g_1(\bar{J}) - g_1(\hat{J}))_{i,j}\|_{L^\infty}$$

$$\leq C\|\nabla(\bar{u} - \hat{u})\|_{L^2} \|\nabla \hat{u}\|_{L^2} \sum_{i,j=1}^{2} \|\bar{J}_{i,j} - \hat{J}_{i,j}\|_{L^2}$$

$$\leq \frac{2C}{z_1} \sum_{i,j=1}^{2} \|\bar{J}_{i,j} - \hat{J}_{i,j}\|_{L^2}^2 \|\nabla \hat{u}\|_{L^2}^2 + \frac{z_1}{2}\|\nabla(\bar{u} - \hat{u})\|_{L^2}^2$$

Reorganizing the above equation, we obtain

$$\frac{d}{dt}\|\bar{u} - \hat{u}\|_{L^2}^2 + z_1\|\nabla(\bar{u} - \hat{u})\|_{L^2}^2 \leq \frac{4C}{z_1} \sum_{i,j=1}^{2} \|\bar{J}_{i,j} - \hat{J}_{i,j}\|_{L^2}^2 \|\nabla \hat{u}\|_{L^2}^2 + \lambda\|\bar{u} - \hat{u}\|_{L^2}^2$$

Therefore,

$$\frac{d}{dt}\|\bar{u}-\hat{u}\|_{L^2}^2 \leq M_1 \sum_{i,j=1}^{2}\|\bar{J}_{i,j}-\hat{J}_{i,j}\|_{L^2}^2\|\nabla\hat{u}\|_{L^2}^2 + \lambda\|\bar{u}-\hat{u}\|_{L^2}^2, \quad M_1=\frac{4C}{z_1} \qquad (35)$$

where $M_1 > 0$. For the second equation in (34), by applying theorem (1), we obtain

$$\frac{\tau}{2}D_c^{\gamma}\|\bar{J}_{i,j}-\hat{J}_{i,j}\|_{L^2}^2 \leq \tau \int_{\Omega} D_c^{\gamma}(\bar{J}_{i,j}-\hat{J}_{i,j})\cdot(\bar{J}_{i,j}-\hat{J}_{i,j})\mathrm{d}x$$

Further, the second equation in (34) can be transformed into

$$\frac{\tau}{2}D_c^{\gamma}\|\bar{J}_{i,j}-\hat{J}_{i,j}\|_{L^2}^2 + \|\bar{J}_{i,j}-\hat{J}_{i,j}\|_{L^2}^2 \leq \int_{\Omega}(\bar{v}_{i,j}-\hat{v}_{i,j})(\bar{J}_{i,j}-\hat{J}_{i,j})\mathrm{d}x$$

Thus,

$$D_c^{\gamma}\sum_{i,j=1}^{2}\|\bar{J}_{i,j}-\hat{J}_{i,j}\|_{L^2}^2 \leq \tau\sum_{i,j=1}^{2}\|\bar{v}_{i,j}-\hat{v}_{i,j}\|_{L^2}^2 - \tau\sum_{i,j=1}^{2}\|\bar{J}_{i,j}-\hat{J}_{i,j}\|_{L^2}^2 \qquad (36)$$

Therefore,

$$D_c^{\gamma}\sum_{i,j=1}^{2}\|\bar{J}_{i,j}-\hat{J}_{i,j}\|_{L^2}^2 \leq \tau\sum_{i,j=1}^{2}\|\bar{v}_{i,j}-\hat{v}_{i,j}\|_{L^2}^2 \qquad (37)$$

For the third equation in (34), similar to the derivation of the first equation, we apply the properties of g_2, the Schwarz inequality, and the Cauchy inequality with ε,

$$\frac{1}{2}\frac{d}{dt}\|\bar{v}_{i,j}-\hat{v}_{i,j}\|_{L^2}^2 + z_2\|\nabla(\bar{v}_{i,j}-\hat{v}_{i,j})\|_{L^2}^2$$

$$\leq \int_{\Omega}|g_2(|\nabla\bar{u}_{\sigma}|)-g_2(|\nabla\hat{u}_{\sigma}|)\nabla\hat{v}_{i,j}|\cdot\nabla(\bar{v}_{i,j}-\hat{v}_{i,j})\mathrm{d}x$$

$$\leq \|\nabla(\bar{v}_{i,j}-\hat{v}_{i,j})\|_{L^2}\left(\int_{\Omega}|(g_2(|\nabla\bar{u}_{\sigma}|)-g_2(|\nabla\hat{u}_{\sigma}|))\nabla\hat{v}_{i,j}|^2\mathrm{d}x\right)^{\frac{1}{2}}$$

$$\leq C_{i,j}\sum_{i,j=1}^{2}\|\nabla\hat{v}_{i,j}\|_{L^2}\|\bar{u}-\hat{u}\|_{L^2}\cdot\|\nabla(\bar{v}_{i,j}-\hat{v}_{i,j})\|_{L^2}$$

$$\leq \frac{2C_{i,j}}{z_2}\sum_{i,j=1}^{2}\|\nabla\hat{v}_{i,j}\|_{L^2}^2\cdot\|\bar{u}-\hat{u}\|_{L^2}^2 + \frac{z_2}{2}\|\nabla(\bar{v}_{i,j}-\hat{v}_{i,j})\|_{L^2}^2$$

After reorganization, it becomes

$$\frac{d}{dt}\|\bar{v}_{i,j}-\hat{v}_{i,j}\|_{L^2}^2 + z_2\|\nabla(\bar{v}_{i,j}-\hat{v}_{i,j})\|_{L^2}^2 \leq \frac{4C_{i,j}}{z_2}\sum_{i,j=1}^{2}\|\nabla\hat{v}_{i,j}\|_{L^2}^2\cdot\|\bar{u}-\hat{u}\|_{L^2}^2$$

Therefore,

$$\frac{d}{dt}\sum_{i,j}^{2}\|\bar{v}_{i,j}-\hat{v}_{i,j}\|_{L^2}^2 \leq M_2\sum_{i,j=1}^{2}\|\nabla\hat{v}_{i,j}\|_{L^2}^2\cdot\|\bar{u}-\hat{u}\|_{L^2}^2, \quad M_2=\max_{i,j}\left(\frac{4C_{i,j}}{z_2}\right) \qquad (38)$$

According to the solution of the fractional-order ordinary differential equation and the formula (37), we obtain

$$\|\bar{J}_{i,j} - \hat{J}_{i,j}\|_{L^2}^2 = \int_0^t (t-s)^{\gamma-1} D_c^{\gamma} \|\bar{J}_{i,j} - \hat{J}_{i,j}\|_{L^2}^2 ds$$
$$\leq \int_0^t (t-s)^{\gamma-1} \tau \|\bar{v}_{i,j} - \hat{v}_{i,j}\|_{L^2}^2 ds \tag{39}$$

Dividing the interval $(0, t]$ equally and assuming that the length between each cell after division is b, each interval can be denoted as $(kb, (k+1)b]$, $k = 0, \cdots, t/b$. Let $\|w\| = \max\limits_{\iota \in (kb, (k+1)b]} \|(\bar{v}_{i,j} - \hat{v}_{i,j})(\iota)\|$. To operate on (39), there are

$$\|\bar{J}_{i,j} - \hat{J}_{i,j}\|_{L^2}^2 \leq \int_{kb}^{(k+1)b} ((k+1)b - s)^{\gamma-1} \tau \|\bar{v}_{i,j} - \hat{v}_{i,j}\|_{L^2}^2 ds$$
$$\leq \|w\|^2 \int_{kb}^{(k+1)b} ((k+1)b - s)^{\gamma-1} \tau ds$$
$$\leq C\|w\|^2$$

Integrating (38) from kb to $(k+1)b$,

$$\|\bar{v}_{i,j} - \hat{v}_{i,j}\|_{L^2}^2 \leq \int_{kb}^{(k+1)b} M_2 \sum_{i,j=1}^2 \|\nabla \hat{v}_{i,j}(s)\|_{L^2}^2 \cdot \|(\bar{u} - \hat{u})(s)\|_{L^2}^2 ds \tag{40}$$

For (40), taking the maximum value at both ends simultaneously, we have

$$\|w\|^2 \leq \max_{s \in (kb, (k+1)b]} \int_0^s M_2 \sum_{i,j=1}^2 \|\nabla \hat{v}_{i,j}(s)\|_{L^2}^2 \cdot \|(\bar{u} - \hat{u})(s)\|_{L^2}^2 ds \tag{41}$$

Let $\|z\| = \max\limits_{\iota \in (kb, (k+1)b]} \|\bar{u} - \hat{u}\|$, $k = 0, \cdots, t/b$, then (41) can be transformed into

$$\|w(t)\|^2 \leq \|z(t)\|^2 \int_0^s M_2 \|\nabla \hat{v}_{i,j}(s)\|_{L^2}^2 ds \tag{42}$$

Integrating (35) from kb to $(k+1)b$

$$\|\bar{u} - \hat{u}\|_{L^2}^2 \leq \int_{kb}^{(k+1)b} M_1 \sum_{i,j=1}^2 \|(\bar{J}_{i,j} - \hat{J}_{i,j})(s)\|_{L^2}^2 \|\nabla \hat{u}(s)\|_{L^2}^2 ds \tag{43}$$
$$+ \lambda \int_{kb}^{(k+1)b} \|(\bar{u} - \hat{u})(s)\|_{L^2}^2 ds \tag{44}$$

For (43), taking the maximum value at both ends simultaneously, we have

$$\|z\|^2 \leq C\|z\|^2 \max_{s \in (kb, (k+1)b]} \int_{kb}^{(k+1)b} \|\nabla \hat{u}(s)\|_{L^2}^2 ds + \lambda \int_{kb}^{(k+1)b} \|z\|^2 ds$$
$$\left(1 - C \max_{s \in (kb, (k+1)b]} \int_{kb}^{(k+1)b} \|\nabla \hat{u}(s)\|_{L^2}^2 ds\right) \|z\|^2 \leq \lambda \int_{kb}^{(k+1)b} \|z\|^2 ds$$

Because b is the length of the divided interval, it is small enough to make the following equation

$$1 - C \max_{s \in (kb, (k+1)b]} \int_{kb}^{(k+1)b} \|\nabla \hat{u}(s)\|_{L^2}^2 ds \leq 1$$

hold. Applying the Gronwall inequality in integral form to z yields

$$\|z\| = \max_{\iota \in (kb, (k+1)b]} \|\bar{u} - \hat{u}\| = 0 \tag{45}$$

Hence, $\bar{u} = \hat{u}$, for a.e. $t \in (0, T]$. Similarly, $\bar{v}_{i,j} = \hat{v}_{i,j}$ and $\bar{J}_{i,j} = \hat{J}_{i,j}$, for a.e. $t \in (0, T]$. Therefore, there exists a unique weak solution for the model. □

3. Numerical Algorithms and Experimental Results

3.1. Numerical Algorithm

In this section, we use the finite difference method [40] to give a simple numerical scheme of the model (3). Denote $J = J_{i,j}$, $v = v_{i,j}$, $(i, j = 1, 2)$. Assume the width and length of the image are N and M, respectively, then

$$x_l = lh_x, \ l = 1, 2, \cdots, N$$
$$y_k = kh_y, \ k = 1, 2, \cdots, M$$
$$t_m = m\Delta t, \ m = 1, 2, \cdots, P$$

where $h_x = 1$, $h_y = 1$ and $\Delta t = \frac{T}{P}$. Define the grid functions by

$$u_{l,k}^m = u(x_l, y_k, t_m), \ J_{l,k}^m = J(x_l, y_k, t_m)$$
$$v_{l,k}^m = v(x_l, y_k, t_m), \ (x_l, y_k) \in \overline{\Omega}_h, \ m = 1, 2, \cdots, P$$

The initial condition on grid point (x_l, y_k) is

$$u_{l,k}^0 = (u_0)_{l,k}, \ J_{l,k}^0 = 0, \ v_{l,k}^0 = (\nabla u_0 \nabla u_0^\top)_{l,k}$$

In this section, we use the scheme in [9] to solve the nonlinear isotropic diffusion equation in the proposed model. Firstly, we discretize the left side of the equation by the forward difference method

$$\frac{\partial v_{l,k}}{\partial t} = \frac{v_{l,k}^{m+1} - v_{l,k}^m}{\Delta t}$$

Next, for the discretization of the divergence term at the right end of the equation, the Laplacian operator is discretized in four directions: north, south, east, and west. Parameter g_2 uses "half-point" discretization. From the definition of the divergence operator, it is obtained that

$$\text{div}(g_2(|\nabla u_\sigma|)_{l,k}^m \nabla v_{l,k}^m) = \frac{\partial}{\partial x}\left(g_2 \frac{\partial v}{\partial x}\right)_{l,k}^m + \frac{\partial}{\partial y}\left(g_2 \frac{\partial v}{\partial y}\right)_{l,k}^m$$

Thus,

$$v_{l,k}^{m+1} = v_{l,k}^m + \Delta t \left(\frac{(g_2)_{l+1,k}^m + (g_2)_{l,k}^m}{2}(v_{l+1,k}^m - v_{l,k}^m) - \frac{(g_2)_{l,k}^m + (g_2)_{l-1,k}^m}{2}(v_{l,k}^m - v_{l-1,k}^m) \right)$$
$$+ \Delta t \left(\frac{(g_2)_{l,k+1}^m + (g_2)_{l,k}^m}{2}(v_{l,k+1}^m - v_{l,k}^m) - \frac{(g_2)_{l,k}^m + (g_2)_{l,k-1}^m}{2}(v_{l,k}^m - v_{l,k-1}^m) \right)$$

where Δt is the unit time step size, and a large number of experiments have shown that when $0 \leq \Delta t \leq 1/4$, the numerical format is stable [9].

For the fractional time-delay equation, we will adopt a general numerical discretization scheme proposed by Diego et al. [41], which is based on a simple quadrature formula to approximate the first-type Volterra integral definition of Caputo fractional derivatives. The numerical format of J at grid nodes (x_l, y_k, t_m) is given by

$$D_c^\gamma J_{l,k}^m = \frac{1}{\Gamma(1-\gamma)} \int_0^{t_m} \frac{\partial J_{l,k}(s)}{\partial t} (J_m - s)^{-\gamma} ds$$

$$= \frac{1}{\Gamma(1-\gamma)} \sum_{p=1}^m \int_{(p-1)\Delta t}^{l\Delta t} \left[\frac{J_{l,k}^p - J_{l,k}^{p-1}}{\Delta t} + O(\Delta t) \right] (m\Delta t - s)^{-\gamma} ds$$

$$= \frac{1}{(1-\gamma)\Gamma(1-\gamma)} \sum_{p=1}^m \left(\left(\frac{J_{l,k}^p - J_{l,k}^{p-1}}{\Delta t} + O(\Delta t) \right) [(m-p+1)^{1-\gamma} - (m-p)^{1-\gamma}] \right)$$

$$(\Delta t)^{1-\gamma}$$

$$= \frac{1}{(1-\gamma)\Gamma(1-\gamma)} \frac{1}{(\Delta t)^\gamma} \sum_{p=1}^m (J_{l,k}^p - J_{l,k}^{p-1})[(m-p+1)^{1-\gamma} - (m-p)^{1-\gamma}]$$

$$+ \frac{1}{(1-\gamma)\Gamma(1-\gamma)} \sum_{p=1}^m [(m-p+1)^{1-\gamma} - (m-p)^{1-\gamma}] O((\Delta t)^{2-\gamma})$$

Let $\sigma_{\gamma,\Delta t} = \frac{(\Delta t)^{-\gamma}}{\Gamma(1-\gamma)(1-\gamma)}$, $\xi_p^{(\gamma)} = p^{1-\gamma} - (p-1)^{1-\gamma}$, $1 = \xi_1^{(\gamma)} > \xi_2^{(\gamma)} > \cdots > \xi_p^{(\gamma)}$, then

$$\frac{\partial^\gamma J_{l,k}^m}{\partial^\gamma u} = D_c^\gamma J_{l,k}^m = \sigma_{\gamma,\Delta t} \sum_{p=1}^m \xi_p^{(\gamma)} \left(J_{l,k}^{m-p+1} - J_{l,k}^{m-p} \right) + \frac{1}{\Gamma(1-\gamma)} \frac{1}{1-\gamma} n^{1-\gamma} O\left((\Delta t)^{2-\gamma}\right)$$

$$= \sigma_{\gamma,\Delta t} \sum_{p=1}^m \xi_p^{(\gamma)} \left(J_{l,k}^{m-p+1} - J_{l,k}^{m-p} \right) + O(\Delta t)$$

Let $\varsigma = \Delta t$, the first-order approximation method for the Caputo fractional derivative is as follows:

$$D_c^\gamma J_{l,k}^{m+1} \cong \sigma_{\gamma,\varsigma} \sum_{p=1}^{m+1} \xi_p^{(\gamma)} \left(J_{l,k}^{(m+1)-p+1} - J_{l,k}^{(m+1)-p} \right)$$

$$= \sigma_{\gamma,\varsigma} \left[J_{l,k}^{(m+1)} - \sum_{p=1}^m \left(\xi_p^{(\gamma)} - \xi_{p+1}^{(\gamma)} \right) J_{l,k}^{(m+1)-p} - \xi_n^{(\gamma)} J_{l,k}^0 \right]$$

Thus,

$$J_{l,k}^{m+1} = \frac{\tau \sigma_{\gamma,\varsigma}}{\tau \sigma_{\gamma,\varsigma} + 1} \left[\sum_{p=1}^{m+1} \left(\xi_p^{(\gamma)} - \xi_{p+1}^{(\gamma)} \right) J_{l,k}^{m+1-p} + \xi_m^{(\gamma)} J_{l,k}^0 \right] + \frac{1}{\tau \sigma_{\gamma,\varsigma} + 1} v_{l,k}^{m+1}$$

$$= \frac{\tau \sigma_{\gamma,\varsigma}}{\tau \sigma_{\gamma,\varsigma} + 1} \sum_{p=1}^m \left(\xi_p^{(\gamma)} - \xi_{p+1}^{(\gamma)} \right) J_{l,k}^{m+1-p} + \frac{\tau \sigma_{\gamma,\varsigma}}{\tau \sigma_{\gamma,\varsigma} + 1} \xi_m^{(\gamma)} J_{l,k}^0 + \frac{1}{\tau \sigma_{\gamma,\varsigma} + 1} v_{l,k}^{m+1}$$

In order to ensure that the discretized scheme is rotationally invariant, can avoid fuzzy artifacts (dissipative), and has high accuracy, the filtering method proposed by [42] is used to perform explicit numerical discretization of the coherent enhanced anisotropic diffusion equation. The divergence operator in the anisotropic diffusion equation is written as

$$\text{div}(D\nabla u) = \frac{\partial}{\partial x}\left(d_{11}\frac{\partial u}{\partial x} + d_{12}\frac{\partial u}{\partial y} \right) + \frac{\partial}{\partial y}\left(d_{12}\frac{\partial u}{\partial x} + d_{22}\frac{\partial u}{\partial y} \right)$$

The total template size of the filter is 5×5, that is, two first-order derivatives with the size of 3×3 are applied consecutively to approach the second derivative. Specifically, the derivative operators F_x and F_y are convolutionally approximated to the first derivative of the original image, respectively. We select the discrete form of the derivative operator as

$$F_x = \frac{1}{32}\begin{pmatrix} -3 & 0 & 3 \\ -10 & 0 & 10 \\ -3 & 0 & 3 \end{pmatrix}, F_y = \frac{1}{32}\begin{pmatrix} 3 & 10 & 3 \\ 0 & 0 & 0 \\ -3 & 10 & -3 \end{pmatrix}$$

Therefore, the divergence operator is discretized as

$$\mathrm{div}\left(D_{l,k}^n \nabla u_{l,k}^m\right) = F_x\left(d_{11}F_x\left(u_{l,k}^m\right) + d_{12}F_y\left(u_{l,k}^m\right)\right) + F_y\left(d_{12}F_x\left(u_{l,k}^m\right) + d_{22}F_y\left(u_{l,k}^m\right)\right)$$

Thus,

$$u_{l,k}^{m+1} = u_{l,k}^m + \Delta t^*\left(\nabla \cdot \left(D_{l,k}^m \nabla u_{l,k}^m\right) + \lambda\left(u_{l,k}^m - \tilde{u}\right)\right)$$

For $\lambda(u - \tilde{u})$, we adaptively choose the parameter λ as

$$\lambda(t) = \frac{p}{(Iter_{OURS} \cdot \Delta t)^{\frac{1}{4}}} \cdot t^{\frac{1}{4}}$$

where we set $0 < p < 0.1$, $Iter_{OURS}$ represents the iteration step size of the proposed model, and Δt is the time step for isotropic diffusion. Choosing appropriate adaptive parameters $\lambda(t)$ not only completes the interruption of line connections but also improves the contrast of the image.

Based on the numerical discretization schemes of the three equations mentioned above, combined with the setting of boundary conditions and initial conditions, a numerical discretization algorithm for the image enhancement model in the text as shown in Algorithm 1 is obtained.

Algorithm 1 The proposed model

Input: Initial image u_0, parameter σ, τ, γ, p, iteration step size $Iter_{OURS}$, time step for isotropic diffusion Δt, and time step for anisotropic diffusion Δt^*.
Initial conditions: $v_{l,k}(x,0) = \left(\nabla u_0 \nabla u_0^\top\right)_{l,k}$.
For $(m = 1, \cdots, P)$

- Choose the diffusivity $g_2(t) = \frac{1}{1+(t/K)^2}$ or $g_2(t) = \frac{1}{\epsilon+t^p}$.
- $v_{l,k}^{m+1} = v_{l,k}^m$
$$+ \Delta t \left(\frac{(g_2)_{l+1,k}^m + (g_2)_{l,k}^m}{2}(v_{l+1,k}^m - v_{l,k}^m) - \frac{(g_2)_{l,k}^m + (g_2)_{l-1,k}^m}{2}(v_{l,k}^m - v_{l-1,k}^m)\right)$$
$$+ \Delta t \left(\frac{(g_2)_{l,k+1}^m + (g_2)_{l,k}^m}{2}(v_{l,k+1}^m - v_{l,k}^m) - \frac{(g_2)_{l,k}^m + (g_2)_{l,k-1}^m}{2}(v_{l,k}^m - v_{l,k-1}^m)\right).$$
- $J_{l,k}^{m+1} = \frac{\tau \sigma_{\gamma,\zeta}}{\tau \sigma_{\gamma,\zeta}+1}\sum_{p=1}^m\left(\xi_p^{(\gamma)} - \xi_{p+1}^{(\gamma)}\right)J_{l,k}^{m+1-p} + \frac{\tau \sigma_{\gamma,\zeta}}{\tau \sigma_{\gamma,\zeta}+1}\xi_m^{(\gamma)}J_{l,k}^0 + \frac{1}{\tau \sigma_{\gamma,\zeta}+1}v_{l,k}^{m+1};$
- Calculate the eigenvalues and eigenfunctions of the structural tensor $J_{l,k}^m$.
- Using the component d_{11}, d_{12}, d_{22} of the diffusion tensor $D = g_1(J)$ as a function of the structural tensor $J_{l,k}^m$;
- Calculate flux components $E_1 := d_{11}F_x u + d_{12}F_y u$ and $E_2 := d_{12}F_x u + d_{22}F_y u$.
- $\nabla \cdot (D(\nabla u)) = F_x E_1 + F_y E_2$.
- $u_{l,k}^{m+1} = u_{l,k}^m + \Delta t^*\left(\nabla \cdot \left(D_{l,k}^m \nabla u_{l,k}^m\right) + \lambda\left(u_{l,k}^m - \tilde{u}\right)\right)$

end
Output: The image u.

3.2. Experimental Results

In this subsection, we attempt to design multiple numerical experiments to justify the efficiency and superiority of the proposed model. We compare the proposed model with several well-known partial differential image enhancement methods, mainly the CED model (1) and CDEs model (2). For all experiments, the best visual effect is selected as the condition to stop iteration. Experiments are implemented in Python.

The test images are shown in Figure 1, which are fingerprint1 with a resolution of 256×256; fingerprint2 with a resolution of 200×200; alphabet with a resolution of 400×561; spring image with a resolution of 400×400; texture1 with a resolution of 256×256; texture image 2, with a resolution of 256×256; weaving diagram with a resolution of 340×342; the Van Gogh, a Dutch Impressionism painter, painting "15 sunflowers in a vase" with a resolution of 255×317; Van Gogh's oil painting "Wheat Field and Cypress Tree" denoted as "cypress" with a rate of 255×200.

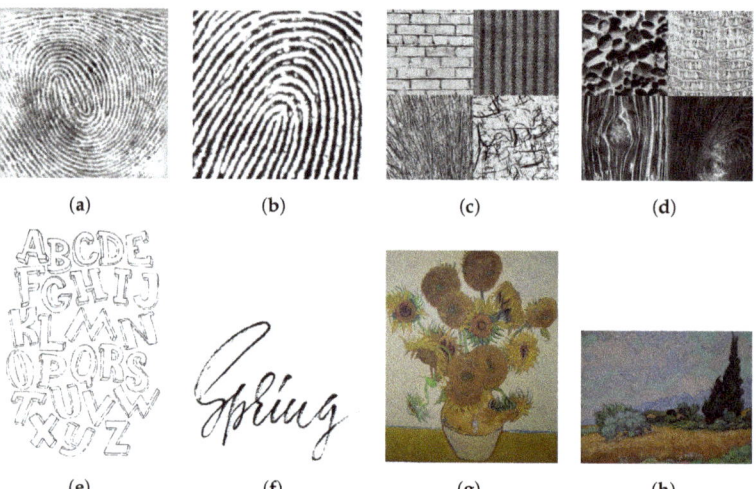

Figure 1. Test figures: (**a**) fingerprint1; (**b**) fingerprint2; (**c**) texture1; (**d**) texture2; (**e**) alphabet; (**f**) spring; (**g**) sunflowers; (**h**) cypress.

The meaning of the experimental parameters for the proposed model, CED model and CDEs model is as follows: σ is the initial image convolution parameter, ρ is a Gaussian kernel parameter, t_{CED} represents the diffusion time of the CED model, $Iter_{CED}$ represents the step size in the iteration for the CED model. t_{1CDEs} denotes the diffusion time of structure tensor J in the CDEs model, t_{2CDEs} denotes the diffusion time of the anisotropic equation in the CDEs model, and $Iter_{CDEs}$ represents the iteration step size of the CDEs model. λ is a source item parameter, τ is the delay regularization parameter, γ is a fractional-order parameter, K is the parameter in g_2-PM, Δt represents the diffusion time of the model structure tensor J in our model, Δt^* denotes the diffusion time of the anisotropic equation in our model, and $Iter_{OURS}$ represents the iteration step size of our model. In the specific experiment, $K = 80$, $\alpha = 0.001$, and more details can be found in the [42]. Select the source term as the average of image u in Ω, which means $\widetilde{u} = \frac{1}{\text{mean}(\Omega)} \int_\Omega u \, dx$. The selection of experimental parameters can be found in Tables 1–3. Due to the subsequent involvement of numerous fingerprint experiments, it is explained that the fingerprint1 parameters in Tables 1–3 refer to Figure 5. The fingerprint2 parameter refers to Figure 7.

Table 1. This is the parameter selection in CED model experiment.

Test Figures	σ	ρ	t_{ced}	$Iter_{CED}$
fingerprint1	0.3	4	0.3	100
fingerprint2	0.5	4	0.5	100
spring	0.5	5	0.2	80
alphabet	0.3	6	0.3	150
texture1	0.3	5	0.5	100
texture2	0.3	7	0.5	150
sunflower	0.2	2	0.6	50
cypress	0.2	2	0.6	50

Table 2. This is the parameter selection in CDEs model experiment.

Test Figures	σ	t_{1cdes}	t_{2cdes}	$Iter_{CDEs}$
fingerprint1	0.5	0.2	0.3	30
fingerprint2	0.5	0.2	0.5	100
spring	0.3	0.1	0.2	50
alphabet	0.3	0.15	0.3	90
texture1	0.5	0.15	0.5	110
texture2	0.5	0.2	0.5	100
sunflower	0.2	0.2	0.6	30
cypress	0.2	0.2	0.6	30

Table 3. This is the parameter selection in our model experiment.

Test Figures	σ	λ	τ	γ	Δt	Δt*	$Iter_{OURS}$
fingerprint1	0.5	0.018	0.5	0.7	0.2	0.3	120
fingerprint2	0.5	0.018	0.5	0.7	0.2	0.5	100
spring	0.3	0.02	0.5	(0.1, 0.5, 0.7)	0.1	0.2	40
alphabet	0.5	0.025	0.3	(0.1, 0.5, 0.7)	0.15	0.3	80
texture1	0.5	0.02	0.5	0.7	0.15	0.5	60
texture2	0.5	0.007	0.5	0.1	0.2	0.5	150
sunflower	0.2	0.02	0.5	0.5	0.2	0.6	30
cypress	0.2	0.02	0.5	0.5	0.2	0.6	30

Since the proposed model can significantly enhance the contrast of image, we use entropy and contrast to quantitatively analyze the model. The contrast of an image is measured from the darkest area to the brightest area, and the calculation formula is as follows:

$$C_{Contrast} = \sum_{i=0}^{L-1}(z_i - m)^2 p(z_i)$$

where z_i is a random variable that represents the grayscale value of pixels in the image, $p(z_i)$ is the probability of pixels with a grayscale value of z_i occupying the entire image, and L represents possible levels of grayscale values. The lower the contrast of the image, the blurrier the image. Entropy is an indicator to measure the information randomness of an image, which reflects the average information contained in the image. The calculation formula is as follows:

$$H_{Entropy}(z) = -\sum_{i=0}^{L-1} p(z_i) \log p(z_i)$$

The rougher areas of the image, the higher the entropy. The smoother the image, the lower the entropy.

In order to verify the importance of the parameters λ, τ, and γ in the proposed model, we give the following three experiments. The results of the numerical experiment about λ, τ, and γ are shown in Figures 2–4.

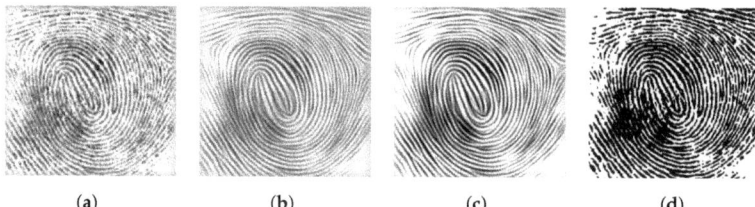

Figure 2. Different values of λ in the proposed model: (**a**) fingerprint1; (**b**) $\lambda = 1.8 \times 10^{-3}$; (**c**) $\lambda = 1.8 \times 10^{-1}$; (**d**) $\lambda = 1.8$.

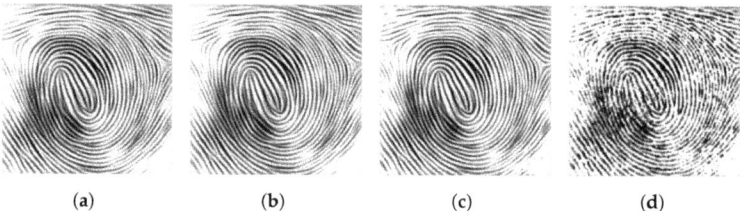

Figure 3. Different values of τ in the proposed model: (**a**) $\tau = 5 \times 10^{-3}$; (**b**) $\tau = 5 \times 10^{-1}$; (**c**) $\tau = 5 \times 10^4$; (**d**) $\tau = 5 \times 10^5$.

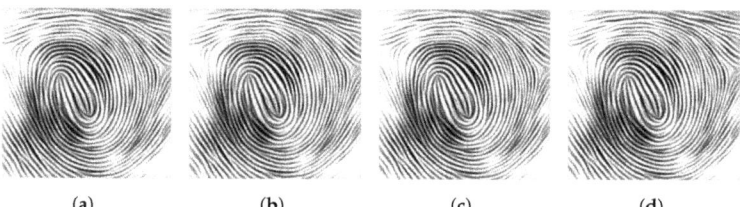

Figure 4. Different values of γ in the proposed model: (**a**) $\gamma = 0.3$; (**b**) $\gamma = 0.5$; (**c**) $\gamma = 0.7$; (**d**) $\gamma = 0.9$.

As shown in Figure 2b,c, the interrupted lines in fingerprint1 are connected but it is obviously that the contrast of Figure 2c is higher and clearer. Meanwhile, the contrast between Figure 2c,d is high and the figures are very clear. However, the connection of the interrupted lines in Figure 2d is very poor, retaining many broken lines, similar to the original image. From the above conclusions, we know that the larger the λ, the stronger the enhancement effect. The smaller the λ, the smoother the enhancement effect. Choosing the appropriate value of λ can complete the connection of the interruption lines, while ensuring good contrast in the model. In this experiment, selecting $\lambda = 0.018$ has the best effect.

Figure 3 shows the different values of τ in the proposed model. It can be seen from the experiment that Figure 3a,b have more enhancement effects than Figure 3c,d. These worse image enhancement phenomena indicate that the larger τ is chosen in the proposed model, which means that the information of the images is not fully utilized, and the information is lost. The experiment should choose a smaller value of τ with $\tau = 5 \times 10^{-1}$.

In Figure 4, the image enhancement effect of γ with different values is relatively good. The consistency between the experiment and theoretical analysis fully demonstrates that the introduction of fractional time delay not only fully utilizes the information of the image but also expands the applicability of the model. Extending the model from traditional time delay to fractional time delay facilitates further exploration of fractional-order models.

Figure 5 presents the experiment results of the fingerprint1 image. Comparing with the CED model and CDEs model, it can be found that the proposed model has a better enhancement effect. While the proposed model completes the fingerprint1 interrupted line connection, it also increases the contrast of the image, and even the clarity of images is better than that of the original image.

However, due to the source term acting on the entire image in Figure 5, the restoration effect of the local area lines is poor as shown in the red box of Figure 5d. To address this issue, the spiral fingerprint image is divided into multiple small images so that the source term can be adapted to each small image.

In this experiment, the spiral fingerprint image is divided into 9 subfigures in the ratio of 3×3, represented by the coordinates location (x, y), $x, y = 1, 2, 3$ subfigure. Based on the experimental results of Figure 5, we select the position (1,1) subfigure, position (2,1) subfigure, and position (3,3) subfigure as examples for demonstration. The experimental results are shown in Figure 6, and the parameter settings are the same as those in Figure 5.

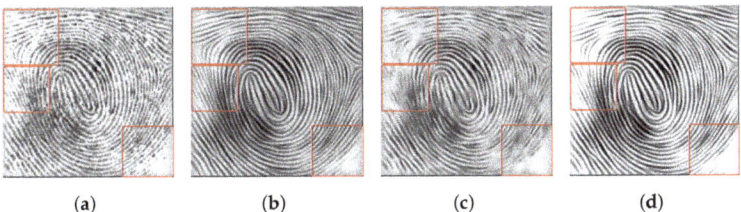

(a)   (b)   (c)   (d)

Figure 5. Fingerprint1 image: (**a**) original image; (**b**) results obtained by CED; (**c**) results obtained by CDEs; (**d**) results obtained by OURS.

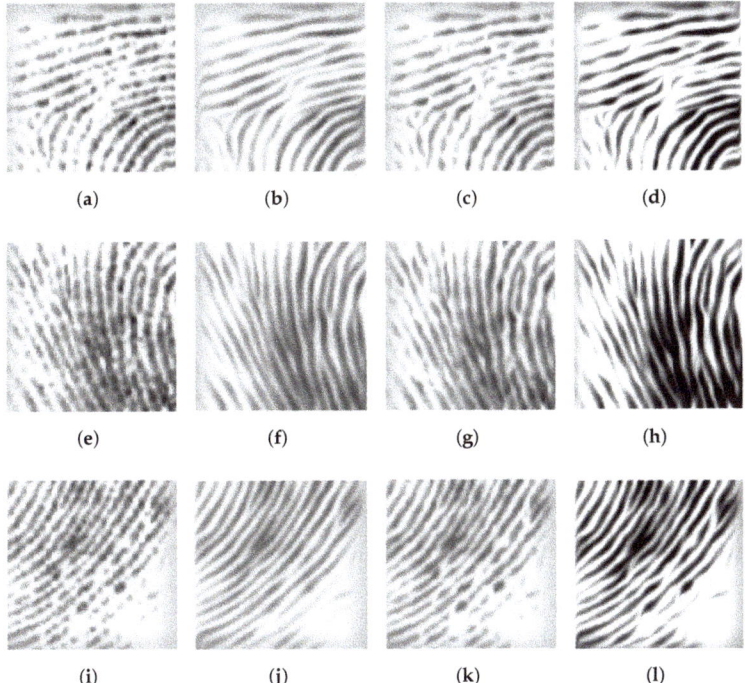

Figure 6. Experimental results of fingerprint1 with subfigures of "positions (1,1), (2,1), and (3,3)": (**a**) (1,1) original subfigure; (**b**) (1,1) results obtained by CED; (**c**) (1,1) results obtained by CDEs; (**d**) (1,1) results obtained by OURS; (**e**) (2,1) original subfigure; (**f**) (2,1) results obtained by CED; (**g**) (2,1) results obtained by CDEs; (**h**) (2,1) results obtained by OURS; (**i**) (3,3) original subfigure; (**j**) (3,3) results obtained by CED; (**k**) (3,3) results obtained by CDEs; (**l**) (3,3) results obtained by OURS.

Observing Figures 5d and 6d, it is found that there are very short lines in the upper right corner of the "position (1,1) subfigure" of the original image. Observing Figures 5d and 6e, it is found that there is a large gap in the left part of the "position (2,1) subfigure" of the original image, which is manifested by only leaving very short fingerprints similar to points. In Figure 6d,h, the corresponding positions of the subgraphs are restored, and the lines are clearer and more distinct. Observing Figure 6l, it is found that after the contrast in the lower right corner of the "position (3,3) subfigure" of the original image is enhanced, the degree of the flattening of the lines with small gray values relative to Figure 5d is decreased. Experiments showed that subdividing the image, which involves local processing of the image and changing the source terms, can achieve better results. On the other hand, in response to the poor restoration effect of the lines in the lower right and upper left corners of the original spiral fingerprint image, we find that this is not a problem with the model itself but rather due to the large grayscale range of the image; the average of the entire image cannot reflect the characteristics of local regions.

To verify the sensitivity of the model to noise, Gaussian noise with a standard deviation of 50 is added to the dustpan-shaped fingerprint image. The experimental results of the fingerprint2 image without Gaussian noise and with Gaussian noise are observed as shown in Figures 7 and 8.

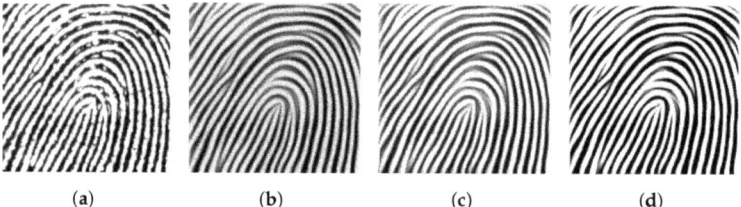

Figure 7. Fingerprint2 image without noise: (**a**) original image; (**b**) results obtained by CED; (**c**) results obtained by CDEs; (**d**) results obtained by OURS.

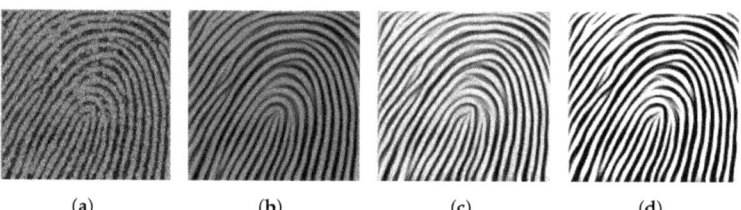

Figure 8. Fingerprint2 image with noise: (**a**) original image; (**b**) results obtained by CED; (**c**) results obtained by CDEs; (**d**) results obtained by OURS.

As shown in Figure 7b,c, the CED model and the CDEs model can complete the interrupted lines, while significantly reducing the contrast between the texture and background. On the contrary, Figure 7d indicates that our model completes the connection of interrupted lines while enhancing the contrast. Looking at Figure 8b,c, it is found that the CED model and the CDEs model are sensitive to noise. Figure 8d shows that the proposed model completely removes noise, and the image restoration effect is very good. This indicates that the proposed model can remove noise while connecting the interrupted lines.

According to the numerical experiments of fingerprint1 and fingerprint2 without/ containing Gaussian noise, Table 4 gives their contrast and entropy of images enhanced by the CED model, CDEs model and OURS model.

Table 4. Contrast and information entropy of two fingerprint images with respect to different models.

	Figure 5	Figure 5	Figure 7	Figure 7	Figure 8	Figure 8
	contrast	entropy	contrast	entropy	contrast	entropy
original	43.59	7.24	80.31	6.62	81.39	6.74
CED	35.27	7.15	71.18	7.27	71.31	7.25
CDEs	-	-	71.95	7.28	75.69	7.15
OURS	**73.57**	**6.49**	**113.56**	**3.75**	**119.13**	**3.05**

Comparing the contrast of different models for the same image, it is found that the proposed model has the highest contrast, indicating that the proposed model effectively improves the contrast of the image and makes it clearer. At the same time, by comparing the information entropy of the same picture with that of different models, it is found that the information entropy of the proposed model is the smallest, which means that the proposed model effectively reduces the chaos of the picture and the image becomes more smooth. The data in the Table 4 use contrast and information entropy to quantitatively demonstrate the effectiveness of the model in enhancing image contrast. In Table 4, the best results are shown in bold face.

The following will conduct numerical experiments on two letter images and provide experimental results for different numerical formats of the CED model, CDEs model, and OURS model with different γ values, which are shown in Figures 9 and 10.

The three pairs of local blocks shown in red line boxes in Figure 9 show that the proposed model can effectively restore blurry lines, successfully solving the problem of handwriting blurring caused by running out of ink or other reasons during writing. The letters "K, N, E, Q, Y" highlighted by the red lines in Figure 10 indicate that the proposed model achieved good connectivity for broken lines in the shapes of "horizontal, vertical, oblique, and arc", and the restored image contrast is more pronounced. Figure 9d–f and 10d–f show that different values of fractional-order γ can achieve the best recovery effect for the proposed model.

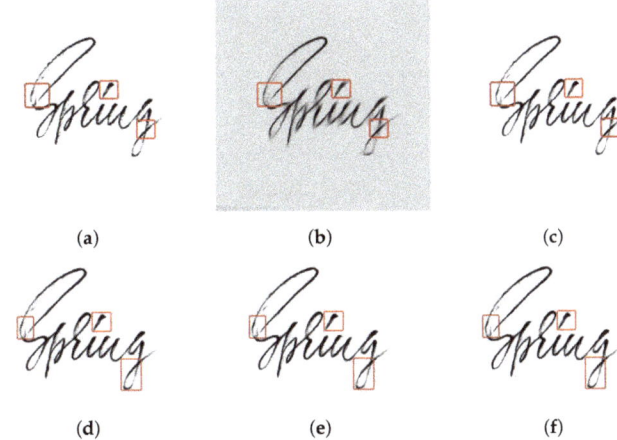

Figure 9. Spring image: (**a**) original image; (**b**) results obtained by CED; (**c**) results obtained by CDEs; (**d**) results obtained by OURS with $\gamma = 0.1$; (**e**) results obtained by OURS with $\gamma = 0.5$; (**f**) results obtained by OURS with $\gamma = 0.7$.

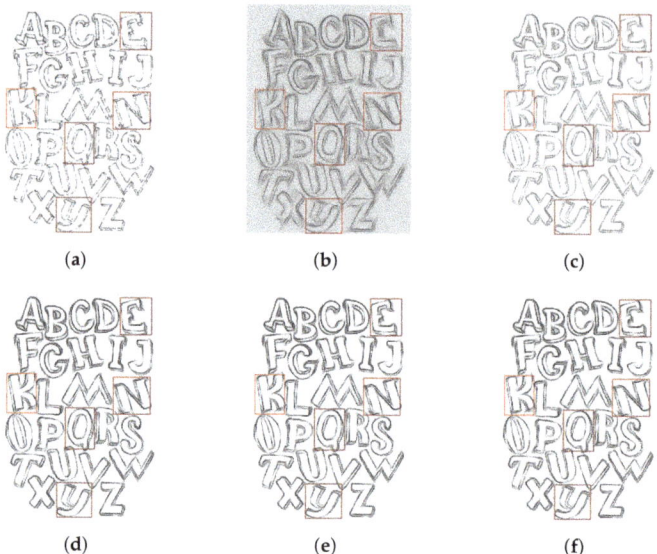

Figure 10. Alphabet image: (**a**) original image; (**b**) results obtained by CED; (**c**) results obtained by CDEs; (**d**) results obtained by OURS with $\gamma = 0.1$; (**e**) results obtained by OURS with $\gamma = 0.5$; (**f**) results obtained by OURS with $\gamma = 0.7$.

In order to observe the impact of the model on the shape and structure of "horizontal, vertical, oblique, and circular" in the text more intuitively, eight texture images are selected to synthesize two texture maps. Figures 11 and 12 provide the processing results.

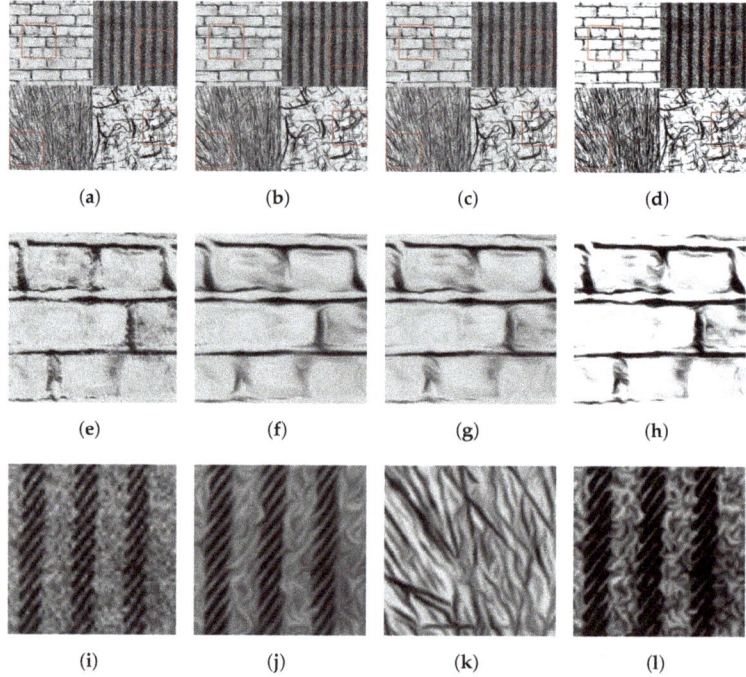

Figure 11. *Cont.*

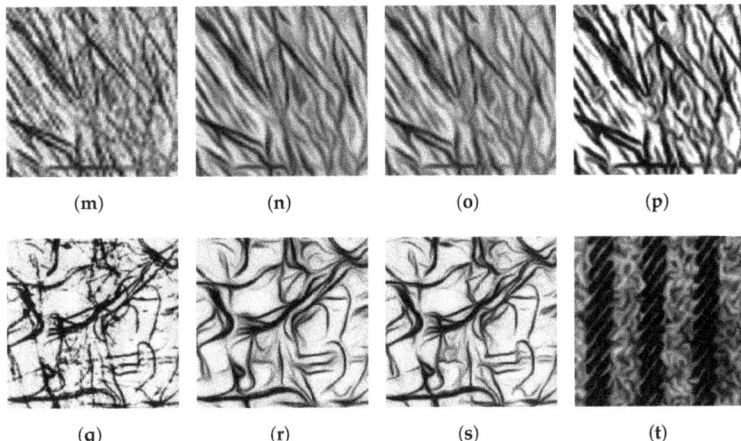

Figure 11. Texture1 image: (**a**) original image; (**b**) results obtained by CED; (**c**) results obtained by CDEs; (**d**) results obtained by OURS; (**e**)/(**i**)/(**m**)/(**q**) enlarged image 01/02/03/04; (**f**)/(**j**)/ (**n**)/(**r**) enlarged image 01/02/03/04 by CED; (**g**)/(**k**)/(**o**)/(**s**) enlarged image 01/02/03/04 by CDEs; (**h**)/(**l**)/(**p**)/(**t**) enlarged image 01/02/03/04 by OURS.

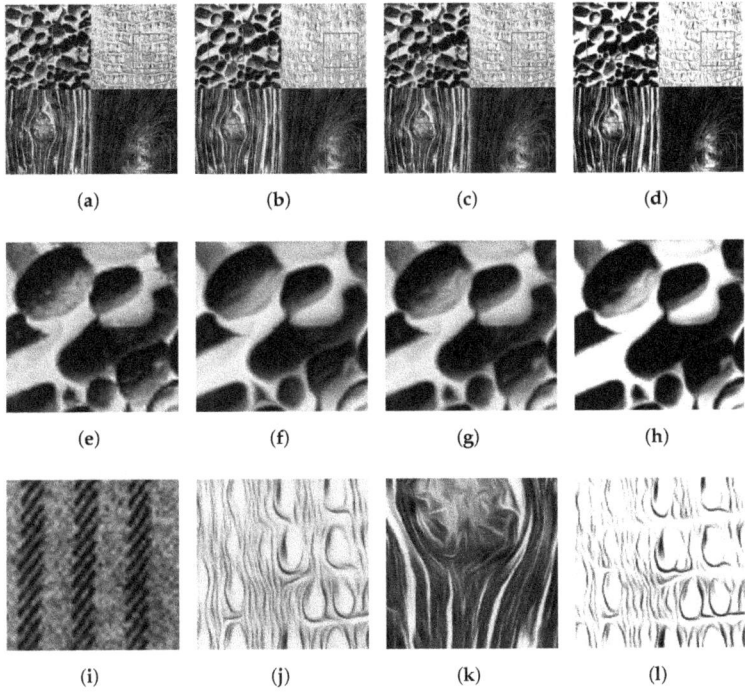

Figure 12. *Cont.*

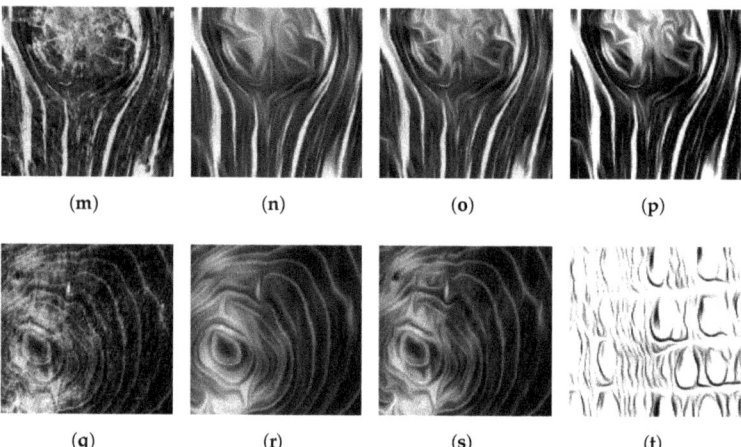

Figure 12. Texture2 image: (**a**) Original image; (**b**) results obtained by CED; (**c**) results obtained by CDEs (**d**) results obtained by OURS; (**e**)/(**i**)/(**m**)/(**q**) enlarged image 01/02/03/04; (**f**)/(**j**)/(**n**)/(**r**) enlarged image 01/02/03/04 by CED; (**g**)/(**k**)/(**o**)/(**s**) enlarged image 01/02/03/04 by CDEs; (**h**)/(**l**)/(**p**)/(**t**) enlarged image 01/02/03/04 by OURS.

The typical "horizontal, vertical, oblique, and circular" shape structures in Figures 11 and 12 have significantly enhanced the flow characteristics of the same type of line. The proposed model further deepens the flow characteristics of the same type of line. The four subimages in Texture1 exhibit the characteristics of spreading along the horizontal, vertical, oblique, and any direction, respectively. Figure 11e–t show the enlarged results of the four subimages in Texture 1. The four subimages in Texture 2 reflect the line features of circular, elliptical, and wavy structures. Figure 12e–t show the enlarged results of the four subimages in Texture 2. Compared with the CED model and CDEs model, the two images of the proposed model have a better enhancement effect, and the contrast of the images is greater, making the images clearer. The enhancement results of the two images further demonstrate the unified texture features of the images.

The proposed model is also applicable to color images, and the RGB channels of Van Gogh's two oil paintings are enhanced separately, and then integrated to obtain the enhanced results.

Figures 13b–d and 14b–d present the restoration results of two paintings under the CED model, CDEs model, and the proposed model. Figures 13e–p and 14e–p, respectively, provide the restoration results of three enlarged images. Observing the cloud in Figure 13h, cypress in Figure 13l, and green plant in Figure 13p, as well as the sunflower with various poses in Figure 14p, it can be found that the proposed model restores the image lines, and the image contrast is more pronounced. Although Van Gogh's works are not typical texture images, they still have characteristics similar to fluidity. As shown in Figures 13d and 14d, the diffusion of the model further enhances the fluidity of the original image, and the image presents unity and coordination, reflecting the unified "texture scale" of the painting and Van Gogh's unique painting style.

Numerical experiments show that, compared with the CED model and CDEs model, the proposed model can effectively not only connect blurred and interrupted lines but also enhance the contrast of images. In addition, the model can effectively remove noise. Experiments on grayscale and color image further illustrate that the model can deepen the fluidity characteristics of various types of lines. In the future, we can further develop other image enhancement methods based on the nonlinear structural tensor and try other numerical algorithms to improve the accuracy and efficiency of the algorithm.

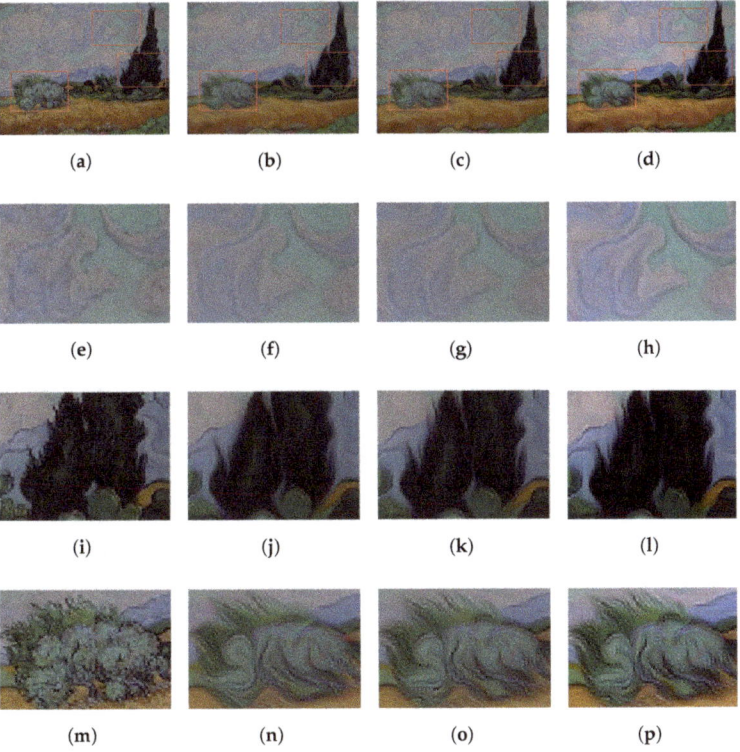

Figure 13. Cypress image: (**a**) Original image; (**b**) results obtained by CED; (**c**) results obtained by CDEs (**d**) results obtained by OURS; (**e**)/(**i**)/(**m**) enlarged image 01/02/03; (**f**)/(**j**)/(**n**) enlarged image 01/02/03 by CED; (**g**)/(**k**)/(**o**) enlarged image 01/02/03 by CDEs; (**h**)/(**l**)/(**p**) enlarged image 01/02/03 by OURS.

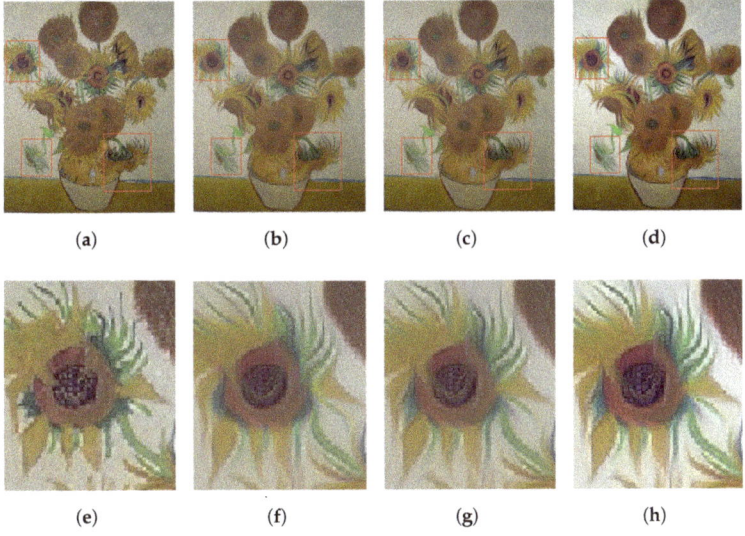

Figure 14. *Cont.*

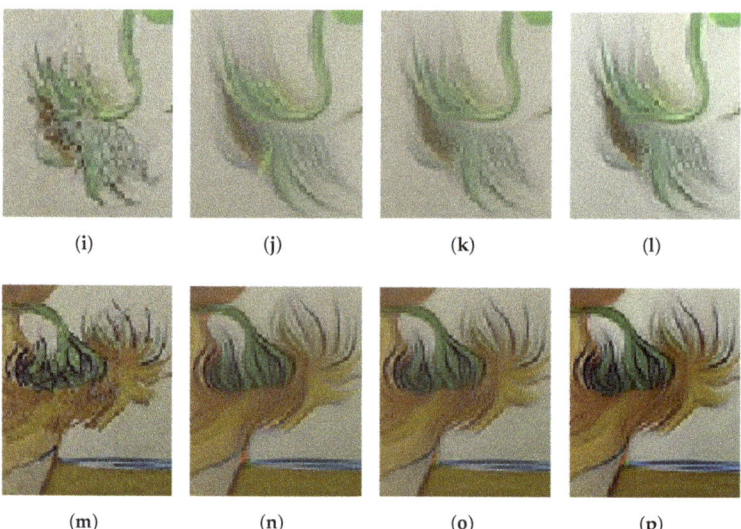

Figure 14. Sunflowers image: (**a**) original image; (**b**) results obtained by CED; (**c**) results obtained by CDEs; (**d**) results obtained by OURS; (**e**)/(**i**)/(**m**) enlarged image 01/02/03; (**f**)/(**j**)/(**n**) enlarged image 01/02/03 by CED; (**g**)/(**k**)/(**o**) enlarged image 01/02/03 by CDEs; (**h**)/(**l**)/(**p**) enlarged image 01/02/03 by OURS.

4. Conclusions

In the framework of partial differential equations, we propose an image enhancement model based on fractional time-delay regularization and diffusion tensor for images with streamlined structures. The structural tensor is spatially regularization using nonlinear isotropic diffusion and is temporally regularized using fractional delay regularization, which makes the structural tensor nonlinear and stable. The proof of the existence and uniqueness of the solution theoretically ensures the feasibility of the model. Through numerical experiments on various streamlined images, the validity and feasibility of the model in this paper are verified.

Author Contributions: Conceptualization, W.Y. and Y.H.; methodology, all authors; software, Y.H. and W.Y.; validation, Z.Z. and B.W.; formal analysis, W.Y. and B.W.; investigation, Y.H. and W.Y.; resources, Z.Z. and B.W.; data curation, W.Y. and Y.H.; writing—original draft preparation, W.Y. and Y.H.; writing—review and editing, W.Y., Z.Z. and B.W.; visualization, Y.H. and W.Y.; supervision, Z.Z. and B.W.; project administration, Z.Z. and B.W.; funding acquisition, W.Y., Z.Z. and B.W. All authors have read and agreed to the published version of the manuscript.

Funding: This research was funded by the National Natural Science Foundation of China (11971131, 12171123, 61873071, 51476047, 11871133, 12271130, U21B2075), the Fundamental Research Funds for the Central Universities (HIT.NSRIF202202, 2022FRFK060014, 2022FRFK060020), China Postdoctoral Science Foundation (2020M670893), Natural Sciences Foundation of Heilongjiang Province (LH2022A011), and the China Society of Industrial and Applied Mathematics Young Women Applied Mathematics Support Research Project.

Data Availability Statement: The data used to support the findings of this study are available from the corresponding author upon request.

Conflicts of Interest: The authors declare no conflict of interest.

References

1. Zou, G.; Li, T.; Li, G.; Peng, X.; Fu, G. A visual detection method of tile surface defects based on spatial-frequency domain image enhancement and region growing. In Proceedings of the 2019 Chinese Automation Congress (CAC), Hangzhou, China, 22–24 November 2019; pp. 1631–1636.
2. Bhandari, A.K. A logarithmic law based histogram modification scheme for naturalness image contrast enhancement. *J. Ambient. Intell. Humaniz. Comput.* **2020**, *11*, 1605–1627. [CrossRef]
3. Yu, T.; Zhu, M. Image enhancement algorithm based on image spatial domain segmentation. *Comput. Inform.* **2021**, *40*, 1398–1421. [CrossRef]
4. Zhao, J.; Fang, Q. Noise reduction and enhancement processing method of cement concrete pavement image based on frequency domain filtering and small world network. In Proceedings of the 2022 International Conference on Edge Computing and Applications (ICECAA), Tamilnadu, India, 13–15 October 2022; pp. 777–780.
5. Fabbri, C.; Islam, M.J.; Sattar, J. Enhancing underwater imagery using generative adversarial networks. In Proceedings of the 2018 IEEE International Conference on Robotics and Automation (ICRA), Brisbane, Australia, 12–15 May 2018; pp. 7159–7165.
6. Huang, J.; Zhu, P.; Geng, M.; Ran, J.; Zhou, X.; Xing, C.; Wan, P.; Ji, X. Range scaling global u-net for perceptual image enhancement on mobile devices. In Proceedings of the European Conference on Computer Vision (ECCV) Workshops, Munich, Germany, 8–14 September 2018.
7. Gabor, D. Information theory in electron microscopy. *Lab. Investig. J. Tech. Methods Pathol.* **1965**, *14*, 801–807.
8. Jain, A.K. Partial differential equations and finite-difference methods in image processing, Part 1: Image represent. *J. Optim. Theory Appl.* **1977**, *23*, 65–91. [CrossRef]
9. Perona, P.; Malik, J. Scale-space and edge detection using anisotropic diffusion. *IEEE Trans. Pattern Anal. Mach. Intell.* **1990**, *12*, 629–639. [CrossRef]
10. Nitzberg, M.; Shiota, T. Nonlinear image filtering with edge and corner enhancement. *IEEE Trans. Pattern Anal. Mach. Intell.* **1992**, *14*, 826–833. [CrossRef]
11. Cottet, G.H.; Germain, L. Image processing through reaction combined with nonlinear diffusion. *Math. Comput.* **1993**, *61*, 659–673. [CrossRef]
12. Hao, Y.; Yuan, C. Fingerprint image enhancement based on nonlinear anisotropic reverse-diffusion equations. In Proceedings of the 26th Annual International Conference of the IEEE Engineering in Medicine and Biology Society, San Francisco, CA, USA, 1–5 September 2004; Volume 1, pp. 1601–1604.
13. Brox, T.; Weickert, J.; Burgeth, B.; Mrázek, P. Nonlinear structure tensors. *Image Vis. Comput.* **2006**, *24*, 41–55. [CrossRef]
14. Wang, W.W.; Feng, X.C. Anisotropic diffusion with nonlinear structure tensor. *Multiscale Model. Simul.* **2008**, *7*, 963–977. [CrossRef]
15. Marin-McGee, M.J.; Velez-Reyes, M. A spectrally weighted structure tensor for hyperspectral imagery. *IEEE J. Sel. Top. Appl. Earth Obs. And Remote Sens.* **2016**, *9*, 4442–4449. [CrossRef]
16. Marin-McGee, M.; Velez-Reyes, M. Coherence enhancement diffusion for hyperspectral imagery using a spectrally weighted structure tensor. In Proceedings of the 2016 8th Workshop on Hyperspectral Image and Signal Processing: Evolution in Remote Sensing (WHISPERS), Los Angeles, CA, USA, 21–24 August 2016; pp. 1–4.
17. Nnolim, U.A. Partial differential equation-based hazy image contrast enhancement. *Comput. Electr. Eng.* **2018**, *72*, 670–681. [CrossRef]
18. Gu, Z.; Chen, Y.; Chen, Y.; Lu, Y. SAR image enhancement based on PM nonlinear diffusion and coherent enhancement diffusion. In Proceedings of the IGARSS 2020—2020 IEEE International Geoscience and Remote Sensing Symposium, Waikoloa, HI, USA, 26 September–2 October 2020; pp. 581–584.
19. Bai, J.; Feng, X.C. Fractional-order anisotropic diffusion for image denoising. *IEEE Trans. Image Process.* **2007**, *16*, 2492–2502. [CrossRef] [PubMed]
20. Sharma, D.; Chandra, S.K.; Bajpai, M.K. Image enhancement using fractional partial differential equation. In Proceedings of the 2019 Second International Conference on Advanced Computational and Communication Paradigms (ICACCP), Gangtok, India, 25–28 February 2019; pp. 1–6.
21. Chandra, S.K.; Bajpai, M.K. Fractional mesh-free linear diffusion method for image enhancement and segmentation for automatic tumor classification. *Biomed. Signal Process. Control* **2020**, *58*, 101841. [CrossRef]
22. Nnolim, U.A. Forward-reverse fractional and fuzzy logic augmented partial differential equation-based enhancement and thresholding for degraded document images. *Optik* **2022**, *260*, 169050. [CrossRef]
23. Ben-loghfyry, A. Reaction-diffusion equation based on fractional-time anisotropic diffusion for textured images recovery. *Int. J. Appl. Comput. Math.* **2022**, *8*, 177. [CrossRef]
24. Weickert, J. Coherence-enhancing diffusion filtering. *Int. J. Comput. Vis.* **1999**, *31*, 111. [CrossRef]
25. Chen, Y.; Levine, S. Image recovery via diffusion tensor and time-delay regularization. *J. Vis. Commun. Image Represent.* **2002**, *13*, 156–175. [CrossRef]
26. Cottet, G.; Ayyadi, M.E. A Volterra type model for image processing. *IEEE Trans. Image Process.* **1998**, *7*, 292–303. [CrossRef]
27. Koeller, R. Applications of fractional calculus to the theory of viscoelasticity. *Trans. ASME J. Appl. Mech.* **1984**, *51*, 299–307. [CrossRef]

28. Benson, D.A.; Wheatcraft, S.W.; Meerschaert, M.M. Application of a fractional advection-dispersion equation. *Water Resour. Res.* **2000**, *36*, 1403–1412. [CrossRef]
29. Butzer, P.L.; Westphal, U. An introduction to fractional calculus. In *Applications of Fractional Calculus in Physics*; World Scientific: Singapore, 2000; pp. 1–85.
30. Dou, F.; Hon, Y. Numerical computation for backward time-fractional diffusion equation. *Eng. Anal. Bound. Elem.* **2014**, *40*, 138–146. [CrossRef]
31. Cuesta-Montero, E.; Finat, J. Image processing by means of a linear integro-differential equation. In Proceedings of the 3rd IASTED International Conference on Visualization, Imaging, and Image Processing, Benalmadena, Spain, 8–10 September 2003; Volume 1.
32. Janev, M.; Pilipović, S.; Atanacković, T.; Obradović, R.; Ralević, N. Fully fractional anisotropic diffusion for image denoising. *Math. Comput. Model.* **2011**, *54*, 729–741. [CrossRef]
33. Li, Y.; Liu, F.; Turner, I.W.; Li, T. Time-fractional diffusion equation for signal smoothing. *Appl. Math. Comput.* **2018**, *326*, 108–116. [CrossRef]
34. Li, L.; Liu, J.G. Some compactness criteria for weak solutions of time fractional PDEs. *SIAM J. Math. Anal.* **2018**, *50*, 3963–3995. [CrossRef]
35. Li, L.; Liu, J.G. A generalized definition of Caputo derivatives and its application to fractional ODEs. *SIAM J. Math. Anal.* **2018**, *50*, 2867–2900. [CrossRef]
36. Alikhanov, A. A priori estimates for solutions of boundary value problems for fractional-order equations. *Differ. Equ.* **2010**, *46*, 660–666. [CrossRef]
37. Agrawal, O. Fractional variational calculus in terms of Riesz fractional derivatives. *J. Phys. A Math. Theor.* **2007**, *40*, 6287. [CrossRef]
38. Dong, G.; Guo, Z.; Zhou, Z.; Zhang, D.; Wo, B. Coherence-enhancing diffusion with the source term. *Appl. Math. Model.* **2015**, *39*, 6060–6072. [CrossRef]
39. Evans, L.C. *Partial Differential Equations*; American Mathematical Society: Providence, RI, USA, 2022; Volume 19.
40. Suri, J.S.; Laxminarayan, S. *PDE and Level Sets*; Springer Science & Business Media: New York, NY, USA, 2002.
41. Murio, D.A. Implicit finite difference approximation for time fractional diffusion equations. *Comput. Math. Appl.* **2008**, *56*, 1138–1145. [CrossRef]
42. Weickert, J.; Scharr, H. A scheme for coherence-enhancing diffusion filtering with optimized rotation invariance. *J. Vis. Commun. Image Represent.* **2002**, *13*, 103–118. [CrossRef]

Disclaimer/Publisher's Note: The statements, opinions and data contained in all publications are solely those of the individual author(s) and contributor(s) and not of MDPI and/or the editor(s). MDPI and/or the editor(s) disclaim responsibility for any injury to people or property resulting from any ideas, methods, instructions or products referred to in the content.

Article

Anomalous Thermally Induced Deformation in Kelvin–Voigt Plate with Ultrafast Double-Strip Surface Heating

Emad Awad [1,*], Sharifah E. Alhazmi [2], Mohamed A. Abdou [1] and Mohsen Fayik [1]

1. Department of Mathematics, Faculty of Education, Alexandria University, Souter St. El-Shatby, Alexandria P.O. Box 21526, Egypt; abdella_777@yahoo.com (M.A.A.); m_fayik@alexu.edu.eg (M.F.)
2. Mathematics Department, Al-Qunfudhah University College, Umm Al-Qura University, Al-Qunfudhah 28821, Mecca, Saudi Arabia; sehazmi@uqu.edu.sa
* Correspondence: emadawad78@alexu.edu.eg

Abstract: The Jeffreys-type heat conduction equation with flux precedence describes the temperature of diffusive hot electrons during the electron–phonon interaction process in metals. In this paper, the deformation resulting from ultrafast surface heating on a "nanoscale" plate is considered. The focus is on the anomalous heat transfer mechanisms that result from anomalous diffusion of hot electrons and are characterized by retarded thermal conduction, accelerated thermal conduction, or transition from super-thermal conductivity in the short-time response to sub-thermal conductivity in the long-time response and described by the fractional Jeffreys equation with three fractional parameters. The recent double-strip problem, Awad et al., *Eur. Phy. J. Plus* 2022, allowing the overlap between two propagating thermal waves, is generalized from the semi-infinite heat conductor case to thermoelastic case in the finite domain. The elastic response in the material is not simultaneous (i.e., not Hookean), rather it is assumed to be of the Kelvin–Voigt type, i.e., $\sigma = E(\varepsilon + \tau_\varepsilon \dot{\varepsilon})$, where σ refers to the stress, ε is the strain, E is the Young modulus, and τ_ε refers to the strain relaxation time. The delayed strain response of the Kelvin–Voigt model eliminates the discontinuity of stresses, a *hallmark* of the Hookean solid. The immobilization of thermal conduction described by the ordinary Jeffreys equation of heat conduction is salient in metals when the heat flux precedence is considered. The absence of the finite speed thermal waves in the Kelvin–Voigt model results in a smooth stress surface during the heating process. The temperature contours and the displacement vector chart show that the anomalous heat transfer characterized by retardation or crossover from super- to sub-thermal conduction may disrupt the ultrafast laser heating of metals.

Keywords: anomalous heat transfer; double-strip problem; fractional Jeffreys equation; Kelvin–Voigt solid

Citation: Awad, E.; Alhazmi, S.E.; Abdou, M.A.; Fayik, M. Anomalous Thermally Induced Deformation in Kelvin–Voigt Plate with Ultrafast Double-Strip Surface Heating. *Fractal Fract.* **2023**, *7*, 563. https://doi.org/10.3390/fractalfract7070563

Academic Editors: Sameerah Jamal and Damian Słota

Received: 14 June 2023
Revised: 12 July 2023
Accepted: 17 July 2023
Published: 22 July 2023

Copyright: © 2023 by the authors. Licensee MDPI, Basel, Switzerland. This article is an open access article distributed under the terms and conditions of the Creative Commons Attribution (CC BY) license (https://creativecommons.org/licenses/by/4.0/).

1. Introduction

In many physical situations, thermal conduction may encounter anomalous behavior deviating from the classical diffusive "Fourier" behavior, e.g., heat transfer in fractals, heterogeneous materials, metals with distributed impurities, and nanoscale materials [1–6]. Fractional kinetic equations are effective mathematical tools for modeling such anomalous behaviors [7–19]. A recent fractional version of the Jeffreys equation has been proposed in [20], and under certain circumstances, it can be connected to the continuous-time random walk scheme [21]. The fractional Jeffreys equation with three fractional parameters is a versatile mathematical tool describing many anomalous heat/mass transition behaviors, e.g., acceleration, retardation, and crossover from super- to subdiffusion.

The stresses generated in elastic materials due to thermal effects may cause the material to reach the yield point. Before the yield point, the linearized thermal stress theories with different heat conduction models [6,22–24] present successful initial engineering assessments for predicting the stresses and deformations in different types of thermal loadings and heat conductors. One of the earliest studies which presented a prediction of stress distribution induced by anomalous heat/mass transfer is the study of Povstenko [25]; see also the comprehensive monograph by the same author [26]. In [27–30], different forms of anomalous heat conduction models are adopted and the corresponding thermal stresses are computed. The main feature in most well known fractional heat conduction models is the disappearance of the finite thermal wave speed, with some exceptions to the Atangana–Baleanu fractional derivative [31,32].

The Kelvin–Voigt model is a crucial tool for defining and studying the viscoelastic behavior of certain solid materials in which there is a retardation time in the material response [33]. It differs from the Hookean solid in the retarded response of strain to an applied stress, namely, $\sigma = E(\varepsilon + \tau_\varepsilon \dot{\varepsilon})$, where τ_ε is the retardation time, or the strain relaxation time [34]. When $\tau_\varepsilon \to 0$, the Hookean response is recovered, i.e., $\sigma = E\varepsilon$. The Kelvin–Voigt thermoelasticity has been considered in a variety of viscoelastic applications, e.g., unbounded thermoviscoelastic domain with spherical cavity [35], vibration of an Euler Bernoulli beam [36,37], and micropolar thermoelasticity [38], and has been extended to the second-gradient media [39].

In order to generalize the Danilovskaya problem in hyperbolic thermoelasticity [40,41] to the finite domains, El-Maghraby [42] solved the Lord–Shulman equations for a thick plate with an internal heat source, and the same author [43] solved the Green–Lindsay equations for a thick plate with body force. A similar setting of the thick plate problem in thermoelasticity has been solved for a transversely isotropic medium [44] and has been considered in Kelvin–Voigt medium when a specific form of the fractional dual-phase lag is considered [45]. For ultrafast thermal heating of metals, the deformation resulting from the electronic conduction was considered in [46] for a one-dimension metal film. The authors considered in their formulation that the driving force describes the effect of free carriers on the lattice [47], mathematically described by the term $T_e \nabla T_e$, where T_e is the electron temperature. In the linearized version, the nonlinear term $T_e \nabla T_e$ is neglected; thus, the coupling factor is lost. A generalized version of ultrafast thermoelasticity was considered in [48], where the stress includes the lattice temperature and the lattice conduction equation is inserted. If the lattice conduction is neglected and the force describing the effect of free carriers on the lattice is neglected, the resulting ultrafast thermoelasticity corresponds to the dual-phase-lag thermoelasticity with flux precedence [6]; see also [49].

In the present article, we consider a Kelvin–Voigt nanoscale two-dimensional plate with infinite extension subject to an ultrafast surface heating on its upper surface taking the double-strip shape [50,51]. The delayed strain response underlying the Kelvin–Voigt assumption, the nanoscale thickness of the plate, and the ultrafast heating method can be considered as reasoning causes for adopting non-Fourier heat transfer mechanisms such as accelerating, retarding, and crossover from super- to sub-thermal conduction. The Laplace–Fourier transform technique is used to obtain exact solutions in the transformed domain. Then, double infinite summations are numerically implemented to obtain the solutions in the physical domain. The relation between the heat flux and the temperature gradient is shown graphically in different critical instants. We organize the paper as follows: In Section 2, we present the governing equations for the Kelvin–Voigt thermoelasticity with the fractional Jeffreys equation with three fractional parameters. The two-dimensional formulation of the Kelvin–Voigt thermoelastic plate problem is given in Section 3. In Section 4, we derive exact solutions for the temperature, hydrostatic stress, and displacement components in the transformed domain. A suitable numerical technique is adopted in Section 5 to obtain the solution to the physical domain numerically. Lastly, we summarize the work findings in Section 6.

2. Mathematical Model

The governing equations for a homogeneous isotropic thermoviscoelastic material of Kelvin–Voigt type [23,33,34] in the context of the fractional Jeffreys heat conduction equation [20,21] consist of the following:

(i) Stress–strain constitutive relation

$$\sigma_{ij} = 2\mu e_{ij} + \lambda e \delta_{ij} - (3\lambda + 2\mu)\alpha_T \theta \delta_{ij} \tag{1}$$

where $\lambda = \lambda_0\left(1 + \lambda_v \frac{\partial}{\partial t}\right)$, $\mu = \mu_0\left(1 + \mu_v \frac{\partial}{\partial t}\right)$, λ_0 and μ_0 are the standard Lamé constants, λ_v and μ_v are viscoelastic relaxation times pertinent to the Kelvin–Voigt solid, α_T is the coefficient of linear thermal expansion, $\sigma_{ij} = \sigma_{ji}$ are the components of the Cauchy stress tensor, e_{ij} is the linear strain tensor, δ_{ij} is the Kronecker delta, $\theta = T - T_0$ is the temperature of the medium, T is the absolute temperature, and T_0 is the temperature of the medium in its natural state; θ is assumed to satisfy the linearized condition $|\theta/T_0| \ll 1$.

(ii) The strain–displacement relation

$$e_{ij} = \frac{1}{2}(u_{i,j} + u_{j,i}), \tag{2}$$

where $e_{ij} = e_{ji}$ is the linear strain tensor, $e = e_{ii} = u_{i,i}$ is the cubical dilation, and u_i is the component of the displacement vector. The subscript i refers to the component of the vector in the x_i-direction, the standard notation $(\cdot)_{,i} = (\partial/\partial x_i)(\cdot)$ has been employed, and x_i is the i-th system coordinate.

(iii) Conservation of momentum

$$\sigma_{ij,j} + \rho F_i = \rho \frac{\partial^2 u_i}{\partial t^2}, \tag{3}$$

where ρ is the material density, assumed to be constant; F_i is the body force component in the x_i-direction; and the tensor convention of summing over repeated indices is used.

Substituting Equation (1) into Equation (3), and using the relations $\lambda = \lambda_0\left(1 + \lambda_v \frac{\partial}{\partial t}\right)$ and $\mu = \mu_0\left(1 + \mu_v \frac{\partial}{\partial t}\right)$, we obtain

$$(\lambda_0 + \mu_0)\left(1 + \delta_v \frac{\partial}{\partial t}\right)e_{,i} + \mu_0\left(1 + \mu_v \frac{\partial}{\partial t}\right)u_{i,jj} - (3\lambda_0 + 2\mu_0)\alpha_T\left(1 + \gamma_v \frac{\partial}{\partial t}\right)\theta_{,i} + \rho F_i = \rho \frac{\partial^2 u_i}{\partial t^2}, \tag{4}$$

where $\gamma_v = \frac{3\lambda_0 \lambda_v + 2\mu_0 \mu_v}{3\lambda_0 + 2\mu_0}$ and $\delta_v = \frac{\lambda_0 \lambda_v + \mu_0 \mu_v}{\lambda_0 + \mu_0}$.

(iv) The balance equation for the entropy

$$-q_{i,i} + Q = \rho T_0 \frac{\partial S}{\partial t}, \tag{5}$$

where q_i is the heat flux generalized component, Q is the strength of the heat source inside the body, and S is the entropy per unit mass.

Starting from the assumption that for a thermally conducting Kelvin–Voigt solid subject to small strain and small temperature changes [23,38], we have

$$\rho T_0 S = \rho c_E \theta + (3\lambda_0 + 2\mu_0)\alpha_T T_0 \left(1 + \gamma_v \frac{\partial}{\partial t}\right)e, \tag{6}$$

where c_E is the specific heat at constant strain.

Hence, the energy balance equation is given from (5) and (6) as

$$\rho c_E \frac{\partial \theta}{\partial t} + (3\lambda_0 + 2\mu_0)\alpha_T T_0 \left(\frac{\partial}{\partial t} + \gamma_v \frac{\partial^2}{\partial t^2}\right)e = -q_{i,i} + Q. \tag{7}$$

The above equations are supplemented with the fractional Jeffery's heat conduction equation [20,21], namely,

$$\left(1 + \tau_q^\alpha \frac{\partial^\alpha}{\partial t^\alpha}\right)q_i = -\check{K}\frac{\partial^{1-\gamma}}{\partial t^{1-\gamma}}\left(1 + \tau_\theta^\beta \frac{\partial^\beta}{\partial t^\beta}\right)\theta_{,i}, \quad \check{K} = K\tau_q^{1-\gamma}, \tag{8}$$

where $\tau_q \geq 0$ and $\tau_\theta \geq 0$ are the heat flux and the temperature gradient phase lags [6], respectively, K is the thermal conductivity, and $0 < \alpha, \beta, \gamma \leq 1$. The assumption $\check{K} = K\tau_q^{1-\gamma}$ is adopted to keep the dimension in order [7,52]. The fractional derivative in (8) is defined in the Riemann–Liouville sense [53]:

$$\frac{\partial^\alpha}{\partial t^\alpha} f(t) = \begin{cases} \frac{1}{\Gamma(1-\alpha)} \frac{\partial}{\partial t} \int_0^t \frac{f(\tau)}{(t-\tau)^\alpha} d\tau, & 0 < \alpha < 1, \\ \frac{\partial}{\partial t} f(t), & \alpha = 1. \end{cases}$$

Substituting Equation (8) into Equation (7), we obtain the energy equation:

$$K\tau_q^{1-\gamma} \frac{\partial^{1-\gamma}}{\partial t^{1-\gamma}} \left(1 + \tau_\theta^\beta \frac{\partial^\beta}{\partial t^\beta}\right) \theta_{,ii} = \left(1 + \tau_q^\alpha \frac{\partial^\alpha}{\partial t^\alpha}\right) \left[\rho c_E \frac{\partial \theta}{\partial t} + (3\lambda_0 + 2\mu_0)\alpha_T T_0 \left(\frac{\partial}{\partial t} + \gamma_v \frac{\partial^2}{\partial t^2}\right) e - Q\right]. \tag{9}$$

3. Problem Formulation

We consider a plate made of a homogeneous isotropic solid occupying the region Ω defined by $\Omega = \{(x,y,z) : -\infty < x, z < \infty, 0 \leq y \leq l\}$. The y-axis is taken perpendicular to the plate plane and pointing inwards, such that $y = 0$ refers to the upper surface and $y = l$ refers to the lower surface. The body is assumed to be initially quiescent. Furthermore, we assume that there are no body forces or heat sources. The upper surface of the plate is assumed to be traction-free and subjected to ultrafast double-strip heating [50], which decays exponentially with time, while the lower surface is assumed to be traction-free and thermally insulated; see Figure 1.

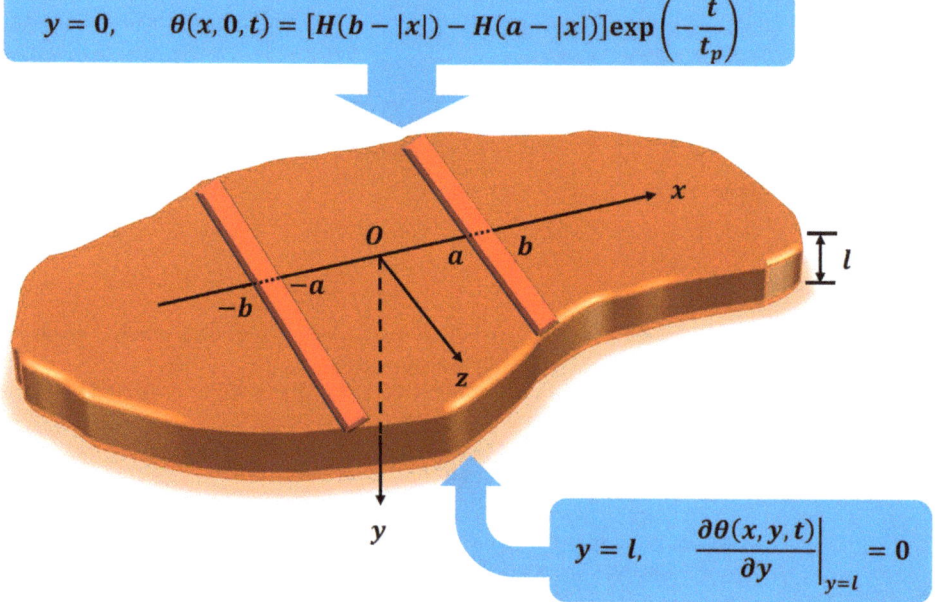

Figure 1. Physical description of the problem.

From the above settings, all the considered functions should depend on x, y, and t. Also, the displacement vector is given in the form

$$\mathbf{u} = \langle u, v, 0 \rangle, \quad u = u(x, y, t), \quad v = v(x, y, t). \tag{10}$$

Hence, the governing equations for Kelvin–Voigt thermoelastic plate on the domain $(x, y, t) \in (-\infty, \infty) \times [0, l] \times (0, \infty)$ consist of the following:

(i) The non-vanishing components of the stress tensor

$$\sigma_{xx} = 2\mu_0\left(1 + \mu_v\frac{\partial}{\partial t}\right)\frac{\partial u}{\partial x} + \lambda_0\left(1 + \lambda_v\frac{\partial}{\partial t}\right)e - (3\lambda_0 + 2\mu_0)\alpha_T\left(1 + \gamma_v\frac{\partial}{\partial t}\right)\theta, \tag{11}$$

$$\sigma_{yy} = 2\mu_0\left(1 + \mu_v\frac{\partial}{\partial t}\right)\frac{\partial v}{\partial y} + \lambda_0\left(1 + \lambda_v\frac{\partial}{\partial t}\right)e - (3\lambda_0 + 2\mu_0)\alpha_T\left(1 + \gamma_v\frac{\partial}{\partial t}\right)\theta, \tag{12}$$

$$\sigma_{zz} = \lambda_0\left(1 + \lambda_v\frac{\partial}{\partial t}\right)e - (3\lambda_0 + 2\mu_0)\alpha_T\left(1 + \gamma_v\frac{\partial}{\partial t}\right)\theta, \tag{13}$$

$$\sigma_{xy} = \sigma_{yx} = \mu_0\left(1 + \mu_v\frac{\partial}{\partial t}\right)\left(\frac{\partial v}{\partial x} + \frac{\partial u}{\partial y}\right). \tag{14}$$

(ii) The non-vanishing components of the strain tensor

$$e_{xx} = \frac{\partial u}{\partial x}, \tag{15}$$

$$e_{yy} = \frac{\partial v}{\partial y}, \tag{16}$$

$$e_{xy} = e_{yx} = \frac{1}{2}\left(\frac{\partial u}{\partial y} + \frac{\partial v}{\partial x}\right). \tag{17}$$

Also, the cubical dilation e is given by

$$e = e_{xx} + e_{yy} = \frac{\partial u}{\partial x} + \frac{\partial v}{\partial y}. \tag{18}$$

(iii) The equations of motion in the absence of body forces along the x- and y-directions, respectively,

$$(\lambda_0 + \mu_0)\left(1 + \delta_v\frac{\partial}{\partial t}\right)\frac{\partial e}{\partial x} + \mu_0\left(1 + \mu_v\frac{\partial}{\partial t}\right)\nabla^2 u - (3\lambda_0 + 2\mu_0)\alpha_T\left(1 + \gamma_v\frac{\partial}{\partial t}\right)\frac{\partial \theta}{\partial x} = \rho\frac{\partial^2 u}{\partial t^2}, \tag{19}$$

$$(\lambda_0 + \mu_0)\left(1 + \delta_v\frac{\partial}{\partial t}\right)\frac{\partial e}{\partial y} + \mu_0\left(1 + \mu_v\frac{\partial}{\partial t}\right)\nabla^2 v - (3\lambda_0 + 2\mu_0)\alpha_T\left(1 + \gamma_v\frac{\partial}{\partial t}\right)\frac{\partial \theta}{\partial y} = \rho\frac{\partial^2 v}{\partial t^2}, \tag{20}$$

By differentiating Equations (19) and (20) with respect to x and y, respectively, adding the resulting equations and utilizing Equation (18), we obtain

$$\left[(\lambda_0 + 2\mu_0) + ((\lambda_0 + \mu_0)\delta_v + \mu_0\mu_v)\frac{\partial}{\partial t}\right]\nabla^2 e - (3\lambda_0 + 2\mu_0)\alpha_t\left(1 + \gamma_v\frac{\partial}{\partial t}\right)\nabla^2\theta = \rho\frac{\partial^2 e}{\partial t^2}, \tag{21}$$

where $\nabla^2 = \left(\frac{\partial^2}{\partial x^2} + \frac{\partial^2}{\partial y^2}\right)$ is the Laplace operator in Cartesian coordinates.

(i) The heat conduction equation in the absence of a heat source

$$K\tau_q^{1-\gamma}\frac{\partial^{1-\gamma}}{\partial t^{1-\gamma}}\left(1 + \tau_\theta^\beta\frac{\partial^\beta}{\partial t^\beta}\right)\nabla^2\theta = \left(1 + \tau_q^\alpha\frac{\partial^\alpha}{\partial t^\alpha}\right)\left[\rho c_E\frac{\partial \theta}{\partial t} + (3\lambda_0 + 2\mu_0)\alpha_T T_0\left(\frac{\partial}{\partial t} + \gamma_v\frac{\partial^2}{\partial t^2}\right)e\right], \tag{22}$$

associated with the following thermal and mechanical boundary conditions:

$$\theta(x, 0, t) = \Theta_0(x, t), \quad \left.\frac{\partial \theta(x, y, t)}{\partial y}\right|_{y=l} = 0, \tag{23}$$

$$\sigma_{yy}(x, 0, t) = \sigma_{yy}(x, l, t) = 0, \tag{24}$$

$$\sigma_{xy}(x,0,t) = \sigma_{xy}(x,l,t) = 0, \tag{25}$$

where $\Theta_0(x,t)$ is a given time-dependent thermal boundary condition, disturbed spatially on the upper surface.

Additionally, it is assumed that the system initiates the experiment in a state of rest with no accelerations, namely,

$$u(x,y,t)|_{t=0} = \left.\frac{\partial u(x,y,t)}{\partial t}\right|_{t=0} = 0, \quad v(x,y,t)|_{t=0} = \left.\frac{\partial v(x,y,t)}{\partial t}\right|_{t=0} = 0,$$
$$\theta(x,y,t)|_{t=0} = \left.\frac{\partial \theta(x,y,t)}{\partial t}\right|_{t=0} = 0, \tag{26}$$

The governing equations can be put in a more convenient form by using the following non-dimensional variables:

$$(x^*, y^*) = c_1 \eta (x,y), \quad (u^*, v^*) = c_1 \eta \frac{\rho c_1^3 \eta}{(3\lambda_0 + 2\mu_0)\alpha_T T_0}(u, v),$$
$$e_{ij}^* = \frac{\rho^2 c_1^2}{(3\lambda_0 + 2\mu_0)\alpha_T T_0} e_{ij}, \quad \theta^* = \frac{\theta}{T_0}, \quad \Theta_0^* = \frac{\Theta_0}{T_0}, \quad \sigma_{ij}^* = \frac{\sigma_{ij}}{(3\lambda_0 + 2\mu_0)\alpha_T T_0},$$
$$\left(t^*, t_p^*, \tau_q^*, \tau_\theta^*, \lambda_v^*, \mu_v^*\right) = c_1^2 \eta \left(t, t_p \tau_q, \tau_\theta, \lambda_v, \mu_v\right), \tag{27}$$

where $c_1 = \sqrt{\frac{\lambda_0 + 2\mu_0}{\rho}}$ and $\eta = \frac{\rho c_E}{K}$.

Using the above non-dimensional variables, Equations (11)–(14), (21), and (22) take the following forms (the asterisks were omitted to avoid confusion):

$$\sigma_{xx} = 2\beta^2\left(1 + \mu_v \frac{\partial}{\partial t}\right)\frac{\partial u}{\partial x} + \left(1 - 2\beta^2\right)\left(1 + \lambda_v \frac{\partial}{\partial t}\right)e - \left(1 + \gamma_v \frac{\partial}{\partial t}\right)\theta, \tag{28}$$

$$\sigma_{yy} = 2\beta^2\left(1 + \mu_v \frac{\partial}{\partial t}\right)\frac{\partial v}{\partial y} + \left(1 - 2\beta^2\right)\left(1 + \lambda_v \frac{\partial}{\partial t}\right)e - \left(1 + \gamma_v \frac{\partial}{\partial t}\right)\theta, \tag{29}$$

$$\sigma_{zz} = \left(1 - 2\beta^2\right)\left(1 + \lambda_v \frac{\partial}{\partial t}\right)e - \left(1 + \gamma_v \frac{\partial}{\partial t}\right)\theta, \tag{30}$$

$$\sigma_{xy} = \beta^2\left(1 + \mu_v \frac{\partial}{\partial t}\right)\left(\frac{\partial v}{\partial x} + \frac{\partial u}{\partial y}\right), \tag{31}$$

$$\left[1 + \left(\left(1 - \beta^2\right)\delta_v + \alpha_1 \beta^2\right)\frac{\partial}{\partial t}\right]\nabla^2 e - \left(1 + \gamma_v \frac{\partial}{\partial t}\right)\nabla^2 \theta = \frac{\partial^2 e}{\partial t^2}, \tag{32}$$

$$\tau_q^{1-\gamma}\frac{\partial^{1-\gamma}}{\partial t^{1-\gamma}}\left(1 + \tau_\theta^\beta \frac{\partial^\beta}{\partial t^\beta}\right)\nabla^2 \theta = \left(1 + \tau_q^\alpha \frac{\partial^\alpha}{\partial t^\alpha}\right)\left[\frac{\partial \theta}{\partial t} + \varepsilon\left(\frac{\partial}{\partial t} + \gamma_v \frac{\partial^2}{\partial t^2}\right)e\right], \tag{33}$$

where $\beta^2 = \frac{\mu_0}{\lambda_0 + 2\mu_0}$ and $\varepsilon = \frac{(3\lambda_0 + 2\mu_0)^2 \alpha_T^2 T_0}{\rho c_E (\lambda_0 + 2\mu_0)}$.

We shall consider the hydrostatic stress as the mean value of the normal stresses σ_{xx}, σ_{yy}, and σ_{zz}, namely,

$$\sigma_H = \frac{\sigma_{xx} + \sigma_{yy} + \sigma_{zz}}{3}. \tag{34}$$

By using Equations (28)–(30), we obtain

$$\sigma_H = \left[\left(1 - \frac{4}{3}\beta^2\right) + \left(\frac{2}{3}\beta^2 \mu_v + \left(1 - 2\beta^2\right)\lambda_v\right)\frac{\partial}{\partial t}\right]e - \left(1 + \gamma_v \frac{\partial}{\partial t}\right)\theta, \tag{35}$$

associated with the following non-dimensional thermal and mechanical boundary conditions

$$\theta(x,0,t) = \Theta_0(x,t), \quad \left.\frac{\partial \theta(x,y,t)}{\partial y}\right|_{y=l} = 0, \tag{36}$$

$$\sigma_{yy}(x,0,t) = \sigma_{yy}(x,l,t) = 0, \tag{37}$$

$$\sigma_{xy}(x,0,t) = \sigma_{xy}(x,l,t) = 0, \tag{38}$$

and non-dimensional homogeneous initial conditions

$$u(x,y,t)|_{t=0} = \left.\frac{\partial u(x,y,t)}{\partial t}\right|_{t=0} = 0, \; v(x,y,t)|_{t=0} = \left.\frac{\partial v(x,y,t)}{\partial t}\right|_{t=0} = 0,$$
$$\theta(x,y,t)|_{t=0} = \left.\frac{\partial \theta(x,y,t)}{\partial t}\right|_{t=0} = 0, \tag{39}$$

4. Solutions in the Integral-Transform Domain

We shall now define the Laplace transform (denoted by a bar) with respect to a function $h(x,y,t)$ by the relation [54]

$$\overline{h}(x,y,s) = \mathcal{L}\{h(x,y,t); t\}(x,y,s) = \int_0^\infty h(x,y,t)e^{-st}dt, \tag{40}$$

where $h(x,y,t)$ is a continuous function over time, s is the Laplace parameter, and the inverse Laplace's transform is defined as

$$\mathcal{L}^{-1}\left(\overline{h}(x,y,s)\right) = \frac{1}{2\pi i}\lim_{\beta\to\infty}\int_{\alpha-i\beta}^{\alpha+i\beta}\overline{h}(x,y,s)e^{st}ds = h(x,y,t), \tag{41}$$

where $i = \sqrt{-1}$, and the Fourier exponential transform (denoted by a hat) to a function $\overline{h}(x,y,s)$ with respect to the variable x is defined by the relation

$$\hat{\overline{h}}(q,y,s) = \mathcal{F}\{\overline{h}(x,y,s); x\}(q,y,s) = \int_0^\infty \overline{h}(x,y,s)e^{-iqx}dx, \tag{42}$$

with its corresponding inversion

$$\mathcal{F}^{-1}\left(\hat{\overline{h}}(q,y,s)\right) = \frac{1}{2\pi}\int_{-\infty}^\infty \hat{\overline{h}}(q,y,s)e^{iqx}dq = \overline{h}(x,y,s), \tag{43}$$

We assume that all the relevant functions are sufficiently smooth on the real line such that the Fourier transform of these functions exists. According to the homogeneous initial conditions (39), upon applying the Laplace transform on both sides of Equations (32) and (33), we arrive at

$$\left[(1+\varsigma s)\nabla^2 - s^2\right]\overline{e} - (1+\gamma_0 s)\nabla^2\overline{\theta} = 0, \tag{44}$$

$$\left(\nabla^2 - sL\right)\overline{\theta} - \varepsilon s(1+\gamma_0 s)L\overline{e} = 0, \tag{45}$$

where

$$\varsigma = \left(1-\beta^2\right)\delta_v + \mu_v\beta^2, \; L(s) = \frac{1+\tau_q^\alpha s^\alpha}{\tau_q^{1-\gamma}s^{1-\gamma}\left(1+\tau_\theta^\beta s^\beta\right)}. \tag{46}$$

Eliminating $\overline{\theta}$ between Equations (44) and (45), we obtain

$$\left[(1+\varsigma s)\nabla^4 - \left(s(1+\varsigma s)L + s^2 + \varepsilon s(1+\gamma_v s)^2 L\right)\nabla^2 + s^3 L\right]\overline{e} = 0, \tag{47}$$

which can be factorized as

$$\prod_{i=1}^{2}\left(\nabla^2 - k_i^2\right)\overline{e} = 0, \tag{48}$$

where k_i^2, ($i = 1, 2$) are the roots with positive real parts of the characteristic equation

$$(1 + \varsigma s)k^4 - \left[s(1 + \varsigma s)L + s^2 + \varepsilon s(1 + \gamma_v s)^2 L\right]k^2 + s^3 L = 0. \tag{49}$$

Upon applying the exponential Fourier transform on Equation (48), we obtain

$$\prod_{i=1}^{2}\left(\mathfrak{D}^2 - m_i^2\right)\hat{\bar{e}} = 0, \tag{50}$$

where $m_i^2 = q^2 + k_i^2$, $i = 1, 2$, and $\mathfrak{D} = \partial/\partial y$. The general solution of Equation (50), bounded for the region $0 \leq y \leq l$, is given as

$$\hat{\bar{e}} = \sum_{i=1}^{2}\left(k_i^2 - sL\right)\left[A_i e^{-m_i y} + B_i e^{m_i y}\right], \tag{51}$$

where A_i, B_i, $i = 1, 2$, are parameters depending on s and q. Similarly, eliminating $\bar{e}$ between Equations (44) and (45) leads to the characteristic equation

$$\left[(1 + \varsigma s)\nabla^4 - \left(s(1 + \varsigma s)L + s^2 + \varepsilon s(1 + \gamma_v s)^2 L\right)\nabla^2 + s^3 L\right]\bar{\theta} = 0. \tag{52}$$

Therefore, the general solution of (52) for $y \in [0, l]$ can be written as

$$\hat{\bar{\theta}} = \varepsilon s(1 + \gamma_v s)L\sum_{i=1}^{2}\left[A'_i e^{-m_i y} + B'_i e^{m_i y}\right], \tag{53}$$

where A'_i, B'_i, $i = 1, 2$, are parameters depending on s and q. In view of Equations (51), (53) and (45), one can deduce the following relations for A'_i and B'_i

$$A'_i(q, s) = A_i(q, s), \quad B'_i(q, s) = B_i(q, s), \quad i = 1, 2. \tag{54}$$

Using the above relations in Equation (53), we obtain

$$\hat{\bar{\theta}} = \varepsilon s(1 + \gamma_v s)L\sum_{i=1}^{2}\left[A_i e^{-m_i y} + B_i e^{m_i y}\right]. \tag{55}$$

On the other hand, Equations (17) and (19) can be written in the non-dimensional form as

$$e = \frac{\partial u}{\partial x} + \frac{\partial v}{\partial y}. \tag{56}$$

$$\beta^2\left(1 + \mu_v \frac{\partial}{\partial t}\right)\nabla^2 v + \left(1 - \beta^2\right)\left(1 + \delta_v \frac{\partial}{\partial t}\right)\mathfrak{D}e - \left(1 + \gamma_v \frac{\partial}{\partial t}\right)\mathfrak{D}\theta = \frac{\partial^2 v}{\partial t^2}, \tag{57}$$

Taking the Laplace–Fourier transforms for Equations (56) and (57), we obtain

$$\hat{\bar{u}} = \frac{1}{iq}\left(\hat{\bar{e}} - \frac{\partial \hat{\bar{v}}}{\partial y}\right), \tag{58}$$

$$\left(\mathfrak{D}^2 - m^2\right)\hat{\bar{v}} = \frac{1}{\beta^2(1 + \mu_v s)}\left((1 + \gamma_v s)\mathfrak{D}\hat{\bar{\theta}} - \left(1 - \beta^2\right)(1 + \delta_v s)\mathfrak{D}\hat{\bar{e}}\right) \tag{59}$$

where $m^2 = q^2 + \frac{s^2}{\beta^2(1+\mu_v s)}$.

Next, substituting Equations (51) and (55) into the right-hand side of Equation (59), we obtain

$$\hat{\bar{v}} = C_1 e^{-my} + C_2 e^{my} + \sum_{i=1}^{2}\psi_i\left[-A_i e^{-m_i y} + B_i e^{m_i y}\right], \tag{60}$$

where $\psi_i = \frac{m_i\left(\varepsilon s(1+\gamma_v s)^2 L - (1-\beta^2)(1+\delta_v s)(k_i^2 - sL)\right)}{\beta^2(1+\mu_v s)(m_i^2 - m^2)}$, and C_i, $i = 1, 2$, are parameters depending on s and q.

To determine the tangential component of the velocity, utilizing Equations (51) and (60) in the right-hand side of Equation (58), we obtain

$$\hat{\bar{u}} = \frac{i}{q}\left(m\left(-C_1 e^{-my} + C_2 e^{my}\right) + \sum_{i=1}^{2}\left(\psi_i m_i - k_i^2 + sL\right)\left[A_i e^{-m_i y} + B_i e^{m_i y}\right]\right). \quad (61)$$

Finally, we combine Equations (51), (55), (60) and (61) with the Laplace and Fourier transforms of Equations (28), (31) and (35), and perform some straightforward calculations; the results are

$$\hat{\bar{\sigma}}_{xx} = 2m\beta^2(1+\mu_v s)\left[C_1 e^{-my} - C_2 e^{my}\right] + \sum_{i=1}^{2}\varphi_i\left[A_i e^{-m_i y} + B_i e^{m_i y}\right], \quad (62)$$

$$\hat{\bar{\sigma}}_{yy} = 2m\beta^2(1+\mu_v s)\left[-C_1 e^{-my} + C_2 e^{my}\right] + \sum_{i=1}^{2}\omega_i\left[A_i e^{-m_i y} + B_i e^{m_i y}\right], \quad (63)$$

$$\hat{\bar{\sigma}}_{zz} = \sum_{i=1}^{2}\chi_i\left[A_i e^{-m_i y} + B_i e^{m_i y}\right], \quad (64)$$

$$\hat{\bar{\sigma}}_{xy} = \frac{i\beta^2(1+\mu_v s)}{q}\left((q^2+m^2)\left[C_1 e^{-my} + C_2 e^{my}\right]\right.$$
$$\left.+ \sum_{i=1}^{2}\left(q^2\psi_i + m_i(\psi_i m_i - k_i^2 + sL)\right)\left[-A_i e^{-m_i y} + B_i e^{m_i y}\right]\right), \quad (65)$$

$$\hat{\bar{\sigma}}_H = \sum_{i=1}^{2}\zeta_i\left[A_i e^{-m_i y} + B_i e^{m_i y}\right], \quad (66)$$

where
$$\varphi_i = -2\beta^2(1+\mu_v s)\psi_i m_i + (k_i^2 - Ls)(2\beta^2(1+\mu_v s) + (1-2\beta^2)(1+\lambda_v s)) - \varepsilon s(1+\gamma_v s)^2 L,$$
$$\omega_i = 2\beta^2(1+\mu_v s)\psi_i m_i + (1-2\beta^2)(1+\lambda_v s)(k_i^2 - sL) - \varepsilon s(1+\gamma_v s)^2 L,$$
$$\chi_i = (1-2\beta^2)(1+\lambda_v s)(k_i^2 - sL) - \varepsilon s(1+\gamma_v s)^2 L,$$
$$\zeta_i = \left(\left(1-\tfrac{4}{3}\beta^2\right) + \left(\tfrac{2}{3}\beta^2\mu_v + (1-2\beta^2)\lambda_v\right)s\right)(k_i^2 - sL) - \varepsilon s(1+\gamma_v s)^2 L.$$

The boundary conditions (36)–(38) in the Laplace–Fourier domain read

$$\hat{\bar{\theta}}(q,0,s) = \hat{\bar{\Theta}}_0(q,s), \quad \left.\frac{\partial\hat{\bar{\theta}}(q,y,s)}{\partial y}\right|_{y=l} = 0, \quad (67)$$

$$\hat{\bar{\sigma}}_{yy}(q,0,s) = \hat{\bar{\sigma}}_{yy}(q,l,s) = 0, \quad (68)$$

$$\hat{\bar{\sigma}}_{xy}(q,0,s) = \hat{\bar{\sigma}}_{xy}(q,l,s) = 0. \quad (69)$$

Without loss of generality, we specify the condition of double-strip heating [50,51]:

$$\Theta_0(x,t) = [H(b-|x|) - H(a-|x|)]\exp\left(-\frac{t}{t_p}\right), \quad (70)$$

where $H(\cdot)$ is the Heaviside unit step function, and t_p is a temporal parameter characterizing the thermalization time, or alternatively, the heating rate. In other words, if we take a dimensional thermalization parameter $t_p = 1$ femtosecond, then at the physical time $t = 1$ picosecond, the surface reaches zero temperature difference $\theta(x,0,t) = 0$, or alternatively, the absolute surface temperature becomes identical with the room temperature, $T(x,0,t) = T_0$. The double-strip heating parameters a and b are taken as nonzero constants such that ($a < b$). The boundary surface temperature in the Laplace–Fourier domain is determined by

$$\hat{\bar{\Theta}}_0(q,s) = \frac{2t_p}{q(1+t_p s)}[\sin(bq) - \sin(aq)]. \tag{71}$$

Equations (67)–(69) immediately give the following system of six linear equations in the unknown parameters $A_i(q,s), B_i(q,s), (i=1, 2)$ and $C_i(q,s), (i=1, 2)$.

$$\varepsilon s L(1+\gamma_v s)\sum_{i=1}^{2}[A_i + B_i] = \frac{t_p}{q(1+t_p s)}(\sin(bq) - \sin(aq)), \tag{72}$$

$$\sum_{i=1}^{2} m_i\left[-A_i e^{-m_i l} + B_i e^{m_i l}\right] = 0, \tag{73}$$

$$2m\beta^2(1+\mu_v s)[-C_1 + C_2] + \sum_{i=1}^{2} \varpi_i[A_i + B_i] = 0, \tag{74}$$

$$2m\beta^2(1+\mu_v s)\left[-C_1 e^{-ml} + C_2 e^{ml}\right] + \sum_{i=1}^{2} \varpi_i\left[A_i e^{-m_i l} + B_i e^{m_i l}\right] = 0, \tag{75}$$

$$\left(q^2 + m^2\right)[C_1 + C_2] + \sum_{i=1}^{2}\left(q^2 \psi_i + m_i\left(\psi_i m_i - k_1^2 + sL\right)\right)[-A_i + B_i] = 0, \tag{76}$$

$$\left(q^2 + m^2\right)\left[C_1 e^{-ml} + C_2 e^{ml}\right] + \sum_{i=1}^{2}\left(q^2 \psi_i + m_i\left(\psi_i m_i - k_1^2 + sL\right)\right)\left[-A_i e^{-m_i l} + B_i e^{m_i l}\right] = 0. \tag{77}$$

This completes the solution of the problem in the Laplace–Fourier-transformed domain.

5. Numerical Results and Discussion

In order to present numerical results, *copper* material [6,55,56] is chosen for the purposes of numerical evaluation, with the parameters in SI units listed in Table 1.

Table 1. Mechanical and thermal properties of copper at reference temperature $T_0 = 293$ °K.

Property	λ_0	μ_0	ρ	c_E	α_T	k	τ_q	τ_θ	$\lambda_v = \mu_v$
Value	7.76×10^{10}	3.86×10^{10}	8954	383.1	1.78×10^{-5}	386.0	0.4648	70.833	0.68831
SI unit	Kg·m^{-1}·s^{-2}	Kg·m^{-1}·s^{-2}	Kg·m^{-3}	J·Kg^{-1}·K^{-1}	K^{-1}	W·m^{-1}·K^{-1}	picoseconds	picoseconds	picoseconds

In addition, we choose the dimensionless plate thickness and the double-strip parameters as

$$l = 1, \quad a = 1, \quad b = 2, \quad t_p = 0.1. \tag{78}$$

According to the choice of the dimensionless thickness, $l = 1$, and the dimensionless thermalization parameter, $t_p = 0.1$, the real thickness of the plate is $1/(c_1 \eta) = 27.063$ nanometers, and the real thermalization parameter equals $0.1/(c_1^2 \eta) = 1.302$ picoseconds; refer to Equation (27), and also see [57].

In this section, we implement two infinite series to calculate the integrals (41) and (43). Thereby, we will bring the temperature, displacement, and hydrostatic stress to the physical domain. Inversion of the Laplace parameter s to the physical time t requires the implementation of Durbin formula, which is the approximation of the integral (41); see [58,59].

$$\hat{h}(q,y,t) = \frac{2\exp(\gamma)}{T_1}\left\{-\frac{1}{2}\hat{\bar{h}}\left(q,y,\frac{\gamma}{t}\right) + \Re\left[\sum_{j=0}^{NSum1} \hat{\bar{h}}\left(q,y,\frac{\gamma}{t} + \frac{2\pi i j}{T_1}\right)\cos\left(\frac{2\pi j t}{T_1}\right)\right] - \Im\left[\sum_{j=0}^{NSum1} \hat{\bar{h}}\left(q,y,\frac{\gamma}{t} + \frac{2\pi i j}{T_1}\right)\sin\left(\frac{2\pi j t}{T_1}\right)\right]\right\}, \tag{79}$$

where $\gamma \cong 4.7 \sim 10$ and T_1 is chosen so that $0 < t \leq 2T_1$. For accelerating the computations time, we use a FORTRAN subroutine [60] for the series with $Nsum1 \cong 10^6$. Inversion of the Fourier transform, i.e., transforming q into x, requires implementing another integral (refer to (43)), which can be approximated by the following Riemann sum

$$\mathcal{F}^{-1}\left(\hat{h}(q,y,t)\right) = \frac{1}{\pi}\begin{cases} \sum_{n=0}^{Nsum2} \hat{h}(q_n,y,t)\cos(q_n x)\Delta q_n, & \text{for even function,} \\ i\sum_{n=0}^{Nsum2} \hat{h}(q_n,y,t)\sin(q_n x)\Delta q_n, & \text{for odd function.} \end{cases} \quad (80)$$

Using a suitable numerical approach, such as a trapezoidal approach, or a nested approach using the Bulirsch–Stoer step method, the rational function extrapolation, and modified midpoint method [61], the series (80) can be implemented. The parameter $Nsum2$ takes a value from 100 to 500. The computation time for 100 points ranges from 30 to 180 s depending on the mathematical model, the numerical technique used for inverting the Fourier transform, and the Intel Core processor version. Because of the evanescence of discontinuities in the stresses of the Kelvin–Voigt model and in the temperature of the fractional Jeffreys equation, the running time of the program is much less than that for the elastic case with finite thermal wave speed [57]. The computation was carried out on two Intel Core processors, Core i5-9600K and Core i7-1165G7. MATLAB R2019a was utilized for graphical representations on an NVIDIA Geforce MX330 graphics card.

The heat flux $\mathbf{q} = \langle q_x, q_y, 0\rangle$ is an important physical vector quantity predicting the actual heat direction inside the conductor. Using the following non-dimensional transformation:

$$\begin{pmatrix} q_x \\ q_y \end{pmatrix} \to kT_0 c_1 \eta \begin{pmatrix} q_x \\ q_y \end{pmatrix}, \quad (81)$$

along with the dimensionless quantities (27) and the fractional Jeffreys Equation (8), the dimensionless heat flux components are given in terms of the temperature gradient as

$$\left(1 + \tau_q^\alpha \frac{\partial^\alpha}{\partial t^\alpha}\right)\begin{Bmatrix} q_x \\ q_y \end{Bmatrix} = -\tau_q^{1-\gamma}\frac{\partial^{1-\gamma}}{\partial t^{1-\gamma}}\left(1 + \tau_\theta^\beta \frac{\partial^\beta}{\partial t^\beta}\right)\begin{Bmatrix} \frac{\partial \theta}{\partial x} \\ \frac{\partial \theta}{\partial y} \end{Bmatrix}. \quad (82)$$

When the combined Laplace–Fourier transform (40) and (42) is invoked, the heat flux components (82) have the following exact formulas in the transformed domain:

$$\begin{Bmatrix} \hat{\bar{q}}_x \\ \hat{\bar{q}}_y \end{Bmatrix} = -\frac{1}{L(s)}\begin{Bmatrix} iq\hat{\bar{\theta}} \\ \mathcal{D}\hat{\bar{\theta}} \end{Bmatrix}, \quad (83)$$

and $L(s) = \frac{1+\tau_q^\alpha s^\alpha}{\tau_q^{1-\gamma}s^{1-\gamma}\left(1+\tau_\theta^\beta s^\beta\right)}$. In view of the temperature (55), the heat flux components (83) are given as

$$\hat{\bar{q}}_x = -iq\varepsilon s(1+\gamma_v s)\sum_{i=1}^{2}[A_i e^{-m_i y} + B_i e^{m_i y}],$$
$$\hat{\bar{q}}_y = -\varepsilon s(1+\gamma_v s)\sum_{i=1}^{2} m_i[-A_i e^{-m_i y} + B_i e^{m_i y}]. \quad (84)$$

In what follows, we will concentrate on four heat transfer models: the ordinary Jeffreys equation with flux precedence, known as the parabolic dual-phase-lag (DPL) model with $\tau_\theta > \tau_q$, the fractional Jeffreys equation with accelerated heat transfer, the fractional Jeffreys equation with retarded transfer, and the fractional Jeffreys equation with crossover from super- to sub-thermal conduction.

In Figure 2, we represent the temporal evolution of the temperature distribution governed by the flux-precedence DPL thermoelasticity and propagating from the upper surface to the lower surface. The heat flux components (84) are also inserted into the figure as a vector plot for anticipating the direction of heat. Before the dimensionless time instant

$t = 0.09$, the heat flux is directed from the upper surface to the lower surface which precedes and stimulates the temperature gradient. In the case of a semi-infinite conductor [50], the temperature peak diffuses with time progress, leaving the boundary surface. Here, in the finite domain setting, because of the presence of the reflecting boundary condition on the lower boundary (36) and the acute heat flux precedence, $\tau_\theta \gg \tau_q$, the heat flux vector reverses its direction between the dimensionless instants $t = 0.08$ and $t = 0.09$, so that the upper surface always has the highest temperature though the overall dissipation of heat (i.e., the decrease in temperature value with time). This behavior is also attributed to the immobilization characteristic of the Jeffreys "DPL" equation referred to in the literature; see [2,21,62]. Because of the cooling of the upper surface, the hot portion begins to move from the upper to the lower surface at a late instant $t = 0.7$ and 0.9; see recent studies on the ultrafast heating of micro- and nanostructures [63,64]. Some numerical results for the temperature at dimensionless time instants $t = 0.05$ and $t = 0.5$ are given in Tables 2 and 3.

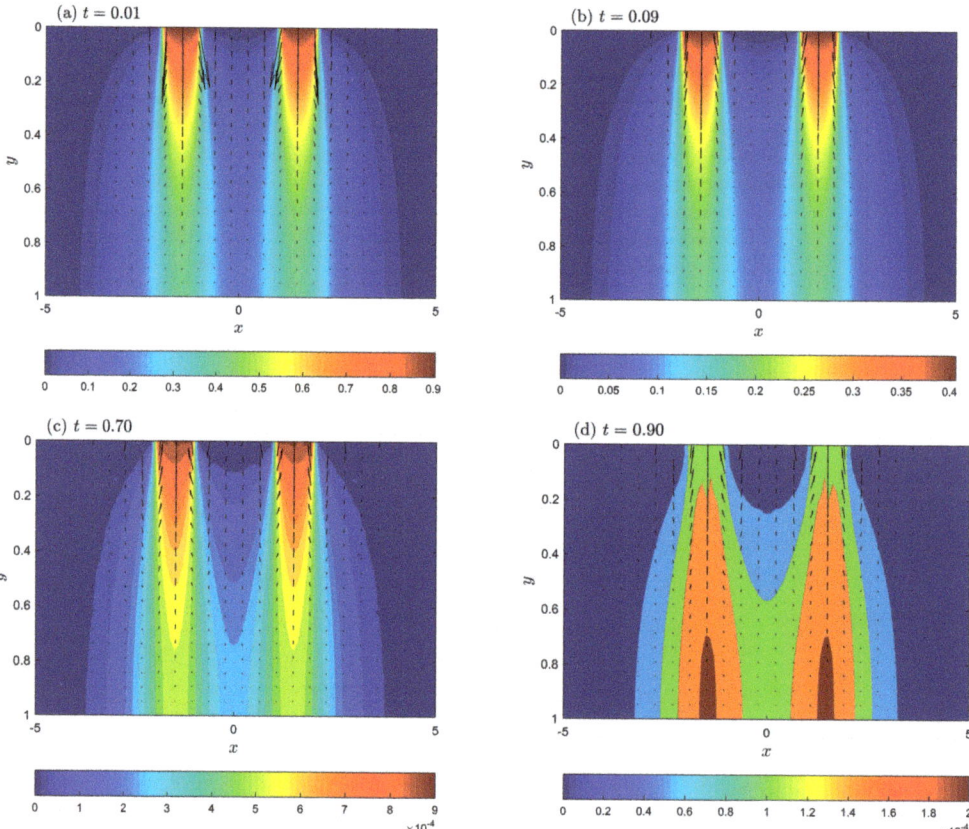

Figure 2. Temperature distribution (contours) and heat flux vector (arrows) for the *"ordinary flux-precedence Jeffreys model"* at four instants: (**a**) $t = 0.01$, (**b**) $t = 0.09$, (**c**) $t = 0.7$, and (**d**) $t = 0.9$.

Table 2. Numerical values of the temperature profile at the dimensionless instant $t = 0.05$.

| | | Ordinary Jeffreys Heat Conduction | | | The Fractional Jeffreys-Type Heat Conduction | | | | | | | |
| | | | | | Accelerated Conduction | | | Retarded Conduction | | | Crossover from Super- to Sub-Conduction | | |
y	x	0.5	1.5	2.5	0.5	1.5	2.5	0.5	1.5	2.5	0.5	1.5	2.5
0.0		0.000017	0.606626	0.000009	0.000017	0.606626	0.000009	0.000017	0.606626	0.000009	0.000017	0.606626	0.000009
0.1		0.032830	0.538056	0.028552	0.027667	0.528095	0.024501	0.008853	0.487462	0.008775	0.007961	0.546885	0.007959
0.2		0.062894	0.475297	0.054399	0.052757	0.457417	0.046500	0.015883	0.381876	0.015723	0.013360	0.469591	0.013353
0.3		0.088464	0.421706	0.076011	0.073675	0.397627	0.064506	0.020156	0.293778	0.019925	0.014976	0.382421	0.014957
0.4		0.109023	0.378412	0.092930	0.090061	0.349397	0.078216	0.021814	0.223230	0.021540	0.013300	0.292004	0.013327
0.5		0.124909	0.344735	0.105599	0.102339	0.311841	0.088122	0.021502	0.168625	0.021190	0.009705	0.205164	0.009689
0.6		0.136780	0.319396	0.114740	0.111189	0.283509	0.094984	0.020134	0.127722	0.019788	0.005969	0.129459	0.005976
0.7		0.145297	0.301096	0.121077	0.117327	0.262969	0.099543	0.018390	0.098306	0.017996	0.003056	0.071513	0.003064
0.8		0.150998	0.288772	0.125192	0.121319	0.249104	0.102376	0.016819	0.078572	0.016355	0.001299	0.033724	0.001296
0.9		0.154272	0.281676	0.127501	0.123560	0.241099	0.103910	0.015675	0.067243	0.015253	0.000497	0.013852	0.000474
1.0		0.155339	0.279372	0.128245	0.124284	0.238483	0.104395	0.015274	0.063551	0.014875	0.000294	0.007668	0.000260

Table 3. Numerical values of the temperature profile at the dimensionless instant $t = 0.5$.

| | | Ordinary Jeffreys Heat Conduction | | | The Fractional Jeffreys-Type Heat Conduction | | | | | | | |
| | | | | | Accelerated Conduction | | | Retarded Conduction | | | Crossover from Super- to Sub-Conduction | | |
y	x	0.5	1.5	2.5	0.5	1.5	2.5	0.5	1.5	2.5	0.5	1.5	2.5
0.0		0.000019	0.006720	0.000020	0.000019	0.006720	0.000020	0.000019	0.006720	0.000020	0.000019	0.006720	0.000020
0.1		0.000376	0.006006	0.000330	0.000535	0.006319	0.000456	0.001648	0.010298	0.001426	0.003184	0.010157	0.002406
0.2		0.000722	0.005325	0.000619	0.001032	0.005914	0.000862	0.003188	0.012555	0.002742	0.006230	0.013075	0.004709
0.3		0.001020	0.004735	0.000872	0.001470	0.005515	0.001225	0.004562	0.013864	0.003915	0.009065	0.015561	0.006847
0.4		0.001252	0.004269	0.001063	0.001830	0.005192	0.001515	0.005728	0.014572	0.004878	0.011628	0.017672	0.008755
0.5		0.001443	0.003896	0.001211	0.002132	0.004929	0.001749	0.006678	0.014898	0.005662	0.013871	0.019431	0.010401
0.6		0.001583	0.003611	0.001321	0.002366	0.004728	0.001929	0.007430	0.015017	0.006280	0.015748	0.020859	0.011785
0.7		0.001683	0.003419	0.001395	0.002540	0.004603	0.002060	0.007996	0.015054	0.006726	0.017237	0.021988	0.012872
0.8		0.001752	0.003287	0.001445	0.002664	0.004520	0.002152	0.008393	0.015067	0.007040	0.018316	0.022795	0.013656
0.9		0.001791	0.003215	0.001473	0.002736	0.004478	0.002204	0.008630	0.015080	0.007225	0.018970	0.023293	0.014129
1.0		0.001803	0.003192	0.001482	0.002760	0.004465	0.002221	0.008706	0.015088	0.007286	0.019190	0.023462	0.014287

The time evolution of the temperature distribution and the heat flux vector governed by the fractional Jeffreys equation with different transport situations are represented in Figures 3–5 for accelerated, retarded, and crossover from super- to sub-thermal conductivity, respectively, at six instants. The terminologies "accelerated", "retarded" and "crossover from super- to sub-" were named based on their deviation from the linear behavior of the mean squared displacement in the case of particle transfer being considered [21]. When the temperature distribution is resulting from anomalous diffusion of hot electrons within the lattice, then the thermal behavior might inherit a similar attitude. As Figure 3 shows, the accelerated case is not dissimilar from the ordinary DPL model in the short time response. The temperature distribution arrives at the lower surface at a very early instant, and the heat flux vector changes its direction to become from the lower surface to the upper surface very fast between the instants $t = 0.01$ and 0.02. Again, the direction reverse of the heat flux vector keeps the peak temperature at the upper surface for a relatively long time; see Figure 3c,d. The cooling of the upper surface due to the exponential function $\exp(-t/t_p)$ enforces the movement of the temperature peak from the upper to the lower surface as the subfigures Figure 3e,f show.

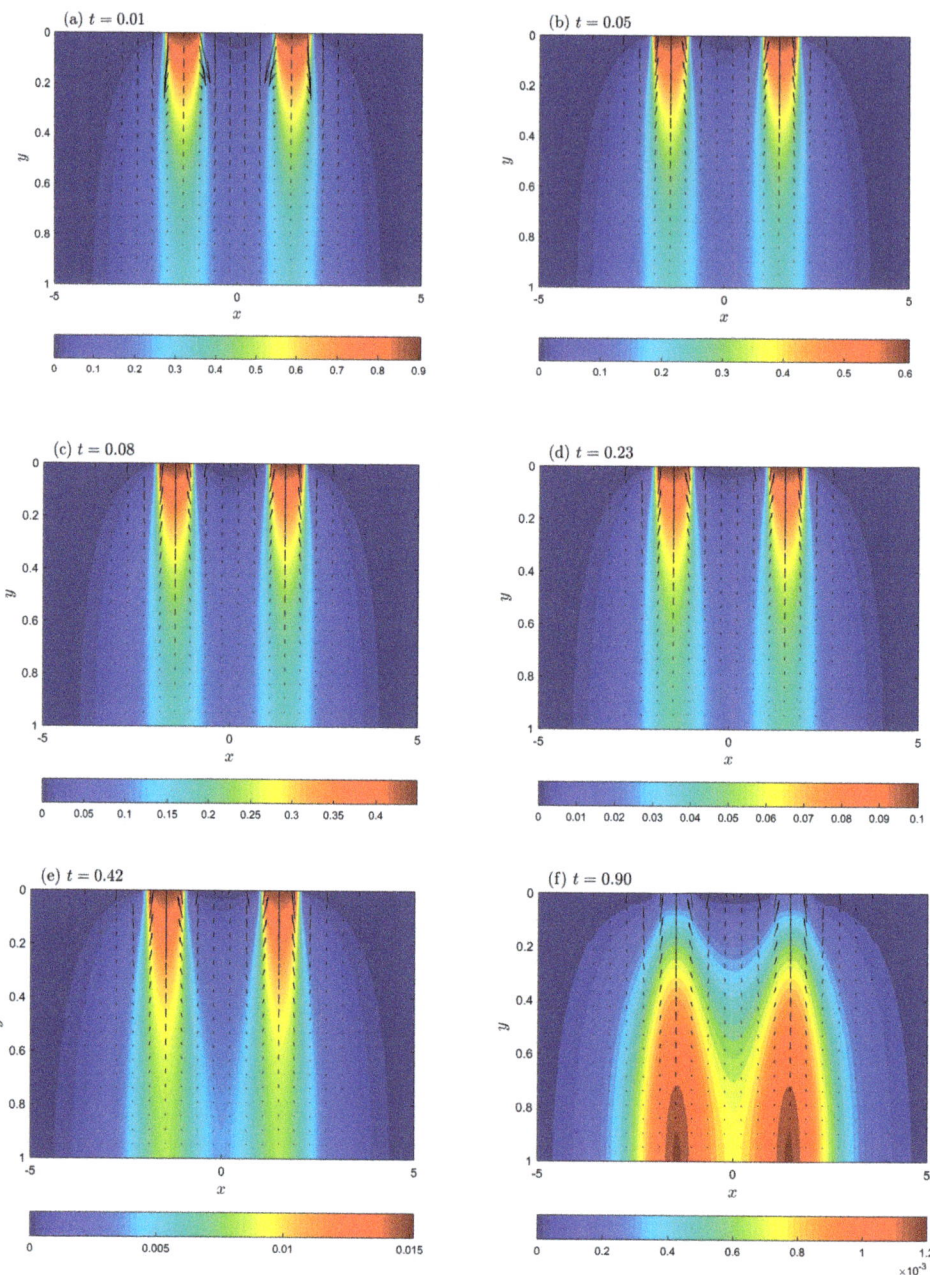

Figure 3. Temperature distribution (contours) and heat flux vector (arrows) governed by the fractional Jeffreys model with *"acceleration"* when $\alpha = 0.2$ and $\beta = \gamma = 0.8$, at six instants: (**a**) $t = 0.01$, (**b**) $t = 0.05$, (**c**) $t = 0.08$, (**d**) $t = 0.23$, (**e**) $t = 0.42$, and (**f**) $t = 0.9$.

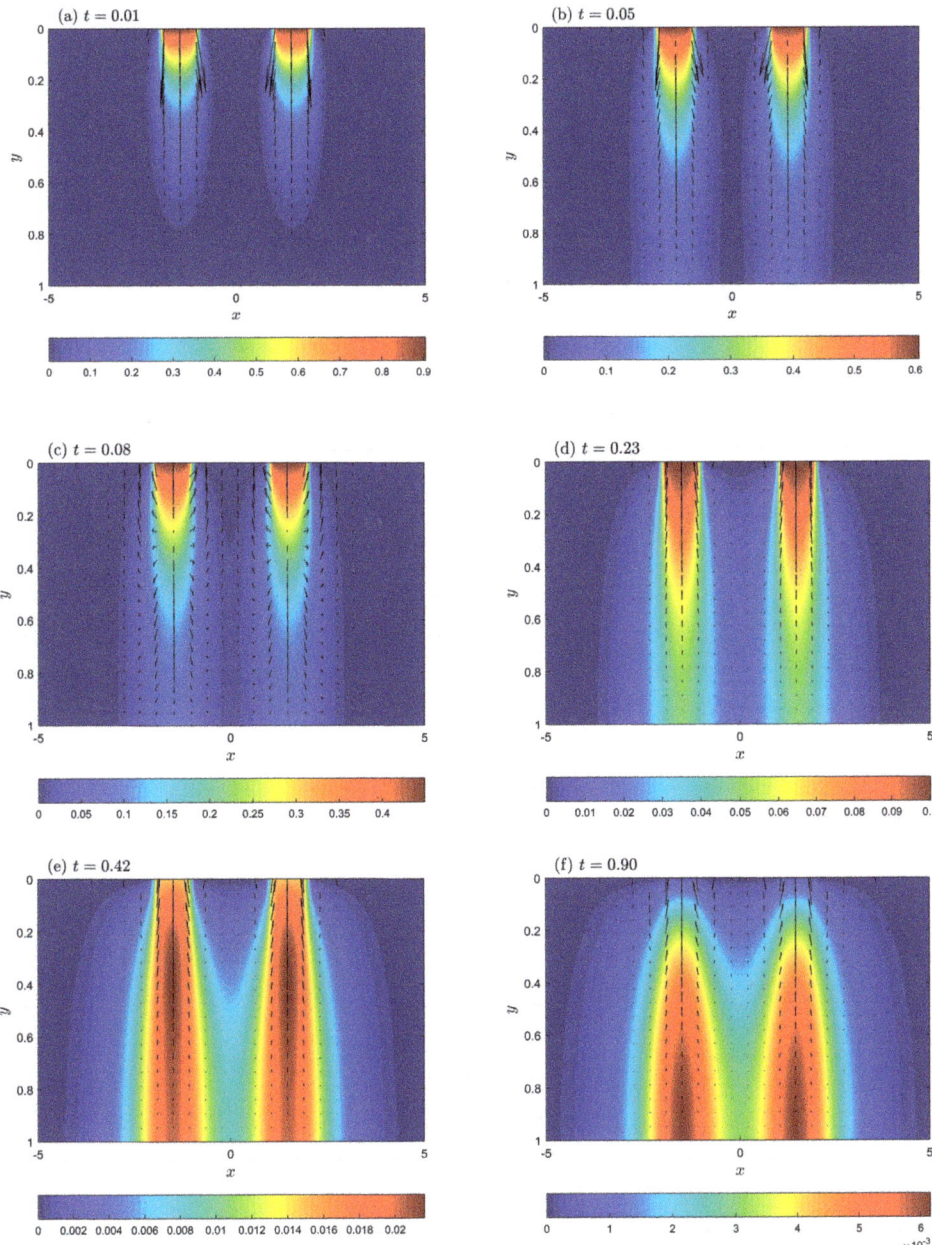

Figure 4. Temperature distribution (contours) and heat flux vector (arrows) governed by the fractional Jeffreys model with *"retardation"*, when $\alpha = 0.6$, $\beta = 0.2$, and $\gamma = 0.4$ at six instants: (**a**) $t = 0.01$, (**b**) $t = 0.05$, (**c**) $t = 0.08$, (**d**) $t = 0.23$, (**e**) $t = 0.42$, and (**f**) $t = 0.9$.

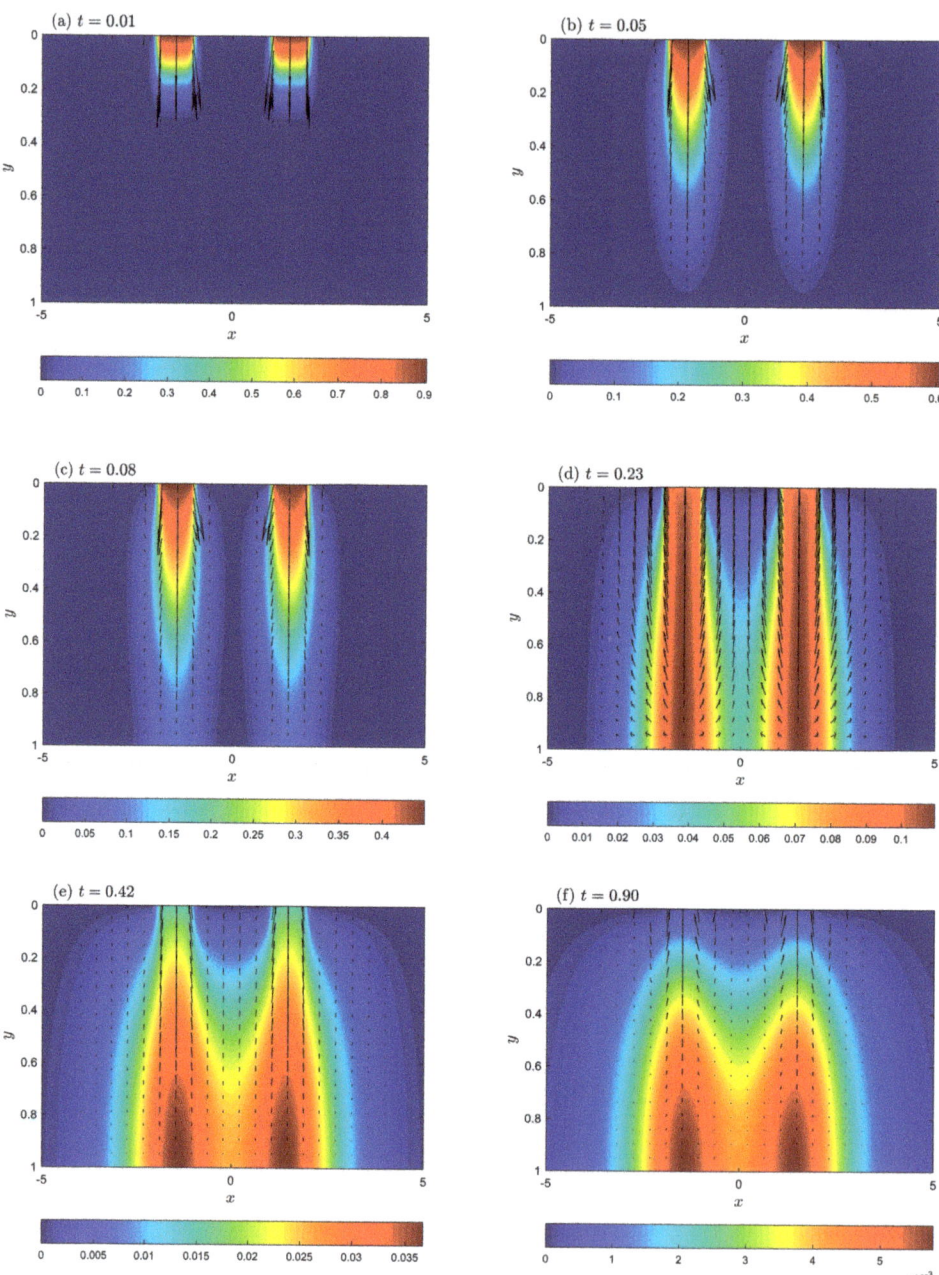

Figure 5. Temperature distribution (contours) and heat flux vector (arrows) governed by the fractional Jeffreys model with *"crossover"*, when $\alpha = 0.8$, $\beta = 0.2$, and $\gamma = 0.8$ at six instants: (**a**) $t = 0.01$, (**b**) $t = 0.05$, (**c**) $t = 0.08$, (**d**) $t = 0.23$, (**e**) $t = 0.42$, and (**f**) $t = 0.9$.

In Figure 4, the retarded heat conduction case represented by the fractional Jeffreys equation is drawn. In comparison with the ordinary Jeffreys equation and the fractional Jeffreys equation of accelerated type, the retardation case moves slower than the accelerated case such that the thermal waves have not yet reached the lower surface at $t = 0.01$. In contrast to the rapid change in the direction of the heat flux in Figures 2 and 3, the heat flux vector spends a longer interval from $t = 0.05$ to $t = 0.1$ to change its direction. The retardation in heat transfer causes lower values for the temperature at the lower surface compared with the ordinary Jeffreys and the acceleration case; compare the instants $t = 0.01$ and 0.05 in Figures 2–4.

The crossover from super- to sub-thermal conduction is represented in Figure 5. Because of its affinity in the temporal behavior to the Cattaneo equation, the temperature distribution of such crossover moves slower than all flux-precedence Jeffreys models (ordinary and fractional), but there is no explicit form for its speed from a mathematical point of view. The heat flux reverses its direction between the instants $t = 0.14$ and $t = 0.3$, i.e., during a longer interval compared with all flux-precedence (ordinary and fractional) Jeffreys models.

In Figure 6, the hydrostatic stress, for the four models of thermoelasticity based on the ordinary and fractional flux-precedence Jeffreys heat conduction equations, is illustrated. At the early instant $t = 0.01$, in Figure 6a, it is salient that the thermal waves resulting from the crossover from super- to sub-thermal conduction are the slowest ones among the four models, followed by those of the retarded heat transfer model. The two peaks near the upper surface are attributed to the mechanical waves of the Kelvin–Voigt model. At the subsequent instant $t = 0.14$, all the thermal waves are reflected from the lower surface and are ready to overlap with the mechanical waves coming from the upper surface; see Figure 6c. It is clear that the Kelvin–Voigt model diminishes the discontinuities of stresses; see the elastic case [57]. To emphasize this merit in the Kelvin–Voigt solid, we compare it with the Hookean response excited by the four thermal transport mechanisms in Figure 7. In the interval $y \in [0, 0.2]$, the curves for both Hookean and Kelvin–Voigt solids are not affected by the thermal transport mechanism, and the discontinuity in the Hookean solid is due to the dominated mechanical wave. The interval $y \in [0.2, 1]$, however, contains the dominated thermal wave, and thus there is a significant difference among the Jeffreys-type conduction models for the single elastic/viscoelastic model. The stresses of Kelvin–Voigt solid record higher values for all models of heat transfer compared with the Hookean elastic case.

In Figure 8, we represent the displacement vector induced by the ordinary Jeffreys-type heat conduction and the crossover from super- to sub-thermal conduction. We do not attach the other models due to the resemblance between their effects on the displacement with the Jeffreys-type heat conduction and crossover from super- to sub-thermal conduction model. The early arrival of the thermal wave to the lower surface, in the case of a Jeffreys-type heat conductor, is very clear in instant $t = 0.01$; see Figure 8a. At the instant $t = 1$, the displacement of the Jeffreys-type heat conduction is on a position of cutting at the double-strip, while the crossover from super- to sub-thermal conduction model is delayed. The contour figures, stress surfaces and displacement vectors are screenshots from full videos in the Supplementary Material section.

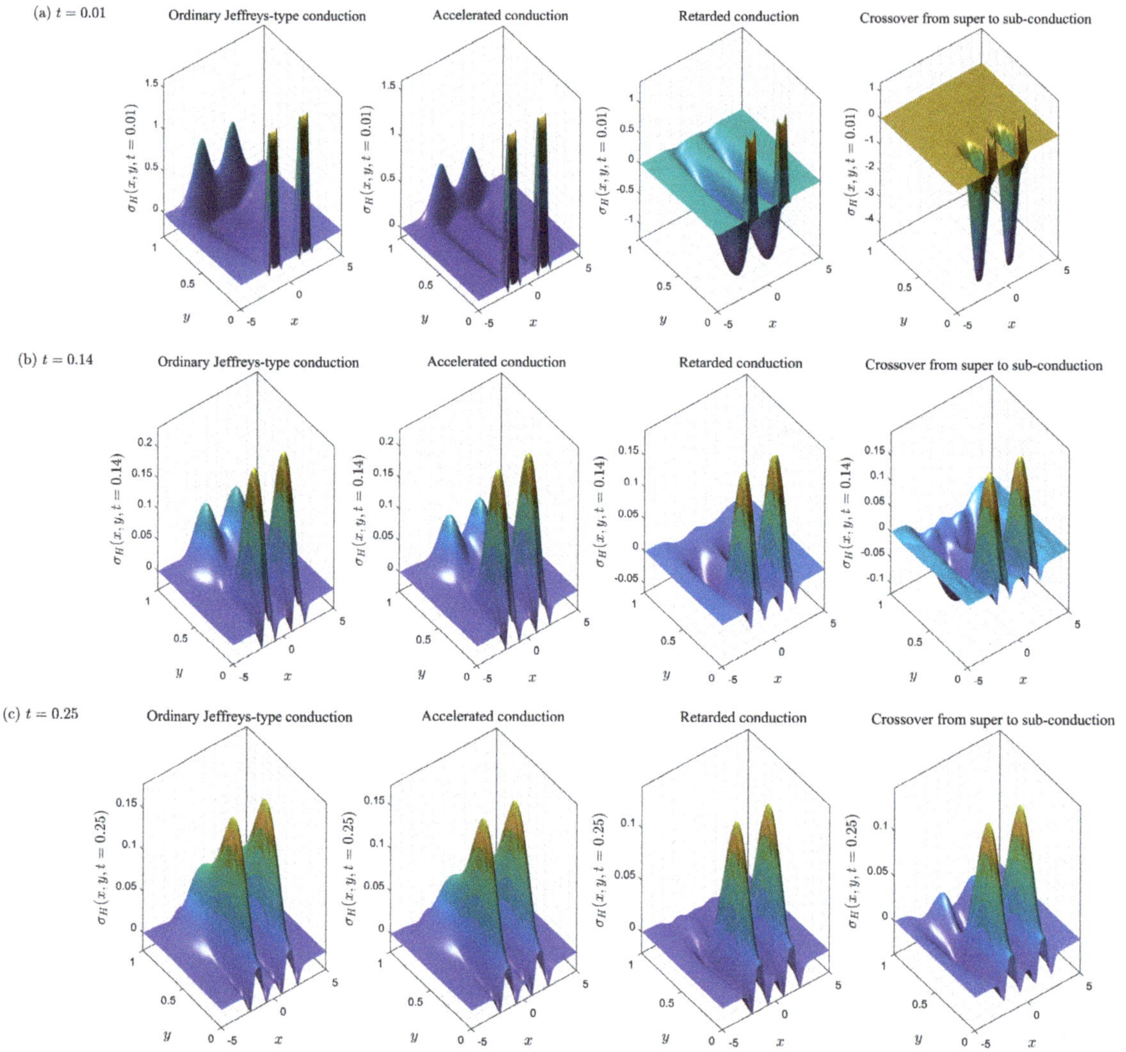

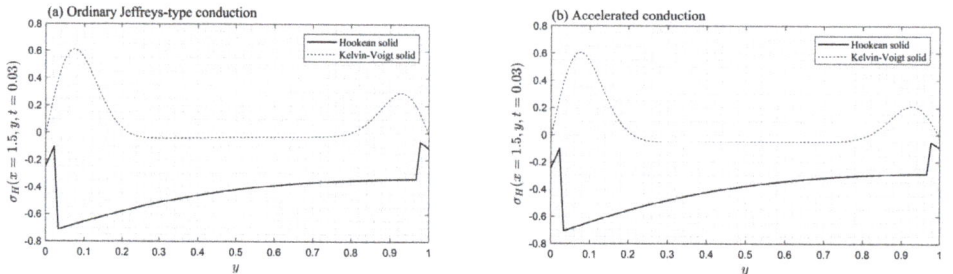

Figure 6. Hydrostatic stress for the ordinary and fractional flux-precedence Jeffreys model at three instants: (**a**) $t = 0.01$, (**b**) $t = 0.14$, and (**c**) $t = 0.25$.

Figure 7. *Cont.*

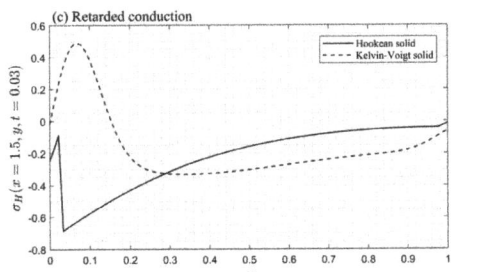
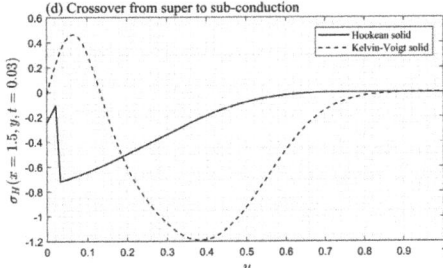

Figure 7. Hydrostatic stress resulting from different Jeffreys-type heat conduction mechanisms at $t = 0.03$ and $x = 1.5$. (**a**) Ordinary Jeffreys-type heat conduction, (**b**) accelerated conduction, (**c**) retarded conduction, and (**d**) crossover from super- to sub-thermal conduction.

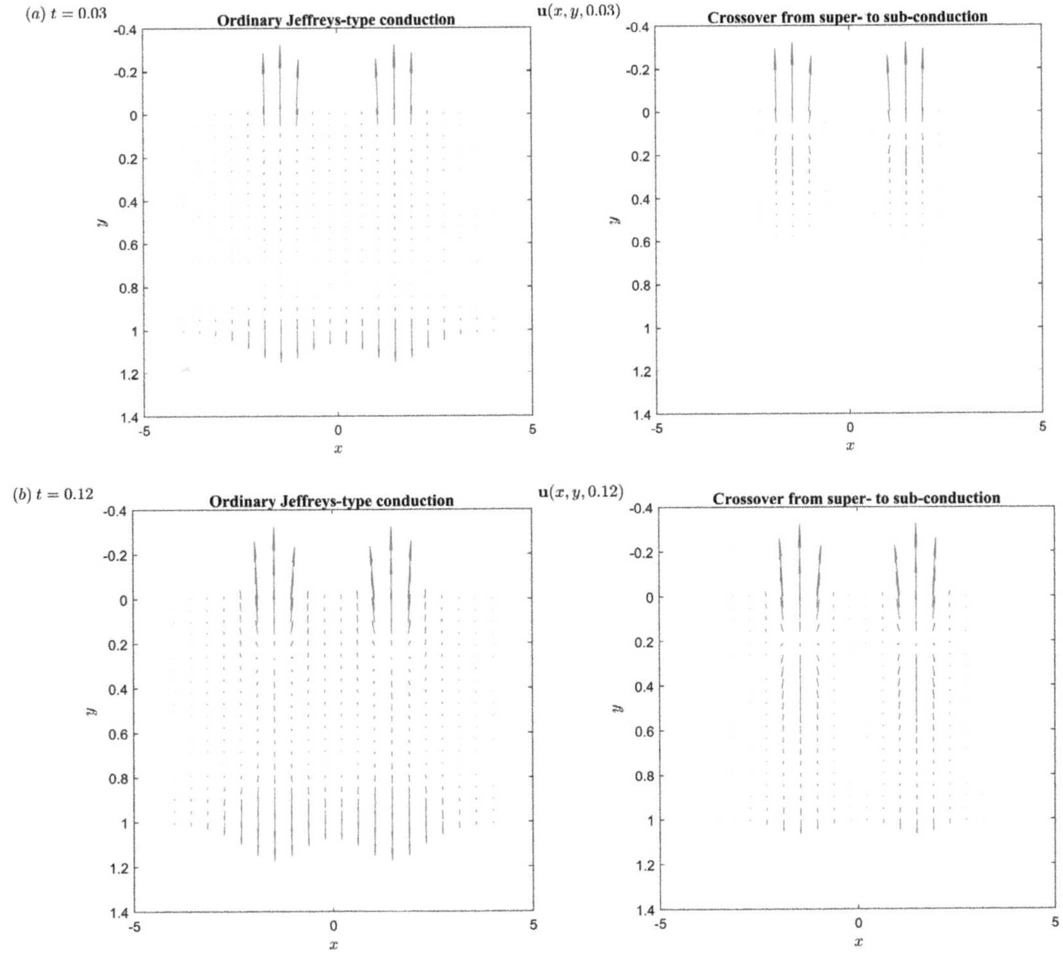

Figure 8. *Cont.*

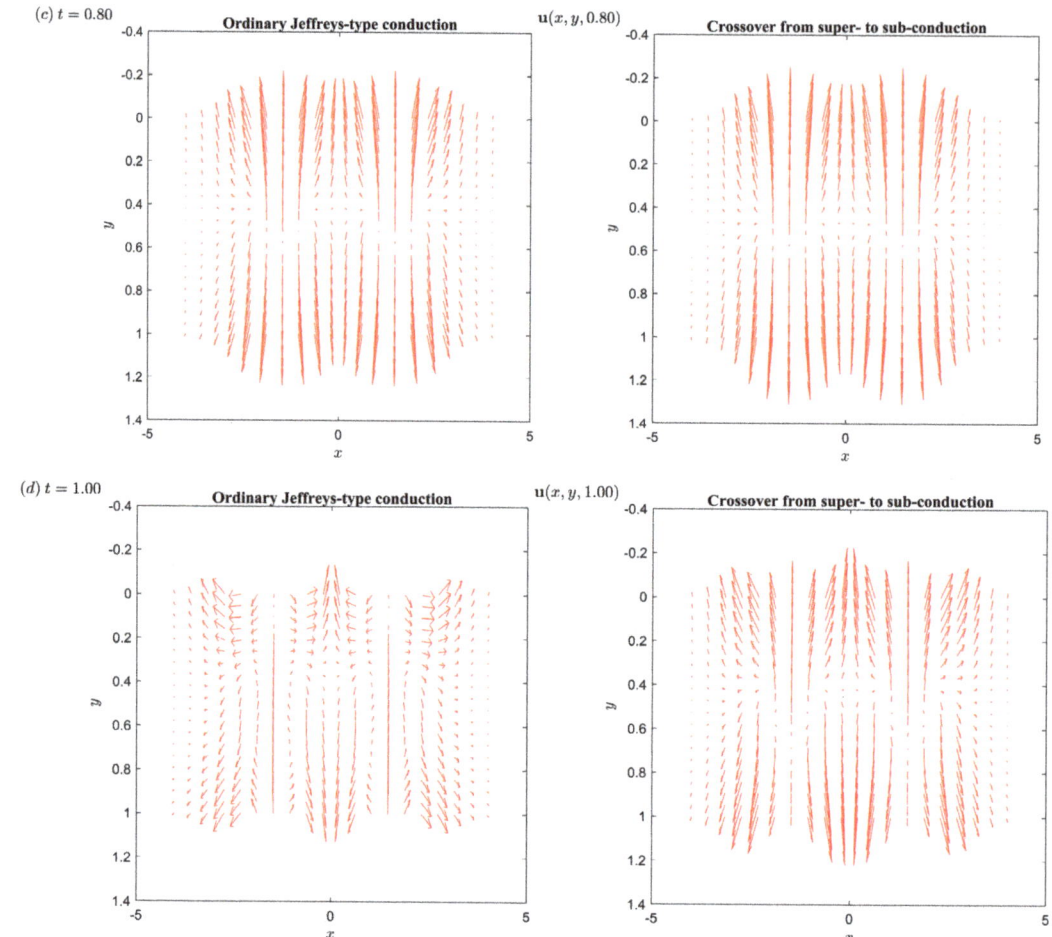

Figure 8. Displacement vector for the ordinary Jeffreys-type heat conduction and the crossover from super- to sub-thermal conduction models, at four instants: (**a**) $t = 0.03$, (**b**) $t = 0.12$, (**c**) $t = 0.8$, and (**d**) $t = 1$.

6. Summary

In this work, we have studied the effect of anomalous heat transfer inherited from the anomalous diffusion of thermal energy carriers throughout the material lattice. The material response is assumed to follow the Kelvin–Voigt assumption in which the stress–strain relation is not instantaneous; however, there is a retardation in the material strain compared with the elastic "Hookean" response. The Kelvin–Voigt hypothesis may be a reason for the occurrence of anomalies during the diffusion of thermal energy carriers and thus anomalous heat transfer. We have considered a two-dimensional plate with nanoscale thickness, heated by an ultrafast double-strip on its upper surface. The Laplace and Fourier transforms have been used to obtain the solution in the transformed domain. A numerical method based on accelerating the implementation of two infinite sums has been used to obtain the solutions in the proper time–space domain.

The thermal wave resulting from the crossover from super- to sub-thermal conduction is slower than that resulting from the retarded conduction, which in turn is slower than that resulting from the accelerated conduction. The ordinary flux-precedence Jeffreys-type heat conduction has the fastest thermal waves among the models considered in this work. The faster models transport thermal energy to the other surface during a short time interval and record the maximum temperature value on the lower surface. The displacement vector chart of the accelerated and ordinary Jeffreys-type heat conduction evolves faster than those in retarded and crossover models.

Supplementary Materials: The following supporting information can be downloaded at: Video S1: Hydrostatic stress https://youtu.be/Mirfq9-nWVo (accessed on 14 June 2023); Video S2: Temperature contours: https://youtu.be/Eg_V8bakMd4 (accessed on 14 June 2023); Video S3: Displacement of ordinary Jeffreys and crossover: https://youtu.be/tmSBJDmM6-g (accessed on 14 June 2023); Video S4: Displacement for retarded case: https://youtu.be/iB93zQzLEWE (accessed on 14 June 2023); Video S5: Displacement for accelerated case: https://youtu.be/W1nXU-GXvH8 (accessed on 14 June 2023).

Author Contributions: Conceptualization, E.A.; Methodology, E.A., M.A.A. and M.F.; Software, E.A. and M.F.; Validation, E.A.; Formal analysis, E.A. and M.F.; Investigation, M.A.A.; Resources, S.E.A.; Data curation, M.F.; Writing—original draft, E.A., S.E.A. and M.F.; Writing—review & editing, S.E.A. and M.A.A.; Visualization, E.A.; Supervision, E.A. and M.A.A.; Funding acquisition, S.E.A. All authors have read and agreed to the published version of the manuscript.

Funding: This research received no external funding.

Data Availability Statement: Data is contained within the article.

Conflicts of Interest: The authors declare no conflict of interest.

References

1. Fournier, D.; Boccara, A. Heterogeneous media and rough surfaces: A fractal approach for heat diffusion studies. *Phys. A Stat. Mech. Its Appl.* **1989**, *157*, 587–592. [CrossRef]
2. Tzou, D.Y.; Chen, J.K. Thermal lagging in random media. *J. Thermophys. Heat Transf.* **1998**, *12*, 567–574. [CrossRef]
3. Choi, S.U.S.; Zhang, Z.G.; Yu, W.; Lockwood, F.E.; Grulke, E.A. Anomalous thermal conductivity enhancement in nanotube suspensions. *Appl. Phys. Lett.* **2001**, *79*, 2252–2254. [CrossRef]
4. Li, B.; Wang, J. Anomalous heat conduction and anomalous diffusion in one-dimensional systems. *Phys. Rev. Lett.* **2003**, *91*, 044301. [CrossRef]
5. Lee, V.; Wu, C.-H.; Lou, Z.-X.; Lee, W.-L.; Chang, C.-W. Divergent and ultrahigh thermal conductivity in millimeter-long nanotubes. *Phys. Rev. Lett.* **2017**, *118*, 135901. [CrossRef]
6. Tzou, D.Y. *Macro-to Microscale Heat Transfer: The Lagging Behavior*, 2nd ed.; John Wiley & Sons: Hoboken, NJ, USA, 2014.
7. Compte, A.; Metzler, R. The generalized Cattaneo equation for the description of anomalous transport processes. *J. Phys. A Math. Gen.* **1997**, *30*, 7277. [CrossRef]
8. Barkai, E. Fractional Fokker-Planck equation, solution, and application. *Phys. Rev. E* **2001**, *63*, 046118. [CrossRef]
9. Klafter, J.; Lim, S.; Metzler, R. *Fractional Dynamics: Recent Advances*; World Scientific: Singapore, 2012.
10. Sierociuk, D.; Dzieliński, A.; Sarwas, G.; Petras, I.; Podlubny, I.; Skovranek, T. Modelling heat transfer in heterogeneous media using fractional calculus. *Phil. Trans. R. Soc. A* **2013**, *371*, 20120146. [CrossRef]
11. Ji, C.-C.; Dai, W.; Sun, Z.-Z. Numerical Method for Solving the Time-Fractional Dual-Phase-Lagging Heat Conduction Equation with the Temperature-Jump Boundary Condition. *J. Sci. Comput.* **2018**, *75*, 1307–1336. [CrossRef]
12. Ji, C.-C.; Dai, W.; Sun, Z.-Z. Numerical Schemes for Solving the Time-Fractional Dual-Phase-Lagging Heat Conduction Model in a Double-Layered Nanoscale Thin Film. *J. Sci. Comput.* **2019**, *81*, 1767–1800. [CrossRef]
13. Bazhlekova, E.; Bazhlekov, I. Transition from Diffusion to Wave Propagation in Fractional Jeffreys-Type Heat Conduction Equation. *Fractal Fract.* **2020**, *4*, 32. [CrossRef]
14. Awad, E.; Metzler, R. Crossover dynamics from superdiffusion to subdiffusion: Models and solutions. *Fract. Calc. Appl. Anal.* **2020**, *23*, 55–102. [CrossRef]
15. Awad, E.; Sandev, T.; Metzler, R.; Chechkin, A. Closed-form multi-dimensional solutions and asymptotic behaviors for subdiffusive processes with crossovers: I. Retarding case. *Chaos Solitons Fractals* **2021**, *152*, 111357. [CrossRef]
16. Awad, E.; Metzler, R. Closed-form multi-dimensional solutions and asymptotic behaviours for subdiffusive processes with crossovers: II. Accelerating case. *J. Phys. A: Math. Gen.* **2022**, *55*, 205003. [CrossRef]
17. Górska, K.; Horzela, A. Subordination and memory dependent kinetics in diffusion and relaxation phenomena. *Fract. Calc. Appl. Anal.* **2023**, *26*, 480–512. [CrossRef]
18. Liu, L.; Zheng, L.; Chen, Y.; Liu, F. Anomalous diffusion in comb model with fractional dual-phase-lag constitutive relation. *Comput. Math. Appl.* **2018**, *76*, 245–256. [CrossRef]

19. Liu, L.; Feng, L.; Xu, Q.; Chen, Y. Anomalous diffusion in comb model subject to a novel distributed order time fractional Cattaneo–Christov flux. *Appl. Math. Lett.* **2020**, *102*, 106116. [CrossRef]
20. Awad, E. Dual-Phase-Lag in the balance: Sufficiency bounds for the class of Jeffreys' equations to furnish physical solutions. *Int. J. Heat Mass Trans.* **2020**, *158*, 119742. [CrossRef]
21. Awad, E.; Sandev, T.; Metzler, R.; Chechkin, A. From continuous-time random walks to the fractional Jeffreys equation: Solution and properties. *Int. J. Heat Mass Transf.* **2021**, *181*, 121839. [CrossRef]
22. Hetnarski, R.B.; Ignaczak, J. Generalized thermoelasticity. *J. Therm. Stress.* **1999**, *22*, 451–476.
23. Ignaczak, J.; Ostoja-Starzewski, M. *Thermoelasticity with Finite Wave Speeds*; Oxford University Press: New York, NY, USA, 2010.
24. Chandrasekharaiah, D.S. Hyperbolic thermoelasticity: A review of recent literature. *Appl. Mech. Rev.* **1998**, *51*, 705–729. [CrossRef]
25. Povstenko, V.Z. Fractional heat conduction equation and associated thermal stress. *J. Therm. Stress.* **2005**, *28*, 83–102. [CrossRef]
26. Povstenko, Y.Z. *Fractional Thermoelasticity*; Springer: Berlin/Heidelberg, Germany, 2015.
27. Sherief, H.H.; El-Sayed, A.M.A.; Abd El-Latief, A.M. Fractional order theory of thermoelasticity. *Int. J. Solids Struct.* **2010**, *47*, 269–275. [CrossRef]
28. Youssef, H.M. Theory of fractional order generalized thermoelasticity. *J. Heat Transf.* **2010**, *132*, 061301. [CrossRef]
29. Ezzat, M.A.; Karamany, A.S.E. Fractional order heat conduction law in magneto-thermoelasticity involving two temperatures. *Z. Fur. Angew. Math. Phys.* **2011**, *62*, 937–952. [CrossRef]
30. Awad, E. On the generalized thermal lagging behavior: Refined aspects. *J. Therm. Stress.* **2012**, *35*, 293–325. [CrossRef]
31. Elhagary, M. Effect of Atangana–Baleanu fractional derivative on a two-dimensional thermoviscoelastic problem for solid sphere under axisymmetric distribution. *Mech. Based Des. Struct. Mach.* **2021**, *51*, 3295–3312. [CrossRef]
32. Sherief, H.H.; Abd El-Latief, A.M.; Fayik, M.A. 2D hereditary thermoelastic application of a thick plate under axisymmetric temperature distribution. *Math. Methods Appl. Sci.* **2022**, *45*, 1080–1092. [CrossRef]
33. Mainardi, F. *Fractional Calculus and Waves in Linear Viscoelasticity: An Introduction to Mathematical Models*; World Scientific: Singapore, 2010.
34. Gurtin, M.E.; Sternberg, E. On the linear theory of viscoelasticity. *Arch. Ration. Mech. Anal.* **1962**, *11*, 291–356. [CrossRef]
35. Mukhopadhyay, S. Effects of thermal relaxations on thermoviscoelastic interactions in an unbounded body with a spherical cavity subjected to a periodic loading on the boundary. *J. Therm. Stress.* **2000**, *23*, 675–684. [CrossRef]
36. Youssef, H.M.; Al-Lehaibi, E.A. The vibration of viscothermoelastic static pre-stress nanobeam based on two-temperature dual-phase-lag heat conduction and subjected to ramp-type heat. *J. Strain Anal. Eng. Des.* **2022**, *58*, 410–421. [CrossRef]
37. Abouelregal, A.; Zenkour, A. Fractional viscoelastic Voigt's model for initially stressed microbeams induced by ultrashort laser heat source. *Waves Random Complex Media* **2020**, *30*, 687–703. [CrossRef]
38. Magaña, A.; Quintanilla, R. On the uniqueness and analyticity of solutions in micropolar thermoviscoelasticity. *J. Math. Anal. Appl.* **2014**, *412*, 109–120. [CrossRef]
39. Fabrizio, M.; Franchi, F.; Nibbi, R. Second gradient Green–Naghdi type thermo-elasticity and viscoelasticity. *Mech. Res. Commun.* **2022**, *126*, 104014. [CrossRef]
40. Sherief, H.H.; Helmy, K.A. A two-dimensional generalized thermoelasticity problem for a half-space. *J. Therm. Stress.* **1999**, *22*, 897–910.
41. Sherief, H.H.; Megahed, F.A. A two-dimensional thermoelasticity problem for a half space subjected to heat sources. *Int. J. Solids Struct.* **1999**, *36*, 1369–1382. [CrossRef]
42. El-Maghraby, N.M. A two-dimensional problem for a thick plate with heat sources in generalized thermoelasticity. *J. Therm. Stress.* **2005**, *28*, 1227–1241. [CrossRef]
43. El-Maghraby, N.M. Two-dimensional thermoelasticity problem for a thick plate under the action of a body force in two relaxation times. *J. Therm. Stress.* **2009**, *32*, 863–876. [CrossRef]
44. Pal, P.; Kanoria, M. Thermoelastic wave propagation in a transversely isotropic thick plate under Green–Naghdi theory due to gravitational field. *J. Therm. Stress.* **2017**, *40*, 470–485. [CrossRef]
45. Kalkal, K.K.; Deswal, S.; Yadav, R. Eigenvalue approach to fractional-order dual-phase-lag thermoviscoelastic problem of a thick plate. *IJST-T Mech. Eng.* **2019**, *43*, 917–927. [CrossRef]
46. Tzou, D.Y.; Beraun, J.E.; Chen, J.K. Ultrafast deformation in femtosecond laser heating. *J. Heat Transf.* **2002**, *124*, 284–292. [CrossRef]
47. Falkovsky, L.A.; Mishchenko, E.G. Electron-lattice kinetics of metals heated by ultrashort laser pulses. *J. Exp. Theor. Phys.* **1999**, *88*, 84–88. [CrossRef]
48. Chen, J.K.; Beraun, J.E.; Tham, C.L. Ultrafast thermoelasticity for short-pulse laser heating. *Int. J. Eng. Sci.* **2004**, *42*, 793–807. [CrossRef]
49. Tzou, D.Y.; Chen, J.K.; Beraun, J.E. Recent development of ultrafast thermoelasticity. *J. Therm. Stress.* **2005**, *28*, 563–594. [CrossRef]
50. Awad, E.; Fayik, M.; El-Dhaba, A. A comparative numerical study of a semi-infinite heat conductor subject to double-strip heating under non-Fourier models. *Eur. Phys. J. Plus* **2022**, *137*, 1303. [CrossRef]
51. Awad, E.; Abo-Dahab, S.M.; Abdou, M.A. Exact solutions for a two-dimensional thermoelectric MHD flow with steady-state heat transfer on a vertical plate with two instantaneous infinite hot suction lines. *arXiv* **2022**, arXiv:2212.01665. [CrossRef]
52. Awad, E. On the time-fractional Cattaneo equation of distributed order. *Phys. A Stat. Mech. Its Appl.* **2019**, *518*, 210–233. [CrossRef]

53. Gorenflo, R.; Mainardi, F. Fractional calculus. In *Fractals and Fractional Calculus in Continuum Mechanics*; Springer: Berlin/Heidelberg, Germany, 1997; pp. 223–276.
54. Duffy, D.G. *Transform Methods for Solving Partial Differential Equations*; Chapman and Hall/CRC: Portsmouth, UK, 2004.
55. Callister, W.D.; Rethwisch, D.G. *Materials Science and Engineering: An Introduction*; Wiley: New York, NY, USA, 2007.
56. Thomas, L.C. *Heat Transfer*; Prentice Hall: Hoboken, NJ, USA, 1992.
57. Fayik, M.; Alhazmi, S.E.; Abdou, M.A.; Awad, E. Transient Finite-Speed Heat Transfer Influence on Deformation of a Nanoplate with Ultrafast Circular Ring Heating. *Mathematics* **2023**, *11*, 1099. [CrossRef]
58. Durbin, F. Numerical inversion of Laplace transforms: An efficient improvement to Dubner and Abate's method. *Comput. J.* **1974**, *17*, 371–376. [CrossRef]
59. Dubner, H.; Abate, J. Numerical inversion of Laplace transforms by relating them to the finite Fourier cosine transform. *J. ACM* **1968**, *15*, 115–123. [CrossRef]
60. Honig, G.; Hirdes, U. A method for the numerical inversion of Laplace transforms. *J. Comput. Appl. Math.* **1984**, *10*, 113–132. [CrossRef]
61. Press, W.H.; Teukolsky, S.A.; Flannery, B.P.; Vetterling, W.T. *Numerical Recipes in Fortran 77: The Art of Scientific Computing*, 2nd ed.; Cambridge University Press: Cambridge, UK, 1992; Volume 1.
62. Rukolaine, S.A.; Samsonov, A.M. Local immobilization of particles in mass transfer described by a Jeffreys-type equation. *Phys. Rev. E* **2013**, *88*, 062116. [CrossRef] [PubMed]
63. Bora, A.; Dai, W.; Wilson, J.P.; Boyt, J.C. Neural network method for solving parabolic two-temperature microscale heat conduction in double-layered thin films exposed to ultrashort-pulsed lasers. *Int. J. Heat Mass Transf.* **2021**, *178*, 121616. [CrossRef]
64. Bora, A.; Dai, W.; Wilson, J.P.; Boyt, J.C.; Sobolev, S. Neural network method for solving nonlocal two-temperature nanoscale heat conduction in gold films exposed to ultrashort-pulsed lasers. *Int. J. Heat Mass Transf.* **2022**, *190*, 122791. [CrossRef]

Disclaimer/Publisher's Note: The statements, opinions and data contained in all publications are solely those of the individual author(s) and contributor(s) and not of MDPI and/or the editor(s). MDPI and/or the editor(s) disclaim responsibility for any injury to people or property resulting from any ideas, methods, instructions or products referred to in the content.

 *fractal and fractional*

Article

Fractional Gradient Optimizers for PyTorch: Enhancing GAN and BERT

Oscar Herrera-Alcántara [1,*] and Josué R. Castelán-Aguilar [2]

[1] Departamento de Sistemas, Universidad Autónoma Metropolitana, Azcapotzalco 02200, Mexico
[2] División de CBI, Universidad Autónoma Metropolitana, Azcapotzalco 02200, Mexico
* Correspondence: oha@azc.uam.mx

Abstract: Machine learning is a branch of artificial intelligence that dates back more than 50 years. It is currently experiencing a boom in research and technological development. With the rise of machine learning, the need to propose improved optimizers has become more acute, leading to the search for new gradient-based optimizers. In this paper, the ancient concept of fractional derivatives has been applied to some optimizers available in PyTorch. A comparative study is presented to show how the fractional versions of gradient optimizers could improve their performance on generative adversarial networks (GAN) and natural language applications with Bidirectional Encoder Representations from Transformers (BERT). The results are encouraging for both state-of-the art algorithms, GAN and BERT, and open up the possibility of exploring further applications of fractional calculus in machine learning.

Keywords: fractional derivative; gradient descent optimizer; machine learning

Citation: Herrera, O.; Castelán, J.R. Fractional Gradient Optimizers for PyTorch: Enhancing GAN and BERT. *Fractal Fract.* **2023**, *7*, 500. https://doi.org/10.3390/fractalfract7070500

Academic Editors: Sameerah Jamal and Riccardo Caponetto

Received: 18 May 2023
Revised: 10 June 2023
Accepted: 19 June 2023
Published: 23 June 2023

Copyright: © 2023 by the authors. Licensee MDPI, Basel, Switzerland. This article is an open access article distributed under the terms and conditions of the Creative Commons Attribution (CC BY) license (https://creativecommons.org/licenses/by/4.0/).

1. Introduction

Several machine learning techniques are posed as optimization problems and owe their success to gradient-based methods. The success is twofold: first, the optimization task itself, and second, the widespread adoption by the AI community. For example, in machine learning and specifically in neural networks, the multilayer perceptron learning technique defines a training error surface that depends on synaptic weights as free parameters that can be optimized with the backpropagation algorithm, which is a gradient-descent-based algorithm. It finds the optimal parameters to minimize the training error. The success lies not only in solving the optimization problem by minimizing the training error but also in maximizing the generalization capacity on a test dataset, avoiding overfitting, which has led to wide use of multilayer perceptrons in various applications by the artificial intelligence community [1].

Recently, with the boom in research and technological development of machine learning, the need to propose improved optimizers has become more acute, leading to the search for new gradient-based optimizers. In this respect, the authors of [2] performed a comparison of 15 optimizers chosen from a large list of 144 optimizers and schedulers, showing the variability of techniques that continues to evolve and grow. Of course, they include the fundamental SGD and Adam optimizers. The former because it is the cornerstone of all gradient-based techniques [3], whereas the latter calculates adaptive learning rates and is considered state of the art in deep learning [4].

Additionally, a survey of optimization algorithms for neural networks is presented in [5], where modifications to basic optimization algorithms are studied. The paper [6] presents the latest contributions for deep learning based on stochastic gradient-descent methods and a summary of applications of network architectures together with the methods used for specific purposes.

A brief summary of relevant variants of SGD, Adam, Adagrad, and Adadelta is also presented in [7], along with a review of their parameter-update formulas that reveals the combination of concepts, including momentum, velocity, learning rate adaptation, parameter normalization, and gradient-memory.

Although the majority of optimizers consider these concepts to enhance the training and the capacity of generalization, in this work, the ancient but powerful concept of fractional derivatives is applied to several gradient-based optimizers available in PyTorch [8,9]. In this way, several fractional versions of optimizers have been implemented for PyTorch, and they are presented as generalizations to the first-order derivative. In other words, the fractional derivative of ν-order ($\nu \in \mathbb{R}^+$) includes the classical first-order gradient when $\nu = 1$. From this point of view, it provides an additional freedom degree to the hyperparameters that allows us to exploit the properties and advantages of fractional derivatives, including the effect of non-locality which obtains information from the neighborhood of the derivation-point by applying integro-differential operators [10,11].

Certainly, the application of fractional derivatives is not recent, and it can be verified in previous works on different areas, including linear viscoelasticity [12], partial differential equations [13], signal processing [14], and image processing [15], among others.

With respect to neural networks, there is also evidence of applications of fractional derivatives. For example, in [16], Fractional Physics-Informed Neural Networks are developed employing partial differential equations embedded in architectures of feedforward neural networks with automatic differentiation to optimize the network parameters. Another work is [17] on the study of two-layer neural networks trained with backpropagation and fractional derivatives. The authors of [18] studied a fractional deep backpropagation algorithm for neural networks with L_2-regularization, and in [19] the stability for Hopfield neural networks of fractional order is investigated, just to mention a few works but the list of fractional-gradient applications seems to grow promisingly.

Although there are many works that use fractional-order derivatives in neural networks, it is notorious that they focus on ad hoc solutions and do not offer easy adaptation or reusability to other applications. Thereupon, it has been identified the need and importance of implementing fractional optimizers in frameworks such as PyTorch [9] that offer versatility and flexibility to apply gradient-based optimizers to different areas of great interest to the machine learning community.

In this regard, about frameworks for machine learning, a related work is [7] that presents a Keras–Tensorflow [20,21] implementation of several fractional optimizers successfully applied to human activity recognition.

Since these frameworks have become a popular and powerful tool that takes advantage of high-performance computing using GPUs and cloud platforms, this article aims to contribute to the implementation of fractional optimizers by extending current versions of integer-order gradient algorithms available in PyTorch. Once described how the implementation of fractional optimizers is done, two case studies are presented, firstly on generative adversarial networks (GAN) [22] and secondly on natural language processing (NLP) with Bidirectional Encoder Representations from Transformers (BERT) [23]. Many other applications may be possible, but for now, only these are shown. The results are encouraging and are expected to provide enough motivation and justification for the success of applying fractional calculus concepts in machine learning.

The remainder of the paper has the following structure. In Section 2, fundamental concepts are revised of fractional derivatives to propose a gradient-update formula based on the Caputo definition. In Section 3, fractional implementations for PyTorch are presented with some comparative experiments that aim to show how the fractional versions of gradient-based optimizers could improve their performance on GAN and NLP applications with BERT. Finally, Section 4 presents some discussions following the experiments and comments on some directions for future work.

2. Materials

The following topics are covered in this section: the Caputo fractional derivative, the backpropagation update formula for multilayer perceptrons (MLP) and the implementations of fractional gradient optimizers for PyTorch. It provides the necessary materials to develop the experiments that support the conclusions.

2.1. Caputo Fractional Derivative

Definition 1. *Let $a, x \in \mathbb{R}$, $\nu > 0$ and $n = [\nu + 1]$. The Caputo fractional derivative of order ν for $f(x)$ is [17]:*

$$_a^C D_x^\nu f(x) = \frac{1}{\Gamma(n-\nu)} \int_a^x (x-y)^{n-\nu-1} f^{(n)}(y) dy. \tag{1}$$

It is one of the most preferred definitions of fractional derivative, since if $f(x) = C$, $C \in \mathbb{R}$, then $_a^C D_x^\nu f(x) = 0$ [18]. In particular, for $\nu = 1$ it corresponds to the classical differential calculus, that means that the derivative of a constant is zero. In general, it is not the same for other definitions such as the Riemman–Liouville or Grünwald–Letnikov [17].

In Equation (1), a convolutional kernel $(x-y)^{n-\nu-1}$ is used and for $f(x) = x^q$ it yields to [24]:

$$D_x^\nu x^q = \frac{\Gamma(q+1) x^{q-\nu}}{\Gamma(q-\nu+1)}. \tag{2}$$

Equation (2) represents a relevant property since it allows to extend the integer-order gradient optimizers to their fractional versions, as described in Section 2.2.

2.2. Backpropagation Update Formula for MLP

Given the original backpropagation formula to update the parameters of MLP, the corresponding fractional versions will be obtained.

Let a training set $\{X^i, O^i\}_{i=1}^N$ with N samples, and a neural network architecture described as follows:

- X is the input layer (input data),
- H hidden layers,
- O is the output layer,
- L layers, $L = H + 1$ because of the hidden layers and the output layer,
- w_{kj}^l is a matrix of synaptic weights, $l \in [1, L-1]$, that connects neuron k of layer $l+1$ with neuron j of layer l,
- w_{kj}^0 are synaptic weights ($l = 0$) that connect the first hidden layer with X,
- o_{ki} is the desired output of neuron k at output layer when the i-th input data is presented,
- $\varphi(x)$ is the activation function in the L layers,
- a_{ki}^L is the output of neuron k at output layer O, when the i-th input data is presented and $a_k^L = \varphi(p_k^L)$ at layer O,
- $p_k^l = \sum w_{kj}^l \cdot a_j^{l-1}$ is the potential activation of neuron k at layer l, $1 \leq l \leq L$, with inputs a_j^{l-1}. For $l - 1 = 0$, $a_j^0 = X_j$ considering the j-th component of X,
- $a_k^l = \varphi(p_k^l)$ is the output of neuron k at a hidden layer l, $1 \leq l < L$.

Note that, at the output layer, the error of neuron k is $e_{ki} = a_{ki}^L - o_{ki}$. Subindex i means that the i-th input pattern is presented to the neural network. For all the n^L neurons, the error E_i at the output layer is:

$$E_i = \frac{1}{2} \sum_{k=1}^{n^L} e_{ki}^2 = \frac{1}{2} \sum_{k=1}^{n^L} (a_{ki}^L - o_{ki})^2 \tag{3}$$

and the cumulative error of the N training samples is E:

$$E = \sum_{i=1}^N E_i = \frac{1}{2} \sum_{i=1}^N \sum_{k=1}^{n^L} (a_{ki}^L - o_{ki})^2. \tag{4}$$

The main goal of the backpropagation algorithm is to find optimal values of the free parameters of the weight matrix that minimize E.

In the backpropagation algorithm, the error of the output layer O is propagated to the hidden layers in reverse order until it reaches the input layer, and the gradient-descent updates are applied to each layer.

The optimization with the gradient-descent method applied to the weight updates Δw_{kj}^l is:

$$\Delta w_{kj}^l = -\eta \frac{\partial E_i}{\partial w_{kj}^l} = -\eta D_{w_{kj}^l} E_i \qquad (5)$$

that points to the direction where E_i decays. Here, $\eta > 0$ is the learning rate.

It should be clarified that Equation (5) uses the nomenclature $D_{w_{kj}^l} E_i$ to match with the Caputo fractional derivative definition of Section 2.1.

At this point, the local gradient is defined as:

$$\delta_k^l = \frac{\partial E_i}{\partial p_k^l} \qquad (6)$$

and since

$$\frac{\partial E_i}{\partial w_{kj}^l} = \frac{\partial E_i}{\partial p_k^l} \cdot \frac{\partial p_k^l}{\partial w_{kj}^l} = \frac{\partial E_i}{\partial p_k^l} \cdot a_j^{l-1} = \delta_k^l a_j^{l-1} \qquad (7)$$

then, Δw_{kj}^l can be expressed as:

$$\Delta w_{kj}^l = -\eta \cdot \delta_k^l \cdot a_j^{l-1}. \qquad (8)$$

For $l = L$, Equation (6) becomes δ_k^L and then, at the output layer O:

$$\delta_k^L = e_{ki} \cdot \varphi'(p_k^L). \qquad (9)$$

For $1 \leq l < L$, the local gradient for hidden layers is:

$$\delta_j^l = \varphi'(p_j^l) \cdot \sum_{k=1}^{n^{l+1}} \delta_k^{l+1} \cdot w_{kj}^{l+1} \qquad (10)$$

and consequently, the weight updates are:

$$\Delta w_{kj}^l = -\eta \delta_k^l a_j^{l-1}. \qquad (11)$$

The Formulas (3) to (11) are well known by the neural network community. However, now, to make way for the fractional optimizers, the same approach for the first-order derivative $D_{w_{kj}^l} E_i$ can be used with the fractional gradient $D_{w_{kj}^l}^\nu E_i$. In such case, the chain rule yields to [18]:

$$D_{w_{kj}^l}^\nu E_i = \frac{\partial E_i}{\partial w_{kj}^l} \cdot D_{w_{kj}^l}^\nu w_{kj}^l = \delta_k^l \cdot a_j^{l-1} \cdot \frac{(w_{kj}^l)^{1-\nu}}{\Gamma(2-\nu)}. \qquad (12)$$

Equation (12) seems identical to Equation (7) except by $\frac{(w_{kj}^l)^{1-\nu}}{\Gamma(2-\nu)}$ that is obtained when Equation (2) is applied to w_{kj}^l. Note that if $\nu = 1$, Equation (12) becomes the classical integer case. So, Equation (12) represents a gradient-descent generalization, for $\nu > 0$.

In practice, it is necessary to avoid two conditions:

- When synaptic weights take zero values that yields to the indetermination of $\frac{(w_{kj}^l)^{1-\nu}}{\Gamma(2-\nu)}$ for $1 - \nu < 0$,

- When $1 - \nu$ is rational, let $1 - \nu = \frac{r}{s}$ and s is even (for example $r = 1$ and $s = 2$) hence if $w_{kj}^l < 0$, then complex values will be generated.

These situations have been explored previously in [7] and a solution consists of replacing w_{kj}^l by $|w_{kj}^l| + \epsilon$, for $\epsilon > 0$. In this way, the fractional gradient factor f_w^ν is defined as:

$$f_w^\nu := \frac{(|w_{kj}^l| + \epsilon)^{1-\nu}}{\Gamma(2 - \nu)} \tag{13}$$

and the limit exists, and is equal to 1, for f_w^ν as $\nu \to 1$.

Hence, Equation (12) becomes:

$$D_{w_{kj}^l}^\nu E_i = \delta_k^l \cdot a_j^{l-1} \cdot f_w^\nu = \delta_k^l \cdot a_j^{l-1} \cdot \frac{(|w_{kj}^l| + \epsilon)^{1-\nu}}{\Gamma(2 - \nu)} \tag{14}$$

that generalizes the known gradient-descent update rule.

It is worth noting that f_w^ν is not negative for $\nu < 2$. Therefore, the fractional gradient of Equation (14) modifies the magnitude of the classical gradient $D_{w_{kj}^l} E_i$, but preserves the negative sign of the gradient-descent of Equation (5). Hence, the fractional gradient also points to the same direction of the gradient-descent on the error surface given by E_i of Equation (3), and thus to the direction in which a loss function for the neural network will decay.

2.3. Fractional Gradient Optimizers for PyTorch

PyTorch is a Python-based scientific computing package for machine learning. As framework, PyTorch follows two purposes: (i) To use GPUs (ii) To provide automatic differentiation for neural networks [9].

The package *torch.optim* [8] implements various optimization algorithms such as SGD [3], Adam [4], Adadelta [25], Adagrad [26], AdamW [27] and RMSProp [28] among others.

To apply an optimizer in PyTorch is enough to use a line of code like the following for the SGD optimizer:

opt=optim.SGD(model.parameters(),learning_rate=0.001,momentum=0.9)

whereas the Adam optimizer can be used as follows:

opt=optim.Adam(model.parameters(),learning_rate=0.001).

Now, since the main idea is to apply Equation (14) to obtain fractional gradient optimizers in PyTorch, simply multiply f_w^ν by the integer-gradient. For this purpose, a new class is defined in PyTorch with the prefix "F" for each existing optimizer. In the case of SGD, the new class is FGSD and the line

__all__ = ['SGD', 'sgd']

is replaced by

__all__ = ['FSGD', 'fsgd'].

Moreover, the source code of the update method *_single_tensor_sgd* is modified as follows, in the Listing 1:

Listing 1. FSGD class definition and single_tensor_sgd method modification.

```
# Parameters: Set v= Cnnu.nnu, 0 < v < 2.0
Cnnu.nnu = 1.75
eps = 0.000001
class FSGD(Optimizer):
...
def _single_tensor_sgd(...):
...
for i, param in enumerate(params):
    d_p = d_p_list[i] if not maximize else -d_p_list[i]
    v = Cnnu.nnu
    t1 = torch.pow(abs(d_p)+eps, 1-v )
    t2 = torch.exp(torch.lgamma(torch.tensor(2.0-v)))
    d_p = d_p * t1/ t2
```

The same procedure can be applied to other gradient-descent optimizers. Let us consider another example with Adam.

The new fractional optimizer is FAdam, and it was obtained by modifying the _single_tensor_adam_ method of the class FAdam, as described below in the Listing 2:

Listing 2. FAdam class definition and single_tensor_adam method modification.

```
#Parameters: Set v= Cnnu.nnu, 0 < v < 2.0
Cnnu.nnu = 1.75
eps = 0.000001
class FAdam(Optimizer):
...
def _single_tensor_adam(...):
...
for i, param in enumerate(params):
    grad = grads[i] if not maximize else -grads[i]
    v = Cnnu.nnu
    t1=torch.pow(abs(grad)+eps, 1-v )
    t2=torch.exp(torch.lgamma(torch.tensor(2.0-v)))
    grad = grad * t1/t2
```

For the purposes of this paper, the fractional versions of AdamW, RMSProp, and Adadelta optimizers were also implemented. However, the same methodology can be applied to other optimizers.

2.4. Fractional GAN

Generative Adversarial Networks (GAN) constitute a representative case of artificial creativity where two artificial neural networks are confronted: the generative G that proposes instances and the discriminative D that tries to detect the degree of falsehood of those instances. After repeating the algorithm, the result is a set of objects that share many characteristics of the training objects but are not identical to them.

If G and D use MLP, then backpropagation can be used to train the whole system [22]. In this way, the generative and discriminative models can apply gradient-descent optimizers, and consequently is possible to create fractional versions of G and D. Thus, a Fractional Generative Adversarial Network (FGAN) is obtained.

In connection with the above, the proposed FGAN minibatch stochastic gradient-descent training algorithm is the one shown in Algorithm 1, which is based on the integer gradient version for GAN-training described in [22]. Essentially, both stochastic gradients for the generator g_{θ_g} and discriminator g_{θ_d} are updated with the fractional factor $f_{\theta_d}^v$ and $f_{\theta_g}^v$ respectively (see lines 5 and 8 of Algorithm 1). In this sense, the FGAN represents a generalization of the GAN version.

Algorithm 1 Fractional GAN minibatch stochastic gradient-descent training algorithm.

1: **for** number of training iterations **do**
2:     **for** k steps **do**
3:         Sample minibatch of m noise samples {z(1), ..., z(m)} from noise prior $p_g(z)$.
4:         Sample minibatch of m examples {x(1), ..., x(m)} from data generating distribution $p_{data}(x)$.
5:         Update the discriminator by ascending its **fractional** stochastic gradient:
$$g_{\theta_d} = \nabla_{\theta_d} \frac{1}{m} \sum_{i=1}^{m} [\log D(x^{(i)}) + \log(1 - D(G(z^{(i)})))]$$
$$f_{\theta_d}^{\nu} = \frac{(|\theta_d^l| + \epsilon)^{1-\nu}}{\Gamma(2-\nu)}$$
$$g_{\theta_d}^{\nu} = g_{\theta_d} * f_{\theta_d}^{\nu}$$
6:     **end for**
7:     Sample minibatch of m noise samples {z(1), ..., z(m)} from noise prior $p_g(z)$.
8:     Update the generator by descending its **fractional** stochastic gradient:
$$g_{\theta_g} = \nabla_{\theta_g} \frac{1}{m} \sum_{i=1}^{m} \log(1 - D(G(z^{(i)})))$$
$$f_{\theta_g}^{\nu} = \frac{(|\theta_g^l| + \epsilon)^{1-\nu}}{\Gamma(2-\nu)}$$
$$g_{\theta_g}^{\nu} = g_{\theta_g} * f_{\theta_g}^{\nu}$$
9: **end for**
    The gradient-based updates can use any **fractional** gradient-based learning rule

2.5. Fractional BERT

BERT is the acronym of Bidirectional Encoder Representations from Transformers and is a machine learning and language representation model that involves the transformer architecture with encoder and decoder modules to extract patterns or representations from data [23]. BERT was developed in the context of computational linguistic and uses bidirectional transformers to learn from both the left and right contexts of a vocabulary. BERT combines two complementary tasks: Pre-training and Fine-tuning. Pre-training uses a lot of unlabeled data to train the model. Fine-tuning is a transfer-learn step where the previous learning is potentiated on specific labeled data for different applications.

The encoder, conformed by a self-attention layer and a feed-forward neural network, aims to map words to intermediate representations together with their relationships.

The decoder has the same structure as the encoder, but inserts a middle layer of Encoder-Decoder Attention.

The main goal is to model patterns of long sequences to improve some drawbacks of previous approaches, such as LSTM [29] that only models a single context direction.

Since BERT includes neural network modules, and they are frequently optimized via gradient methods, fractional gradient optimizers can be applied to obtain a Fractional BERT version (FBERT). Essentially, the unique difference is the use of fractional optimizers, described in Section 2.3, instead of others based on integer-order derivatives.

The fractional optimizers of this paper have been included in a torch.Foptim package that refers to Fractional Optimization for PyTorch. Then, instead of using a PyTorch optimizer such as Adam from the package torch.optim with a line of code like this

```
optim = optim.Adam(model.parameters(), learning_rate=0.001)
```

a fractional optimizer from the package torch.Foptim can be used. In case of the fractional Adam (FAdam) the code is as follows:

```
optim = Foptim.FAdam(model.parameters(), learning_rate=0.001).
```

It is emphasized that for $\nu = 1.0$, the fractional case is reduced to the well-known integer case.

3. Results

In this section, two experiments are described, and their results are shown.

3.1. Experiment 1: FGAN

A first experiment implements an FGAN based on [30] that presents a GAN trained with the MNIST [31] dataset of grayscale images of 28 × 28 pixels. The discriminator network D considers both real and fake images as unidimensional 1 × 784 vectors. The cost function is:

$$D_{cost} = -log(D_{l2rA}) + log(1.0 - D_{l2fA}) \qquad (15)$$

where D_{l2rA} is the output of D with real images as inputs, and D_{l2fA} corresponds to the output of D with fake images as inputs.

The FGAN was executed 30 times with FSGD and FAdam for different values of $\nu \in (0, 2)$. Figures 1 and 2 allow us to compare FSGD and FAdam with $\nu = 1.0$. In other words, it represents the integer case of GAN+SGD vs. GAN+Adam (here + means "optimized with"). Note that in Figure 1, GAN+SGD fails completely since it does not produce any digit shape, whereas in Figure 2 GAN+Adam is better since it produces 22 of 30 digit images successfully.

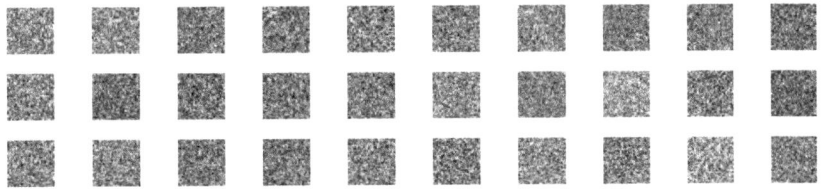

Figure 1. GAN + SGD: FGAN with FSGD and $\nu = 1.0$.

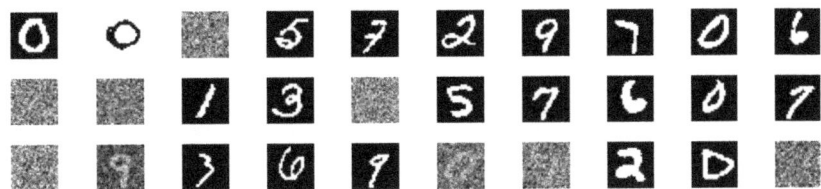

Figure 2. GAN + Adam: FGAN with FADAM and $\nu = 1.0$.

Other experiments were developed with $\nu \in (0, 2)$, but for reasons of space, only a few of them are reported. From these experiments, it was observed that FGAN + FSGD with $\nu = 1.9$ gave the best results because it produced a digit shape in all the 30 executions, as illustrated in Figure 3.

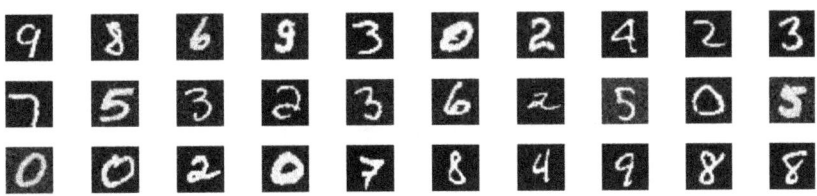

Figure 3. FGAN + FSGD and $\nu = 1.9$.

In an attempt to obtain a similar result with FAdam, the FGAN was trained with some values of $\nu \in (0, 2)$. The results for $\nu = 0.1, 0.3, 0.7, 0.9$ and 1.9 are reported in Figures 4–8, respectively. From these figures, it can be deduced that as ν grows, there is a greater number of failures because more images look noisy (no shape of some digit is visible), and the best of FGAN+FAdam was for $\nu = 0.1$ with 3 fails, as shown in Figure 4.

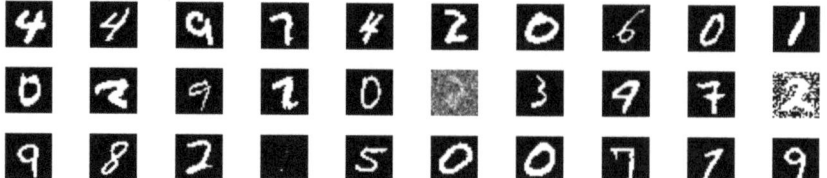

Figure 4. FGAN + FAdam and $\nu = 0.1$.

Experimentally, it was not possible to find a ν-value for FGAN+FAdam that always produced digits like FSGD. This suggests that SGD is still competitive in certain applications, such as GANs, by introducing the fractional gradient.

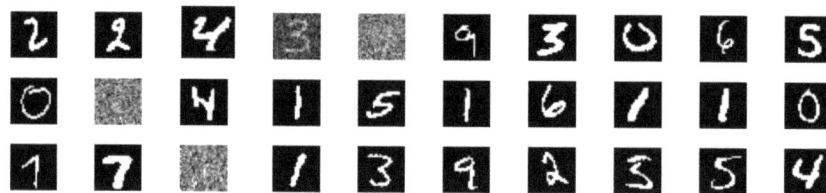

Figure 5. FGAN with FAdam and $\nu = 0.3$.

Figure 6. FGAN with FAdam and $\nu = 0.7$.

Figure 7. FGAN with FAdam and $\nu = 0.9$.

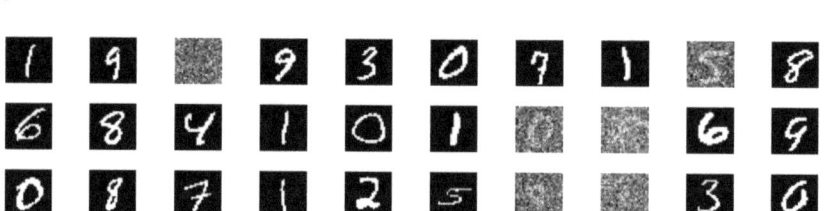

Figure 8. FGAN with FAdam and $\nu = 1.9$.

3.2. Experiment 2: FBERT

The second experiment is based on [32] that implements a BERT architecture in PyTorch and has 4 modules: Preprocessing, Building model, Loss and Optimization, and Training.

Preprocessing section. Defines a text data and applies several tasks, including those where the sentences are converted to lowercase and a vocabulary is created, as well as others where special tokens are defined as follows:

- hCLS: token classification,
- SEP: sentence separation,
- END: end of sentence,
- PAD: equal length and sentence truncation,
- MASK: mask creation and word replacement.

Additionally, embedding and masking tasks are included, and they are briefly described below.

Embedding tasks. Three embedding tasks are developed: token embedding to insert the special tokens and to replace each token with its index, segment embedding to separate two sentences from each other, and position embedding that assigns positions to the embeddings of a sequence.

Masking tasks. Randomly assign masks to 15% of the sequence except to the special tokens and then aim to predict these masked words. Additionally, a padding is used to ensure that all sentences are equally long.

The experiment focuses on the Next-Word Prediction case of study where a label is created to predict consecutive sentences. A *true* value is assigned for consecutive sentences in the sense that the first sentence and the second sentence positions are in the same context.

Building model section. Given the previously described tasks, the building model section involves 4 components for BERT: Embedding layer, Attention Mask, Encoder layer, and BERT Assembling.

An Embedding layer applies the embedding tasks. The Attention Mask applies the masking tasks and attempts to predict a masked word randomly selected from the input. The encoder establishes representations and patterns from the embedding and masking tasks by combining the embedding information via three variables Query, Key, and Value, and the attention information to produce a score via an operator of the scaled dot product. This operator has two outputs, the attention and the context vectors evaluated in a linear layer.

Loss and Optimization section. The original experiment of [23] uses only the Adam optimizer. In this experiment, fractional Foptim.FAdam, Foptim.FSGD (with and without momentum), Foptim.FAdamW, Foptim.FAdan, Foptim.FRMSProp and Foptim.FAdadelta optimizers are used. Essentially, it is enough to change the optimizer of the original line:

```
optim = optim.Adam(model.parameters(), learning_rate=0.001)
```

to the corresponding fractional. For example, for the fractional Foptim.FAdam, the following line of code can be used:

```
optim = Foptim.FAdam(model.parameters(), learning_rate=0.001)
```

and similarly for the other fractional optimizers.

The loss function is the same from [23] and it is the CrossEntropyLoss defined in Equation (15).

Training section. Like the original work, it runs 100 epochs and reports the loss function for each 10 epoch.

In our experiment, seven fractional optimizers were considered with the self-descriptive labels FSGD, FSGDm (using momentum), FAdam, FAdamW, FAdan, FRMSProp, and FAdadelta. The ν-derivative is controlled by the *FSGDTorch.Cnu.nu* variable and the values in this experiment were $\nu = 0.3, 0.65, 1.0, 1.35, 1.7$, and 1.9. As previously stated, for $\nu = 1.0$ the fractional optimizers becomes the first-order integer case.

The text for training was the same originally used in [23]. The FBERT training results are reported in the boxplot of Figure 9, where the following can be observed:

- Focused on FAdam, and considering the original experiment with Adam (i.e., FAdam with $\nu = 1.0$), it is suboptimal and is outperformed by others with fractional derivatives
- Focused on FSGD and FSGDm, the best results are for $\nu = 1.7$ and 1.9
- Focused on FAdan, the best results are for $\nu = 1.7$ and 1.9
- FRMSProp and FAdadelta do not show a competitive performance
- From all the 42 bars in the boxplot, the best results are for FSGD, FSGDm, and FAdam, and the minimum is for FSGD with $\nu = 1.9$.

In addition to the fact that the best optimizers turned out to be fractional, they achieved better consistency in the boxplot with respect to others with $\nu = 1.0$. The numerical data of Figure 9 were not included because of simplicity and space-saving.

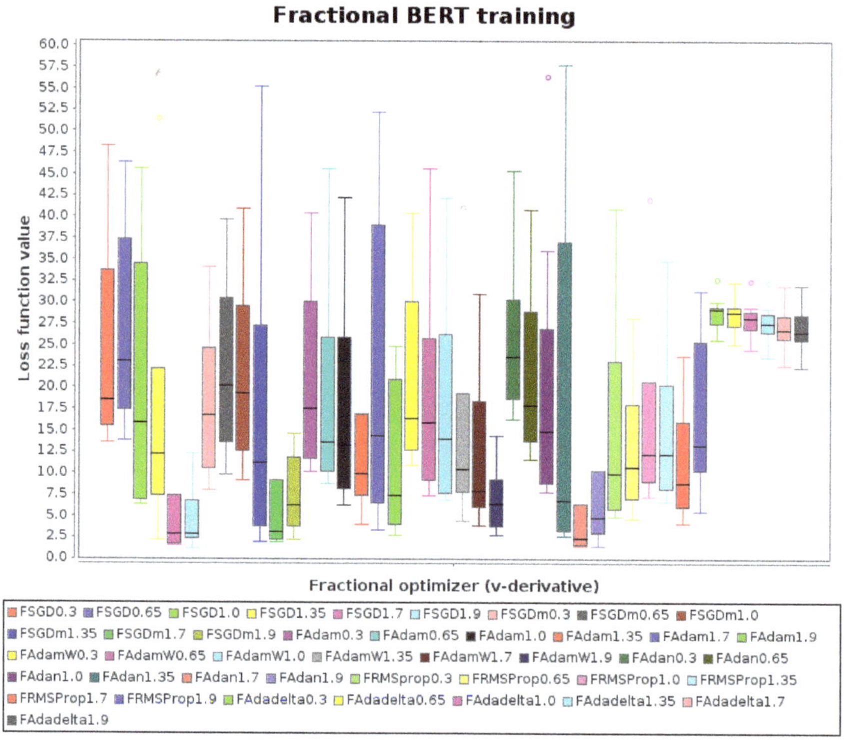

Figure 9. Boxplot of loss functions for FBERT trained with fractional optimizers and $\nu = \{0.3, 0.65, 1.0, 1.35, 1.7, 1.9\}$.

The source code of all fractional optimizers of this paper are available for download.

4. Discussion

One of the optimizers considered state of the art in machine learning is Adam, along with "Adam-flavors", which focus mainly on the history and self-tuning of hyperparameters, in particular of the learning rate. In contrast, this work focuses on applying the ancient but powerful concept of fractional derivative to give an additional degree of freedom to existing optimizers.

Two experiments were developed to show how the fractional versions of gradient-based optimizers could improve their performance on GAN and natural language applications with BERT.

For Experiment 1, it is worth mentioning that the author of the original program admits the complexity of finding a set of hyperparameters that gives satisfactory results with GAN+Adam over MNIST (SGD is not even considered by many authors). This paper shows that using Adam (i.e., FAdam with $\nu = 1.0$) does not always lead to successful results, and on the contrary, SGD does (not for $\nu = 1.0$ but $\nu > 1.7$). With these encouraging results, there are reasons to affirm that fractional gradients favor controlled artificial creativity, useful in neural networks such as GAN.

In Experiment 2, the fractional BERT was successfully implemented. Certainly, it was not trained on a large data set because the objective was to appreciate and compare the influence of the fractional gradient. The running time for each combination of fractional optimizer and ν-derivative was not prohibitive and were successfully executed with a single GPU.

The experimental results show that SGD can be as competitive as other optimizers, which can also improve their performance when considering the fractional gradient. Indeed, fractional SGD has shown better performance in artificial creativity applications with GAN and NLP applications with BERT.

In future work, with the current background, it is proposed to apply fractional optimizers on large data sets, with transfer-learning from pre-trained models, as well as explore other application areas.

An open research area is to study the existence of some optimal value of the fractional derivative given by the data, the self-tuning of the fractional ν-value, as well as the use of other fractional derivatives definitions.

The source code of the fractional optimizers for PyTorch resulting from this work are available online with the aim of being used and improved. At the same time, we hope that more members of the AI community will learn, apply and see the benefits of applying fractional calculus concepts.

Author Contributions: Conceptualization, O.H.-A.; Methodology, O.H.-A.; Software, O.H.-A. and J.R.C.-A.; Validation, O.H.-A. and J.R.C.-A.; Writing—review and editing, O.H.-A. and J.R.C.-A. All authors have read and agreed to the published version of the manuscript.

Funding: This research received no external funding.

Data Availability Statement: The source code of the fractional optimizers of this paper are available for download at: http://ia.azc.uam.mx/ (accessed on 1 May 2023).

Conflicts of Interest: The authors declare no conflict of interest.

References

1. Haykin, S.S. *Neural Networks and Learning Machines*, 3rd. ed.; Pearson Education: Upper Saddle River, NJ, USA, 2009.
2. Schmidt, R.M.; Schneider, F.; Hennig, P. Descending through a Crowded Valley—Benchmarking Deep Learning Optimizers. In Proceedings of the Proceedings of the 38th International Conference on Machine Learning, PMLR, Virtual Event, 18–24 July 2021; Meila, M.; Zhang, T., Eds.; 2021; Volume 139, pp. 9367–9376.
3. Robbins, H.; Monro, S. A stochastic approximation method. *Ann. Math. Stat.* **1951**, 400–407. [CrossRef]
4. Kingma, D.P.; Ba, J. Adam: A Method for Stochastic Optimization. *arXiv* **2014**, arXiv:1412.6980.
5. Abdulkadirov, R.; Lyakhov, P.; Nagornov, N. Survey of Optimization Algorithms in Modern Neural Networks. *Mathematics* **2023**, *11*, 2466. [CrossRef]
6. Tian, Y.; Zhang, Y.; Zhang, H. Recent Advances in Stochastic Gradient Descent in Deep Learning. *Mathematics* **2023**, *11*, 682. [CrossRef]
7. Herrera-Alcántara, O. Fractional Derivative Gradient-Based Optimizers for Neural Networks and Human Activity Recognition. *Appl. Sci.* **2022**, *12*, 9264. [CrossRef]
8. PyTorch-Contributors. TOPTIM: Implementing Various Optimization Algorithms. 2023. Available online: https://pytorch.org/docs/stable/optim.html (accessed on 1 May 2023).

9. Paszke, A.; Gross, S.; Massa, F.; Lerer, A.; Bradbury, J.; Chanan, G.; Killeen, T.; Lin, Z.; Gimelshein, N.; Antiga, L.; et al. PyTorch: An Imperative Style, High-Performance Deep Learning Library. In *Advances in Neural Information Processing Systems 32*; Curran Associates, Inc.: Red Hook, NY, USA, 2019; pp. 8024–8035.
10. Oldham, K.B.; Spanier, J. *The Fractional Calculus*; Academic Press [A Subsidiary of Harcourt Brace Jovanovich, Publishers]: New York, NY, USA; London, UK, 1974; Volume 111, pp. xiii+234.
11. Miller, K.; Ross, B. *An Introduction to the Fractional Calculus and Fractional Differential Equations*; Wiley: Hoboken, NJ, USA, 1993.
12. Mainardi, F. *Fractional Calculus and Waves in Linear Viscoelasticity*, 2nd ed.; Number 2; World Scientific: Singapore, 2022; p. 628.
13. Yousefi, F.; Rivaz, A.; Chen, W. The construction of operational matrix of fractional integration for solving fractional differential and integro-differential equations. *Neural Comput. Applic* **2019**, *31*, 1867–1878. [CrossRef]
14. Gonzalez, E.A.; Petráš, I. Advances in fractional calculus: Control and signal processing applications. In Proceedings of the 2015 16th International Carpathian Control Conference (ICCC), Szilvasvarad, Hungary, 27–30 May 2015; pp. 147–152. [CrossRef]
15. Henriques, M.; Valério, D.; Gordo, P.; Melicio, R. Fractional-Order Colour Image Processing. *Mathematics* **2021**, *9*, 457. [CrossRef]
16. Pang, G.; Lu, L.; Karniadakis, G.E. fPINNs: Fractional Physics-Informed Neural Networks. *SIAM J. Sci. Comput.* **2019**, *41*, A2603–A2626,
17. Wang, J.; Wen, Y.; Gou, Y.; Ye, Z.; Chen, H. Fractional-order gradient descent learning of BP neural networks with Caputo derivative. *Neural Netw.* **2017**, *89*, 19–30. [CrossRef] [PubMed]
18. Bao, C.; Pu, Y.; Zhang, Y. Fractional-Order Deep Backpropagation Neural Network. *Comput. Intell. Neurosci.* **2018**, *2018*, 7361628. [CrossRef] [PubMed]
19. Wang, H.; Yu, Y.; Wen, G. Stability analysis of fractional-order Hopfield neural networks with time delays. *Neural Netw.* **2014**, *55*, 98–109. [CrossRef] [PubMed]
20. Chollet, F.; Zhu, Q.; Rahman, F.; Lee, T.; Marmiesse, G.; Zabluda, O.; Qian, C.; Jin, H.; Watson, M.; Chao, R.; et al. Keras. 2015. Available online: https://keras.io/ (accessed on 1 May 2023).
21. Abadi, M.; Agarwal, A.; Barham, P.; Brevdo, E.; Chen, Z.; Citro, C.; Corrado, G.S.; Davis, A.; Dean, J.; Devin, M.; et al. TensorFlow: Large-Scale Machine Learning on Heterogeneous Systems. 2015. Available online: https://tensorflow.org (accessed on 1 May 2023).
22. Goodfellow, I.; Pouget-Abadie, J.; Mirza, M.; Xu, B.; Warde-Farley, D.; Ozair, S.; Courville, A.; Bengio, Y. Generative adversarial nets. In Proceedings of the Advances in Neural Information Processing Systems, Montreal, QC, Canada, 8–13 December 2014; pp. 2672–2680.
23. Devlin, J.; Chang, M.W.; Lee, K.; Toutanova, K. BERT: Pre-training of Deep Bidirectional Transformers for Language Understanding. In *Proceedings of the 2019 Conference of the North American Chapter of the Association for Computational Linguistics: Human Language Technologies, Volume 1 (Long and Short Papers)*; Association for Computational Linguistics: Minneapolis, MN, USA, 2019; pp. 4171–4186. [CrossRef]
24. Garrappa, R.; Kaslik, E.; Popolizio, M. Evaluation of Fractional Integrals and Derivatives of Elementary Functions: Overview and Tutorial. *Mathematics* **2019**, *7*, 407. [CrossRef]
25. Zeiler, M.D. ADADELTA: An Adaptive Learning Rate Method. *arXiv* **2012**, arXiv:1212.5701. [CrossRef]
26. Duchi, J.; Hazan, E.; Singer, Y. Adaptive Subgradient Methods for Online Learning and Stochastic Optimization. *J. Mach. Learn. Res.* **2011**, *12*, 2121–2159.
27. Zhuang, Z.; Liu, M.; Cutkosky, A.; Orabona, F. Understanding adamw through proximal methods and scale-freeness. *arXiv* **2022**, arXiv:2202.00089.
28. Tieleman, T.; Hinton, G. *Neural Networks for Machine Learning*; Technical Report; COURSERA: Napa County, CA, USA, 2012.
29. Hochreiter, S.; Schmidhuber, J. Long short-term memory. *Neural Comput.* **1997**, *9*, 1735–1780. [CrossRef] [PubMed]
30. Seo, J.D. Only Numpy: Implementing GAN (General Adversarial Networks) and Adam Optimizer Using Numpy with Interactive Code. 2023. Available online: https://towardsdatascience.com/only-numpy-implementing-gan-general-adversarial-networks-and-adam-optimizer-using-numpy-with-2a7e4e032021 (accessed on 1 May 2023).
31. Deng, L. The mnist database of handwritten digit images for machine learning research. *IEEE Signal Process. Mag.* **2012**, *29*, 141–142. [CrossRef]
32. Barla, N. How to code BERT using PyTorch. Available online: https://neptune.ai/blog/how-to-code-bert-using-pytorch-tutorial (accessed on 1 May 2023).

Disclaimer/Publisher's Note: The statements, opinions and data contained in all publications are solely those of the individual author(s) and contributor(s) and not of MDPI and/or the editor(s). MDPI and/or the editor(s) disclaim responsibility for any injury to people or property resulting from any ideas, methods, instructions or products referred to in the content.

fractal and fractional

Article

The Effect of Fractional Derivatives on Thermo-Mechanical Interaction in Biological Tissues during Hyperthermia Treatment Using Eigenvalues Approach

Aatef Hobiny [1] and Ibrahim Abbas [1,2,*]

1. Mathematics Department, Faculty of Science, King Abdulaziz University, Jeddah 21589, Saudi Arabia; ahobany@kau.edu.sa
2. Mathematics Department, Faculty of Science, Sohag University, Sohag 82524, Egypt
* Correspondence: ibrabbas7@science.sohag.edu.eg

Abstract: This article studies the effects of fractional time derivatives on thermo-mechanical interaction in living tissue during hyperthermia treatment by using the eigenvalues approach. A comprehensive understanding of the heat transfer mechanism and the related thermo-mechanical interactions with the patient's living tissues is crucial for the effective implementation of thermal treatment procedures. The surface of living tissues is traction-free and is exposed to a pulse boundary heat flux that decays exponentially. The Laplace transforms and their associated techniques are applied to the generalized bio-thermo-elastic model, and analytical procedures are then implemented. The eigenvalue approach is utilized to obtain the solution of governing equations. Graphical representations are given for the temperature, the displacement, and the thermal stress results. Afterward, a parametric study was carried out to determine the best method for selecting crucial design parameters that can improve the precision of hyperthermia therapies.

Keywords: living tissue; fractional time derivatives; analytical solutions; thermo-mechanical interactions; Laplace transform; thermal relaxation time

Citation: Hobiny, A.; Abbas, I. The Effect of Fractional Derivatives on Thermo-Mechanical Interaction in Biological Tissues during Hyperthermia Treatment Using Eigenvalues Approach. *Fractal Fract.* **2023**, *7*, 432. https://doi.org/10.3390/fractalfract7060432

Academic Editors: Corina S Drapaca and Sameerah Jamal

Received: 3 May 2023
Revised: 20 May 2023
Accepted: 24 May 2023
Published: 26 May 2023

Copyright: © 2023 by the authors. Licensee MDPI, Basel, Switzerland. This article is an open access article distributed under the terms and conditions of the Creative Commons Attribution (CC BY) license (https://creativecommons.org/licenses/by/4.0/).

1. Introduction

The temperature behavior of living tissue is still not fully understood due to the difficulty in accurately measuring it in vivo. This is because necropsy can alter tissue temperature characteristics and examining tissue outside of the body lacks perfusion effects. Various in vivo techniques exist to measure thermal behavior, but they yield varying results, and precise measurement of tissue temperature in vivo remains elusive. For effective treatment, it is critical to control the body's heat transmission pathways. Thermal therapies aim to freeze or heat tumors without damaging surrounding healthy tissue. If doctors could predict how tissue would react thermally, they could plan therapy dosages and durations before surgery. Tissue and blood perfusion's temperature response is associated with a range of diseases and injuries, including diabetes, skin grafts, and frostbites. The severity of these diseases is influenced by the extent to which blood can reach a certain location. If the thermal characteristics of damaged tissue can be precisely monitored before problems arise, appropriate and efficient therapy can be provided immediately. Heat transport analysis in living tissue is challenging due to its diverse internal structure, which includes perfusion via capillary tubes, convection between blood and tissues, thermal conduction between solid tissues and blood arteries, and heating generation through metabolism, evaporation, and other factors. Pennes' [1] bioheat model, which is based on Fourier's law of thermal conduction, is used to represent heat transmission in living tissues. Various thermotherapy procedures, such as laser tissue welding [2], laser operations [3], and hyperthermia [4], are frequently utilized in modern medicine. Skin tissue temperature distributions are influenced by complex factors such as metabolic heating generation and blood circulation, so researchers have expanded on basic relationships by incorporating a wide range of phenomenological mechanisms, such as metabolic heating production, thermal conduction, blood perfusions, radiation, and phase change. Biological tissues undergo diverse stages of change, which can take many different forms. Modified versions of Pennes' bioheat models, which employ various numerical methods, are available in the relevant literature. Several techniques have been used to study heat transmission in living tissues, including the homotopy perturbation technique [5], Legendre wavelets Galerkin approaches [6,7], and the finite element approach [8]. When a person's body temperature was unusually low, Esneault and Dillenseger [9] used finite difference approaches to investigate the time-dependent increase in temperature. During thermal therapy, Ghanmi and Abbas [10] performed an analytical investigation of the fractional time derivative in skin tissue. Marin et al. [11] utilized finite element analysis to study the nonlinear bio-heat model in skin tissue caused by external heating sources, while Hobiny and Abbas [12] explored the analytical solution for the fractional bioheat model in tissues with a spherical shape. On the other hand, Keangin and Phadungsak [13] conducted an analysis on the heat transport in porous liver during microwave ablation, specifically focusing on local thermal non-equilibrium. In their research, Keangin et al. [14] investigated the analysis of heat transfer in a deformed liver cancer model treated with a microwave coaxial antenna. Andreozzi et al. [15] studied the effects of a pulsating heat source on interstitial fluid transport in tumor tissues in which the effects of modulating-heat strategies to influence interstitial fluid transport in tissues were analyzed.

Different methods can be used to solve the time-dependent heat transfer equation and model infinite thermal propagations based on classical Fourier heat conduction. Fractional computation has recently proved to be a successful method for modifying many physical models. Fractional derivatives have received significant attention, and various definitions and methods have been developed. The use of fractional time derivatives has enabled the successful modification of many physical models' processes. Ezzat and colleagues introduced a novel bio-heat model based on the fractional heat conduction formulation, as described in their publications [16,17], while the investigation of transient heating in skin tissues caused by time-dependent thermal therapy, utilizing a heat transport law that incorporates memory, was carried out by Mondal and colleagues in reference [18]. Researchers have conducted several studies on the use of thermal transfer on living tissue [19] to improve treatment methods, develop more accurate temperature prediction technologies, and ultimately, find a cure for cancer. Over the past forty years, a wide range of researchers from various fields, including high-energy particle accelerators, continuum mechanics, acoustics, nuclear engineering, and aeronautics have expressed significant interest in generalized thermo-elastic models from both a technical and mathematical standpoint. The concepts of heat transfer and elasticity are linked in this model. Lord and Shulman [20] developed the thermo-elasticity hypothesis with multiple generalizations. Mondal et al. [21] employed the memory-dependent derivatives on a sliding interval within the framework of the Lord–Shulman model to investigate the heat transfer equation for this problem. Diaz et al. [22] used the finite element method to obtain the solutions of thermo-diffusion types present in living tissue to develop thermal damage. Zhu et al. [22] used the diffusion theory to consider rate process models for the results of thermal damages and the sedimentation of lighting energy in the tissue. When studying the actual phenomena of thermal transfer in finite media, the nonlinear and linear models of heating transfer are extended, and many authors have sought numerical or analytical solutions to the problems posed by these models [23–33]. Despite the growing popularity of laser, microwave, and other forms of thermal therapy in dermatology, thermo-mechanical interactions are seldom considered in current research, despite being central to the thermo-mechanically linked nature of these therapies. Generalized thermo-elastic models govern tissue thermo-elastic behaviors, which include the G-N model, the G-NII model, the DPL, the fractional model, and Li et al. [34–36], who further investigated the effects of heat-induced mechanical responses in skin tissues under temperature-dependent properties.

This research aims to create an analytical approach to examine the thermo-mechanical interactions with fractional time derivatives in living tissue that experiences instantaneous heating and has varying thermal and mechanical properties. A generalized thermo-elastic model is constructed that takes into account the tissue structure and variable thermal and mechanical characteristics within the bioheat transfer equation framework. The effect of fractional parameter in temperature, displacement, and thermal stress variations are shown in the graphics.

2. Materials and Methods

The field of bio-thermo-elasticity merges the principles of elasticity and bioheat conduction. The basic equations under fractional time derivatives in the living tissues can be given by [20,37,38]:

$$(\lambda + \mu)u_{j,ij} + \mu u_{i,jj} - \gamma T_{,i} = \rho \frac{\partial^2 u_i}{\partial t^2}, \tag{1}$$

$$k\nabla^2 T = \left(1 + \frac{\tau_o^\beta}{\Gamma(\beta+1)}\frac{\partial^\beta}{\partial t^\beta}\right)\left(\rho c_e \frac{\partial T}{\partial t} + \omega_b \rho_b c_b (T - T_b) + \gamma T_o \frac{\partial^2 u}{\partial t \partial x} - Q_m\right), 0 < \beta \leq 1, \tag{2}$$

$$\sigma_{ij} = \mu(u_{i,j} + u_{j,i}) + (\lambda u_{k,k} - \gamma(T - T_o))\delta_{ij}, \tag{3}$$

where t is the time, τ_o is the thermal relaxation time, T_b is the blood temperature, c_e refers to the specific heat at constant strain, ρ is the tissue mass density, $\gamma = (3\lambda + 2\mu)\alpha_t$, α_t refers to the linear thermal expansion coefficient, λ, μ refer to the Lame's constants, T is the tissue temperature, k is the tissue thermal conductivity, ω_b is the blood perfusion rate, Q_m is the metabolic heat generation in skin tissues, e_{ij} are the strain components, σ_{ij} are the stress components, u_i are the displacement components, δ_{ij} is the Kronecker symbol and c_b is the blood specific heat. The definition of the fractional order derivative is as follows:

$$\frac{\partial^\beta h(r,t)}{\partial t^\beta} = \begin{cases} h(r,t) - h(r,0), & \beta \to 0, \\ I^{\beta-1}\frac{\partial h(r,t)}{\partial t}, & 0 < \beta < 1, \\ \frac{\partial h(r,t)}{\partial t}, & \beta = 1, \end{cases} \tag{4}$$

$$I^\nu h(r,t) = \int_0^t \frac{(t-s)^\nu}{\Gamma(\nu)} h(r,s)ds, \ \nu > 0, \tag{5}$$

$$\lim_{\nu \to 1} \frac{\partial^\nu h(r,t)}{\partial t^\nu} = \frac{\partial h(r,t)}{\partial t}, \tag{6}$$

Equation (4) illustrates how the range of local thermal conduction can be characterized by two types of conductivity: standard thermal conduction and heat ballistic conduction. The fractional parameter is β, where $0 < \beta \leq 1$ is used to define these conductivities. For normal conductivity, $\beta = 1$, while for low conductivity $0 < \beta < 1$. Here, we assume that the surface and the bottom boundary of a limited domain of tissues with thickness L. As a result, the displacement components can be expressed as follows:

$$u_x = u(x,t), u_y = 0, u_z = 0. \tag{7}$$

So that the model has the following form

$$(\lambda + 2\mu)\frac{\partial^2 u}{\partial x^2} - \gamma \frac{\partial T}{\partial x} = \rho \frac{\partial^2 u}{\partial t^2}, \tag{8}$$

$$k\frac{\partial^2 T}{\partial x^2} = \left(1 + \frac{\tau_o^\beta}{\Gamma(\beta+1)}\frac{\partial^\beta}{\partial t^\beta}\right)\left(\rho c \frac{\partial T}{\partial t} + \omega_b \rho_b c_b (T - T_b) + \gamma T_o \frac{\partial^2 u}{\partial t \partial x} - Q_m\right), \tag{9}$$

$$\sigma_{xx} = (\lambda + 2\mu)\frac{\partial u}{\partial x} - \gamma(T - T_o). \tag{10}$$

To obtain a solution for the equations, it is necessary to have two sets of initial and boundary conditions that align with the physical model description:

$$T(x,0) = T_b, \frac{\partial T(x,0)}{\partial t} = 0, u(x,0) = 0, \frac{\partial u(x,0)}{\partial t} = 0, \qquad (11)$$

$$\sigma_{xx}(0,t) = 0,\ \sigma_{xx}(L,t) = 0,\ -k\frac{\partial T(x,t)}{\partial x}\bigg|_{x=0} = q_0 \frac{t^2 e^{-\frac{t}{t_p}}}{16 t_p^2},\ -k\frac{\partial T(x,t)}{\partial x}\bigg|_{x=L} = 0, \qquad (12)$$

where t_p points to the characteristic time of pulsing heat flux and q_0 is constant. Now, the dimensionless quantities may be utilized for ease by employing:

$$T' = \frac{T - T_o}{T_o},\ (t', \tau'_o, t'_p) = \eta c^2 (t, \tau_o, t_p),\ (x', u') = \eta c(x, u),$$

$$\sigma'_{xx} = \frac{\sigma_{xx}}{\lambda + 2\mu},\ q'_o = \frac{q_0}{\eta c T_o K},\ Q'_m = \frac{Q_m}{T_o K \eta^2 c^2}, \qquad (13)$$

where $\eta = \frac{\rho c_e}{K}$ and $c^2 = \frac{\lambda + 2\mu}{\rho}$.

The primary equations can be expressed in a non-dimensional form by removing the dashes and introducing appropriate parameters, as shown in Equation (13):

$$\frac{\partial^2 u}{\partial x^2} - \varepsilon_1 \frac{\partial T}{\partial x} = \frac{\partial^2 u}{\partial t^2}, \qquad (14)$$

$$\frac{\partial^2 T}{\partial x^2} = \left(1 + \frac{\tau_o^\beta}{\Gamma(\beta + 1)} \frac{\partial^\beta}{\partial t^\beta}\right) \left(\frac{\partial T}{\partial t} + \varepsilon_2 T + \varepsilon_3 \frac{\partial^2 u}{\partial t \partial x} - Q_m\right), \qquad (15)$$

$$\sigma_{xx} = \frac{\partial u}{\partial x} - \varepsilon_1 T, \qquad (16)$$

$$u(x,0) = 0, \frac{\partial u(x,0)}{\partial t} = 0, T(x,0) = 0, \frac{\partial T(x,0)}{\partial t} = 0, \qquad (17)$$

$$\sigma_{xx}(0,t) = 0, \sigma_{xx}(L,t) = 0, \frac{\partial T(x,t)}{\partial x}\bigg|_{x=0} = -q_0 \frac{t^2 e^{-\frac{t}{t_p}}}{16 t_p^2}, \frac{\partial T(x,t)}{\partial x}\bigg|_{x=L} = 0, \qquad (18)$$

where $\varepsilon_1 = \frac{T_o \gamma_e}{(\lambda_e + 2\mu_e)},\ \varepsilon_2 = \frac{\rho_b c_b \omega_b}{K \eta^2 c^2},\ \varepsilon_3 = \frac{\gamma_e}{\rho c_e}$.

3. Analytical Solutions in the Transform Domain

Equations (14)–(18) can be transformed using Laplace transforms, as in

$$\overline{f}(x,s) = L[f(x,t)] = \int_0^\infty f(x,t) e^{-st} dt. \qquad (19)$$

Therefore, the following equations can be obtained

$$\frac{d^2 \overline{u}}{dx^2} = s^2 \overline{u} + \varepsilon_1 \frac{d\overline{T}}{dx}, \qquad (20)$$

$$\frac{d^2 \overline{T}}{dx^2} = \left(1 + \frac{s^\beta \tau_o^\beta}{\Gamma(\beta + 1)}\right) \left((s + \varepsilon_2) \overline{T} + s \varepsilon_3 \frac{d\overline{u}}{dx}\right) - \frac{Q_m}{s}, \qquad (21)$$

$$\overline{\sigma}_{xx} = \frac{d\overline{u}}{dx} - \varepsilon_1 \overline{T}, \qquad (22)$$

$$\overline{\sigma}_{xx}(0,s) = 0,\ \overline{\sigma}_{xx}(L,s) = 0,\ \frac{d\overline{T}(x,s)}{dx}\bigg|_{x=0} = \frac{-q_0 t_p}{8(s t_p + 1)^3},\ \frac{d\overline{T}(x,s)}{dx}\bigg|_{x=L} = 0. \qquad (23)$$

Equations (20) and (21) can be used to represent the vector–matrix differential equation as follows:

$$\frac{dM}{dx} = BM - f, \quad (24)$$

where $M = \begin{pmatrix} \overline{u} \\ \overline{T} \\ \frac{d\overline{u}}{dx} \\ \frac{d\overline{T}}{dx} \end{pmatrix}$, $B = \begin{pmatrix} 0 & 0 & 1 & 0 \\ 0 & 0 & 0 & 1 \\ s^2 & 0 & 0 & \varepsilon_1 \\ 0 & \left(1+\frac{s^\beta \tau_0^\beta}{\Gamma(\beta+1)}\right)(s+\varepsilon_2) & \left(1+\frac{s^\beta \tau_0^\beta}{\Gamma(\beta+1)}\right)s\varepsilon_3 & 0 \end{pmatrix}$, $f = \begin{pmatrix} 0 \\ 0 \\ 0 \\ \frac{Q_m}{s} \end{pmatrix}$.

To solve Equation (24) using the eigenvalue techniques described in [39–48], Matrix B's characteristic equation is expressed as:

$$\alpha^4 - \left(s^2 + \left(1+\frac{s^\beta \tau_0^\beta}{\Gamma(\beta+1)}\right)(s+\varepsilon_2) + \left(1+\frac{s^\beta \tau_0^\beta}{\Gamma(\beta+1)}\right)s\varepsilon_3\varepsilon_1\right)\alpha^2 + \left(1+\frac{s^\beta \tau_0^\beta}{\Gamma(\beta+1)}\right)(s+\varepsilon_2)s^2 = 0, \quad (25)$$

Relation (25) has four roots, which are the eigenvalues of matrix B, which are defined by $\pm\alpha_1, \pm\alpha_2$. The general solutions to the nonhomogeneous system (24) can be obtained by adding the complementary solution of the corresponding homogeneous system to a particular solution of the nonhomogeneous system. To find the particular solution to the nonhomogeneous Equation (24), we need to consider that the inhomogeneous terms in (24) contain functions of the Laplace parameter s. As a result, the particular solution can be expressed as:

$$M(x,s) = A_1 X_1 e^{-\alpha_1 x} + A_2 X_2 e^{\alpha_1 x} + A_3 X_3 e^{-\alpha_2 x} + A_4 X_4 e^{\alpha_2 x} + \begin{pmatrix} 0 \\ R \\ 0 \\ 0 \end{pmatrix}. \quad (26)$$

where $R = \dfrac{Q_m}{s(s+\varepsilon_2)\left(1+\frac{s^\beta \tau_0^\beta}{\Gamma(\beta+1)}\right)}$. Hence, in the Laplace domain, the general solutions of displacement, temperature, and stress can be given by:

$$\overline{u}(x,s) = A_1 U_1 e^{-\alpha_1 x} + A_2 U_2 e^{\alpha_1 x} + A_3 U_3 e^{-\alpha_2 x} + A_4 U_4 e^{\alpha_2 x}. \quad (27)$$

$$\overline{T}(x,s) = A_1 T_1 e^{-\alpha_1 x} + A_2 T_2 e^{\alpha_1 x} + A_3 T_3 e^{-\alpha_2 x} + A_4 T_4 e^{\alpha_2 x} + R. \quad (28)$$

$$\overline{\sigma}_{xx} = A_1(-\alpha_1 U_1 - \varepsilon_1 T_1)e^{-\alpha_1 x} + A_2(\alpha_1 U_2 - \varepsilon_1 T_2)e^{\alpha_1 x} + A_3(-\alpha_2 U_3 - \varepsilon_1 T_3)e^{-\alpha_2 x} + A_4(\alpha_2 U_4 - \varepsilon_1 T_4)e^{\alpha_2 x} + R, \quad (29)$$

where U_i, T_i refer to the eigenvectors of displacement and temperature, respectively. The problem boundary conditions can be utilized to determine the values of A_1, A_2, A_3, and A_4. To obtain the final solutions for the displacement, temperature, and stress distributions, the Stehfest approach [49] can be used, which has an inverse function $f(x,t)$ defined by a specific formulation:

$$f(x,t) = \frac{\ln 2}{t} \sum_{j=1}^{M} V_j \overline{f}\left(x, j\frac{\ln 2}{t}\right), \quad (30)$$

where V_j can be given by

$$V_j = (-1)^{\frac{M}{2}+1} \sum_{k=\frac{i+1}{2}}^{\min(i,\frac{M}{2})} \frac{k^{\frac{M}{2}+1}(2k)!}{\left(\frac{M}{2}-k\right)!k!(i-k)!(2k-1)!}$$

4. Numerical Outcomes and Discussion

To demonstrate the theoretical results discussed in the above sections, the numerical values of the physical parameters are presented. The material parameters for living tissues at the reference temperature, used in the following calculation, are denoted as follows [35]:

$$\lambda = 8.27 \times 10^8 (N)(m^{-2}), \alpha_t = 1 \times 10^{-4}(k^{-1}), T_o = 310(k), t_p = 0.15,$$

$$\mu = 3.446 \times 10^7 (N)(m^{-2}), c_b = 3770 \, (J)(kg^{-1})(k^{-1}), \rho_b = 1060(kg)(m^{-3}),$$

$$\tau_o = 0.05, K = 0.235 \, (W)(m^{-1})(k^{-1}), Q_m = 1.19 \times 10^3 (W)(m^{-3}), \rho = 1190(kg)(m^{-3}), c_e = 3600 \, (J)(kg^{-1})(k^{-1})$$

The numerical values of the calculated physical quantities under the fractional biothermo-elastic model, considering one thermal relaxation time and using the previous parameters, are displayed in Figures 1–12. Numerical calculations have been performed at time t = 0.2 to determine the temperature variations, the variation of displacement, and stress variation along the distance x under different values of the studied parameters as in Figures 1–12. Figures 1, 4, 7 and 10 display the temperature variation along the distance x. It can be observed from the figures that the temperature initially peaks at the tissue surface $(x = 0)$ due to the exponentially decaying pulse boundary heat flux. As the distance x increases, the temperature steadily decreases. Figures 2, 5, 8 and 11 display the variations of displacement along the distance x. Observing the figures, it can be noted that the displacement reaches its highest negative values at the tissue surface $(x = 0)$. Subsequently, it progressively increases towards peak values near the surface before decreasing back to zero. Figures 3, 6, 9 and 12 show the variation of stress σ_{xx} along the distance x. It can be observed that the stress σ_{xx} starts from zero and ends at zero to comply with the boundary condition of the problem. Figures 1–12 can be classified into four distinct groups.

In the first group, Figures 1–3 show the variations of temperature, displacement, and stress under various models. In Figures 1–3, the solid line (—) refers to the Pennes model (Pennes model) without thermal relaxation time ($\tau_o = 0$) and without fractional time derivative ($\beta = 1$), the dashed line (—) points to the single-phase lag model (SPL model) with one thermal relaxation time ($\tau_o = 0.02$) and without fractional time derivative ($\beta = 1$), while the dotted line (...) refers to the single-phase lag model under fractional time derivative (FSPL model) with one thermal relaxation time ($\tau_o = 0.02$) and with fractional time derivative ($\beta = 0.5$). The significant effects on the quantities under consideration are evident due to the various models.

In the second group, Figures 4–6 display the variation of temperature, displacement, and stress under different values of the fractional parameter ($\beta = 1, 0.5, 0.1$) when ($\tau_o = 0.02$). It is evident that the fractional time derivatives are responsible for the evident significant impacts on the quantities under consideration. A decrease in fractional time derivatives weakens the effect of thermo-mechanical propagation, as evidenced by a decrease in the maximum amplitude of temperature, displacement, and stress.

In the third group, Figures 7–9 show the variation of temperature, displacement, and stress under various values of thermal relaxation time ($\tau_o = 0, 0.02, 0.2$) under fractional time derivative when ($\beta = 0.5$). It is evident that the thermal relaxation time has significant effects on the quantities under consideration. The maximum amplitude of the temperature, displacement, and stress decreases with the increase the thermal relaxation time, which means that the thermal relaxation time is apt to weaken the effect of thermo-mechanical propagation.

In the fourth group, Figures 10–12 show the variations of temperature, displacement, and stress under various of the characteristic time of pulsing heat flux ($t_p = 0.1, 0.15, 0.2$) with one thermal relaxation time ($\tau_o = 0.02$) under fractional time derivative when ($\beta = 0.5$). It is observed that the characteristic time of pulsing heat flux has a significant effect on the quantities under consideration. An increase in the characteristic time of pulsing heat flux weakens the effect of thermo-mechanical propagation, as evidenced by a decrease in the maximum amplitude of temperature, displacement, and stress.

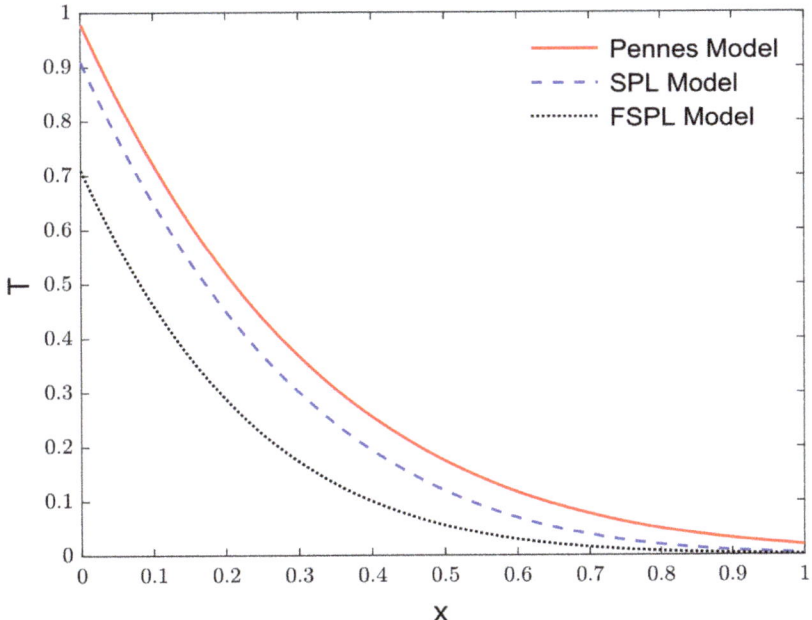

Figure 1. The temperature variations T via x under three different models.

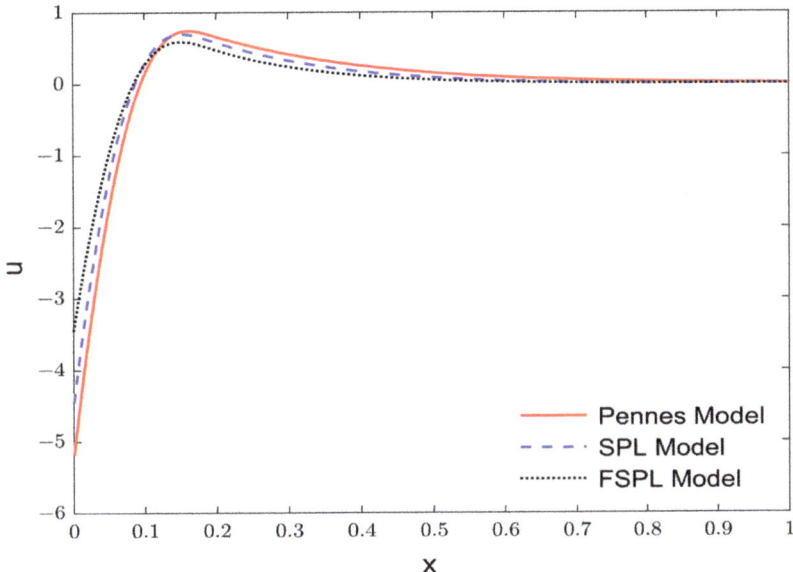

Figure 2. The variations of displacement u via x under three different models.

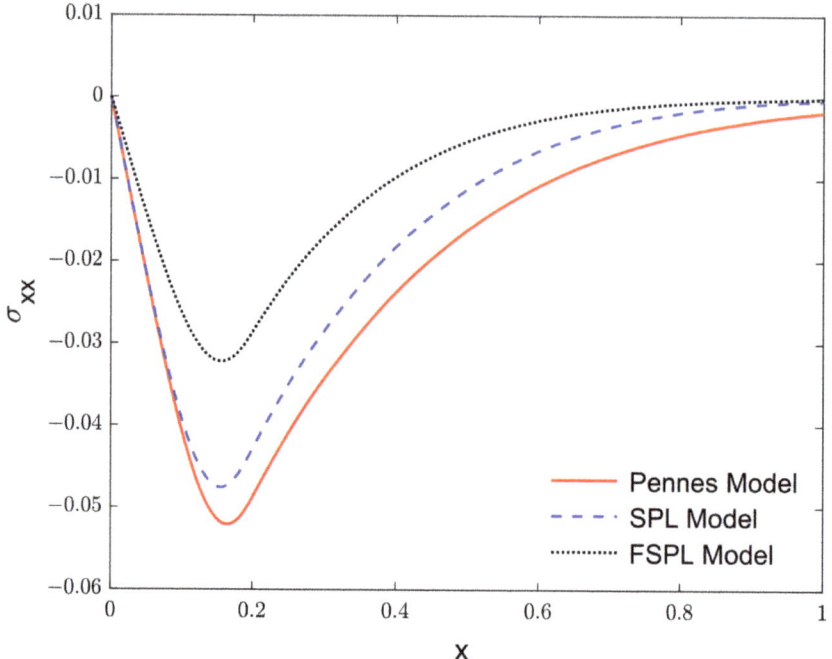

Figure 3. The variations of stress σ_{xx} via x under three different models.

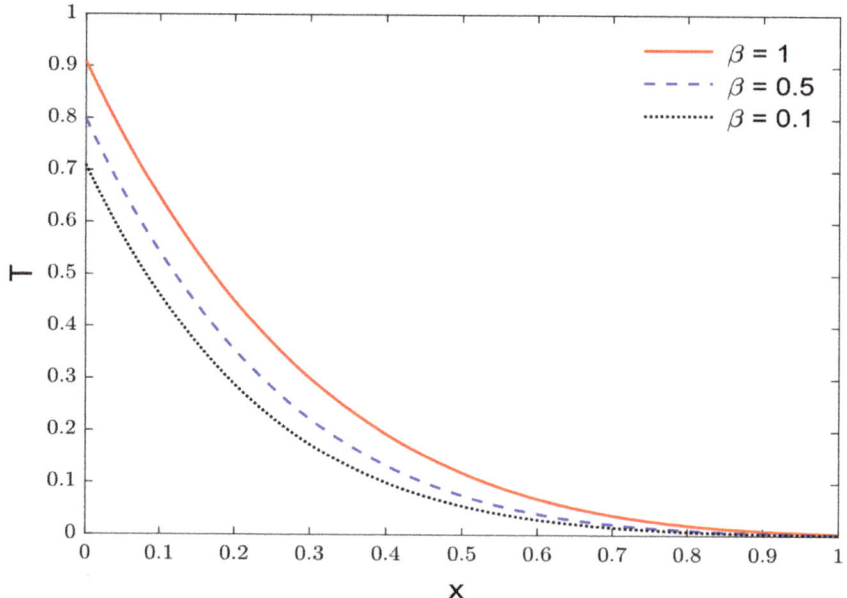

Figure 4. The temperature variations T via x under varying fractional parameter β.

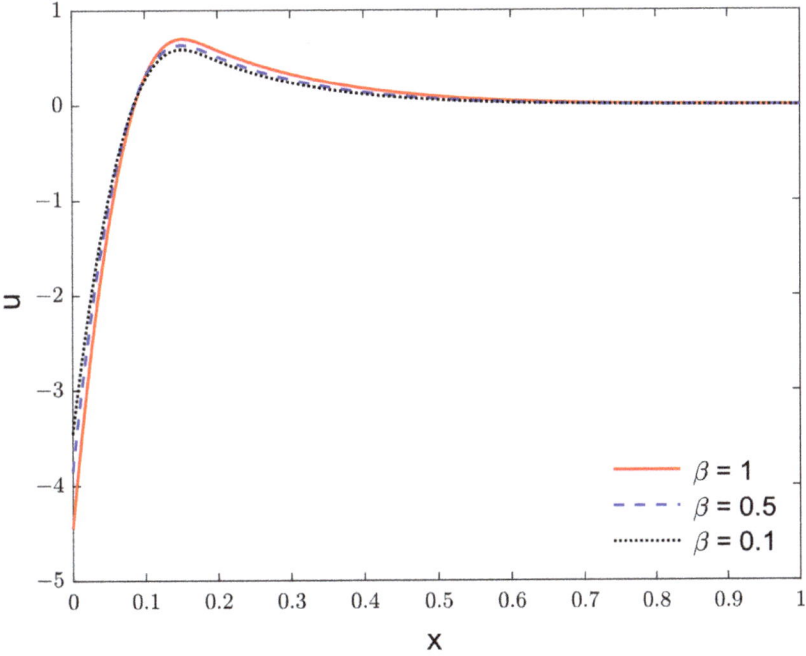

Figure 5. The variations of displacement u via x under varying fractional parameter β.

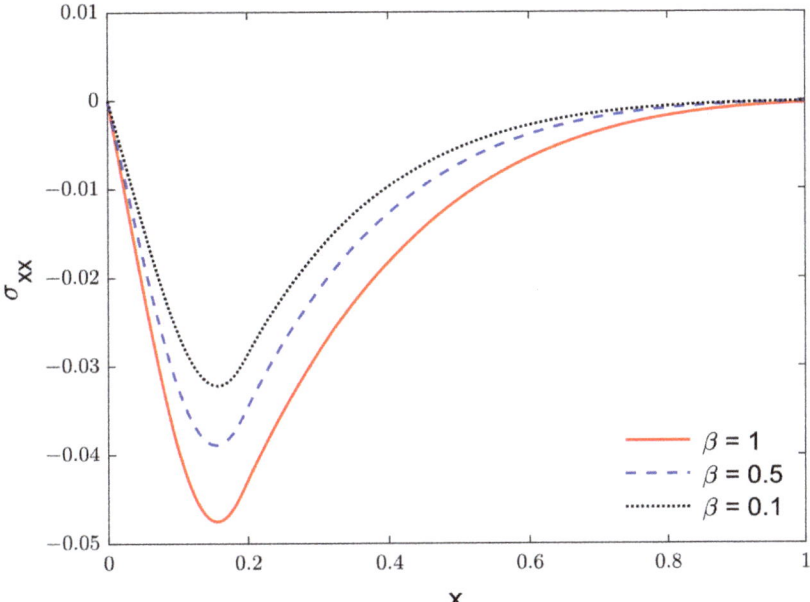

Figure 6. The variations of stress σ_{xx} via x under varying fractional parameter β.

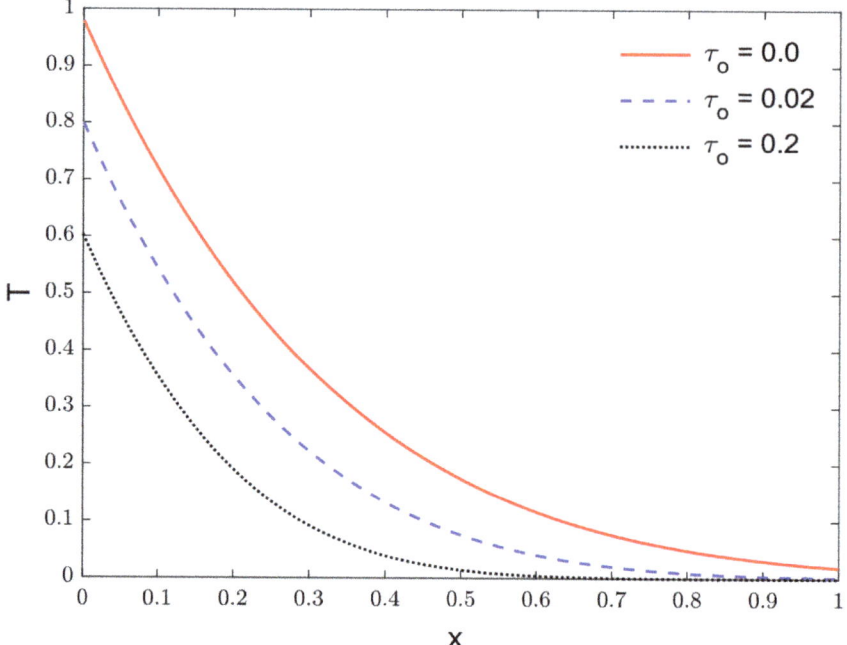

Figure 7. The temperature variations T via x under varying thermal relaxation time τ_o.

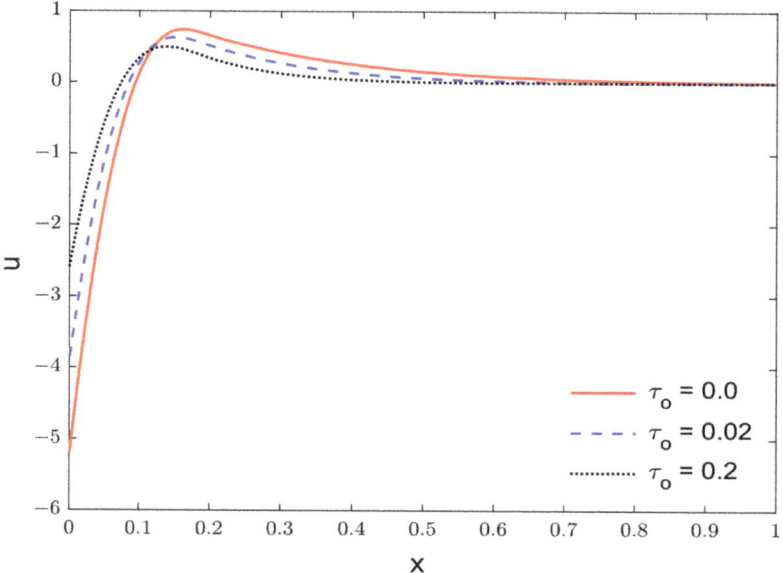

Figure 8. The variations of displacement u via x under varying thermal relaxation time τ_o.

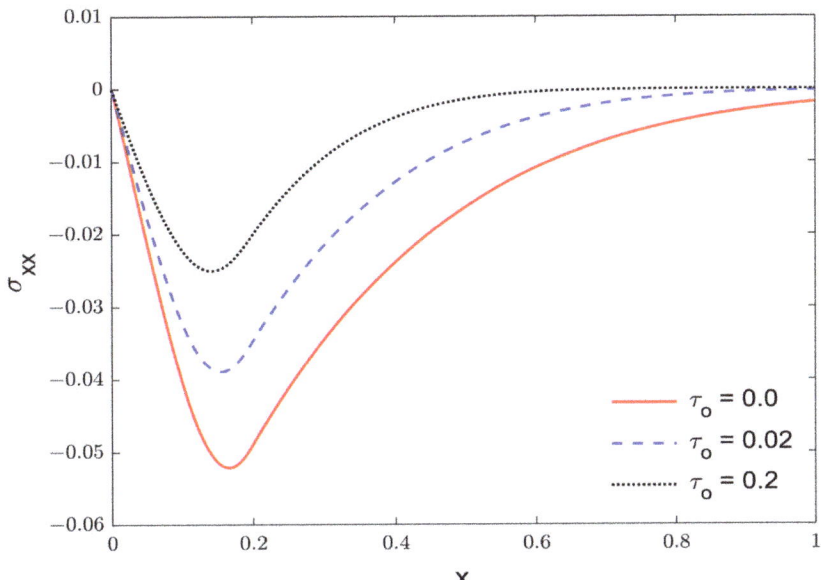

Figure 9. The variations of stress σ_{xx} via x under varying thermal relaxation time τ_o.

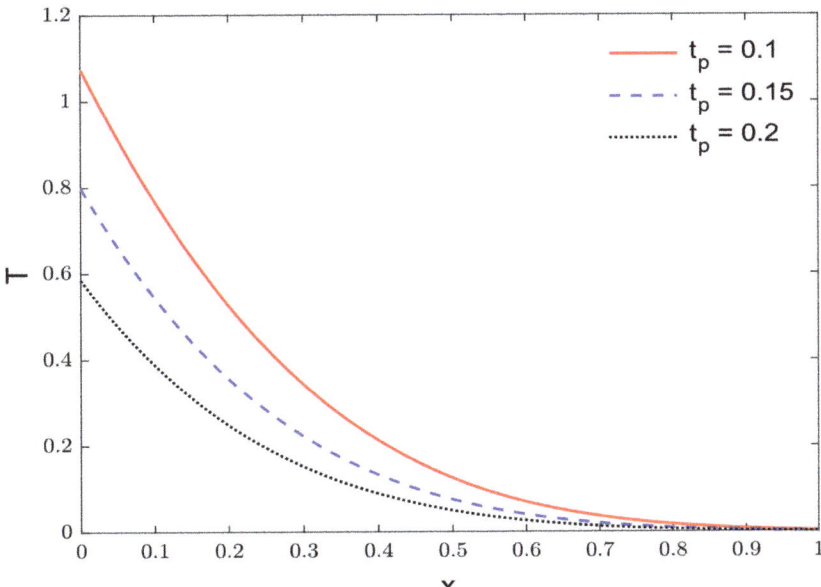

Figure 10. The temperature variations T via x under varying pulsing heat flux characteristic time t_p.

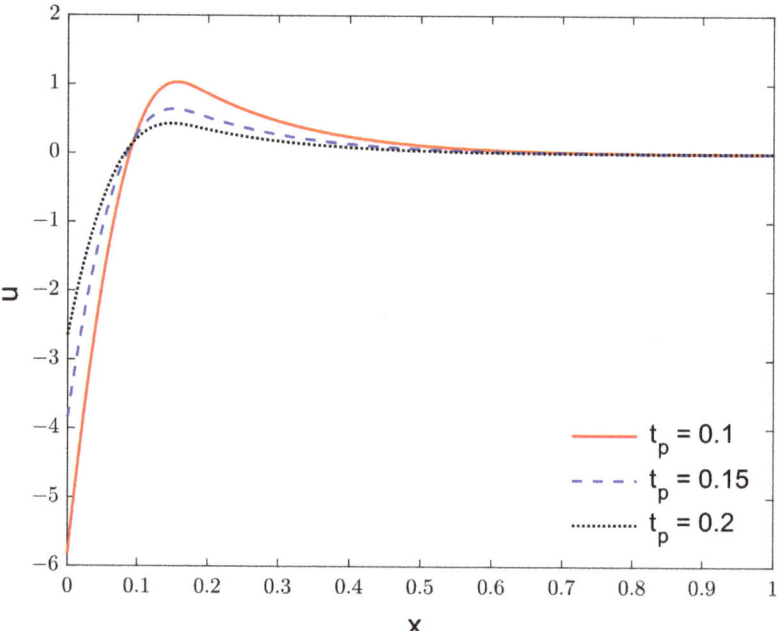

Figure 11. The variations of displacement u via x under varying pulsing heat flux characteristic time t_p.

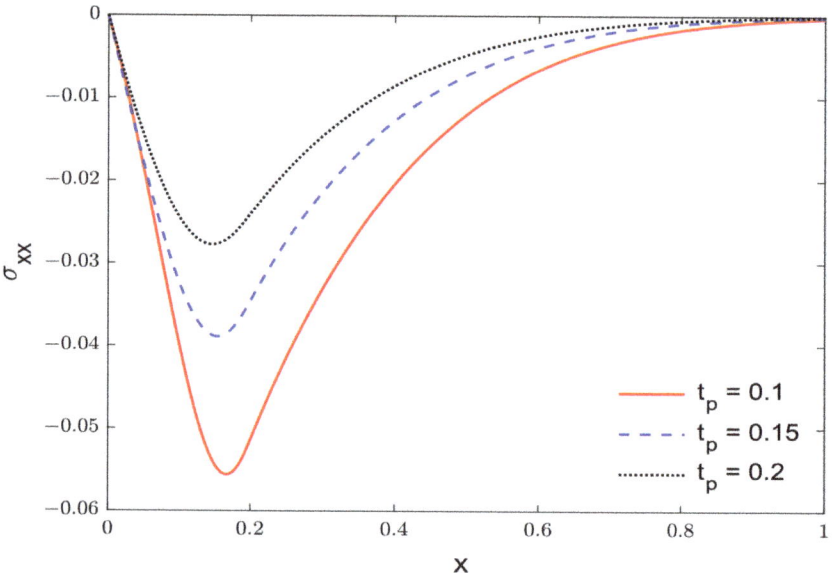

Figure 12. The variations of stress σ_{xx} via x under varying pulsing heat flux characteristic time t_p.

5. Conclusions

The aim of this research paper was to examine how biological tissues react to a sudden pulsing heat flux load by employing generalized thermo-elasticity under the fractional time derivatives framework, which incorporates one thermal relaxation time.

- This study specifically focused on the impacts of fractional parameter, thermal relaxation time, and the pulsing heat flux characteristic time on bio-thermo-elastic behaviors.
- A comparative analysis was conducted between the fractional single-phase lag model (FSPL model) and previous single-phase lag (SPL model) and Pennes (Pennes model) models.
- The findings of this study, which presented a modified thermo-elasticity approach, offered a fresh perspective on the propagation of thermal waves, representing the first attempts in this area.
- These results significantly contribute to enhancing our understanding of thermo-elastic behavior in living tissue.

Author Contributions: Conceptualization, A.H. and I.A.; methodology: A.H. and I.A.; validation: A.H. and I.A.; formal analysis: A.H. and I.A.; investigation: A.H. and I.A.; resources: I.A.; data curation: A.H. and I.A.; writing—original draft preparation: A.H. and I.A.; writing—review and editing: A.H.: visualization: I.A.; supervision: A.H. and I.A.; project administration: I.A. All authors have read and agreed to the published version of the manuscript.

Funding: This research work was funded by Institutional Fund Projects under grant no. (IFPIP: 93-130-1443). The authors gratefully acknowledge the technical and financial support provided by the Ministry of Education and King Abdulaziz University, DSR, Jeddah, Saudi Arabia.

Institutional Review Board Statement: Not applicable.

Informed Consent Statement: Not applicable.

Data Availability Statement: Not applicable.

Conflicts of Interest: The authors declare no conflict of interest.

References

1. Pennes, H.H. Analysis of tissue and arterial blood temperatures in the resting human forearm. *J. Appl. Physiol.* **1948**, *1*, 93–122. [CrossRef] [PubMed]
2. Gabay, I.; Abergel, A.; Vasilyev, T.; Rabi, Y.; Fliss, D.M.; Katzir, A. Temperature-controlled two-wavelength laser soldering of tissues. *Lasers Surg. Med.* **2011**, *43*, 907–913. [CrossRef] [PubMed]
3. Zhou, J.; Chen, J.; Zhang, Y. Dual-phase lag effects on thermal damage to biological tissues caused by laser irradiation. *Comput. Biol. Med.* **2009**, *39*, 286–293. [CrossRef] [PubMed]
4. Mahjoob, S.; Vafai, K. Analytical characterization of heat transport through biological media incorporating hyperthermia treatment. *Int. J. Heat Mass Transf.* **2009**, *52*, 1608–1618. [CrossRef]
5. Gupta, P.K.; Singh, J.; Rai, K. Numerical simulation for heat transfer in tissues during thermal therapy. *J. Therm. Biol.* **2010**, *35*, 295–301. [CrossRef]
6. Kumar, P.; Kumar, D.; Rai, K. A numerical study on dual-phase-lag model of bio-heat transfer during hyperthermia treatment. *J. Therm. Biol.* **2015**, *49*, 98–105. [CrossRef]
7. Yadav, S.; Kumar, D.; Rai, K.N. Finite Element Legendre Wavelet Galerkin Approch to Inward Solidification in Simple Body under Most Generalized Boundary Condition. *Z. Nat. A* **2014**, *69*, 501–510. [CrossRef]
8. Gupta, P.K.; Singh, J.; Rai, K.; Rai, S. Solution of the heat transfer problem in tissues during hyperthermia by finite difference–decomposition method. *Appl. Math. Comput.* **2013**, *219*, 6882–6892. [CrossRef]
9. Dillenseger, J.-L.; Esneault, S. Fast FFT-based bioheat transfer equation computation. *Comput. Biol. Med.* **2010**, *40*, 119–123. [CrossRef]
10. Ghanmi, A.; Abbas, I.A. An analytical study on the fractional transient heating within the skin tissue during the thermal therapy. *J. Therm. Biol.* **2019**, *82*, 229–233. [CrossRef]
11. Marin, M.; Hobiny, A.; Abbas, I. Finite element analysis of nonlinear bioheat model in skin tissue due to external thermal sources. *Mathematics* **2021**, *9*, 1459. [CrossRef]
12. Hobiny, A.; Abbas, I. Analytical solutions of fractional bioheat model in a spherical tissue. *Mech. Based Des. Struct. Mach.* **2021**, *49*, 430–439. [CrossRef]
13. Keangin, P.; Rattanadecho, P. Analysis of heat transport on local thermal non-equilibrium in porous liver during microwave ablation. *Int. J. Heat Mass Transf.* **2013**, *67*, 46–60. [CrossRef]
14. Keangin, P.; Wessapan, T.; Rattanadecho, P. Analysis of heat transfer in deformed liver cancer modeling treated using a microwave coaxial antenna. *Appl. Therm. Eng.* **2011**, *31*, 3243–3254. [CrossRef]

15. Andreozzi, A.; Iasiello, M.; Netti, P. Effects of pulsating heat source on interstitial fluid transport in tumour tissues. *J. R. Soc. Interface* **2020**, *17*, 20200612. [CrossRef]
16. Ezzat, M.A.; AlSowayan, N.S.; Al-Muhiameed, Z.I.; Ezzat, S.M. Fractional modelling of Pennes' bioheat transfer equation. *Heat Mass Transf.* **2014**, *50*, 907–914. [CrossRef]
17. Ezzat, M.A.; El-bary, A.A.; Al-sowayan, N.S. Tissue responses to fractional transient heating with sinusoidal heat flux condition on skin surface. *Anim. Sci. J.* **2016**, *87*, 1304–1311. [CrossRef]
18. Mondal, S.; Sur, A.; Kanoria, M. Transient heating within skin tissue due to time-dependent thermal therapy in the context of memory dependent heat transport law. *Mech. Based Des. Struct. Mach.* **2019**, *49*, 271–285. [CrossRef]
19. Andreozzi, A.; Brunese, L.; Iasiello, M.; Tucci, C.; Vanoli, G.P. Modeling Heat Transfer in Tumors: A Review of Thermal Therapies. *Ann. Biomed. Eng.* **2019**, *47*, 676–693. [CrossRef]
20. Lord, H.W.; Shulman, Y. A generalized dynamical theory of thermoelasticity. *J. Mech. Phys. Solids* **1967**, *15*, 299–309. [CrossRef]
21. Sur, A.; Mondal, S.; Kanoria, M. Influence of Moving Heat Source on Skin Tissue in the Context of Two-Temperature Caputo–Fabrizio Heat Transport Law. *J. Multiscale Model.* **2019**, *11*, 2050002. [CrossRef]
22. Díaz, S.H.; Nelson, J.S.; Wong, B.J. Rate process analysis of thermal damage in cartilage. *Phys. Med. Biol.* **2002**, *48*, 19. [CrossRef] [PubMed]
23. Ghazanfarian, J.; Saghatchi, R.; Patil, D. Implementation of Smoothed-Particle Hydrodynamics for non-linear Pennes' bioheat transfer equation. *Appl. Math. Comput.* **2015**, *259*, 21–31. [CrossRef]
24. Li, L.; Liang, M.; Yu, B.; Yang, S. Analysis of thermal conductivity in living biological tissue with vascular network and convection. *Int. J. Therm. Sci.* **2014**, *86*, 219–226. [CrossRef]
25. Selvi, C.; Srinivas, A.; Sreenadh, S. Peristaltic transport of a power-law fluid in an elastic tube. *J. Taibah Univ. Sci.* **2018**, *12*, 687–698. [CrossRef]
26. Khan, A.A.; Bukhari, S.R.; Marin, M.; Ellahi, R. Effects of chemical reaction on third-grade MHD fluid flow under the influence of heat and mass transfer with variable reactive index. *Heat Transf. Res.* **2019**, *50*, 1061–1080. [CrossRef]
27. Lata, P.; Himanshi. Orthotropic magneto-thermoelastic solid with higher order dual-phase-lag model in frequency domain. *Struct. Eng. Mech.* **2021**, *77*, 315–327. [CrossRef]
28. Abbas, I.A. A GN model for thermoelastic interaction in an unbounded fiber-reinforced anisotropic medium with a circular hole. *Appl. Math. Lett.* **2013**, *26*, 232–239. [CrossRef]
29. Abbas, I.A. Analytical solution for a free vibration of a thermoelastic hollow sphere. *Mech. Based Des. Struct. Mach.* **2015**, *43*, 265–276. [CrossRef]
30. Hobiny, A.; Abbas, I. A GN model on photothermal interactions in a two-dimensions semiconductor half space. *Results Phys.* **2019**, *15*, 102588. [CrossRef]
31. Marin, M.; Ellahi, R.; Vlase, S.; Bhatti, M. On the decay of exponential type for the solutions in a dipolar elastic body. *J. Taibah Univ. Sci.* **2020**, *14*, 534–540. [CrossRef]
32. Abo-Dahab, S.M.; Abouelregal, A.E.; Marin, M. Generalized thermoelastic functionally graded on a thin slim strip non-Gaussian laser beam. *Symmetry* **2020**, *12*, 1094. [CrossRef]
33. Alzahrani, F.; Hobiny, A.; Abbas, I.; Marin, M. An Eigenvalues Approach for a Two-Dimensional Porous Medium Based upon Weak, Normal and Strong Thermal Conductivities. *Symmetry* **2020**, *12*, 848. [CrossRef]
34. Li, X.; Li, C.; Xue, Z.; Tian, X. Analytical study of transient thermo-mechanical responses of dual-layer skin tissue with variable thermal material properties. *Int. J. Therm. Sci.* **2018**, *124*, 459–466. [CrossRef]
35. Li, X.; Xue, Z.; Tian, X. A modified fractional order generalized bio-thermoelastic theory with temperature-dependent thermal material properties. *Int. J. Therm. Sci.* **2018**, *132*, 249–256. [CrossRef]
36. Li, X.; Li, C.; Xue, Z.; Tian, X. Investigation of transient thermo-mechanical responses on the triple-layered skin tissue with temperature dependent blood perfusion rate. *Int. J. Therm. Sci.* **2019**, *139*, 339–349. [CrossRef]
37. Xu, F.; Seffen, K.; Lu, T. Non-Fourier analysis of skin biothermomechanics. *Int. J. Heat Mass Transf.* **2008**, *51*, 2237–2259. [CrossRef]
38. Ahmadikia, H.; Fazlali, R.; Moradi, A. Analytical solution of the parabolic and hyperbolic heat transfer equations with constant and transient heat flux conditions on skin tissue. *Int. Commun. Heat Mass Transf.* **2012**, *39*, 121–130. [CrossRef]
39. Abbas, I.A. Eigenvalue approach on fractional order theory of thermoelastic diffusion problem for an infinite elastic medium with a spherical cavity. *Appl. Math. Model.* **2015**, *39*, 6196–6206. [CrossRef]
40. Othman, M.I.A.; Abbas, I.A. Eigenvalue approach for generalized thermoelastic porous medium under the effect of thermal loading due to a laser pulse in DPL model. *Indian J. Phys.* **2019**, *93*, 1567–1578. [CrossRef]
41. Kumar, R.; Miglani, A.; Rani, R. Eigenvalue formulation to micropolar porous thermoelastic circular plate using dual phase lag model. *Multidiscip. Model. Mater. Struct.* **2017**, *13*, 347–362. [CrossRef]
42. Kumar, R.; Miglani, A.; Rani, R. Analysis of micropolar porous thermoelastic circular plate by eigenvalue approach. *Arch. Mech.* **2016**, *68*, 423–439.
43. Gupta, N.D.; Das, N.C. Eigenvalue approach to fractional order generalized thermoelasticity with line heat source in an infinite medium. *J. Therm. Stress.* **2016**, *39*, 977–990. [CrossRef]
44. Santra, S.; Lahiri, A.; Das, N.C. Eigenvalue Approach on Thermoelastic Interactions in an Infinite Elastic Solid with Voids. *J. Therm. Stress.* **2014**, *37*, 440–454. [CrossRef]

45. Baksi, A.; Roy, B.K.; Bera, R.K. Eigenvalue approach to study the effect of rotation and relaxation time in generalized magneto-thermo-viscoelastic medium in one dimension. *Math. Comput. Model.* **2006**, *44*, 1069–1079. [CrossRef]
46. Das, N.C.; Lahiri, A.; Giri, R.R. Eigenvalue approach to generalized thermoelasticity. *Indian J. Pure Appl. Math.* **1997**, *28*, 1573–1594.
47. Abbas, I.A.; Abdalla, A.-E.-N.N.; Alzahrani, F.S.; Spagnuolo, M. Wave propagation in a generalized thermoelastic plate using eigenvalue approach. *J. Therm. Stress.* **2016**, *39*, 1367–1377. [CrossRef]
48. Abbas, I.; Hobiny, A.; Marin, M. Photo-thermal interactions in a semi-conductor material with cylindrical cavities and variable thermal conductivity. *J. Taibah Univ. Sci.* **2020**, *14*, 1369–1376. [CrossRef]
49. Stehfest, H. Algorithm 368: Numerical inversion of Laplace transforms [D5]. *Commun. ACM* **1970**, *13*, 47–49. [CrossRef]

Disclaimer/Publisher's Note: The statements, opinions and data contained in all publications are solely those of the individual author(s) and contributor(s) and not of MDPI and/or the editor(s). MDPI and/or the editor(s) disclaim responsibility for any injury to people or property resulting from any ideas, methods, instructions or products referred to in the content.

Article

Combined Liouville–Caputo Fractional Differential Equation

McSylvester Ejighikeme Omaba *, Hamdan Al Sulaimani, Soh Edwin Mukiawa, Cyril Dennis Enyi and Tijani Abdul-Aziz Apalara

Department of Mathematics, College of Science, University of Hafr Al Batin, P.O. Box 1803, Hafr Al Batin 31991, Saudi Arabia
* Correspondence: mcomaba@uhb.edu.sa

Abstract: This paper studies a fractional differential equation combined with a Liouville–Caputo fractional differential operator, namely, ${}^{LC}\mathcal{D}_\eta^{\beta,\gamma} Q(t) = \lambda \vartheta(t, Q(t))$, $t \in [c,d]$, $\beta, \gamma \in (0,1]$, $\eta \in [0,1]$, where $Q(c) = q_c$ is a bounded and non-negative initial value. The function $\vartheta : [c,d] \times \mathbb{R} \to \mathbb{R}$ is Lipschitz continuous in the second variable, $\lambda > 0$ is a constant and the operator ${}^{LC}\mathcal{D}_\eta^{\beta,\gamma}$ is a convex combination of the left and the right Liouville–Caputo fractional derivatives. We study the well-posedness using the fixed-point theorem, estimate the growth bounds of the solution and examine the asymptotic behaviours of the solutions. Our findings are illustrated with some analytical and numerical examples. Furthermore, we investigate the effect of noise on the growth behaviour of the solution to the combined Liouville–Caputo fractional differential equation.

Keywords: well-posedness; growth estimate; asymptotic behaviours; combined Liouville–Caputo fractional derivative; numerical simulations; stochastic models; second moment bound

Citation: Omaba, M.E.; Al Sulaimani, H.; Mukiawa, S.E.; Enyi, C.D.; Apalara, T.A.-A. Combined Liouville–Caputo Fractional Differential Equation. *Fractal Fract.* **2023**, *7*, 366. https://doi.org/10.3390/fractalfract7050366

Academic Editors: Hari Mohan Srivastava, Riccardo Caponetto and Sameerah Jamal

Received: 28 January 2023
Revised: 4 March 2023
Accepted: 29 March 2023
Published: 28 April 2023

Copyright: © 2023 by the authors. Licensee MDPI, Basel, Switzerland. This article is an open access article distributed under the terms and conditions of the Creative Commons Attribution (CC BY) license (https://creativecommons.org/licenses/by/4.0/).

1. Introduction

Fractional-order derivatives are known to give more accurate and realistic mathematical models when compared to the classical-order models. The Liouville–Caputo fractional derivative is unarguably a useful operator that mostly models nonlocal behaviours by fractional DEs [1]. The Liouville–Caputo fractional derivative and others alike have found applications in different science and engineering fields and have been used to model many real-life problems. For example, they are used in the mathematical modelling of a human brain tissue (HBT) constitutive model in the framework of anisotropic hyperelasticity [2]; modelling the growth of many economical processes, specifically memory effect on the economic growth model, that is, in the application of economic growth models with memory effect [3] in physics and the environment; studying the chaotic behaviour(s) of dynamical systems; and developing the fractional-order models of neurons [4] and porous media, among others. See also [5,6] for other fractional models. It is worthy of note that all of the above fractional differential equations and more studied in the literature make use of one-sided (left- or right-sided) fractional derivative operators.

The new operator is a convex combination of left and right Liouville–Caputo fractional operators. There is little that one can find in the literature regarding this combined fractional derivative operators. Importantly, this new combined fractional operator is more general than other fractional derivatives [7]. The new operators were studied and defined by Malinowska and Torres [7] as follows:

$${}^{LC}\mathcal{D}_\eta^{\beta,\gamma} = \eta \, {}^{LC}_c\mathcal{D}_t^\beta + (1-\eta) \, {}^{LC}_t\mathcal{D}_d^\gamma, \; \beta, \gamma \in (0,1] \, \& \, \eta \in [0,1], \qquad (1)$$

where

$${}^{LC}\mathcal{D}_0^{\beta,\gamma} Q(t) = {}^{LC}_t\mathcal{D}_d^\gamma Q(t),$$

and

$${}^{LC}\mathcal{D}_1^{\beta,\gamma} Q(t) = {}^{LC}_c\mathcal{D}_t^\beta Q(t).$$

Another advantage of this new fractional derivative $^{LC}\mathcal{D}_\eta^{\beta,\gamma}$ is that it can describe variational problems in a broad perspective [7]. By drawing inspirations from the diamond-alpha derivative on a time scale, which is a linear combination of the delta and nabla derivatives [8–10], the model (1) was birthed. Malinowska and Torres [8] showed that the approximation of exact derivatives by the diamond-alpha derivative was better that those of the delta and nabla derivatives.

Therefore, this research considered a special operator by studying the combined Liouville–Caputo fractional differential equation as follows:

$$^{LC}\mathcal{D}_\eta^{\beta,\gamma} Q(t) = \lambda \vartheta(t, Q(t)), \quad \beta, \gamma \in (0,1] \ \& \ \eta \in [0,1], \tag{2}$$

where $Q(c) = q_c$ is the initial condition, $\vartheta : [c,d] \times \mathbb{R} \to \mathbb{R}$ is Lipschitz in the second variable, $\lambda > 0$ and $^{LC}\mathcal{D}_\eta^{\beta,\gamma}$ is known as the combined Liouville–Caputo fractional derivative operator. The operator $^{LC}\mathcal{D}_\eta^{\beta,\gamma}$ is a convex combination of left and right Liouville–Caputo fractional derivatives. Thus, our contribution and aim in this research paper was to examine the qualitative properties, the well-posedness, estimates of the growth bounds, and the asymptotic behaviour of the solution to a class of combined fractional differential equations.

The organization of the paper is as follows. Section 2 contains the preliminary concepts and definitions needed in the article; Section 3 contains the main results—existence, uniqueness, upper growth estimate, asymptotic behaviour of solution to the combined L–C fractional differential equation. Numerical and analytical illustration of our results are given in Section 4. In Section 5, we consider the stochastic (non-deterministic) case of our equation. Summary of the paper is given in Section 6.

2. Preliminary Concepts

Here, we give some definitions and basic materials. Readers can refer to [5] for further materials on fractional calculus.

Definition 1 ([7]). *For $\beta, \gamma \in (0,1)$ and $0 \leq \eta \leq 1$, the combined Liouville–Caputo fractional derivative operator $^{LC}\mathcal{D}_\eta^{\beta,\gamma}$ is a convex combination of left and right Liouville–Caputo fractional derivatives, defined by*

$$^{LC}\mathcal{D}_\eta^{\beta,\gamma} = \eta \, _c^{LC}\mathcal{D}_t^\beta + (1-\eta) \, _t^{LC}\mathcal{D}_d^\gamma.$$

Definition 2 ([11]). *Let $0 < c < d$ and $f : [c,d] \to \mathbb{R}$ be an integrable function. The left-sided Katugampola fractional integral of order $\beta > 0$ and parameter $\sigma > 0$ is given by*

$$\mathcal{I}_{c+}^{\beta,\sigma} u(t) = \frac{\sigma^{1-\beta}}{\Gamma(\beta)} \int_c^t s^{\sigma-1} (t^\sigma - s^\sigma)^{\sigma-1} u(s) ds,$$

provided the integral converges.

For $\sigma = 1$, we define the fractional integral as follows.

Definition 3 ([11]). *Let $u : [c,d] \to \mathbb{R}$ be an integrable function where $c,d > 0$ with $c < d$. Then,*

$$_c\mathcal{I}_t^\beta u(t) = \frac{1}{\Gamma(\beta)} \int_c^t (t-s)^{\beta-1} u(s) ds, \tag{3}$$

is the left-sided Riemann–Liouville fractional integral of u of order $0 < \beta < 1$, provided the integral converges.

Definition 4 ([5]). *Let $u : [c,d] \to \mathbb{R}$, then*

$$_c\mathcal{D}_t^\beta u(t) = \frac{1}{\Gamma(1-\beta)} \frac{d}{dt} \int_c^t (t-s)^{-\beta} u(s) ds,$$

is the Riemann–Liouville fractional derivative of u of order $0 < \beta < 1$ provided the integral converges.

Definition 5 ([11]). *Let $c, d > 0$ with $c < d$, $\sigma > 0$, $\beta \in \mathbb{R}^+$ and $m \in \mathbb{N}$ satisfying $m - 1 < \beta < m$. Let $u : [c, d] \to \mathbb{R}$ be a C^m-function. Then,*

$$^C\mathcal{D}_{c^+}^{\beta,\sigma} u(t) = \mathcal{I}_{c^+}^{\beta,\sigma}\left(t^{1-\sigma}\frac{d}{dt}\right)^m u(t) = \frac{\sigma^{1-m+\beta}}{\Gamma(m-\beta)}\int_c^t s^{\sigma-1}(t^\sigma - s^\sigma)^{\beta-1}\left(t^{1-\sigma}\frac{d}{ds}\right)^m u(s)ds$$

is the left-sided Caputo–Katugampola fractional derivative of u of order β and parameter σ.

For $\sigma = 1$ and $m = 1$, we define the Liouville–Caputo fractional derivative as follows.

Definition 6. *Given $c, d > 0$ with $c < d$, $\beta \in \mathbb{R}^+$ so that $0 < \beta < 1$, and a C^1-function $u : [c, d] \to \mathbb{R}$. The left-sided Liouville–Caputo fractional derivative of order β is given by*

$$_c^{LC}\mathcal{D}_t^\beta u(t) = \frac{1}{\Gamma(1-\beta)} \int_c^t (t-s)^{-\beta} u'(s) ds,$$

provided that the integral converges. Similarly, the right-sided Liouville–Caputo fractional derivative of order γ is given by

$$_t^{LC}\mathcal{D}_d^\gamma u(t) = \frac{1}{\Gamma(1-\beta)} \int_t^d (s-t)^{-\gamma} u'(s) ds,$$

provided that the integral converges.

Lemma 1 ([12]). *The Liouville–Caputo derivative is connected to the Riemann–Liouville derivatives by*

$$_c^{LC}\mathcal{D}_t^\beta u(t) = {_c\mathcal{D}_t^\beta} u(t) - \sum_{k=0}^{m-1} \frac{(t-c)^{k-\beta}}{\Gamma(k-\beta+1)} u^{(k)}(c), \quad m - 1 < \beta \leq m.$$

In particular, when $m = 1$, one obtains

$$_c^{LC}\mathcal{D}_t^\beta u(t) = {_c\mathcal{D}_t^\beta} u(t) - \frac{(t-c)^{-\beta}}{\Gamma(1-\beta)} u(c).$$

Suppose the function $u : [c, d] \to \mathbb{R}$ is defined as $u(t) = t^a$. Then,

$$_c\mathcal{D}_t^\beta u(t) = \frac{\Gamma(a+1)}{\Gamma(a-\beta+1)} t^{a-\beta}.$$

Theorem 1 ([11]). *Suppose $u \in C^m[c, d]$, then for $m - 1 < \beta \leq m$, $0 < \sigma \leq 1$*

$$\mathcal{I}_{c^+}^{\beta,\sigma} {^C\mathcal{D}_{c^+}^{\beta,\sigma}} u(t) = u(t) - \sum_{k=0}^{m-1} \frac{\sigma^{-k}}{k!}(t^\sigma - c^\sigma)^k u_{(k)}(c).$$

Note that if $u \in C^1[c, d]$ and $\sigma = 1$, then

$$\mathcal{I}_{c^+}^\beta {^{LC}\mathcal{D}_{c^+}^\beta} u(t) = u(t) - u(c).$$

Thus,

Corollary 1. *Suppose $u \in C^1[c, d]$, $0 < \beta \leq 1$ and $\sigma = 1$, we have*

$$_c\mathcal{I}_t^\beta {_c^{LC}\mathcal{D}_t^\beta} u(t) = u(t) - u(c). \qquad (4)$$

The next result is a formula for the generalized fractional integration by parts:

Theorem 2 ([11]). *Suppose $u \in C[c,d]$ and $v \in C^m[c,d]$. Then, for $m-1 < \beta \leq m$, $0 < \sigma \leq 1$,*

$$\int_c^d u(t)\,^C\mathcal{D}_{c+}^{\beta,\sigma} v(t)dt = \int_c^d t^{\sigma-1} v(t) \mathcal{D}_{d-}^{\beta,\sigma}(t^{1-\sigma}) u(t) dt$$
$$+ \left[\sum_{j=0}^{m-1} \left(-t^{1-\sigma}\frac{d}{dt} \right)^j \mathcal{I}_{d-}^{m-\beta,\sigma}(t^{1-\beta}u(t)) v_{(m-j-1)}(t) \right]_{t=c}^{t=d}.$$

Particularly for $m=1$ and $\sigma = 1$, we have

$$\int_c^d u(t)\,^{LC}\mathcal{D}_{c+}^{\beta} v(t) dt = \int_c^d v(t)\mathcal{D}_{d-}^{\beta} u(t) dt.$$

Therefore,

Corollary 2. *Suppose $u \in C[c,d]$ and $v \in C^1[c,d]$, then for $0 < \gamma \leq 1$ and $\sigma = 1$,*

$$\int_c^d u(t)\,^{LC}_t\mathcal{D}_d^{\gamma} v(t) dt = \int_c^d v(t)\,_c\mathcal{D}_t^{\gamma} u(t) dt. \qquad (5)$$

Formulation of the Solution

Here, we apply the properties or relationship between the fractional integral and fractional differential operators in Equation (4) to make sense of the solution to problem (2).

Lemma 2. *Let $\eta \in (0,1]$. Then, the solution to fractional differential Equation (2) is defined as*

$$Q(t) = q_c + \frac{1-\eta}{\eta\Gamma(\beta-\gamma)} \int_c^t (t-s)^{\beta-\gamma-1} Q(s) ds + \frac{\lambda}{\eta\Gamma(\beta)} \int_c^t (t-s)^{\beta-1} \vartheta(s,Q(s)) ds.$$

Proof. The application of the integral operator $_c\mathcal{I}_t^\beta$ to Equation (2) on both sides gives

$$_c\mathcal{I}_t^\beta \left[{}^{LC}\mathcal{D}_\eta^{\beta,\gamma} Q(t) \right] = \lambda \,_c\mathcal{I}_t^\beta [\vartheta(t,Q(t))].$$

That is,

$$_c\mathcal{I}_t^\beta \left[\eta \,^{LC}_c\mathcal{D}_t^\beta Q(t) + (1-\eta) \,^{LC}_t\mathcal{D}_d^\gamma Q(t) \right] = \lambda \,_c\mathcal{I}_t^\beta [\vartheta(t,Q(t))].$$

By the linearity of the operator $_c\mathcal{I}_t^\beta$, we have

$$\eta \,_c\mathcal{I}_t^\beta \,^{LC}_c\mathcal{D}_t^\beta Q(t) + (1-\eta) \,_c\mathcal{I}_t^\beta \,^{LC}_t\mathcal{D}_d^\gamma Q(t) = \lambda \,_c\mathcal{I}_t^\beta [\vartheta(t,Q(t))].$$

From Equation (4) in Corollary 1 and Equation (3), we get

$$\eta[Q(t) - q_c] + \frac{1-\eta}{\Gamma(\beta)} \int_c^t (t-s)^{\beta-1} \,^{LC}_s\mathcal{D}_d^\gamma Q(s) ds = \frac{\lambda}{\Gamma(\beta)} \int_c^t (t-s)^{\beta-1} \vartheta(s,Q(s)) ds.$$

By Equation (5) in Corollary 2, we obtain

$$\eta[Q(t) - q_c] + \frac{1-\eta}{\Gamma(\beta)} \int_c^t Q(s) \,_c\mathcal{D}_s^\gamma [(t-s)^{\beta-1}] ds = \frac{\lambda}{\Gamma(\beta)} \int_c^t (t-s)^{\beta-1} \vartheta(s,Q(s)) ds. \qquad (6)$$

The derivative $_c\mathcal{D}_s^\gamma\left((t-s)^{\beta-1}\right)$ is evaluated as,

$$_c\mathcal{D}_s^\gamma\left((t-s)^{\beta-1}\right) = -\frac{\Gamma(\beta-1+1)}{\Gamma(\beta-1-\gamma+1)}(t-s)^{\beta-\gamma-1} = -\frac{\Gamma(\beta)}{\Gamma(\beta-\gamma)}(t-s)^{\beta-\gamma-1}.$$

101

From Equation (6), one gets

$$\eta[Q(t) - q_c] - \frac{1-\eta}{\Gamma(\beta-\gamma)} \int_c^t (t-s)^{\beta-\gamma-1} Q(s) ds = \frac{\lambda}{\Gamma(\beta)} \int_c^t (t-s)^{\beta-1} \vartheta(s, Q(s)) ds.$$

Thus, for $\eta \in (0,1]$, one obtains

$$Q(t) = q_c + \frac{1-\eta}{\eta\Gamma(\beta-\gamma)} \int_c^t (t-s)^{\beta-\gamma-1} Q(s) ds + \frac{\lambda}{\eta\Gamma(\beta)} \int_c^t (t-s)^{\beta-1} \vartheta(s, Q(s)) ds.$$

□

The following sup-norm on Q defined by

$$\|Q\| := \sup_{c \le t \le d} |Q(t)|,$$

is useful in the next section.

3. Main Results

The following global Lipschitz condition on the function $\vartheta(., Q)$ with respect to the second variable is important for establishing our main result.

Condition 1. *Suppose $0 < \text{Lip}_\vartheta < \infty$, $t \in [c,d]$ and $\forall Q, R \in \mathbb{R}$, we assume*

$$|\vartheta(t, Q) - \vartheta(t, R)| \le \text{Lip}_\vartheta |Q - R|. \tag{7}$$

For convenience, we shall set $\vartheta(t, 0) = 0$ in our computations.

3.1. Well-Posedness

Here, we apply the Banach's fixed-point theorem to prove the existence and uniqueness of the solution to our problem (2). We begin by defining the operator

$$\mathcal{A}Q(t) = q_c + \frac{1-\eta}{\eta\Gamma(\beta-\gamma)} \int_c^t (t-s)^{\beta-\gamma-1} Q(s) ds + \frac{\lambda}{\eta\Gamma(\beta)} \int_c^t (t-s)^{\beta-1} \vartheta(s, Q(s)) ds, \tag{8}$$

and show that $\mathcal{A}$ has a unique fixed point which gives the solution to problem (2).

Lemma 3. *Suppose Q is a solution to problem (2) and Condition 1 holds. Then, for $0 < \gamma < \beta < 1$ and $\eta \in (0,1]$, we have*

$$\|\mathcal{A}Q\| \le q_c + c_1 \|Q\|, \tag{9}$$

with positive constant

$$c_1 := \left[\frac{1-\eta}{\eta\Gamma(\beta-\gamma+1)} (d-c)^{\beta-\gamma} + \frac{\lambda \text{Lip}_\vartheta}{\eta\Gamma(\beta+1)} (d-c)^\beta \right] < \infty.$$

Proof. Taking the absolute value of Equation (8) leads to

$$|\mathcal{A}Q(t)| \le q_c + \frac{1-\eta}{\eta\Gamma(\beta-\gamma)} \int_c^t (t-s)^{\beta-\gamma-1} |Q(s)| ds + \frac{\lambda}{\eta\Gamma(\beta)} \int_c^t (t-s)^{\beta-1} |\vartheta(s, Q(s))| ds.$$

Applying Equation (7) of Condition 1, we have

$$|\mathcal{A}Q(t)| \le q_c + \frac{1-\eta}{\eta\Gamma(\beta-\gamma)}\int_c^t (t-s)^{\beta-\gamma-1}|Q(s)|ds + \frac{\lambda\mathrm{Lip}_\vartheta}{\eta\Gamma(\beta)}\int_c^t (t-s)^{\beta-1}|Q(s)|ds$$

$$\le q_c + \frac{1-\eta}{\eta\Gamma(\beta-\gamma)}\|Q\|\int_c^t (t-s)^{\beta-\gamma-1}ds + \frac{\lambda\mathrm{Lip}_\vartheta}{\eta\Gamma(\beta)}\|Q\|\int_c^t (t-s)^{\beta-1}ds$$

$$= q_c + \frac{1-\eta}{\eta\Gamma(\beta-\gamma)}\|Q\|\frac{(t-c)^{\beta-\gamma}}{\beta-\gamma} + \frac{\lambda\mathrm{Lip}_\vartheta}{\eta\Gamma(\beta)}\|Q\|\frac{(t-c)^\beta}{\beta}$$

$$= q_c + \left[\frac{1-\eta}{\eta\Gamma(\beta-\gamma+1)}(t-c)^{\beta-\gamma} + \frac{\lambda\mathrm{Lip}_\vartheta}{\eta\Gamma(\beta+1)}(t-c)^\beta\right]\|Q\|.$$

Next, we take the supremum over $t \in [c,d]$ to get

$$\|\mathcal{A}Q\| \le q_c + \left[\frac{1-\eta}{\eta\Gamma(\beta-\gamma+1)}(d-c)^{\beta-\gamma} + \frac{\lambda\mathrm{Lip}_\vartheta}{\eta\Gamma(\beta+1)}(d-c)^\beta\right]\|Q\|,$$

and the result is obtained. □

Lemma 4. *Let Condition 1 hold. Suppose Q_1 and Q_2 are two solutions of (2); for $0 < \gamma < \beta < 1$ and $\eta \in (0,1]$, we have*

$$\|\mathcal{A}Q_1 - \mathcal{A}Q_2\| \le c_1\|Q_1 - Q_2\|. \tag{10}$$

Proof. Proceeding with similar steps as in the proof of Lemma 3, we arrive at the desired result. □

Theorem 3. *Suppose Condition 1 holds, $0 < \gamma < \beta < 1$ and $\eta \in (0,1]$. There exists a constant $0 < c_1 < 1$ such that Equation (2) possesses a unique solution.*

Proof. Applying the Banach fixed point theorem gives $Q(t) = \mathcal{A}Q(t)$. It follows from Equation (9) in Lemma 3 that

$$\|Q\| = \|\mathcal{A}Q\| \le q_c + c_1\|Q\|.$$

This gives $\|Q\|[1 - c_1] \le q_c$ and therefore, $\|Q\| < \infty$ whenever $c_1 < 1$.

Next, suppose for a contradiction that $Q_1 \ne Q_2$ are solutions of Equation (2). Then, from Equation (10) of Lemma 4, we have

$$\|Q_1 - Q_2\| = \|\mathcal{A}Q_1 - \mathcal{A}Q_2\| \le c_1\|Q_1 - Q_2\|.$$

Therefore, $\|Q_1 - Q_2\|[1 - c_1] \le 0$. However, $1 - c_1 > 0$, therefore $\|Q_1 - Q_2\| < 0$. This is a contradiction, hence $\|Q_1 - Q_2\| = 0$. By the contraction principle, the existence and uniqueness result follows. □

3.2. Upper Growth Bound

Agarwal et al. [13] presented the following retarded Gronwall type inequality:

$$u(t) \le f(t) + \sum_{i=1}^n \int_{r_i(t_0)}^{r_i(t)} h_i(t,s)w_i(u(s))ds, \quad t_0 \le t < t_1. \tag{11}$$

Theorem 4 (Theorem 2.1 of [13]). *Assume the hypotheses of (Theorem 2.1 of [13]) hold and $u(t)$ is a non-negative continuous function on $[t_0, t_1)$ satisfying (11). Then,*

$$u(t) \le X_n^{-1}\left[X_n(q_n(t)) + \int_{r_n(t_0)}^{r_n(t)} \max_{t_0 \le \tau \le t} h_n(\tau,s)ds\right], \quad t_0 \le t \le T_1,$$

103

where $q_n(t)$ is determined recursively by

$$q_1(t) := f(t_0) + \int_{t_0}^{t} |f'(s)| ds,$$

$$q_{i+1} := X_i^{-1}\left[X_i(q_i(t)) + \int_{r_i(t_0)}^{r_i(t)} \max_{t_0 \leq \tau \leq t} h_i(\tau, s) ds\right], \ i = 1, \ldots, n-1,$$

and $X_i(\tau, \tau_i) := \int_{\tau_i}^{\tau} \frac{d\omega}{w_i(\omega)}$.

Remark 1. For the case $n = 2$, if

$$u(t) \leq f(t) + \int_{r_1(t_0)}^{r_1(t)} h_1(t,s) w_1(u(s)) ds + \int_{r_2(t_0)}^{r_2(t)} h_2(t,s) w_2(u(s)) ds,$$

then

$$u(t) \leq X_2^{-1}\left[X_2(q_2(t)) + \int_{r_2(t_0)}^{r_2(t)} \max_{t_0 \leq \tau \leq t} h_2(\tau, s) ds\right],$$

with $q_2(t) = X_1^{-1}\left[X_1(r_1(t)) + \int_{r_1(t_0)}^{r_1(t)} \max_{t_0 \leq \tau \leq t} h_1(\tau, s) ds\right]$.

Here, we take $w_i(u(s)) = u(s)$, $r_i(t_0) = t_0 = c$, and $r_i(t) = t$ for $i = 1, 2$.

Consequently, we present the upper growth bound estimate for the solution.

Theorem 5. Assume Condition 1 holds. Then, $\forall t \in [c,d]$, $0 < c < d$, and $c_2, c_3 > 0$, we have

$$|Q(t)| \leq \frac{q_c}{\exp\left(c_2(c-t)^{\beta-\gamma} + c_3(c-t)^{\beta}\right)},$$

with $c_2 = \frac{1-\eta}{\eta\Gamma(\beta-\gamma+1)}$, $c_3 = \frac{\lambda \text{Lip}_\vartheta}{\eta\Gamma(\beta+1)}$, for $\eta \in (0,1]$, $0 < \gamma < \beta < 1$.

Proof. We already obtained from Lemma 3 that

$$|Q(t)| \leq q_c + \frac{1-\eta}{\eta\Gamma(\beta-\gamma)} \int_c^t (t-s)^{\beta-\gamma-1} |Q(s)| ds + \frac{\lambda \text{Lip}_\vartheta}{\eta\Gamma(\beta)} \int_c^t (t-s)^{\beta-1} |Q(s)| ds.$$

Let $g(t) := |Q(t)|$, $t \in [c,d]$; it follows that

$$g(t) \leq q_c + \frac{1-\eta}{\eta\Gamma(\beta-\gamma)} \int_c^t (t-s)^{\beta-\gamma-1} g(s) ds + \frac{\lambda \text{Lip}_\vartheta}{\eta\Gamma(\beta)} \int_c^t (t-s)^{\beta-1} g(s) ds. \quad (12)$$

Applying Theorem 4 to (12), we take $w_i(\omega) = \omega$ for $i = 1, 2$ and it follows that

$$X_2(\tau, \tau_2) = \int_{\tau_2}^{\tau} \frac{d\omega}{\omega} = \ln\left(\frac{\tau}{\tau_2}\right).$$

If one takes $\tau_2 = 1$ for convenience, then $X_2(\tau) = \ln \tau$ with the inverse $X_2^{-1}(\tau) = e^{\tau}$. Similarly, $X_1(\tau) = \ln \tau$ has the inverse $X_1^{-1}(\tau) = e^{\tau}$. Moreover, $f(t) = q_c$ and $f'(t) = 0$, hence $q_1(t) = q_c$. Now, we define the non-negative functions $h_1, h_2 : [c,d] \times [c,d] \to \mathbb{R}_+$ as follows:

$$h_1(\zeta, s) := \frac{1-\eta}{\eta\Gamma(\beta-\gamma)} (\zeta-s)^{\beta-\gamma-1},$$

and
$$h_2(\zeta,s) := \frac{\lambda \text{Lip}_\vartheta}{\eta \Gamma(\beta)}(\zeta-s)^{\beta-1}.$$

Let $c \leq s < \zeta$; since $\beta - \gamma - 1 < 0$, then h_1 is decreasing and continuous, thus
$$\max_{c \leq \tau \leq t} h_1(\zeta,s) = \frac{1-\eta}{\eta \Gamma(\beta-\gamma)}(c-s)^{\beta-\gamma-1},$$

and it follows that
$$\begin{aligned}
q_2(t) &= \exp\left[\ln(q_c) + \frac{1-\eta}{\eta\Gamma(\beta-\gamma)}\int_c^t (c-s)^{\beta-\gamma-1}ds\right] \\
&= \exp\left[\ln(q_c) - \frac{1-\eta}{\eta\Gamma(\beta-\gamma)}\frac{(c-t)^{\beta-\gamma}}{\beta-\gamma}\right] \\
&= \exp\left[\ln(q_c) - \frac{1-\eta}{\eta\Gamma(\beta-\gamma+1)}(c-t)^{\beta-\gamma}\right].
\end{aligned}$$

In addition, for $c \leq s < \zeta$, and for all $\beta < 1$, h_2 is decreasing and continuous, and
$$\max_{c \leq \zeta \leq t} h_2(\zeta,s) = \frac{\lambda \text{Lip}_\vartheta}{\eta\Gamma(\beta)}(c-s)^{\beta-1}.$$

Thus,
$$\begin{aligned}
g(t) &\leq \exp\left[\ln(q_2(t)) + \frac{\lambda \text{Lip}_\vartheta}{\eta\Gamma(\beta)}\int_c^t (c-s)^{\beta-1}ds\right] \\
&= \exp\left[\ln(q_c) - \frac{1-\eta}{\eta\Gamma(\beta-\gamma+1)}(c-t)^{\beta-\gamma} - \frac{\lambda \text{Lip}_\vartheta}{\eta\Gamma(\beta)}\frac{(c-t)^\beta}{\beta}\right] \\
&= q_c \exp\left[-\frac{1-\eta}{\eta\Gamma(\beta-\gamma+1)}(c-t)^{\beta-\gamma} - \frac{\lambda \text{Lip}_\vartheta}{\eta\Gamma(\beta+1)}(c-t)^\beta\right],
\end{aligned}$$

and this completes the proof. □

3.3. Asymptotic Behaviours

Here, we show that the solution exhibits some asymptotic properties. By the growth bound in Theorem 5, we have
$$|Q(t)| \leq q_c \exp\left[-\frac{1}{\eta}\left(\frac{1-\eta}{\Gamma(\beta-\gamma+1)}(c-t)^{\beta-\gamma} + \frac{\lambda \text{Lip}_\vartheta}{\Gamma(\beta+1)}(c-t)^\beta\right)\right].$$

Now, taking the limit as $\eta \to 0$, we obtain
$$\lim_{\eta \to 0}|Q(t)| = 0.$$

Next, taking limit as $t \to c^+$, we get
$$\lim_{t \to c^+}|Q(t)| \leq q_c.$$

4. Examples

The example below illustrates Theorem 3 as follows: For $\beta = \frac{9}{10}$, $\gamma = \frac{1}{10}$, $\eta = \frac{1}{2}$, and the nonlinear Lipschitz continuous function $\vartheta : [0.01, 0.05] \times \mathbb{R} \to \mathbb{R}$ defined by

$\vartheta(t, Q(t)) = \sin(Q(t))$ having a Lipschitz constant $\text{Lip}_\vartheta = 1$, the Combined Liouville–Caputo fractional differential equation

$$\begin{cases} {}^{LC}\mathcal{D}_{\frac{1}{2}}^{\frac{9}{10}, \frac{1}{10}} Q(t) = \lambda \sin(Q(t)), & 0.01 < t \leq 0.05, \\ Q(0.01) = q_c, \end{cases}$$

has a unique solution provided by

$$c_1 := \frac{(1 - \frac{1}{2})}{\frac{1}{2}\eta(\frac{9}{10} - \frac{1}{10} + 1)}(0.04)^{0.8} + \frac{\lambda}{\frac{1}{2}\eta(\frac{9}{10} + 1)}(0.04)^{0.9} < 1,$$

if and only if $c_1 = 0.081756 + \frac{0.0551892\lambda}{0.480883} < 1$. That is, for all λ such that $0 < \lambda < 8.00099$.

Numerical Comparisons

We present numerical simulations and different plots of the upper growth bound functions $q_c \exp\left[-\frac{1}{\eta}\left(\frac{1-\eta}{\Gamma(\beta-\gamma+1)}(c-t)^{\beta-\gamma} + \frac{\lambda \text{Lip}_\vartheta}{\eta(\beta+1)}(c-t)^\beta\right)\right]$ and compare their behaviours for various values of parameters β, γ, η and λ over different time intervals. See Figures 1–6 below.

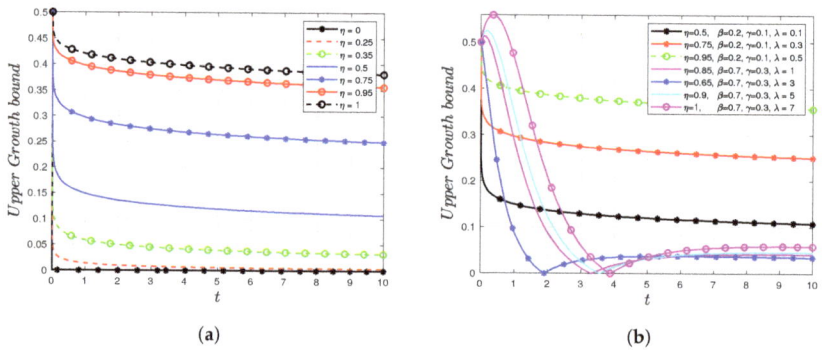

Figure 1. Behaviour of the upper growth bound for different η and λ values: (**a**) $0.01 \leq t \leq 10$, $\beta = 0.2$, $\gamma = 0.1$, $\lambda = 1$; (**b**) $0.01 \leq t \leq 10$.

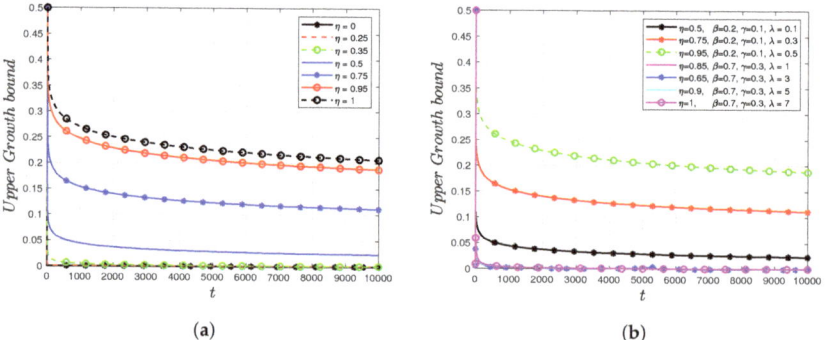

Figure 2. Behaviour of the upper growth bound for different η and λ values: (**a**) $0.01 \leq t \leq 10^4$, $\beta = 0.2$, $\gamma = 0.1$, $\lambda = 1$; (**b**) $0.01 \leq t \leq 10^4$.

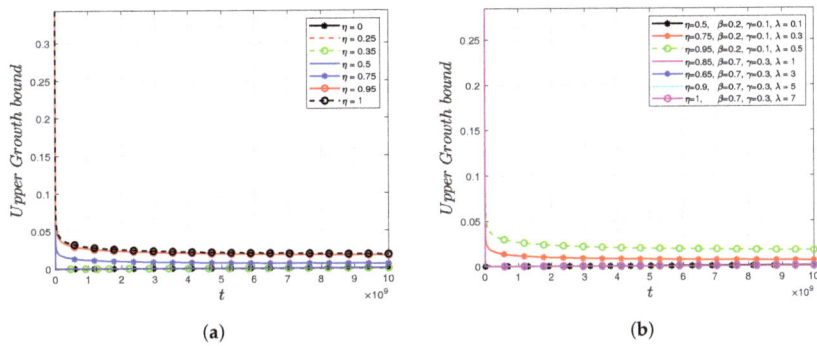

Figure 3. Behaviour of the upper growth bound for different η and λ values: (**a**) $0.01 \leq t \leq 10^{10}$, $\beta = 0.2$, $\gamma = 0.1$, $\lambda = 1$; (**b**) $0.01 \leq t \leq 10^{10}$.

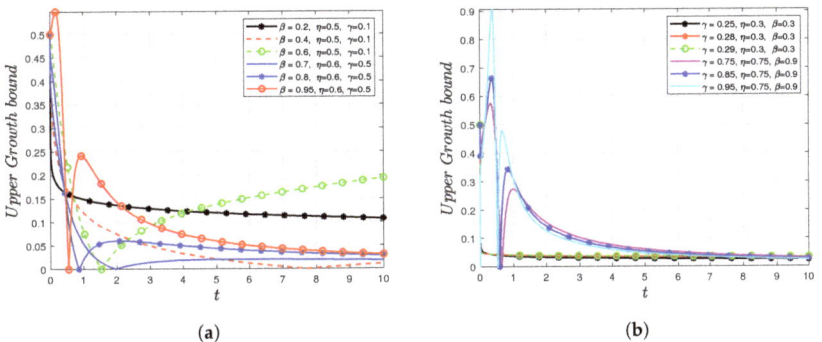

Figure 4. Behaviour of the upper growth bound for different η, β and γ values: (**a**) $0.01 \leq t \leq 10$, $\lambda = 1$; (**b**) $0.01 \leq t \leq 10$, $\lambda = 1$.

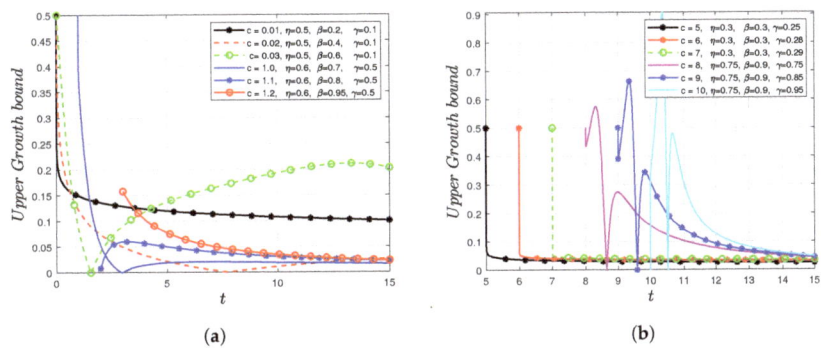

Figure 5. Behaviour of the upper growth bound for different initial points $t = c$: (**a**) $c \leq t \leq 15$, $\lambda = 1$; (**b**) $c \leq t \leq 15$, $\lambda = 1$.

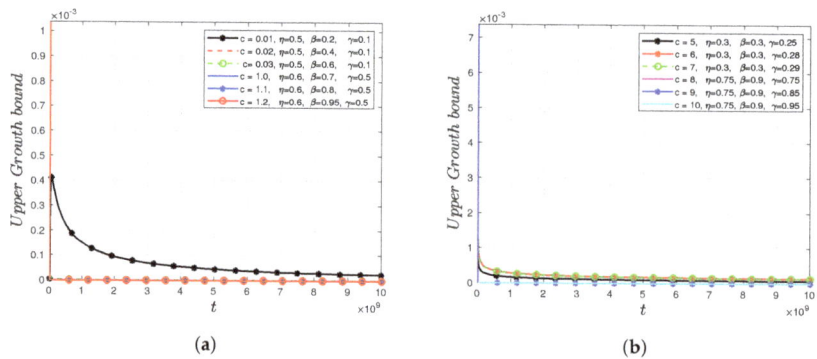

Figure 6. Behaviour of the upper growth bound for different initial points $t = c$: (**a**) $c \leq t \leq 10^{10}$, $\lambda = 1$; (**b**) $c \leq t \leq 10^{10}$, $\lambda = 1$.

5. Stochastic Combined Fractional Differential Equation

In this section, we study the effect of an external force (a noise term) on the growth behaviour of Equation (2). Thus, we perturb the combined L–C fractional differential equation with a multiplicative noise term $\dot{w}(t)$ known as the generalized derivative of a Wiener process $w(t)$ (a Gaussian white noise process) and consider the following stochastic combined L–C fractional differential equation:

$$^{LC}\mathcal{D}_{\eta}^{\beta,\gamma}\Phi(t) = \lambda \vartheta(t, \Phi(t))\dot{w}(t), \quad \beta, \gamma \in (0,1] \ \& \ \eta \in [0,1], \tag{13}$$

where $\Phi(c) = \rho_c$ is the initial condition, $\vartheta : [c,d] \times \mathbb{R} \to \mathbb{R}$ is Lipschitz in the second variable, $^{LC}\mathcal{D}_{\eta}^{\beta,\gamma}$ is known as the combined Liouville–Caputo fractional derivative operator, $\dot{w}(t)$ is the noise term and $\lambda > 0$ denotes the level of the noise term. For recent work on stochastic fractional differential equations, see [14,15] and their references.

Following the formulation of solution in Lemma 2, the solution of Equation (13) is given by

$$\Phi(t) = \rho_c + \frac{1-\eta}{\eta\Gamma(\beta-\gamma)}\int_c^t (t-s)^{\beta-\gamma-1}\Phi(s)ds + \frac{\lambda}{\eta\Gamma(\beta)}\int_c^t (t-s)^{\beta-1}\vartheta(s,\Phi(s))dw(s). \tag{14}$$

5.1. Well-Posedness of the Solution to Equation (13)

We define the norm of the solution (14) above by

$$\|\Phi\|_2^2 := \sup_{c \leq t \leq d} \mathbb{E}|\Phi(t)|^2$$

and define the operator as follows:

$$\mathcal{L}\Phi(t) = \rho_c + \frac{1-\eta}{\eta\Gamma(\beta-\gamma)}\int_c^t (t-s)^{\beta-\gamma-1}\Phi(s)ds + \frac{\lambda}{\eta\Gamma(\beta)}\int_c^t (t-s)^{\beta-1}\vartheta(s,\Phi(s))dw(s). \tag{15}$$

We show that the fixed point of the operator $\mathcal{L}$ gives the solution to Equation (13).

Lemma 5. *Suppose Φ is a solution to problem (13) and Condition 1 holds. Then, for $0 < \gamma < \beta < 1$ and $\eta \in (0,1]$, we have*

$$\|\mathcal{L}\Phi\|_2^2 \leq 3\rho_c^2 + c_4\|\Phi\|_2^2,$$

with positive constant

$$c_4 := \left[\frac{3(1-\eta)^2}{\eta^2\Gamma^2(\beta-\gamma)[2(\beta-\gamma)-1]}(d-c)^{2(\beta-\gamma)} + \frac{3\lambda^2 \text{Lip}_\vartheta^2}{\eta^2\Gamma^2(\beta)[2\beta-1]}(d-c)^{2\beta-1}\right] < \infty.$$

Proof. Take the second moment of Equation (15) to get

$$E|\mathcal{L}\Phi(t)|^2 \leq 3\rho_c^2 + \frac{3(1-\eta)^2}{\eta^2\Gamma^2(\beta-\gamma)} E \left| \int_c^t (t-s)^{\beta-\gamma-1}\Phi(s)ds \right|^2$$

$$+ \frac{3\lambda^2}{\eta^2\Gamma^2(\beta)} E \left| \int_c^t (t-s)^{\beta-1}\vartheta(s,\Phi(s))dw(s) \right|^2.$$

Applying Holder's inequality on the first integral and Itô isometry on the second integral, we obtain

$$E|\mathcal{L}\Phi(t)|^2 \leq 3\rho_c^2 + \frac{3(1-\eta)^2}{\eta^2\Gamma^2(\beta-\gamma)} E\left[\left(\int_c^t (t-s)^{2(\beta-\gamma-1)}ds \right)^{\frac{1}{2}} \left(\int_c^t |\Phi(s)|^2 ds \right)^{\frac{1}{2}} \right]^2$$

$$+ \frac{3\lambda^2}{\eta^2\Gamma^2(\beta)} \int_c^t (t-s)^{2(\beta-1)} E|\vartheta(s,\Phi(s))|^2 ds.$$

Next, we apply Equation (7) of Lipschitz Condition 1 to arrive at

$$E|\mathcal{L}\Phi(t)|^2 \leq 3\rho_c^2 + \frac{3(1-\eta)^2}{\eta^2\Gamma^2(\beta-\gamma)} \int_c^t (t-s)^{2(\beta-\gamma-1)} ds \int_c^t E|\Phi(s)|^2 ds$$

$$+ \frac{3\lambda^2 \text{Lip}_\vartheta}{\eta^2\Gamma^2(\beta)} \int_c^t (t-s)^{2(\beta-1)} E|\Phi(s)|^2 ds$$

$$\leq 3\rho_c^2 + \frac{3(1-\eta)^2}{\eta^2\Gamma^2(\beta-\gamma)} \int_c^t (t-s)^{2(\beta-\gamma-1)} ds \|\Phi\|_2^2 \int_c^t 1 ds$$

$$+ \frac{3\lambda^2 \text{Lip}_\vartheta}{\eta^2\Gamma^2(\beta)} \|\Phi\|_2^2 \int_c^t (t-s)^{2(\beta-1)} ds$$

$$= 3\rho_c^2 + \frac{3(1-\eta)^2}{\eta^2\Gamma^2(\beta-\gamma)} \frac{(t-c)^{2(\beta-\gamma)-1}}{2(\beta-\gamma)-1} \|\Phi\|_2^2 (t-c) + \frac{3\lambda^2 \text{Lip}_\vartheta}{\eta^2\Gamma^2(\beta)} \|\Phi\|_2^2 \frac{(t-c)^{2\beta-1}}{2\beta-1}$$

$$= 3\rho_c^2 + \frac{3(1-\eta)^2}{\eta^2\Gamma^2(\beta-\gamma)} \frac{(t-c)^{2(\beta-\gamma)}}{2(\beta-\gamma)} \|\Phi\|_2^2 + \frac{3\lambda^2 \text{Lip}_\vartheta}{\eta^2\Gamma^2(\beta)} \|\Phi\|_2^2 \frac{(t-c)^{2\beta-1}}{2\beta-1}.$$

For $0 < \gamma < \beta < 1$ such that $\beta > \frac{1}{2}$ and $\beta - \gamma > \frac{1}{2}$, we take the supremum over $t \in [c,d]$ to arrive at

$$\|\mathcal{L}\Phi\|_2^2 \leq 3\rho_c^2 + \left[\frac{3(1-\eta)^2}{\eta^2\Gamma^2(\beta-\gamma)} \frac{(d-c)^{2(\beta-\gamma)}}{2(\beta-\gamma)} + \frac{3\lambda^2 \text{Lip}_\vartheta}{\eta^2\Gamma^2(\beta)} \frac{(d-c)^{2\beta-1}}{2\beta-1} \right] \|\Phi\|_2^2,$$

and the result follows. □

Similarly, we obtain the following result:

Lemma 6. *Let Condition 1 hold. Suppose Φ and Θ are two solutions of (13); for $0 < \gamma < \beta < 1$ and $\eta \in (0,1]$, we have*

$$\|\mathcal{L}\Phi - \mathcal{L}\Theta\|_2^2 \leq c_4 \|\Phi - \Theta\|_2^2.$$

Applying Lemmas 5 and 6, we obtain the following existence and uniqueness result:

Theorem 6. *Suppose Condition 1 holds, $0 < \gamma < \beta < 1$ and $\eta \in (0,1]$. There exists a constant $0 < c_4 < 1$ such that Equation (13) possesses a unique solution.*

5.2. Growth Moment Bound

Here, we state and prove the second moment growth estimate for the solution to Equation (13):

Theorem 7. *Assume Condition 1 holds. Then, $\forall\, t \in [c,d]$, $0 < c < d$ and $c_5, c_6 > 0$, we have*

$$E|\Phi(t)|^2 \leq \frac{3\rho_c^2}{\exp\left(c_5(c-t)^{2(\beta-\gamma)-1} + c_6(c-t)^{2\beta-1}\right)},$$

with $c_5 = \frac{3(1-\eta)^2}{\eta^2 \Gamma^2(\beta-\gamma)\left(2(\beta-\gamma)-1\right)}$, $c_6 = \frac{3\lambda^2 \text{Lip}_\vartheta^2}{\eta^2 \Gamma^2(\beta)(2\beta-1)}$, *for* $\eta \in (0,1]$, $0 < \gamma < \beta < 1$.

Proof. Following the proof of Lemma 5, we obtain that

$$E|\Phi(t)|^2 \leq 3\rho_c^2 + \frac{3(1-\eta)^2}{\eta^2 \Gamma^2(\beta-\gamma)} E\left|\int_c^t (t-s)^{\beta-\gamma-1}\Phi(s)ds\right|^2$$
$$+ \frac{3\lambda^2}{\eta^2 \Gamma^2(\beta)} E\left|\int_c^t (t-s)^{\beta-1}\vartheta(s,\Phi(s))dw(s)\right|^2.$$

According to Holder's inequality and Itô isometry on the first and second integrals, respectively, together with Equation (7) of Condition 1, one arrives at

$$E|\Phi(t)|^2 \leq 3\rho_c^2 + \frac{3(1-\eta)^2}{\eta^2 \Gamma^2(\beta-\gamma)} E\left[\left(\int_c^t (t-s)^{2(\beta-\gamma-1)}|\Phi(s)|^2 ds\right)^{1/2}\left(\int_c^t 1 ds\right)^{1/2}\right]^2$$
$$+ \frac{3\lambda^2 \text{Lip}_\vartheta^2}{\eta^2 \Gamma^2(\beta)} \int_c^t (t-s)^{2(\beta-1)} E|\Phi(s)|^2 ds$$
$$= 3\rho_c^2 + \frac{3(1-\eta)^2}{\eta^2 \Gamma^2(\beta-\gamma)}(t-c)\int_c^t (t-s)^{2(\beta-\gamma-1)} E|\Phi(s)|^2 ds$$
$$+ \frac{3\lambda^2 \text{Lip}_\vartheta^2}{\eta^2 \Gamma^2(\beta)} \int_c^t (t-s)^{2(\beta-1)} E|\Phi(s)|^2 ds$$
$$\leq 3\rho_c^2 + \frac{3(1-\eta)^2}{\eta^2 \Gamma^2(\beta-\gamma)}(d-c)\int_c^t (t-s)^{2(\beta-\gamma-1)} E|\Phi(s)|^2 ds$$
$$+ \frac{3\lambda^2 \text{Lip}_\vartheta^2}{\eta^2 \Gamma^2(\beta)} \int_c^t (t-s)^{2(\beta-1)} E|\Phi(s)|^2 ds.$$

The last line follows since $t \in [c,d]$. Let $g(t) := E|\Phi(t)|^2$, $t \in [c,d]$; it follows that

$$g(t) \leq 3\rho_c^2 + \frac{3(1-\eta)^2}{\eta^2 \Gamma^2(\beta-\gamma)}(d-c)\int_c^t (t-s)^{2(\beta-\gamma-1)} g(s)ds + \frac{3\lambda^2 \text{Lip}_\vartheta^2}{\eta^2 \Gamma^2(\beta)} \int_c^t (t-s)^{2(\beta-1)} g(s)ds. \quad (16)$$

Next, we apply the retarded Gronwall-type inequality of Theorem 4 on Equation (16) and follow the proof of Theorem 5. Consequently, the non-negative functions $h_1, h_2 : [c,d] \times [c,d] \to \mathbb{R}_+$ are defined as follows:

$$h_1(\zeta, s) := \frac{3(1-\eta)^2(d-c)}{\eta^2 \Gamma^2(\beta-\gamma)}(\zeta-s)^{2(\beta-\gamma-1)},$$

and

$$h_2(\zeta, s) := \frac{3\lambda^2 \text{Lip}_\vartheta^2}{\eta^2 \Gamma^2(\beta)}(\zeta-s)^{2(\beta-1)}.$$

For $c \leq s < \zeta$ and $\beta - \gamma - 1 < 0$, it follows that h_1 is continuous and decreasing and one obtains

$$\max_{c \leq \tau \leq t} h_1(\zeta, s) = \frac{3(1-\eta)^2(d-c)}{\eta^2 \Gamma^2(\beta-\gamma)}(c-s)^{2(\beta-\gamma-1)}.$$

This gives (for $\beta - \gamma > \frac{1}{2}$),

$$\begin{aligned} q_2(t) &= \exp\left[\ln(3\rho_c^2) + \frac{3(1-\eta)^2(d-c)}{\eta^2\Gamma^2(\beta-\gamma)}\int_c^t (c-s)^{2(\beta-\gamma-1)}ds\right] \\ &= \exp\left[\ln(3\rho_c^2) - \frac{3(1-\eta)^2(d-c)}{\eta^2\Gamma^2(\beta-\gamma)}\frac{(c-t)^{2(\beta-\gamma)-1}}{2(\beta-\gamma)-1}\right]. \end{aligned}$$

Similarly, for h_2, we have that, given $c \leq s < \zeta$ and $\beta < 1$, h_2 is decreasing, continuous and

$$\max_{c \leq \zeta \leq t} h_2(\zeta,s) = \frac{3\lambda^2\text{Lip}_\theta^2}{\eta^2\Gamma^2(\beta)}(c-s)^{2(\beta-1)}.$$

Then, it follows that (for $\beta > \frac{1}{2}$ and $\beta - \gamma > \frac{1}{2}$)

$$\begin{aligned} g(t) &\leq \exp\left[\ln(q_2(t)) + \frac{3\lambda^2\text{Lip}_\theta^2}{\eta^2\Gamma^2(\beta)}\int_c^t (c-s)^{2(\beta-1)}ds\right] \\ &= \exp\left[\ln(3\rho_c^2) - \frac{3(1-\eta)^2(d-c)}{\eta^2\Gamma^2(\beta-\gamma)}\frac{(c-t)^{2(\beta-\gamma)-1}}{2(\beta-\gamma)-1} - \frac{3\lambda^2\text{Lip}_\theta^2}{\eta^2\Gamma^2(\beta)}\frac{(c-t)^{2\beta-1}}{2\beta-1}\right] \\ &= 3\rho_c^2 \exp\left[-\frac{3(1-\eta)^2(d-c)}{\eta^2\Gamma^2(\beta-\gamma)}\frac{(c-t)^{2(\beta-\gamma)-1}}{2(\beta-\gamma)-1} - \frac{3\lambda^2\text{Lip}_\theta^2}{\eta^2\Gamma^2(\beta)}\frac{(c-t)^{2\beta-1}}{2\beta-1}\right], \end{aligned}$$

and this proves the result. □

Remark 2. *The mild solution in Equation (14) also satisfies the same asymptotic properties of Section 3.3. Since*

$$E|\Phi(t)|^2 \leq 3\rho_c^2 \exp\left[-\frac{3}{\eta^2}\left(\frac{(1-\eta)^2(d-c)}{\Gamma^2(\beta-\gamma)}\frac{(c-t)^{2(\beta-\gamma)-1}}{2(\beta-\gamma)-1} + \frac{\lambda^2\text{Lip}_\theta^2}{\Gamma^2(\beta)}\frac{(c-t)^{2\beta-1}}{2\beta-1}\right)\right],$$

then, taking limits as $\eta \to 0$ and $t \to c^+$, we obtain the following: $\lim_{\eta \to 0} E|\Phi(t)|^2 = 0$ *and* $\lim_{t \to c^+} E|\Phi(t)|^2 \leq 3\rho_c^2.$

6. Conclusions

The combined Liouville–Caputo fractional derivative operator plays a major role in describing a more general class of variational problems. We used this new operator to investigate the behaviour of the solution to a class of combined Liouville–Caputo fractional differential equations. The existence and uniqueness of the solution was established through Banach's fixed-point theorem. The solution's growth bound and asymptotic behaviours were also established. Moreover, in Figures 1–6, we presented a numerical simulation of the behaviour of the combined Liouville–Caputo fractional differential equations via the upper growth bound, with respect to different initial points $t = c$, different values β and γ of the fractional orders, different convex combination parameters η, as well as different values of λ. In general, the solution function Q of problem (2) decayed to zero; however, the speed of decay was determined by the values of the parameters η, β, γ and λ. We further investigated the effects of a noise term on the growth of the solution to the combined fractional differential equation and observed that the presence or introduction of the noise term does not affect the growth behaviour of the solution to the combined fractional differential equation. For future work, we will study the dependence of the solution(s) on the initial condition and will also estimate the lower bounds, etc.

Author Contributions: Conceptualization, M.E.O.; methodology, M.E.O., H.A.S., S.E.M., C.D.E. and T.A.-A.A.; software, C.D.E.; validation, M.E.O., H.A.S., S.E.M., C.D.E. and T.A.-A.A.; software, C.D.E.; formal analysis, M.E.O., H.A.S., S.E.M., C.D.E. and T.A.-A.A.; investigation, M.E.O., H.A.S., S.E.M., C.D.E. and T.A.-A.A.; writing—original draft preparation, M.E.O.; writing—review and editing, M.E.O., H.A.S., S.E.M., C.D.E. and T.A.-A.A.; project administration, M.E.O.; funding acquisition, M.E.O. All authors have read and agreed to the published version of the manuscript.

Funding: This research was funded by the University of Hafr Al Batin, Institutional Financial Program under project number IFP-A-2022-2-1-09.

Data Availability Statement: Not applicable.

Acknowledgments: The authors gratefully acknowledge the technical and financial support from the Agency for Research and Innovation, Ministry of Education and University of Hafr Al Batin, Saudi Arabia.

Conflicts of Interest: The authors declare no conflict of interest.

References

1. Baleanu, D.; Fernadez, A.; Akgul, A. On a Fractional Combining proportional and Classical Differintegrals. *Mathematics* **2020**, *8*, 360. [CrossRef]
2. Voyiadjis, G.Z.; Sumelka, W. Brain modelling in the framework of anisotropic hyperelasticity with time fractional damage evolution governed by the Caputo–Almeida fractional derivative. *J. Mech. Behav. Biomed. Mater.* **2019**, *89*, 209–216. [CrossRef] [PubMed]
3. Johansyah, M.D.; Supriatna, A.K.; Rusyaman, E.; Saputra, J. Application of fractional differential equation in economic growth model: A Systematic review approach. *Aims Math.* **2021**, *6*, 10266–10280. [CrossRef]
4. Mu'lla, M. Fractional calculus, Fractional Differential Equations and Applications. *Open Access Libr. J.* **2020**, *7*, 1–9. [CrossRef]
5. Kilbas, A.A.; Srivastava, H.M.; Trujillo, J.J. *Theory and Applications of Fractional Differential Equations*, 1st ed.; North–Holland Mathematics Studies; Elsevier: Amsterdam, The Netherlands, 2006; Volume 204, pp. 1–523.
6. Baleanu, D.; Machado, J.A.T.; Luo, A.C. *Fractional Dynamics and Control*; Springer Science and Business Mdeia: Berlin, Germany, 2011.
7. Malinowska, A.B.; Torres, D.F.M. Fractional calculus of variations for a combined Caputo derivative. *Fract. Calc. Appl. Anal.* **2011**, *14*, 523–537. [CrossRef]
8. Malinowska, A.B.; Torres, D.F.M. The diamond-alpha Riemann integral and mean value theorems on time scales. *Dynam. Syst. Appl.* **2009**, *18*, 469–482.
9. Sidi Ammi, M.R.; Ferreira, R.A.C.; Torres, D.F.M. Diamond-α Jensen's Inequality on time scales. *J. Inequal. Appl.* **2008**, 576876. [CrossRef]
10. Atasever, N.A. On Diamond-Alpha Dynamic Equations and Inequalities. Master's Thesis, Georgia Southern University, Statesboro, GA, USA, 2011.
11. Almeida, R. A Gronwall inequality for a general Caputo fractional operator. *Math. Inequalities Appl.* **2017**, *20*, 1089–1105. [CrossRef]
12. Abdeljawad, T. On Riemann and Caputo fractional differences. *Comput. Math. Appl.* **2011**, *62*, 1602–1611. [CrossRef]
13. Agarwal, R.P.; Deng, S.; Zhang, W. Generalization of a retarded Gronwall-like inequality and its applications. *Appl. Math. Comput.* **2005**, *165*, 599–612. [CrossRef]
14. Omaba, M.E.; Enyi, C.D. Atangana–Baleanu time-fractional stochastic integro-differential equation. *Partial. Differ. Equations Appl. Math.* **2021**, *4*, 100100. [CrossRef]
15. Omaba, M.E.; Nweze, E.R. A Nonlinear Fractional Langevin Equation of Two Fractional Orders with Multiplicative Noise. *Fractal Fract.* **2022**, *6*, 290. [CrossRef]

Disclaimer/Publisher's Note: The statements, opinions and data contained in all publications are solely those of the individual author(s) and contributor(s) and not of MDPI and/or the editor(s). MDPI and/or the editor(s) disclaim responsibility for any injury to people or property resulting from any ideas, methods, instructions or products referred to in the content.

Article

Lie Symmetries and Third- and Fifth-Order Time-Fractional Polynomial Evolution Equations

Jollet Truth Kubayi and Sameerah Jamal *

School of Mathematics, University of the Witwatersrand, Johannesburg 2001, South Africa
* Correspondence: sameerah.jamal@wits.ac.za

Abstract: This paper is concerned with a class of ten time-fractional polynomial evolution equations. The one-parameter Lie point symmetries of these equations are found and the symmetry reductions are provided. These reduced equations are transformed into nonlinear ordinary differential equations, which are challenging to solve by conventional methods. We search for power series solutions and demonstrate the convergence properties of such a solution.

Keywords: time fractional; Lie symmetry; Erdélyi–Kober

Citation: Kubayi, J.T.; Jamal, S. Lie Symmetries and Third- and Fifth-Order Time-Fractional Polynomial Evolution Equations. *Fractal Fract.* **2023**, *7*, 125. https://doi.org/10.3390/fractalfract7020125

Academic Editor: Riccardo Caponetto

Received: 7 January 2023
Revised: 25 January 2023
Accepted: 28 January 2023
Published: 29 January 2023

Copyright: © 2023 by the authors. Licensee MDPI, Basel, Switzerland. This article is an open access article distributed under the terms and conditions of the Creative Commons Attribution (CC BY) license (https://creativecommons.org/licenses/by/4.0/).

1. Introduction

Decades ago, Fujimoto-Watanabe [1] derived a complete list of the third-order polynomial evolution equations that admit nontrivial Lie–Bäcklund symmetries. Recursion operators map symmetries to symmetries so that certain integrable evolution equations admit infinitely many symmetries [2]. If the recursion operator is hereditary [3], the infinite series of symmetries commute with each other (see [1], Equation (2.7), p. 2). Most of these equations possess a hereditary recursion operator so that the Lie algebras of their Lie–Bäcklund symmetries are infinitely dimensional and commutative. From the third-order equations, all except the seventh equation admit a recursion operator (see Remark 1 in [1], p. 3).

Further, two fifth-order equations were also presented. In this work, we consider the time-fractional version of this class of equations. They are the following eight equations:

$$\frac{\partial^\alpha u}{\partial t^\alpha} = u_x^3 u_{xxx} + au_x^4, \tag{1}$$

$$\frac{\partial^\alpha u}{\partial t^\alpha} = u_x^3 u_{xxx} + au_x^3, \tag{2}$$

$$\frac{\partial^\alpha u}{\partial t^\alpha} = u^3 u_{xxx} + 3u^2 u_x u_{xx} + a(u^3 u_{xx} + u^2 u_x^2) + \frac{2}{9}a^2 u^3 u_x, \tag{3}$$

$$\frac{\partial^\alpha u}{\partial t^\alpha} = u^3 u_{xxx} + 3u^2 u_x u_{xx} + 4au^3 u_x, \tag{4}$$

$$\frac{\partial^\alpha u}{\partial t^\alpha} = u^3 u_{xxx} + 3u^2 u_x u_{xx} + 3au^2 u_x, \tag{5}$$

$$\frac{\partial^\alpha u}{\partial t^\alpha} = u^3 u_{xxx} + au^3 u_x, \tag{6}$$

$$\frac{\partial^\alpha u}{\partial t^\alpha} = u^3 u_{xxx} + \frac{3}{2} u^2 u_x u_{xx} + a(u^3 u_{xx} + u^2 u_x^2) + \frac{2}{9} a^2 u^3 u_x, \tag{7}$$

$$\frac{\partial^\alpha u}{\partial t^\alpha} = u^3 u_{xxx} + \frac{3}{2} u^2 u_x u_{xx} + au^2 u_x, \tag{8}$$

where $a > 0$ is a constant, and also two fifth-order equations that do not belong to the above hierarchies of equations

$$\frac{\partial^\alpha u}{\partial t^\alpha} = u^5 u_{xxxxx} + 5u^4(u_x u_{xxxx} + 2u_{xx} u_{xxx}), \tag{9}$$

$$\frac{\partial^\alpha u}{\partial t^\alpha} = u^5 u_{xxxxx} + 5u^4(u_x u_{xxxx} + \frac{1}{2} u_{xx} u_{xxx}) + \frac{15}{4} u^3 u_x^2 u_{xxx}. \tag{10}$$

Moreover, it is possible to construct chains of differential substitutions that connect the Fujimoto-Watanabe equations with the KdV, Sawada–Kotera, and Kaup equations [4]. These equations find applications in different areas such as mathematical physics, but they are primarily studied from the perspective of waves and ocean science [5].

Lie symmetry analysis has been widely applied to investigate nonlinear differential equations arising in both mathematics and physics [6,7], particularly for constructing their exact solutions. A Lie symmetry group of a system of differential equations is a group of transformations. The group of transformations relies on continuous parameters and maps any solution to another solution of the system. Lie group analysis is a systematic and direct method for deriving new exact and explicit solutions. The above equations were considered in [5,8] from the classical integer derivative perspective. Fractional derivatives are of superior interest in recent literature, see for example [9–13]. FDEs are often considered superior to classical integer-order equations since the latter experience memory effects and FDEs allow for the study of intermediate evolutionary behaviour at fractional time. Fractional differential equations, or FDEs, may most commonly contain Riemann and Liouville or Caputo derivatives. Symmetry methods have been extended to FDEs [14–17].

The plan of the paper is as follows. In Section 2, we define the preliminary mathematical notation and definitions required for this study. Thereafter, in Section 3, we list the symmetries for each of the ten equations under study. Section 4 contains the series solutions and reductions of the equations. A demonstration for testing of convergence of the series is given, and finally, in Section 5, we conclude.

2. Fractional Calculus and Symmetries

In this section, we present the mathematical framework required in subsequent sections of this paper. In existence, there are several different definitions of fractional derivatives. Time-fractional derivatives are commonly discussed in terms of Caputo, Grünwald–Letnikov, or Riemann–Liouville derivatives [18–20]. In this work, we limit ourselves to the latter—that is, we shall introduce the linear operators of differentiation in the framework of Riemann–Liouville fractional calculus, followed by the procedure for determining point symmetries of time-fractional PDEs.

$$G := \frac{\partial^\alpha u}{\partial t^\alpha} - \kappa(x, t, u, u_x, u_{xx}, \ldots) = 0. \tag{11}$$

Here, $0 < \alpha < 1$ is the parameter describing the order of the fractional time derivative.

The Riemann–Liouville fractional derivative is defined by

$$D_t^\alpha u(t, x) = \begin{cases} \frac{\partial^n u}{\partial t^n}, & \alpha = n \in \mathbb{N} \\ \frac{1}{\Gamma(n-\alpha)} \frac{\partial^n}{\partial t^n} \int_0^t \frac{u(\theta, x)}{(t-\theta)^{\alpha+1-n}} d\theta, & n-1 \leq \alpha \leq n, n \in \mathbb{N} \end{cases} \tag{12}$$

where $\Gamma(z)$ is the Euler gamma function.

Suppose that (1) is invariant under the one-parameter Lie group of point transformations

$$\begin{aligned}
\bar{t} &= t + \epsilon\tau(x,t,u) + O(\epsilon^2), \\
\bar{x} &= x + \epsilon\xi(x,t,u) + O(\epsilon^2), \\
\bar{u} &= u + \epsilon\eta(x,t,u) + O(\epsilon^2), \\
\frac{\partial^\alpha \bar{u}}{\partial \bar{t}^\alpha} &= \frac{\partial^\alpha u}{\partial t^\alpha} + \epsilon\eta_\alpha^0(x,t,u) + O(\epsilon^2), \\
\frac{\partial \bar{u}}{\partial \bar{x}} &= \frac{\partial u}{\partial x} + \epsilon\eta^x(x,t,u) + O(\epsilon^2), \\
\frac{\partial^2 \bar{u}}{\partial \bar{x}^2} &= \frac{\partial^2 u}{\partial x^2} + \epsilon\eta^{xx}(x,t,u) + O(\epsilon^2), \\
&\vdots
\end{aligned} \tag{13}$$

where ϵ is an infinitesimal parameter and, for example, the individual terms in the above expression are

$$\begin{aligned}
\eta^x &= \eta_x + \eta_u u_x - (\xi_x + \xi_u u_x)u_x - (\tau_x + \tau_u u_x)u_t, \\
\eta^{xx} &= \eta_{xx} + 2\eta_{xu}u_x - 2\xi_{xu}u_x^2 - \xi_{xx}u_x - 2\tau_{xu}u_t u_x - \tau_{xx}u_t - \xi_{uu}u_x^3 \\
&\quad - \tau_{uu}u_x^2 u_t + \eta_{uu}u_x^2 - 3\xi_u u_x u_{xx} - \tau_u u_t u_{xx} + \eta_u u_{xx} - 2\xi_x u_{xx} \\
&\quad - 2\tau_u u_x u_{tx} - 2\tau_x u_{tx}.
\end{aligned} \tag{14}$$

Using the generalised Leibniz rule [21–23] and a generalisation of the chain rule, we have that [15]

$$\begin{aligned}
\eta_\alpha^0 &= \frac{\partial^\alpha \eta}{\partial t^\alpha} + (\eta - \alpha D_t(\tau))\frac{\partial^\alpha u}{\partial t^\alpha} - u\frac{\partial^\alpha \eta_u}{\partial t^\alpha} + \mu + \sum_{n=1}^{\infty}\binom{\alpha}{n}D_t^n(\xi)D_t^{\alpha-n}(u_x) \\
&\quad + \sum_{n=1}^{\infty}\left[\binom{\alpha}{n}\frac{\partial^n}{\partial t^n}\eta_u - \binom{\alpha}{n+1}D_t^{n+1}(\tau)\right]D_t^{\alpha-n}.
\end{aligned} \tag{15}$$

The D_t^α is the total fractional derivative operator, and

$$\begin{aligned}
\mu &= \sum_{n=2}^{\infty}\sum_{m=2}^{n}\sum_{k=2}^{m}\sum_{r=0}^{k-1}\binom{\alpha}{n}\binom{n}{m}\binom{k}{r}\frac{1}{k!}\frac{t^{n-\alpha}}{\Gamma(n+1-\alpha)} \\
&\quad \times (-u)^r \frac{\partial^m}{\partial t^m}\left(u^{k-r}\right)\frac{\partial^{n-m+k}\eta}{\partial t^{n-m}\partial u^k}.
\end{aligned} \tag{16}$$

It is important to remark that by convention in the literature, $\eta(x,t,u)$ is taken to be linear in the variable u so that μ vanishes. We adopt this idea in the work hereafter as well.

Let the generator

$$X = \tau(x,t,u)\frac{\partial}{\partial t} + \xi(x,t,u)\frac{\partial}{\partial x} + \eta(x,t,u)\frac{\partial}{\partial u}, \tag{17}$$

span the associated Lie algebra—that is,

$$\tau(x,t,u) = \frac{dt^*}{d\epsilon}\bigg|_{\epsilon=0}, \quad \xi(x,t,u) = \frac{dx^*}{d\epsilon}\bigg|_{\epsilon=0}, \quad \eta(x,t,u) = \frac{du^*}{d\epsilon}\bigg|_{\epsilon=0}.$$

The infinitesimal criterion for invariance is given by $XG = 0$, when $G = 0$, where X is extended to all derivatives appearing in the equation through an appropriate prolongation. Moreover, it is essential that the transformation (13) leaves the lower limit of the fractional derivative invariant $\frac{\partial^\alpha u}{\partial t^\alpha}$, which translates into the additional constraint condition

$$\tau(x,t,u)\bigg|_{t=0} = 0. \tag{18}$$

We further require the following two definitions. The definition of the Erdélyi–Kober fractional integral operator given by

$$\left(K_\beta^{l,m} g\right)(z) = \begin{cases} g(z), & m = 0, \\ \frac{1}{\Gamma(m)} \int_1^\infty (u-1)^{m-1} u^{-(l+m)} g(zu^{\frac{1}{\beta}}) du, & m > 0, \end{cases} \quad (19)$$

and the Erdélyi–Kober fractional differential operator is

$$P_\beta^{q,r} w = \prod_{j=0}^{n-1} \left(q + j - \frac{1}{\beta} z \frac{\partial}{\partial t}\right) \left(K_\beta^{q+r,n-r} w\right)(z), \quad (20)$$

At this stage, we also recall the formula [24]

$$\frac{d^\alpha x^\beta}{dx^\alpha} = \frac{x^{-\alpha+\beta} \Gamma(1+\beta)}{\Gamma(1-\alpha+\beta)}, \quad \beta > -1, \quad (21)$$

which is useful in the reduction of the FDE.

In the next two sections, we shall study the main equations of the paper. The definitions and formulas discussed above will be used to investigate each of the cases.

3. Symmetry Analysis

The application of the theory of Section 2 shows that we have the following symmetries (see Table 1) corresponding to each of the above ten Equations (1)–(10), corresponding to Cases 1–10. Detailed calculations of these symmetries are omitted due to their volume.

Table 1. Lie point symmetries of Equations (1)–(10).

Case	Symmetries	Dimension
1	$X_1 = \partial_x$, $X_2 = 3t\partial_t - u\alpha\partial_u$, $X_u = \partial_u$,	The Lie algebra spanned by point symmetries is 3 dimensional.
2	X_1, $X_3 = -3t\partial_t + 3u\alpha\partial_u + x\alpha\partial_x$, X_u,	The Lie algebra spanned by point symmetries is 3 dimensional.
3	X_1, X_2, $X_a = e^{-\frac{ax}{3}} u\partial_u - \frac{3}{a} e^{-\frac{ax}{3}} \partial_x$,	The Lie algebra spanned by point symmetries is 3 dimensional.
4	X_1, X_2,	The Lie algebra spanned by point symmetries is 2 dimensional.
5,8	X_1, $X_4 = -3t\partial_t + 2u\alpha\partial_u + x\alpha\partial_x$,	The Lie algebra spanned by point symmetries is 2 dimensional.
6	X_1, X_2, $X_5 = u\cos(\sqrt{a}x)\sqrt{a}\partial_u + \sin(\sqrt{a}x)\partial_x$, $X_6 = u\sin(\sqrt{a}x)\sqrt{a}\partial_u - \cos(\sqrt{a}x)\partial_x$,	The Lie algebra spanned by point symmetries is 4 dimensional.
7	X_1, X_2, $X_{aa} = 2e^{-\frac{2ax}{3}} u\partial_u - \frac{3}{a} e^{-\frac{2ax}{3}} \partial_x$,	The Lie algebra spanned by point symmetries is 3 dimensional.
9, 10	X_1, $X_7 = 5t\partial_t - \alpha u\partial_u$, $X_8 = u\partial_u + x\partial_x$, $X_9 = 2ux\partial_u + x^2\partial_x$,	The Lie algebra spanned by point symmetries is 4 dimensional.

The Lie brackets are given in Tables 2–8. As for Cases 1, 3, and 7, the algebra is solvable. Case 4 is abelian, nilpotent, and solvable—all commutators vanish. Cases 2, 5, and 8 are indecomposable and solvable. Cases 6, 9, and 10 are decomposable.

Table 2. Lie brackets for Case 1.

[,]	X_1	X_2	X_u
X_1	0	0	0
X_2	0	0	αX_u
X_u	0	$-\alpha X_u$	0

Table 3. Lie brackets for Case 2.

[,]	X_1	X_3	X_u
X_1	0	αX_1	0
X_3	$-\alpha X_1$	0	$-3\alpha X_u$
X_u	0	$3\alpha X_u$	0

Table 4. Lie brackets for Case 3.

[,]	X_1	X_2	X_a
X_1	0	0	$-\frac{a}{3} X_a$
X_2	0	0	0
X_a	$\frac{a}{3} X_a$	0	0

Table 5. Lie brackets for Cases 5 and 8.

[,]	X_1	X_4
X_1	0	αX_1
X_4	$-\alpha X_1$	0

Table 6. Lie brackets for Case 6.

[,]	X_1	X_2	X_5	X_6
X_1	0	0	$-\sqrt{a} X_6$	$\sqrt{a} X_5$
X_2	0	0	0	0
X_5	$\sqrt{a} X_6$	0	0	$\sqrt{a} X_1$
X_6	$-\sqrt{a} X_5$	0	$-\sqrt{a} X_1$	0

Table 7. Lie brackets for Case 7.

[,]	X_1	X_2	X_{aa}
X_1	0	0	$-\frac{2a}{3} X_{aa}$
X_2	0	0	0
X_{aa}	$\frac{2a}{3} X_{aa}$	0	0

Table 8. Lie brackets for Cases 9 and 10.

[,]	X_1	X_7	X_8	X_9
X_1	0	0	X_1	$2 X_8$
X_7	0	0	0	0
X_8	$-X_1$	0	0	X_9
X_9	$-2 X_8$	0	$-X_9$	0

4. Reductions and Power Series Solutions

In this section, we consider several transformed equations via the symmetries listed above. The solutions are found with power series or, alternatively, the equation is reduced with the use of Erdélyi–Kober operators. We consider Cases 1, 3, 4, 6, 7, and Cases 9 and 10, which admit the symmetries X_2 and where the last two cases admit X_7. The symmetry X_2 produces the invariants

$$u(x,t) = w(x)t^{-\frac{\alpha}{3}}, \tag{22}$$

while X_7 produces the invariants

$$u(x,t) = w(x)t^{-\frac{\alpha}{5}}. \tag{23}$$

In each case, these invariants will provide us with a fractional-order ODE, whereupon the fractional terms are manipulated with the application of (21) to obtain an integer-order ODE. The latter ODE is solved using the power series method [25]. The convergence and uniqueness of the solution can then be determined via the implicit functional theorem. Case 1 is performed in detail. Cases 2, 5, and 8 are best reduced with Erdélyi–Kober operators given the symmetries they admit.

4.1. Case 1

Consider Equation (1), a reduction using (22) followed by application of (21) generates the following ODE to solve, viz.

$$w(x)\Gamma\left(1-\frac{\alpha}{3}\right)\left(\Gamma\left(1-\frac{4\alpha}{3}\right)\right)^{-1} - \left(\frac{d}{dx}w(x)\right)^3 \frac{d^3}{dx^3}w(x) - a\left(\frac{d}{dx}w(x)\right)^4 = 0. \tag{24}$$

This ODE is very difficult to solve using most techniques. We show that power series are highly effective. Thus, the power series

$$w(x) = \sum_{r_1=0}^{\infty} a_{r_1} x^{r_1}, \tag{25}$$

is substituted into (24). We find that a_0, a_1, a_2 are arbitrary and that a solution may be expressed as

$$\begin{aligned}
w(x) &= a_0 + a_1 x + a_2 x^2 + \\
&\quad x^3 \frac{a_0 \Gamma\left(1-\frac{\alpha}{3}\right) - a a_1^4 \Gamma\left(1-\frac{4\alpha}{3}\right)}{6 a_1^3 \Gamma\left(1-\frac{4\alpha}{3}\right)} + \\
&\quad x^4 \frac{-8aa_2 a_1^2 \Gamma\left(1-\frac{4\alpha}{3}\right) - \frac{6a_2\left(a_0 \Gamma\left(1-\frac{\alpha}{3}\right) - a a_1^4 \Gamma\left(1-\frac{4\alpha}{3}\right)\right)}{a_1^2} + \Gamma\left(1-\frac{\alpha}{3}\right)}{24 a_1^2 \Gamma\left(1-\frac{4\alpha}{3}\right)} \\
&\quad + \ldots
\end{aligned} \tag{26}$$

with graphical solution expressed in Figure 1.

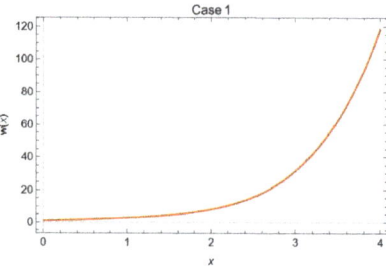

Figure 1. We let $a_0 = a_1 = a_2 = a = 1, \alpha = \frac{1}{2}$, for the graphical solution.

Testing for Convergence

A natural question that arises is whether or not the above series solution converges. The following illustrates how to test for convergence. Suppose we consider (24) with the power series (25) substituted into it; then, we have that

$$\sum_{r_1=0}^{\infty} \left(a_{r_1} \Gamma\left(1 - \frac{\alpha}{3}\right) \Gamma\left(1 - \frac{4\alpha}{3}\right)^{-1} - \right.$$

$$\sum_{r_2=3}^{r_1+6} \sum_{r_3=1}^{r_2} \sum_{r_4=1}^{r_3} r_4 a_{r_4} (r_3 - r_4) a_{r_3-r_4} (r_2 - r_3) a_{r_2-r_3} (r_1 + 6 - r_2)(r_1 + -r_2)(r_1 + -r_2) a_{r_1+6-r_2} - \tag{27}$$

$$\left. a \sum_{r_2=3}^{r_1+4} \sum_{r_3=1}^{r_2} \sum_{r_4=1}^{r_3} r_4 a_{r_4} (r_3 - r_4) a_{r_3-r_4} (r_2 - r_3) a_{r_2-r_3} (r_1 + 4 - r_2) a_{r_1+4-r_2} \right) x^{r_1} = 0.$$

Hence, by formal calculations we have that, in general, the coefficients in the above sum are given by

$$a_{r_1+3} = \frac{\frac{a_{r_1} \Gamma(1-\frac{\alpha}{3})}{\Gamma(1-\frac{4\alpha}{3})}}{a_1^3 (r_1+3)(r_1+2)(r_1+1)}$$

$$-\frac{\sum_{r_2=4}^{r_1+6} \sum_{r_3=1}^{r_2} \sum_{r_4=1}^{r_3} r_4 a_{r_4}(r_3-r_4) a_{r_3-r_4}(r_2-r_3)}{a_1^3(n_1+3)(r_1+2)(r_1+1)} \times$$

$$a_{r_2-r_3}(r_1+6-r_2)(r_1+5-r_2)(r_1+4-r_2) a_{r_1+6-r_2}$$

$$-\frac{a \sum_{r_2=2}^{r_1+4} \sum_{r_3=1}^{r_2} \sum_{r_4=1}^{r_3} r_4 a_{r_4}(r_3-r_4) a_{r_3-r_4}(r_2-r_3) a_{r_2-r_3}(r_1+4-r_2) a_{r_1+4-r_2}}{a_1^3(r_1+3)(r_1+2)(r_1+1)}, \tag{28}$$

for $r_1 \geq 0$, such that (26) reads as

$$w(x) = a_0 + a_1 x + a_2 x^2 + \sum_{r_1=0}^{\infty} a_{r_1+3} x^{r_1+3}. \tag{29}$$

Next, we prove the convergence of the power series solution (29). From (28), we obtain

$$|a_{r_1+3}| \leq M \left(|a_{r_1}| + \sum_{r_2=4}^{r_1+6} \sum_{r_3=1}^{r_2} \sum_{r_4=1}^{r_3} |a_{r_4}||a_{r_3-r_4}||a_{r_2-r_3}||a_{r_1+6-r_2}| \right.$$

$$\left. + \sum_{r_2=2}^{r_1+4} \sum_{r_3=1}^{r_2} \sum_{r_4=1}^{r_3} |a_{r_4}||a_{r_3-r_4}||a_{r_2-r_3}||a_{r_1+4-r_2}| \right), \tag{30}$$

where $r_1 = 0, 1, 2...$, and $M = max\{\frac{\Gamma(1-\frac{\alpha}{3})}{\Gamma(1-\frac{4\alpha}{3})}, \frac{|a|}{a_1^3}\}$.

Suppose we have the power series $\mu = R(x) = \sum_{r_1=0}^{\infty} p_{r_1} x^{r_1}$ where

$$p_k = |a_k|, \ k = 0, 1, 2 \tag{31}$$

and

$$p_{r_1+3} = M \left(p_{r_1} + \sum_{r_2=4}^{r_1+6} \sum_{r_3=1}^{r_2} \sum_{r_4=1}^{r_3} p_{r_4} p_{r_3-r_4} p_{r_2-r_3} p_{r_1+6-r_2} \right.$$

$$\left. + \sum_{r_2=2}^{r_1+4} \sum_{r_3=1}^{r_2} \sum_{r_4=1}^{r_3} p_{r_4} p_{r_3-r_4} p_{r_2-r_3} p_{r_1+4-r_2} \right). \tag{32}$$

Hence,
$$|a_{r_1}| \le p_{r_1}, \quad r_1 = 0, 1, 2 \ldots \tag{33}$$

Next, we prove that μ is convergent in a neighbourhood of a point. Note that μ is a majorant series of Equation (29) and can be written as follows:

$$\begin{aligned}
R(x) &= p_0 + p_1 x + p_2 x^2 + \sum_{r_1=0}^{\infty} p_{r_1+3} x^{r_1+3} \\
&= p_0 + p_1 x + p_2 x^2 + \\
&\quad M \sum_{r_1=0}^{\infty} \left(p_{r_1} + \sum_{r_2=4}^{r_1+6} \sum_{r_3=1}^{r_2} \sum_{r_4=1}^{r_3} p_{r_4} p_{r_3-r_4} p_{r_2-r_3} p_{r_1+6-r_2} \right. \\
&\quad + \left. \sum_{r_2=2}^{r_1+4} \sum_{r_3=1}^{r_2} \sum_{r_4=1}^{r_3} p_{r_4} p_{r_3-r_4} p_{r_2-r_3} p_{r_1+4-r_2} \right) x^{r_1+3} \\
&= p_0 + p_1 x + p_2 x^2 \\
&\quad + M[R^4 + R^2 \rho(x) + R\sigma(x) + \nu(x)],
\end{aligned} \tag{34}$$

where $\nu(x) = \theta(x) - p_0^4$ and $\theta(x), \rho(x)$, and $\sigma(x)$ are polynomials with each term having a degree of x of at least one. Hence, let

$$\begin{aligned}
F(x, \mu) &= \mu - p_0 - p_1 x - p_2 x^2 \\
&\quad - M[R^4 + R^2 \rho(x) + R\sigma(x) + \nu(x)],
\end{aligned} \tag{35}$$

be the implicit function equation, where we obtain that $F(0, p_0) = 0$ and $F_\mu(0, r_0) = 1 - 4Mp_0^3 \ne 0$. By virtue of the implicit function theorem [26], $\mu = R(x)$ is analytic and convergent in a neighbourhood of the point $(0, p_0)$ in the plane and with a positive radius. Then, the power series solution (29) is convergent in the neighbourhood of a point $(0, p_0)$. Therefore, (29) can be written as

$$\begin{aligned}
w(x) =\ & a_0 + a_1 x + a_2 x^2 + \\
& \Sigma_{r_1=0}^{\infty} \left(\frac{\frac{a_{r_1} \Gamma(1-\frac{\alpha}{3})}{\Gamma(1-\frac{\alpha}{3})}}{a_1^3 (r_1+3)(r_1+2)(r_1+1)} \right. \\
& - \frac{\sum_{r_2=4}^{r_1+6} \sum_{r_3=1}^{r_2} \sum_{r_4=1}^{r_3} r_4 a_{r_4}(r_3-r_4) a_{r_3-r_4}(r_2-r_3)}{a_1^3 (n_1+3)(r_1+2)(r_1+1)} \times \\
& a_{r_2-r_3}(r_1+6-r_2)(r_1+5-r_2)(r_1+4-r_2) a_{r_1+6-r_2} \\
& - \frac{a \sum_{r_2=2}^{r_1+4} \sum_{r_3=1}^{r_2} \sum_{r_4=1}^{r_3} r_4 a_{r_4}(r_3-r_4) a_{r_3-r_4}(r_2-r_3) a_{r_2-r_3}(r_1+4-r_2) a_{r_1+4-r_2}}{a_1^3 (r_1+3)(r_1+2)(r_1+1)} \left.\right) x^{r_1+3}.
\end{aligned} \tag{36}$$

Thus, the exact power series solution of Equation (1) can be written as

$$u(x, t) = \left(a_0 + a_1 x + a_2 x^2 + \Sigma_{r_1=0}^{\infty} a_{r_1+3} x^{r_1+3} \right) t^{-\frac{\alpha}{3}} \tag{37}$$

where $a_0 \ne 0, a_1, a_2$, are arbitrary constants and the rest of the constants are to be determined by (28). This produces the solution (26).

Similarly, and very tediously, we can construct convergent power series solutions to all reduced equations in this paper. The solutions can then be transformed back into original variables, given the invertible transformations stated for each reduction. Due to how lengthy the above test for convergence is, we omit the convergence details for all other cases.

4.2. Case 2

As mentioned above, this case is best reduced by the elegant Erdélyi–Kober operators instead of the how we treated Case 1. Suppose we take X_3; then, we have the invariants $z = xt^{\frac{\alpha}{3}}$ and $u(x,t) = w(x,t)t^{-\alpha}$. Now, we transform the LHS of (2) using the following transformation:

$$u_t^\alpha = \frac{\partial^n}{\partial t^n}\left[\frac{1}{\Gamma(n-\alpha)}\int_0^t (t-s)^{n-\alpha-1}w(s^{-\frac{\alpha}{3}}x)s^{-\alpha}ds\right]. \tag{38}$$

Let $s = t/v$; then, $ds = -\frac{t}{v^2}dv$ so that the above becomes

$$u_t^\alpha = \frac{\partial^n}{\partial t^n}\left[\frac{1}{\Gamma(n-\alpha)}\int_\infty^1 \left(t-\frac{t}{v}\right)^{n-\alpha-1}w\left(\left(\frac{t}{v}\right)^{-\frac{\alpha}{3}}x\right)\left(\frac{t}{v}\right)^{-\alpha}\left(-\frac{t}{v^2}\right)dv\right]$$

$$= \frac{\partial^n}{\partial t^n}\left[\frac{1}{\Gamma(n-\alpha)}\int_\infty^1 \left(t-\frac{t}{v}\right)^{n-\alpha-1}w\left(\left(\frac{t}{v}\right)^{-\frac{\alpha}{3}}x\right)\left(\frac{t}{v}\right)^{-\alpha}\left(-\frac{t}{v^2}\right)dv\right]$$

$$= \frac{\partial^n}{\partial t^n}\left[\frac{t^{n-2\alpha}}{\Gamma(n-\alpha)}\int_1^\infty (v-1)^{n-\alpha-1}w\left(zv^{\frac{\alpha}{3}}\right)(v)^{-(n-2\alpha-1)}dv\right].$$

Then, by the definition of the Erdélyi–Kober fractional integral operator (19), $\beta = \frac{3}{\alpha}$ and $m = n - \alpha$, and from the powers of v we have $-(n-2\alpha+1) \implies -[(n-\alpha)-1-\alpha] \implies -[m+l]$, where $l = -1 - \alpha$.

So, the above becomes

$$u_t^\alpha = \frac{\partial^n}{\partial t^n}\left[\frac{t^{n-2\alpha}}{\Gamma(n-\alpha)}\left(K_{\frac{3}{\alpha}}^{-1-\alpha,n-\alpha}w\right)(z)\right]. \tag{39}$$

From $z = xt^{-\frac{\alpha}{3}}$, by the chain rule, we obtain

$$t\frac{\partial}{\partial t}\phi(z) = -\frac{\alpha}{3}z\frac{\partial}{\partial t}. \tag{40}$$

Therefore, the RHS of (39) is

$$\frac{\partial^n}{\partial t^n}\left[t^{n-2\alpha}\left(K_{\frac{3}{\alpha}}^{1-\alpha,n-\alpha}w\right)(z)\right] = \frac{\partial^{n-1}}{\partial t^{n-1}}\left[\frac{\partial}{\partial t}t^{n-2\alpha}\left(K_{\frac{3}{\alpha}}^{-1-\alpha,n-\alpha}w\right)(z)\right], \tag{41}$$

which by product rule gives

$$\frac{\partial^{n-1}}{\partial t^{n-1}}\left[(n-2\alpha)t^{n-2\alpha-1}\left(K_{\frac{3}{\alpha}}^{-1-\alpha,n-\alpha}w\right)(z) + t^{n-2\alpha-1}t\left(K_{\frac{3}{\alpha}}^{-1-\alpha,n-\alpha}w\right)'(z)\right]. \tag{42}$$

Now, we will have

$$\frac{\partial^{n-1}}{\partial t^{n-1}}\left[(n-2\alpha)t^{n-2\alpha-1}\left(n-2\alpha-\frac{\alpha}{3}z\frac{\partial}{\partial t}\right)\left(K_{\frac{3}{\alpha}}^{-1-\alpha,n-\alpha}w\right)(z)\right].$$

Then, by repeating this $n-1$ times, we obtain

$$\frac{\partial^n}{\partial t^n}\left[t^{n-2\alpha}\left(K_{\frac{3}{\alpha}}^{-1-\alpha,n-\alpha}w\right)(z)\right] = t^{-2\alpha}\prod_{j=0}^{n-1}\left(1+j-2\alpha-\frac{\alpha}{3}z\frac{\partial}{\partial t}\right)K_{\frac{3}{\alpha}}^{-1-\alpha,n-\alpha}. \tag{43}$$

By the definition of the fractional operator (20) and by comparing the subscripts in the $K_\beta^{q+r,n-r}$ term, we have that $r = \alpha$ and $q = -1 - 2\alpha$, and (43) can be written as

$$\frac{\partial^n}{\partial t^n}\left[t^{n-2\alpha}\left(K_{\frac{3}{\alpha}}^{-1-\alpha,n-\alpha}w\right)(z)\right] = t^{-2\alpha}\left(P_{\frac{3}{\alpha}}^{-1-2\alpha,\alpha}w\right)(z). \tag{44}$$

Then, from (39), we will have

$$u_t^\alpha = t^{-2\alpha}\left(P_{\frac{3}{\alpha}}^{-1-2\alpha,\alpha}w\right)(z). \tag{45}$$

Hence, Equation (2) transforms to

$$\left(P_{\frac{3}{\alpha}}^{-1-2\alpha,\alpha}w\right)(z) = (w'(z))^3(w'''(z) + a).$$

4.3. Case 3

Similar to Case 1, consider a reduction using (22) followed by application of (21) to generate the following ODE

$$w(x)\Gamma\left(1 - \frac{\alpha}{3}\right)\left(\Gamma\left(1 - \frac{4\alpha}{3}\right)\right)^{-1} - (w(x))^3\frac{d^3}{dx^3}w(x) - 3(w(x))^2\left(\frac{d^2}{dx^2}w(x)\right)\frac{d}{dx}w(x)$$
$$-a\left((w(x))^3\frac{d^2}{dx^2}w(x) + (w(x))^2\left(\frac{d}{dx}w(x)\right)^2\right) - \frac{2a^2(w(x))^3\frac{d}{dx}w(x)}{9} = 0,$$

which we solve with a power series $w(x) = \sum_{r_1=0}^{\infty} a_{r_1}x^{r_1}$ to obtain a_0, a_1, a_2 as arbitrary and where

$$w(x) = a_0 + a_1 x + a_2 x^2 +$$
$$\frac{x^3}{54 a_0^3 \Gamma\left(1 - \frac{4\alpha}{3}\right)}\left(-2a^2 a_1 a_0^3 \Gamma\left(1 - \frac{4\alpha}{3}\right) - 18 a a_2 a_0^3 \Gamma\left(1 - \frac{4\alpha}{3}\right)\right.$$
$$\left. - 9 a a_1^2 a_0^2 \Gamma\left(1 - \frac{4\alpha}{3}\right) - 54 a_1 a_2 a_0^2 \Gamma\left(1 - \frac{4\alpha}{3}\right) + 9 a_0 \Gamma\left(1 - \frac{\alpha}{3}\right)\right)$$
$$+ \ldots \tag{46}$$

with graphical solution expressed in Figure 2.

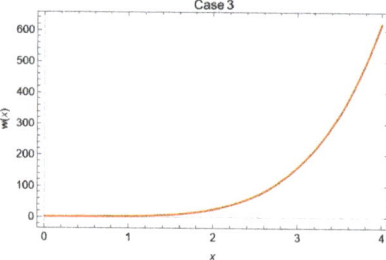

Figure 2. We let $a_0 = 1, a_1 = 1, a_2 = 1, \alpha = \frac{1}{2}, a = 1$.

4.4. Case 4

In this case again, consider a reduction using (22) followed by application of (21) to generate the following ODE

$$w(x)\Gamma\left(1-\frac{\alpha}{3}\right)\left(\Gamma\left(1-\frac{4\alpha}{3}\right)\right)^{-1} - (w(x))^3 \frac{d^3}{dx^3}w(x) - 3(w(x))^2\left(\frac{d^2}{dx^2}w(x)\right)\frac{d}{dx}w(x)$$
$$-4a(w(x))^3\frac{d}{dx}w(x) = 0,$$

which we solve with a power series $w(x) = \sum_{r_1=0}^{\infty} a_{r_1} x^{r_1}$ to obtain a_0, a_1, a_2 as arbitrary and where

$$w(x) = a_0 + a_1 x + a_2 x^2 +$$
$$\frac{x^3}{6a_0^2 \Gamma\left(1-\frac{4\alpha}{3}\right)}\left(-4aa_1 a_0^2 \Gamma\left(1-\frac{4\alpha}{3}\right)\right.$$
$$\left.-9aa_1^2 a_0^2 \Gamma\left(1-\frac{4\alpha}{3}\right) - 54a_1 a_2 a_0^2 \Gamma\left(1-\frac{4\alpha}{3}\right) + 9a_0 \Gamma\left(1-\frac{\alpha}{3}\right)\right)$$
$$+ \ldots \tag{47}$$

with graphical solution expressed in Figure 3.

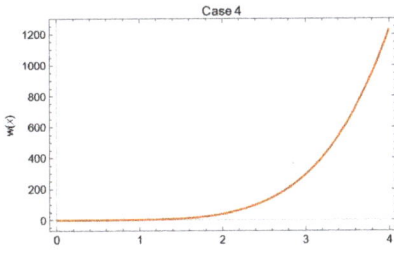

Figure 3. We let $a_0 = 1, a_1 = 1, a_2 = 1, \alpha = \frac{1}{2}, a = 1$.

4.5. Case 5

This case admits the symmetry X_4, which gives the invariants $z = xt^{\frac{\alpha}{3}}$ and $w(z) = ut^{\frac{2\alpha}{3}}$. This case was considered in [27] with $a = 1$, where it is shown that

$$u_t^\alpha = t^{\frac{-5\alpha}{3}}\left(P_{\frac{3}{\alpha}}^{-1-\frac{5\alpha}{3},\alpha} w\right)(z). \tag{48}$$

Hence, for our case, using the above, we obtain that (5) transforms to

$$\left(P_{\frac{3}{\alpha}}^{-1-2\alpha,\alpha} w\right)(z) = 3w^2(z)\left((a+w''(z))w'(z) - \frac{1}{3}w(z)w'''(z)\right).$$

4.6. Case 6

Similar to Case 1, consider a reduction using (22) followed by application of (21) to generate the following ODE

$$w(x)\Gamma\left(1-\frac{\alpha}{3}\right)\left(\Gamma\left(1-\frac{4\alpha}{3}\right)\right)^{-1} - (w(x))^3 \frac{d^3}{dx^3}w(x) - a(w(x))^3 \frac{d}{dx}w(x) = 0,$$

which we solve with a power series $w(x) = \sum_{r_1=0}^{\infty} a_{r_1} x^{r_1}$ to obtain a_0, a_1, a_2 as arbitrary and where

$$\begin{aligned} w(x) &= a_0 + a_1 x + a_2 x^2 + \\ &\quad \frac{x^3}{6 a_1^3 \Gamma\left(1 - \frac{4\alpha}{3}\right)} \left(a_0 \Gamma\left(1 - \frac{\alpha}{3}\right) - a a_0 a_1 \Gamma\left(1 - \frac{4\alpha}{3}\right) \right) \\ &\quad + \ldots \end{aligned} \qquad (49)$$

with graphical solution expressed in Figure 4.

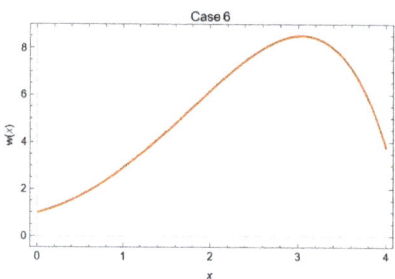

Figure 4. We let $a_0 = 1, a_1 = 1, a_2 = 1, \alpha = \frac{1}{2}, a = 1$.

4.7. Case 7

Similar to Case 1, consider a reduction using (22) followed by application of (21) to generate the following ODE

$$w(x) \Gamma\left(1 - \frac{\alpha}{3}\right) \left(\Gamma\left(1 - \frac{4\alpha}{3}\right)\right)^{-1} - (w(x))^3 \frac{d^3}{dx^3} w(x) - \frac{3 (w(x))^2 \left(\frac{d^2}{dx^2} w(x)\right) \frac{d}{dx} w(x)}{2}$$
$$- a \left((w(x))^3 \frac{d^2}{dx^2} w(x) + (w(x))^2 \left(\frac{d}{dx} w(x)\right)^2 \right) - \frac{2 a^2 (w(x))^3 \frac{d}{dx} w(x)}{9} = 0,$$

which we solve with a power series $w(x) = \sum_{r_1=0}^{\infty} a_{r_1} x^{r_1}$ to obtain a_0, a_1, a_2 as arbitrary and where

$$\begin{aligned} w(x) &= a_0 + a_1 x + a_2 x^2 + \\ &\quad \frac{x^3}{54 a_0^3 \Gamma\left(1 - \frac{4\alpha}{3}\right)} \Bigg(-2 a^2 a_1 a_0^3 \Gamma\left(1 - \frac{4\alpha}{3}\right) - 18 a a_2 a_0^3 \Gamma\left(1 - \frac{4\alpha}{3}\right) \\ &\quad -9 a a_1^2 a_0^2 \Gamma\left(1 - \frac{4\alpha}{3}\right) - 27 a_1 a_2 a_0^2 \Gamma\left(1 - \frac{4\alpha}{3}\right) + 9 a_0 \Gamma\left(1 - \frac{\alpha}{3}\right) \Bigg) \\ &\quad + \ldots \end{aligned} \qquad (50)$$

with graphical solution expressed in Figure 5.

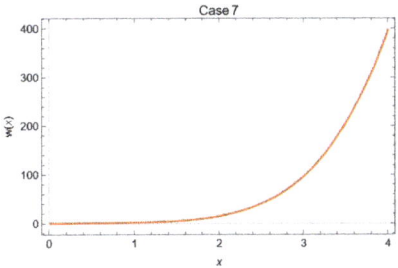

Figure 5. We let $a_0 = 1, a_1 = 1, a_2 = 1, \alpha = \frac{1}{2}, a = 1$.

4.8. Case 8

This case shares the symmetry X_4 with Case 5; hence, the reduction is the same for the LHS of the equation, but the RHS differs, so that (8) transforms to

$$\left(P_{\frac{3}{\alpha}}^{-1-2\alpha,\alpha}w\right)(z) = w^2(z)\left((a + \frac{3}{2}w''(z))w'(z) + w(z)w'''(z)\right).$$

4.9. Case 9

Similar to Case 1, consider a reduction using (22) followed by application of (21) to generate the following ODE

$$w(x)\Gamma\left(1 - \frac{\alpha}{5}\right)\left(\Gamma\left(1 - \frac{6\alpha}{5}\right)\right)^{-1} - (w(x))^5 \frac{d^5}{dx^5}w(x) - 5(w(x))^4\left(\left(\frac{d^4}{dx^4}w(x)\right)\frac{d}{dx}w(x)\right. \\ \left. + 2\left(\frac{d^2}{dx^2}w(x)\right)\frac{d^3}{dx^3}w(x)\right) = 0,$$

which we solve with a power series $w(x) = \sum_{r_1=0}^{\infty} a_{r_1} x^{r_1}$ to obtain a_0, a_1, a_2, a_3, a_4 as arbitrary and where

$$\begin{aligned} w(x) &= a_0 + a_1 x + a_2 x^2 + a_3 x^3 + a_4 x^4 \\ &\quad + \frac{x^5}{120 a_0^4 \Gamma\left(1 - \frac{6\alpha}{5}\right)} \left(-120 a_2 a_3 a_0^3 \Gamma\left(1 - \frac{6\alpha}{5}\right)\right. \\ &\quad \left. -120 a_1 a_4 a_0^3 \Gamma\left(1 - \frac{6\alpha}{5}\right) + \Gamma\left(1 - \frac{\alpha}{5}\right)\right) \\ &\quad + \ldots \end{aligned} \tag{51}$$

with graphical solution expressed in Figure 6.

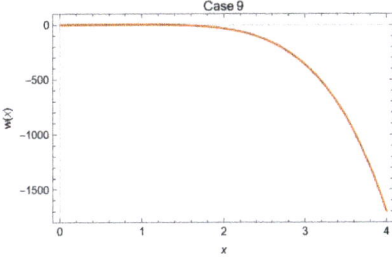

Figure 6. We let $a_0 = 1, a_1 = 1, a_2 = 1, a_3 = 1, a_4 = 1, \alpha = \frac{1}{2}, a = 1$.

4.10. Case 10

Finally, consider a reduction using (22) followed by application of (21) to generate the following ODE

$$w(x)\Gamma\left(1-\tfrac{\alpha}{5}\right)\left(\Gamma\left(1-\tfrac{6\alpha}{5}\right)\right)^{-1} - (w(x))^5 \tfrac{d^5}{dx^5}w(x)$$
$$-5(w(x))^4\left(\left(\tfrac{d^4}{dx^4}w(x)\right)\tfrac{d}{dx}w(x) + 1/2\left(\tfrac{d^2}{dx^2}w(x)\right)\tfrac{d^3}{dx^3}w(x)\right)$$
$$-\tfrac{15(w(x))^3\left(\tfrac{d}{dx}w(x)\right)^2 \tfrac{d^3}{dx^3}w(x)}{4} = 0,$$

which we solve with a power series $w(x) = \sum_{r_1=0}^{\infty} a_{r_1} x^{r_1}$ to obtain a_0, a_1, a_2, a_3, a_4 as arbitrary and where

$$\begin{aligned}
w(x) &= a_0 + a_1 x + a_2 x^2 + a_3 x^3 + a_4 x^4 + \\
&\quad \frac{x^5}{240 a_0^5 \Gamma\left(1-\tfrac{6\alpha}{5}\right)}\left(-60 a_2 a_3 a_0^4 \Gamma\left(1-\tfrac{6\alpha}{5}\right)\right. \\
&\quad \left. - 240 a_1 a_4 a_0^4 \Gamma\left(1-\tfrac{6\alpha}{5}\right) - 45 a_1^2 a_3 a_0^3 \Gamma\left(1-\tfrac{6\alpha}{5}\right)\right. \\
&\quad \left. + 2 a_0 \Gamma\left(1-\tfrac{\alpha}{5}\right)\right) + \ldots
\end{aligned} \tag{52}$$

with graphical solution expressed in Figure 7.

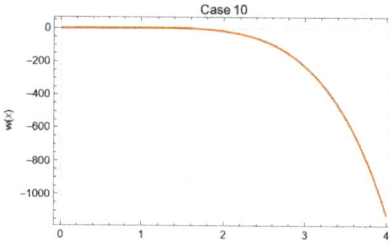

Figure 7. We let $a_0 = 1, a_1 = 1, a_2 = 1, a_3 = 1, a_4 = 1, \alpha = \tfrac{1}{2}, a = 1$.

5. Concluding Remarks

It has remained a topic of debate as to how to find the solutions of highly nonlinear equations. There are many challenges associated with finding reductions and solutions of FDEs in particular. We have shown that Lie symmetries combined with power series methods are extremely effective in the analysis. The purpose of this study is to show how power series may be applied to Lie symmetry reductions. We have restricted our attention to FDEs with the Riemann–Liouville derivative; however, reductions from Caputo fractional derivatives will work in practice. In this regard, power series may be used to address problems in solving reduced equations obtained from other methods as well.

Author Contributions: J.T.K. conducted formal analysis, software applications and wrote the first draft. S.J. conceptualised the study and reviewed and edited the manuscript. All authors have read and agreed to the published version of the manuscript.

Funding: National Research Foundation of South Africa.

Data Availability Statement: This study did not report any data.

Conflicts of Interest: The authors declare no conflict of interest.

References

1. Fujimoto, A.; Watanabe, Y. Polynomial evolution equations of not normal type admitting nontrivial symmetries. *Phys. Lett. A* **1989**, *136*, 294–299. [CrossRef]
2. Olver, P.J. Evolution equations possessing infinitely many symmetries. *J. Math. Phys.* **1977**, *18*, 1212. [CrossRef]
3. Fuchssteiner, B. Application of Hereditary Symmetries to Nonlinear Evolution Equations. *Nonlin. Anal. Theory Meth. Appl.* **1979**, *3*, 849–862. [CrossRef]
4. Sakovich, S.Y. Fujimoto-Watanabe equations and differential substitutions. *J. Phys. A Math. Gen.* **1991**, *24*, L519. [CrossRef]
5. Dong, H.; Fang, Y.; Guo, B.; Liu, Y. Lie point symmetry, conservation laws and exact power series solutions to the Fujimoto-Watanabe equation. *Quaest. Math.* **2019**, *43*, 1349–1365. [CrossRef]
6. Muatjetjeja, B. On the symmetry analysis and conservation laws of the (1 + 1)-dimensional Hénon-Lane-Emden system. *Math. Methods Appl. Sci.* **2017**, *40*, 1531–1537. [CrossRef]
7. Muatjetjeja, B. Coupled Lane-Emden-Klein-Gordon-Fock system with central symmetry: Symmetries and conservation laws. *J. Differ. Equ.* **2017**, *263*, 8322–8328. [CrossRef]
8. Gwaxa, B.; Jamal, S.; Johnpillai, A.G. On the conservation laws, Lie symmetry analysis and power series solutions of a class of third-order polynomial evolution equations, to appear in. *Arab. J. Math.* **2023**.
9. Dubey, S.; Chakraverty, S. Application of modified extended tanh method in solving fractional order coupled wave equations. *Math. Comput. Simul.* **2022**, *198*, 509–520. [CrossRef]
10. Wang, G.; Shen, B.; He, M.; Guan, F.; Zhang, L. Symmetry Analysis and PT-Symmetric Extension of the Fifth-Order Korteweg-de Vries-Like Equation. *Fractal Fract.* **2022**, *6*, 468. [CrossRef]
11. Mnguni, N.; Jamal, S. Invariant solutions of fractional-order spatio-temporal partial differential equations. *Int. J. Nonlinear Sci. Numer.* **2021**, *22*, 1011–1022. [CrossRef]
12. El-Ajou, A.; Abu Arqub, O.; Al Zhour, Z.; Momani, S. New results on fractional power series: Theories and applications. *Entropy* **2013**, *15*, 5305–5323. [CrossRef]
13. Jamal, S.; Mnguni, N. Moving front solutions of a time-fractional power-law fluid under gravity. *Quaest. Math.* **2021**, *44*, 1295–1304. [CrossRef]
14. Buckwar, E.; Luchko, Y. Invariance of a partial differential equation of fractional order under the Lie group of scaling transformations. *J. Math. Anal. Appl.* **1998**, *227*, 81–97. [CrossRef]
15. Gazizov, R.K.; Kasatkin, A.A.; Lukashchuk, S.Y. Symmetry properties of fractional diffusion equations. *Phys. Scr.* **2009**, *T136*, 014016. [CrossRef]
16. Bakkyaraj, T. Lie symmetry analysis of system of nonlinear fractional partial differential equations with Caputo fractional derivative. *Eur. Phys. J. Plus* **2020**, *135*, 126. [CrossRef]
17. Hashemi, M.S.; Baleanu, D. *Lie Symmetry Analysis of Fractional Differential Equations*; CRC Press: Boca Raton, FL, USA, 2020.
18. Caputo, M. Linear Models of Dissipation whose Q is almost Frequency Independent-II. *Geophys. J. R. Astr. Soc.* **1967**, *13*, 529. [CrossRef]
19. Miller, K.S.; Ross, B. *An Introduction to the Fractional Calculus and Fractional Differential Equations*; Wiley: New York, NY, USA, 1993.
20. Kiryakova, V. *Generalised Fractional Calculus and Applications*; Pitman Res. Notes in Math; CRC Press: Boca Raton, FL, USA, 1994.
21. Leibniz, G.W. Letter from Hanover; Germany; to G.F.A L'Hospital, 30 September 1695. In *Leibniz Mathematische Schriften*; Olms: Hildesheim, Germany, 1962; pp. 301–302.
22. Leibniz, G.W. Letter from Hanover; Germany; to Johann Bernoulli, 28 December 1695. In *Leibniz Mathematische Schriften*; Olms: Hildesheim, Germany, 1962; p. 226.
23. Leibniz, G.W. Letter from Hanover; Germany; to John Wallis, 30 May 1697. In *Leibniz Mathematische Schriften*; Olms: Hildesheim, Germany, 1962; p. 25.
24. Atangana, A.; Secer, A. A note on fractional order derivatives and table of fractional derivatives of some special functions. *Abstr. Appl. Anal.* **2013**, *2013*, 279681. [CrossRef]
25. Asmar, N.H. *Partial Differential Equations with Fourier Series and Boundary Value Problems*, 2nd ed.; China Machine Press: Beijing, China, 2005.
26. Rudin, W. *Principles of Mathematical Analysis*, 3rd ed.; China Machine Press: Beijing, China, 2004.
27. Guo, B.; Dong, H.; Fang, Y. Symmetry Groups, Similarity Reductions, and Conservation Laws of the Time-Fractional Fujimoto-Watanabe Equation Using Lie Symmetry Analysis Method. *Complexity* **2020**, *2020*, 4830684. [CrossRef]

Disclaimer/Publisher's Note: The statements, opinions and data contained in all publications are solely those of the individual author(s) and contributor(s) and not of MDPI and/or the editor(s). MDPI and/or the editor(s) disclaim responsibility for any injury to people or property resulting from any ideas, methods, instructions or products referred to in the content.

Article

New Results for Homoclinic Fractional Hamiltonian Systems of Order $\alpha \in (1/2, 1]$

Abdelkader Moumen [1,†], Hamid Boulares [2,†], Jehad Alzabut [3,4,†,*], Fathi Khelifi [5,†] and Moheddine Imsatfia [6,†]

1 Department of Mathematics, Faculty of Science, University of Ha'il, Ha'il 55425, Saudi Arabia
2 Laboratory of Analysis and Control of Differential Equations "ACED", Faculty MISM, Department of Mathematics, University of Guelma, Guelma 24000, Algeria
3 Department of Mathematics and Sciences, Prince Sultan University, Riyadh 11586, Saudi Arabia
4 Department of Industrial Engineering, Ostim Technical University, Ankara 06374, Türkiye
5 Lycée Secondaire Avenue Tahar, Sousse 4000, Tunisia
6 Department of Mathematics, College of Science, King Khalid University, Abha 61413, Saudi Arabia
* Correspondence: jalzabut@psu.edu.sa
† These authors contributed equally to this work.

Abstract: In this manuscript, we are interested in studying the homoclinic solutions of fractional Hamiltonian system of the form $-_\varsigma\mathcal{D}_\infty^\alpha(_{-\infty}\mathcal{D}_\varsigma^\alpha Z(\varsigma)) - \mathcal{A}(\varsigma)Z(\varsigma) + \nabla\omega(\varsigma, Z(\varsigma)) = 0$, where $\alpha \in (\frac{1}{2}, 1]$, $Z \in H^\alpha(\mathbb{R}, \mathbb{R}^N)$ and $\omega \in C^1(\mathbb{R} \times \mathbb{R}^N, \mathbb{R})$ are not periodic in ς. The characteristics of the critical point theory are used to illustrate the primary findings. Our results substantially improve and generalize the most recent results of the proposed system. We conclude our study by providing an example to highlight the significance of the theoretical results.

Keywords: fractional Hamiltonian systems; Mountain Pass Theorem; genus properties critical point

Citation: Moumen, A.; Boulares, H.; Alzabut, J.; Khelifi, F.; Imsatfia, M. New Results for Homoclinic Fractional Hamiltonian Systems of Order $\alpha \in (1/2, 1]$. *Fractal Fract.* **2023**, *7*, 39. https://doi.org/10.3390/fractalfract7010039

Academic Editors: António Lopes, Riccardo Caponetto and Sameerah Jamal

Received: 4 November 2022
Revised: 16 December 2022
Accepted: 26 December 2022
Published: 29 December 2022

Copyright: © 2022 by the authors. Licensee MDPI, Basel, Switzerland. This article is an open access article distributed under the terms and conditions of the Creative Commons Attribution (CC BY) license (https://creativecommons.org/licenses/by/4.0/).

1. Introduction

In physics, mechanics, control theory, biology, bioengineering, and economics, processes are frequently simulated using fractional ordinary and partial differential equations. The theory of fractional differential equations has consequently attracted a lot of attention in recent years. For instance, existence and stability are addressed in [1–3], and several resolution strategies are in [4–6]. The monographs [7,8] are exceptional sources for numerous techniques that are thought to be extensions of various differential equations. Recent discussions have focused in particular on equations that have both left and right fractional derivatives. With regard to their numerous applications, these kinds of equations are significant and are considered as a novel subject in the theory of fractional differential equations. Using nonlinear analytic techniques such as fixed point theory, there have appeared many results dealing with the existence and multiplicity of solutions to nonlinear fractional differential equations in this field. For instance, we name here Leray–Schauder nonlinear alternative [9], topological degree theory [10], and the comparison method, which includes upper and lower solutions and monotone iterative method [11,12], and so on. On the other hand, it has been demonstrated that the critical point theory and variational techniques are crucial for assessing whether or not differential equations have solutions. With the help of this theory, one can search for solutions to a specific boundary value problem by locating the critical points of an appropriate energy functional defined on a suitable function space. In light of this, the critical point theory has developed into a potent tool for investigating the existence of solutions to differential equations with variational forms (see [13,14] and the references therein).

Adopting the aforementioned classic research, Zhou and Lu [15] implemented the critical point theory to tackle the existence of solutions for the following fractional BVP

$$\begin{cases} {}_\varsigma\mathfrak{D}_T^\alpha({}_0\mathfrak{D}_\varsigma^\alpha Z(\varsigma)) = \nabla\varpi(\varsigma, Z(\varsigma)), & \text{a.e. } \varsigma \in [0, T], \\ Z(0) = Z(T), \end{cases} \quad (1)$$

where α in $(\frac{1}{2}, 1)$, $Z \in \mathbb{R}^N$, $\varpi \in C^1([0, T] \times \mathbb{R}^N, \mathbb{R})$ and $\nabla\varpi(\varsigma, Z)$ is the gradient of ϖ at Z. It is significant to note that many of the premises made in order to arrive at the conclusions in [15] weaken the fundamental theorems. Inspired by their work, Torres [16] studied the following fractional Hamiltonian systems

$$\begin{cases} -{}_\varsigma\mathfrak{D}_\infty^\alpha(-{}_\infty\mathfrak{D}_\varsigma^\alpha Z(\varsigma)) - \mathcal{A}(\varsigma)Z(\varsigma) + \nabla\varpi(\varsigma, Z(\varsigma)) = 0, \\ Z \in H^\alpha(\mathbb{R}, \mathbb{R}^N), \end{cases} \quad (2)$$

where $-{}_\infty\mathfrak{D}_\varsigma^\alpha$ and ${}_\varsigma\mathfrak{D}_\infty^\alpha$ are left and right Liouville–Weyl fractional derivatives of order α and $\mathcal{A}(\varsigma) \in C(\mathbb{R}, \mathbb{R}^{N^2})$ is symmetric and positive definite matrix for all $\varsigma \in \mathbb{R}$. The Mountain Pass Theorem was used in [16] to show that equations accept at least one nontrivial solution as long as $\mathcal{A}$ and ϖ can validate the following four hypotheses:

(Y_0) $\mathcal{A}(\varsigma)$ is symmetric and positive definite matrix $\forall\, \varsigma \in \mathbb{R}$, and there exists functional $l \in C(\mathbb{R}, (0, \infty))$ while $l(\varsigma) \to \infty$ as $|\varsigma| \to \infty$ and $(\mathcal{A}(\varsigma)Z, Z) \geq l(\varsigma)|Z|^2$, for any $\varsigma \in \mathbb{R}$ and $Z \in \mathbb{R}^N$;

($\mathcal{F}_1$) $|\nabla\varpi(\varsigma, Z)| = o(|Z|)$ as $|Z| \to 0$ uniformly in $\varsigma \in \mathbb{R}$;

($\mathcal{F}_2$) There exists $\overline{\varpi} \in C(\mathbb{R}^N, \mathbb{R})$ such that $|\varpi(\varsigma, Z)| + |\nabla\varpi(\varsigma, Z)| \leq |\overline{\varpi}(Z)|$ for all $(\varsigma, Z) \in \mathbb{R} \times \mathbb{R}^N$;

($\mathcal{F}_3$) There exists some constant $\mu > 2$ such as $0 < \mu\varpi(\varsigma, Z) \leq (\nabla\varpi(\varsigma, Z), Z)$, for any $\varsigma \in \mathbb{R}$ and $Z \in \mathbb{R}^N \setminus \{0\}$.

For $\alpha = 1$, Equation (2) is downloaded to the following standard second-order Hamiltonian system

$$\ddot{Z}(\varsigma) - \mathcal{A}(\varsigma)Z(\varsigma) + \nabla\varpi(\varsigma, Z(\varsigma)) = 0. \quad (3)$$

Several papers including [17–24] investigated the existence of homoclinic solutions for the Hamiltonian system (3) when $\mathcal{A}(\varsigma)$ and $\varpi(\varsigma, Z)$ are either independent of or periodic in ς.

In this work, we impose new standards based on the critical point theory to demonstrate the existence of infinitely many homoclinic solutions of fractional Hamiltonian system (2) where $\varpi(\varsigma, Z)$ is sub-quadratic as $|Z| \to +\infty$. In addition to condition (Y_0), we assume that $\varpi(\varsigma, Z)$ fulfills the following three conditions:

(Λ_1) $\varpi \in C^1(\mathbb{R} \times \mathbb{R}^N, \mathbb{R})$, and there exists γ_1, γ_2 satisfying $1 < \gamma_1 < \gamma_2 < 2$ and two functional a_1, a_2 in $\mathcal{L}^{\frac{2}{2-\gamma_1}}(\mathbb{R}, \mathbb{R}^+)$ such that

$$|\varpi(\varsigma, Z)| \leq a_1(\varsigma)|Z|^{\gamma_1}, \text{ for all } (\varsigma, Z) \text{ in } \mathbb{R} \times \mathbb{R}^N, |Z| \leq 1,$$

and

$$|\varpi(\varsigma, Z)| \leq a_2(\varsigma)|Z|^{\gamma_2}, \text{ for all } (\varsigma, Z) \text{ in } \mathbb{R} \times \mathbb{R}^N, |Z| \geq 1.$$

(Λ_2) There exists b in $\mathcal{L}^{\frac{2}{2-\gamma_1}}(\mathbb{R}, \mathbb{R}^+)$ and φ in $C([0, +\infty), [0, +\infty))$ such that

$$|\nabla\varpi(\varsigma, Z)| \leq b(\varsigma)\varphi(|Z|), \text{ for all } (\varsigma, Z) \text{ in } \mathbb{R} \times \mathbb{R}^N,$$

and $\varphi(s) = O(s^{\gamma_1 - 1})$ as $s \to 0^+$.

(Λ_3) There exists an open set $J \subset \mathbb{R}$ and two constants $\gamma_3 \in (1, 2)$, $\eta > 0$ such that

$$\varpi(\varsigma, Z) \geq \eta|Z|^{\gamma_3}, \,\forall\, (\varsigma, Z) \in J \times \mathbb{R}^N, |Z| \leq 1.$$

It is worthy mentioning here that the results given in [14] were obtained under the condition $(\mathcal{F}_3)$, which is known as the global Ambrosetti–Rabinowitz condition. That is, $\varpi(\varsigma, Z)$ is super-quadratic when $|Z| \to \infty$. Moreover, it was assumed that Z and ϖ are periodic in ς. In this paper, however, the main results are proved under less restrictive condition where $\mathcal{A}$ is coercive at infinity, ϖ is sub-quadratic growth as $|Z| \to \infty$ ($\frac{\varpi}{|Z|^2} = 0$ if $|Z| \to \infty$) and Z and ϖ are not periodic in ς. Our results supply substantial generalizations to the recent results existing in the literature.

Significant findings of our paper are described in the following two theorems.

Theorem 1. *If conditions (Y_0), (Λ_1), (Λ_2), and (Λ_3) hold. So, (2) accepts one nontrivial homoclinic solution.*

Theorem 2. *Assuming that (Y_0), (Λ_1), (Λ_2) and (Λ_3) hold. In addition, assume that $\varpi(\varsigma, Z)$ is even in Z. Then, (2) has infinitely many nontrivial homoclinic solutions $(Z_k)_{k \in \mathbb{N}}$ such that, as $k \to \infty$,*

$$\int_{\mathbb{R}} \left[\frac{1}{2} |_{-\infty}\mathcal{D}_{\varsigma}^{\alpha} Z_k(\varsigma)|^2 + \frac{1}{2} (\mathcal{A}(\varsigma) Z_k(\varsigma), Z_k(\varsigma)) - \varpi(\varsigma, Z_k(\varsigma)) \right] d\varsigma \to 0^-. \quad (4)$$

The proofs of Theorems 1 and 2 are given in Section 3.

2. Essential Preliminaries

This section is devoted to stating and demonstrating some fundamental definitions and lemmas that are required in the work that follows.

Definition 1. *The left and right Liouville–Weyl fractional integrals of order α on $\mathbb{R}$, $(0 < \alpha < 1)$ are, respectively, given by*

$$_{-\infty}I_{\varkappa}^{\alpha} Z(\varkappa) = \frac{1}{\Gamma(\alpha)} \int_{-\infty}^{\varkappa} (\varkappa - \xi)^{\alpha-1} Z(\xi) \, d\xi, \quad \varkappa \in \mathbb{R}, \quad (5)$$

and

$$_{\varkappa}I_{\infty}^{\alpha} Z(\varkappa) = \frac{1}{\Gamma(\alpha)} \int_{\varkappa}^{\infty} (\xi - \varkappa)^{\alpha-1} Z(\xi) \, d\xi, \quad \varkappa \in \mathbb{R}.$$

Definition 2. *The left and the right Liouville–Weyl fractional derivatives of order α on $\mathbb{R}$, $(0 < \alpha < 1)$ are, respectively, given by*

$$_{-\infty}\mathcal{D}_{\varkappa}^{\alpha} Z(\varkappa) = \frac{d}{d\varkappa} {}_{-\infty}I_{\varkappa}^{1-\alpha} Z(\varkappa), \quad \varkappa \in \mathbb{R} \quad (6)$$

and

$$_{\varkappa}\mathcal{D}_{\infty}^{\alpha} Z(\varkappa) = -\frac{d}{d\varkappa} {}_{\varkappa}I_{\infty}^{1-\alpha} Z(\varkappa), \quad \varkappa \in \mathbb{R}.$$

Remark 1. *The operators (5) and (6) can be written in the form*

$$_{-\infty}\mathcal{D}_{\varkappa}^{\alpha} Z(\varkappa) = \frac{\alpha}{\Gamma(1-\alpha)} \int_0^{\infty} \frac{Z(\varkappa) - Z(\varkappa - \xi)}{\xi^{\alpha+1}} d\xi,$$

and

$$_{\varkappa}\mathcal{D}_{\infty}^{\alpha} Z(\varkappa) = \frac{\alpha}{\Gamma(1-\alpha)} \int_0^{\infty} \frac{Z(\varkappa) - Z(\varkappa + \xi)}{\xi^{\alpha+1}} d\xi.$$

Definition 3. *A solution x of (2) is called homoclinic (to 0) if $x \in C^2(\mathbb{R}, \mathbb{R}^N)$, $x \neq 0$, $x(t) \to 0$ and $\dot{x}(t) \to 0$ as $|t| \to \infty$. A function φ is said to be coercive if $\varphi(t) \to \infty$ as $|t| \to \infty$.*

We recall that the Fourier transform of $Z(\cdot)$ is

$$\widehat{Z}(w) = \int_{-\infty}^{\infty} e^{-i\varkappa \cdot w} Z(\varkappa)\, d\varkappa.$$

The semi–norm is given by

$$|Z|_{I_{-\infty}^{\alpha}} := \|_{-\infty}\mathfrak{D}_{\varkappa}^{\alpha} Z\|_{\mathbb{L}^2},\ \alpha > 0,$$

while the norm is

$$\|Z\|_{I_{-\infty}^{\alpha}} := \left(\|Z\|_{\mathbb{L}^2}^2 + |Z|_{I_{-\infty}^{\alpha}}^2\right)^{1/2}.$$

We denote by $I_{-\infty}^{\alpha}(\mathbb{R})$ the completion of $C_0^{\infty}(\mathbb{R})$ coupled with the norm $\|\cdot\|_{I_{-\infty}^{\alpha}}$, that is

$$I_{-\infty}^{\alpha}(\mathbb{R}) = \overline{C_0^{\infty}(\mathbb{R})}^{\|\cdot\|_{I_{-\infty}^{\alpha}}}.$$

Further, we define the semi-norm by

$$|Z|_{\alpha} = \||w|^{\alpha}\widehat{Z}\|_{\mathbb{L}^2},\ 0 < \alpha < 1,$$

and the norm by

$$\|Z\|_{\alpha} = (\|Z\|_{\mathbb{L}^2}^2 + |Z|_{\alpha}^2)^{1/2}.$$

We define the fractional Sobolev space $H^{\alpha}(\mathbb{R})$ in terms of the Fourier transform as follows:

$$H^{\alpha}(\mathbb{R}) := \overline{C_0^{\infty}(\mathbb{R})}^{\|\cdot\|_{\alpha}}.$$

Noting that $Z \in \mathbb{L}^2(\mathbb{R})$ is an element of $I_{-\infty}^{\alpha}(\mathbb{R})$ if and only if

$$|w|^{\alpha}\widehat{Z} \in \mathbb{L}^2(\mathbb{R}).$$

In particular, we obtain

$$|Z|_{I_{-\infty}^{\alpha}} = \||w|^{\alpha}\widehat{Z}\|_{\mathbb{L}^2(\mathbb{R})}.$$

Therefore, if the semi-norm and the norm are equivalent, then $H^{\alpha}(\mathbb{R})$ and $I_{-\infty}^{\alpha}(\mathbb{R})$ are also equivalent [16].

Similar to $I_{-\infty}^{\alpha}(\mathbb{R})$, we define $I_{\infty}^{\alpha}(\mathbb{R})$. Thus, the semi-norm $|Z|_{I_{\infty}^{\alpha}}$ and the norm $|Z|_{I_{\infty}^{\alpha}}$ of Z are, respectively, given by

$$|Z|_{I_{\infty}^{\alpha}} := \|_{\varkappa}\mathfrak{D}_{\infty}^{\alpha}\|_{\mathbb{L}^2(\mathbb{R})},$$

and

$$\|Z\|_{I_{\infty}^{\alpha}} := (\|Z\|_{\mathbb{L}^2}^2 + |Z|_{I_{\infty}^{\alpha}}^2)^{1/2}.$$

Letting

$$I_{-\infty}^{\alpha}(\mathbb{R}) := \overline{C_0^{\infty}(\mathbb{R})}^{\|\cdot\|_{I_{-\infty}^{\alpha}}}.$$

Additionally, if the semi-norm and the norm are equivalent, then $I_{\infty}^{\alpha}(\mathbb{R})$ and $I_{-\infty}^{\alpha}(\mathbb{R})$ are equivalent.

Lemma 1 ([16]). *If $\alpha > \frac{1}{2}$, then $H^{\alpha}(\mathbb{R})$ is included in the continuous real functions space $C(\mathbb{R})$, and there exists a constant C_{α} (noted by C) such that*

$$\|Z\|_{\mathbb{L}^{\infty}} = \sup_{Z \in \mathbb{R}} |Z(\varkappa)| \leq C\|Z\|_{\alpha}. \tag{7}$$

Remark 2. If $Z \in H^\alpha(\mathbb{R})$, then $Z \in \mathbb{L}^q(\mathbb{R})$ for any q in $[2, \infty]$, as

$$\int_\mathbb{R} |Z(\varkappa)|^q d\varkappa \leq \|Z\|_{\mathbb{L}^\infty}^{q-2} \|Z\|_{\mathbb{L}^2}^2.$$

Next, we define the fractional space and construct the variational framework of the fractional Hamiltonian systems (2). To this end, letting

$$E = X^\alpha = \left\{ Z \text{ in } H^\alpha(\mathbb{R}, \mathbb{R}^n) : \int_\mathbb{R} |_{-\infty}\mathfrak{D}_\varsigma^\alpha Z(\varsigma)|^2 + (\mathcal{A}(\varsigma)Z(\varsigma), Z(\varsigma))\, d\varsigma < \infty \right\}. \tag{8}$$

The space X^α is a reflexive and separable Hilbert space under the inner product

$$(Z, v)_{X^\alpha} = \int_\mathbb{R} (_{-\infty}\mathfrak{D}_\varsigma^\alpha Z(\varsigma)._{-\infty}\mathfrak{D}_\varsigma^\alpha v(\varsigma)) + (\mathcal{A}(\varsigma)Z(\varsigma), v(\varsigma))d\varsigma,$$

with the norm

$$\|Z\|^2 = (Z, Z)_{X^\alpha}.$$

Lemma 2. *If $\mathcal{A}$ satisfies (Y_0), then X^α is continuously embedded in $H^\alpha(\mathbb{R}, \mathbb{R}^n)$.*

Proof. Since $l \in C(\mathbb{R}, (0, \infty))$ and l is coercive, then $l_* := \min_{\varsigma \in \mathbb{R}} l(\varsigma)$ exists. So, we obtain

$$(\mathcal{A}(\varsigma)Z(\varsigma), Z(\varsigma)) \geq l(\varsigma)|\varsigma|^2 \geq l_*|\varsigma|^2, \text{ for any real } \varsigma.$$

Thus,

$$\|Z\|_\alpha^2 = \int_\mathbb{R} (|_{-\infty}\mathfrak{D}_\varsigma^\alpha Z(\varsigma)|^2 + (\mathcal{A}(\varsigma)Z(\varsigma), Z(\varsigma)))d\varsigma$$
$$\leq \int_\mathbb{R} |_{-\infty}\mathfrak{D}_\varsigma^\alpha Z(\varsigma)|^2 d\varsigma + \frac{1}{l_*} \int_\mathbb{R} (\mathcal{A}(\varsigma)Z(\varsigma), Z(\varsigma))d\varsigma.$$

Therefore,

$$\|Z\|_\alpha^2 \leq K\|Z\|^2, \tag{9}$$

where $K := \max\left(1, \frac{1}{l_*}\right)$. □

It is difficult to demonstrate that there are infinitely many solutions to the Hamiltonian systems (2) because the Sobolev embedding is not compact under the assumptions of Theorems 1 and 2. We will utilize the following lemma to ensure that the task is made simple:

Lemma 3. *If $\mathcal{A}$ satisfies the condition (Y_0), then the embedding of X^α in $\mathbb{L}^2(\mathbb{R})$ is compact.*

Proof. Form Lemma 2 and Remark 2, we obtain the continuity of $X^\alpha \hookrightarrow \mathbb{L}^2(\mathbb{R})$. Let $(Z_k) \in X^\alpha$ be a sequence such that $Z_k \rightharpoonup Z$ in X^α. We will prove that $Z_k \to Z$ in $\mathbb{L}^2(\mathbb{R})$ functional. The Banach–Steinhauss theorem implies that

$$A := \sup_{k \in \mathbb{N}} \|Z_k - Z\| < \infty.$$

Let $\epsilon > 0$. Since $\lim_{|\varsigma| \to \infty} l(\varsigma) = \infty$, there exits a real $T_0 > 0$ such that

$$\frac{1}{l(\varsigma)} \leq \epsilon, \text{ for all } |\varsigma| \geq T_0.$$

Therefore,

$$\int_{|\varsigma|\geq T_0} |Z_k(\varsigma) - Z(\varsigma)|^2 d\varsigma \leq \epsilon \int_{|\varsigma|\geq T_0} l(\varsigma)|Z_k(\varsigma) - Z(\varsigma)|^2 d\varsigma$$
$$\leq \epsilon \|Z_k - Z\|^2 \leq \epsilon A^2. \tag{10}$$

Moreover, Sobolev's theorem ([13]) implies that $Z_k \to Z$ uniformly on $[-T_0, T_0]$. Thus, there is $k_0 \in \mathbb{N}$ such that

$$\int_{|\varsigma|\leq T_0} |Z_k(\varsigma) - Z(\varsigma)|^2 d\varsigma \leq \epsilon, \text{ for all } k \geq k_0. \tag{11}$$

By combining (10) and (11), we obtain that $Z_k \to Z$ in $\mathbb{L}^2(\mathbb{R})$. □

Remark 3. *We note that Remark 2 and Lemma 3 assure the embedding of X^α in $L^q(\mathbb{R})$. For $q \in (2, \infty)$, the operator X^α is also continuous and compact. Consequently, by the Lemma 1, there exists a constant C_α satisfies*

$$\|Z_q\| \leq C_q \|Z\| \text{ for any } q \in [2, \infty]. \tag{12}$$

Lemma 4. *Under the condition of Theorem 1, if $Z_k \rightharpoonup Z$ in X^α, then $\nabla\omega(\varsigma, Z_k) \to \nabla\omega(\varsigma, Z)$ in $\mathbb{L}^2(\mathbb{R})$.*

Proof. Assuming $Z_k \rightharpoonup Z$ in X^α. Consequently, by using the Banach–Steinhauss theorem, there exists $M > 0$ such that

$$\sup_{k\in\mathbb{N}}\|Z_k\| \leq M \text{ and } \|Z\| \leq M. \tag{13}$$

By (Λ_2), there exists $M_1 > 0$ such as

$$\varphi(|Z|) \leq M_1 |Z|^{\gamma_1 - 1}, \text{ for all } |Z| \leq M. \tag{14}$$

Further, by (8), for any $Z \in X^\alpha$, there exists $T \overset{\circ}{>} 0$ such that

$$|Z(\varsigma)| \leq M, \text{ for all } |\varsigma| \geq T. \tag{15}$$

Therefore, from the inequalities (12), (13), (14) and (15), and by using Hölder inequality, we obtain

$$\int_{|\varsigma|\geq T} |\nabla\omega(\varsigma, Z_k(\varsigma)) - \nabla\omega(\varsigma, Z(\varsigma))|^2 d\varsigma$$
$$\leq 2\int_{|\varsigma|\geq T} \left(|\nabla\omega(\varsigma, Z_k(\varsigma))|^2 + |\nabla\omega(\varsigma, Z(\varsigma))|^2\right) d\varsigma$$
$$\leq 2M_1^2 \int_{|\varsigma|\geq T} |b(\varsigma)|^2 \left(|Z_k(\varsigma)|^{2(\gamma_1-1)} + |Z(\varsigma)|^{2(\gamma_1-1)}\right) d\varsigma$$
$$\leq 2M_1^2 \left(\int_{|\varsigma|\geq T} |b(\varsigma)|^{\frac{2}{2-\gamma_1}} d\varsigma\right)^{2-\gamma_1} \left(\int_{|\varsigma|\geq T} |Z_k(\varsigma)|^2 d\varsigma\right)^{\gamma_1-1}$$
$$+ 2M_1^2 \left(\int_{|\varsigma|\geq T} |b(\varsigma)|^{\frac{2}{2-\gamma_1}} d\varsigma\right)^{2-\gamma_1} \left(\int_{|\varsigma|\geq T} |Z(\varsigma)|^2 d\varsigma\right)^{\gamma_1-1}$$
$$\leq 2M_1^2 \|b\|_{\frac{2}{2-\gamma_1}}^2 \left(\|Z_k\|_2^{2(\gamma_1-1)} + \|Z\|_2^{2(\gamma_1-1)}\right)$$
$$\leq 4M_1^2 M^{2(\gamma_1-1)} C_2^{2(\gamma_1-1)} \|b\|_{\frac{2}{2-\gamma_1}}^2. \tag{16}$$

Moreover, since $\nabla\omega(\varsigma, Z)$ is continuous, there is a constant $d > 0$ such that

$$\int_{|\varsigma|\leq T}|\nabla\omega(\varsigma, Z_k(\varsigma)) - \nabla\omega(\varsigma, Z(\varsigma))|^2 d\varsigma \leq d. \tag{17}$$

Thus, by combining (16) and (17), we obtain

$$\int_{\mathbb{R}}|\nabla\omega(\varsigma, Z_k(\varsigma)) - \nabla\omega(\varsigma, Z(\varsigma))|^2 d\varsigma \leq d + 4M_1^2 M^{2(\gamma_1-1)} C_2^{2(\gamma_1-1)} \|b\|_{\frac{2}{2-\gamma_1}}^2. \tag{18}$$

However, by Lemma 3, the fact $Z_k \rightharpoonup Z$ implies the existence of a subsequence $(Z_k)_{k\in\mathbb{N}}$ such that $Z_k \to Z \in \mathbb{L}^2(\mathbb{R})$, which yields $Z_k(\varsigma) \to Z(\varsigma)$ for almost every $\varsigma \in \mathbb{R}$. Thus, the proof is completed by applying the Lebesgue's convergence Theorem. $\square$

Lemma 5 ([13]). *Let $I \in C^1(B, \mathbb{R})$ satisfying the Palais–Smale condition (PS) and bounded below. Then, $c = \inf_B I$ is a critical value of I.*

To find solutions of (2) under the conditions of Theorem 2, we use the genus properties. For this, we recall some definitions and results from [14]. Denote by B the real Banach space. For $I \in C^1(B, \mathbb{R})$ and $c \in \mathbb{R}$, let us define the following sets:

$$\Sigma := \{A \subset B \backslash \{0\} \text{ such that } A \text{ symmetric with respect to } 0 \text{ and closed in } B\},$$

$$K_c := \{Z \in B : I(Z) = c, I'(Z) = 0\},$$

and

$$I^c := \{Z \in B : I(Z) \leq c\}.$$

Definition 4. *For $A \in \Sigma$, we call the genus of A is j (denoted by $\Gamma(A) = j$) if there is an odd map ψ in $C(A, \mathbb{R}^j \backslash \{0\})$, where j is the smallest integer satisfy this property.*

Lemma 6 ([14]). *Let $I \in C^1$ be an even functional on B that satisfies the Palais–Smale (PS) condition. Further, for every $j \in \mathbb{N}$, let $\Sigma_j = \{A \in \Sigma : \Gamma(A) \geq j\}$ and $c_j = \inf_{A \in \Sigma_j} \sup_{Z \in A} I(Z)$.*

(i) *If $\Sigma_j \neq \emptyset$ and $c_j \in \mathbb{R}$, then c_j is a critical value of I.*
(ii) *If there exists a natural number r such that $c_j = c_{j+1} = \ldots = c_{j+r} = c \in \mathbb{R}$, and $c \neq I(0)$, then $\Gamma(K_c) \geq r + 1$.*

Remark 4 ([14]). *If K_c belongs to Σ and $\Gamma(K_c) > 1$, then K_c has infinitely many distinct points. Thus, I contains infinitely many distinct critical points in B.*

3. Proofs of Main Results

First, we construct the variational framework to prove the existence of solutions for (2). We define $I : X^\alpha \to \mathbb{R}$, by

$$I(Z) = \int_{\mathbb{R}}\left[\frac{1}{2}|_{-\infty}\mathfrak{D}_\varsigma^\alpha Z(\varsigma)|^2 + \frac{1}{2}(\mathcal{A}(\varsigma)Z(\varsigma), Z(\varsigma)) - \omega(\varsigma, Z(\varsigma))\right]d\varsigma$$

$$= \frac{1}{2}\|Z\|^2 - \int_{\mathbb{R}}\omega(\varsigma, Z(\varsigma))d\varsigma. \tag{19}$$

Under the assumptions of Theorem 1, we obtain

$$I'(Z)v = \int_{\mathbb{R}}\left[\left(_{-\infty}\mathfrak{D}_\varsigma^\alpha Z(\varsigma), _{-\infty}\mathfrak{D}_\varsigma^\alpha v(\varsigma)\right) + (\mathcal{A}(\varsigma)Z(\varsigma), v(\varsigma)) - (\nabla\omega(\varsigma, Z(\varsigma)), v(\varsigma))\right]d\varsigma \tag{20}$$

for any $Z, v \in X^\alpha$. This implies that

$$I'(v)v = \|v\|^2 - \int_\mathbb{R} (\nabla \varpi(\varsigma, Z(\varsigma)), v(\varsigma)) d\varsigma. \qquad (21)$$

Furthermore, I is defined on X^α and continuously Fréchet-differentiable functional; that is $I \in C^1(X^\alpha, \mathbb{R})$.

3.1. Proof of Theorem 1

First, we prove that I is bounded below. From the hypothesis (Λ_1) and Hölder inequality, we obtain

$$\begin{aligned} I(Z) &\geq \frac{1}{2}\|Z\|^2 - \int_{\mathbb{R}(|Z(\varsigma)| \leq 1)} a_1(\varsigma)|Z(\varsigma)|^{\gamma_1} d\varsigma - \int_{\mathbb{R}(|Z(\varsigma)| \geq 1)} a_2(\varsigma)|Z(\varsigma)|^{\gamma_2} d\varsigma \\ &\geq \frac{1}{2}\|Z\|^2 - \left(\int_{\mathbb{R}(|Z(\varsigma)| \leq 1)} |a_1(\varsigma)|^{\frac{2}{2-\gamma_1}} d\varsigma \right)^{\frac{2-\gamma_1}{2}} \|Z(\varsigma)\|_2^{\gamma_1} \\ &\quad - \left(\int_{\mathbb{R}(|Z(\varsigma)| \leq 1)} |a_2(\varsigma)|^{\frac{2}{2-\gamma_2}} d\varsigma \right)^{\frac{2-\gamma_2}{2}} \left(\int_{\mathbb{R}(|Z(\varsigma)| \geq 1)} |Z(\varsigma)|^{\frac{2\gamma_2}{\gamma_1}} d\varsigma \right)^{\frac{\gamma_1}{2}} \\ &\geq \frac{1}{2}\|Z\|^2 - C_2^{\gamma_1} \|a_1\|_{\frac{2}{2-\gamma_1}} \|Z\|^{\gamma_1} - C_2^{\gamma_1} \|a_2\|_{\frac{2}{2-\gamma_1}} \|Z\|_\infty^{\gamma_2-\gamma_1} \|Z\|^{\gamma_2} \\ &\geq \frac{1}{2}\|Z\|^2 - C_2^{\gamma_1} \|a_1\|_{\frac{2}{2-\gamma_1}} \|Z\|^{\gamma_1} - C_2^{\gamma_1} C_\infty^{\gamma_2-\gamma_1} \|a_2\|_{\frac{2}{2-\gamma_1}} \|Z\|^{\gamma_2}. \end{aligned} \qquad (22)$$

Since $1 < \gamma_1 < \gamma_2$, from (22), we conclude

$$I(Z) \to \infty \text{ as } \|Z\| \to \infty.$$

Thus, I is bounded below.

Now, we show that I satisfies the (PS) condition. To this end, let $(Z_k)_{k \in \mathbb{N}}$ be a sequence in X^α such that $(I(Z_k))$ is bounded and $I'(Z_k) \to 0$ as $k \to \infty$. So, by (19) and (22), it follows that there exists a positive real constant A such that

$$\|Z_k\| \leq A, \text{ for all } k \in \mathbb{N}. \qquad (23)$$

It follows from (21) that

$$(I'(Z_k) - I'(Z))(Z_k - Z) = \|Z_k - Z\|^2 - \int_\mathbb{R} (\nabla \varpi(\varsigma, Z_k(\varsigma)) - \nabla \varpi(\varsigma, Z(\varsigma)), Z_k - Z(\varsigma)) d\varsigma.$$

Since $(I'(Z_k) - I'(Z))(Z_k - Z) \to 0$ as $k \to \infty$, by the Lemma 4, we deduce that

$$\|Z_k - Z\|^2 \to 0 \text{ as } k \to \infty.$$

Consequently, I validates the Palais–Smale condition (PS) as desired.

Now, by Lemma 5, it follows that $c = \inf_{X^\alpha} I(Z)$ is a critical value of I. Thus, there exists a critical point $Z_* \in X^\alpha$ such that $I(Z_*) = c$.

It is remaining to show that $Z_* \neq 0$. Let $Z_0 \in (\mathcal{W}_0^{1,2}(J) \cap X^\alpha) \setminus \{0\}$ and $\|Z_0\|_\infty \leq 1$. Then, by (Λ_1), (Λ_3) and (19), we obtain

$$\begin{aligned} I(sZ_0) &= \frac{s^2}{2}\|Z_0\|^2 - \int_\mathbb{R} \varpi(\varsigma, sZ_0(\varsigma)) d\varsigma = \frac{s^2}{2}\|Z_0\|^2 - \int_J \varpi(\varsigma, sZ_0(\varsigma)) d\varsigma \\ &\leq \frac{s^2}{2}\|Z_0\|^2 - \eta s^{\gamma_3} \int_J |Z_0|^{\gamma_3} d\varsigma, \ 0 < s < 1. \end{aligned} \qquad (24)$$

Since $1 < \gamma_3 < 2$, it follows from (24) that $I(sZ_0) < 0$ for $s > 0$ small enough. Hence $I(Z_*) = c < 0$, and thus Z_* is nontrivial critical point of I. Therefore, $Z_* = Z(\varsigma)$ is nontrivial solution of (2).

3.2. Proof of Theorem 2

By Lemma 5 and the proof of Theorem 1, $I \in C^1(X^\alpha, \mathbb{R})$ is bounded below and satisfies the (PS) condition. It is clear that I is even and $I(0) = 0$. In order to apply the Lemma 6, we show that

$$\forall\, n \in \mathbb{N}\ \exists\, \epsilon > 0 \text{ such that } \gamma(I^{-\epsilon}) \geq n. \tag{25}$$

For any natural n, take n disjoint open sets J_i such that $\bigcup_{i=1}^{n} J_i \subset J$. For $i = 1, 2, \ldots, n$, choose $Z_i \in \left(\mathcal{W}_0^{1,2}(J_i) \cap X^\alpha\right) \setminus \{0\}$ such that $\|Z_i\| = 1$. Letting

$$E_n := \mathrm{span}\{Z_1, Z_2, \ldots, Z_n\} \text{ and } S_n := \{Z \in E_n : \|Z\| = 1\}.$$

For each $Z \in E_n$, there exist $\lambda_i \in \mathbb{R}, i = 1, 2, \ldots, n$ such that

$$Z(\varsigma) = \sum_{i=1}^{n} \lambda_i Z_i(\varsigma) \text{ for } \varsigma \in \mathbb{R}. \tag{26}$$

Hence,

$$\|Z\|_{\gamma_3} = \left(\int_\mathbb{R} |Z(\varsigma)|^{\gamma_3} d\varsigma\right)^{\frac{1}{\gamma_3}} = \left(\sum_{i=1}^{n} |\lambda_i|^{\gamma_3} \int_{J_i} |Z_i(\varsigma)|^{\gamma_3} d\varsigma\right)^{\frac{1}{\gamma_3}}, \tag{27}$$

and hence

$$\|Z\|^2 = \int_\mathbb{R} (|{}_{-\infty}\mathfrak{D}_\varsigma^\alpha Z(\varsigma)|^2 + (\mathcal{A}(\varsigma)Z(\varsigma), Z(\varsigma))) d\varsigma$$
$$= \sum_{i=1}^{n} \lambda_i^2 \int_\mathbb{R} (|{}_{-\infty}\mathfrak{D}_\varsigma^\alpha Z_i(\varsigma)|^2 + (\mathcal{A}(\varsigma)Z_i(\varsigma), Z_i(\varsigma))) d\varsigma = \sum_{i=1}^{n} \lambda_i^2. \tag{28}$$

There exists a constant $c > 0$ such that all norms of a finite dimensional normed space are similar

$$c\|Z\| \leq \|Z\|_{\gamma_3} \text{ for } Z \in E_n. \tag{29}$$

So, by $(\Lambda_1), (\Lambda_3)$, (27)–(29), we have

$$I(sZ) = \frac{s^2}{2}\|Z\|^2 - \int_\mathbb{R} \omega(\varsigma, sZ(\varsigma))d\varsigma = \frac{s^2}{2}\|Z\|^2 - \sum_{i=1}^{n} \int_{J_i} \omega(\varsigma, s\lambda_i Z_i(\varsigma))d\varsigma$$
$$\leq \frac{s^2}{2}\|Z\|^2 - \eta s^{\gamma_3} \sum_{i=1}^{n} |\lambda_i|^{\gamma_3} \int_{J_i} |Z_i(\varsigma)|^{\gamma_3} d\varsigma$$
$$= \frac{s^2}{2}\|Z\|^2 - \eta s^{\gamma_3} \|Z\|_{\gamma_3}^{\gamma_3} \leq \frac{s^2}{2}\|Z\|^2 - \eta(cs)^{\gamma_3}\|Z\|^{\gamma_3}$$
$$= \frac{s^2}{2} - \eta(cs)^{\gamma_3}, \text{ for all } Z \in S_n, \text{ with } 0 < s \leq 1. \tag{30}$$

From (30), it follows that there exists $\epsilon > 0$ and $\sigma > 0$ such as

$$I(\sigma Z) < -\epsilon \text{ for } Z \in S_n. \tag{31}$$

Letting

$$S_n^\sigma := \{\sigma Z : Z \in S_n\} \text{ and } \Omega := \left\{(\lambda_1, \lambda_2, \cdots, \lambda_n) \in \mathbb{R}^n : \sum_{i=1}^{n} \lambda_i^2 < \sigma^2\right\}.$$

Thus, from (31), is results that $I(Z) < -\epsilon$ for $Z \in S_n^\sigma$. In addition, we have $I \in C^1(X^\alpha, \mathbb{R})$ and even. This implies that
$$S_n^\sigma \subset I^{-\epsilon} \in \Sigma. \tag{32}$$

From (26) and (28) we deduce that there exists $\psi \in C(S_n^\sigma, \partial\Omega)$ an odd homeomorphism mapping ([14]), we obtain
$$\Gamma(I^{-\epsilon}) \geq \Gamma(S_n^\sigma) = n, \tag{33}$$

Let $c_n = \inf_{A \in \Sigma_n} \sup_{Z \in A} I(Z)$. Since I is bounded below on E, from (33) we obtain $-\infty < c_n \leq -\epsilon < 0$, and so $c_n \in \mathbb{R}_+$. We know that I has infinitely many nontrivial critical points (by using Lemma 3). Thus, the system 2 possesses infinitely many non trivial solutions.

Next, we show that $c_n \to 0^-$ as $n \to +\infty$. Define
$$X_n := \text{span}\{e_n\}, \quad Z_n = \overline{\bigoplus_{k=n}^{\infty} X_k},$$

where $\{e_n\}_{n=1}^{\infty}$ the standard orthogonal basis of X^α, and let
$$\beta_n = \sup_{Z \in Z_n, \|Z\|=1} \|Z\|_{\mathbb{L}^2}. \tag{34}$$

We claim that $\beta_n \to 0$ as $n \to +\infty$. Indeed, $0 < \beta_{n+1} \leq \beta_n$, and so $\beta_n \to \beta \geq 0$ as $n \to +\infty$. Now, for all $n \geq 1$, there exists $Z_n \in Z_n$ as such $\|Z_n\| = 1$ and $\|Z_n\| \geq \frac{\beta_n}{2}$. By definition of Z_n, it follows that $Z_n \to 0$ in X^α. Thus, by Lemma 3, we obtain $Z_n \to 0$ in $\mathbb{L}^2(\mathbb{R})$, and so $\beta = 0$. This proves our claim. Moreover, we have
$$I(Z) \geq \frac{1}{2}\|Z\|^2 - C_2^{\gamma_1}\|a_1\|_{\frac{2}{2-\gamma_1}}\|Z\|^{\gamma_1} - C_2^{\gamma_1} C_\infty^{\gamma_2-\gamma_1}\|a_2\|_{\frac{2}{2-\gamma_1}}\|Z\|^{\gamma_2}.$$

This implies that $I(Z)$ is coercive and $I(Z) \to +\infty$ as $\|Z\| \to +\infty$. Hence, there exists a $\tau > 0$ such that $I(Z) \to 0$ for $\|Z\| \geq \tau$. Moreover, for any $A \in \Sigma_n$, $\Gamma(A) \geq n$, and so $A \cap Z_n \neq \emptyset$. Thus, (34), yields
$$\sup_{Z \in A} I(Z) \geq \inf_{Z \in Z_n, \|Z\| \leq \tau} I(Z)$$
$$\geq \inf_{Z \in Z_n, \|Z\| \leq \tau} \left(\frac{1}{2}\|Z\|^2 - \beta_n^{\gamma_1}\|a_1\|_{\frac{2}{2-\gamma_1}}\|Z\|^{\gamma_1} - \beta_n^{\gamma_1} C_\infty^{\gamma_2-\gamma_1}\|a_2\|_{\frac{2}{2-\gamma_1}}\|Z\|^{\gamma_2}\right)$$
$$\geq -\beta_n^{\gamma_1}\|a_1\|_{\frac{2}{2-\gamma_1}}\tau^{\gamma_1} - \beta_n^{\gamma_1} C_\infty^{\gamma_2-\gamma_1}.$$

Therefore,
$$c_n = \inf_{A \in \Sigma_n} \sup_{Z \in A} I(Z) \geq -\beta_n^{\gamma_1}\|a_1\|_{\frac{2}{2-\gamma_1}}\tau^{\gamma_1} - \beta_n^{\gamma_1} C_\infty^{\gamma_2-\gamma_1}\|a_2\|_{\frac{2}{2-\gamma_1}}\tau^{\gamma_2}.$$

Combining this with $c_n < 0$ and $\beta_n \to 0$, we obtain $c_n \to 0^-$ as $n \to +\infty$ as desired.

4. Example

Consider system (2) with $\mathcal{A}(\varsigma) = (1+\varsigma^2)I_N$, where I_N is the identity matrix of order N and
$$\omega(\varsigma, Z) = \frac{e^{-\varsigma^2}\cos(\varsigma)}{1+|\varsigma|}|Z|^{\frac{4}{3}} + \frac{e^{-\varsigma^2}\sin(\varsigma)}{1+|\varsigma|}|Z|^{\frac{3}{2}}.$$

Then, we obtain

$$\nabla \omega(\varsigma, Z) = \frac{4e^{-\varsigma^2}\cos(\varsigma)}{3(1+|\varsigma|)}|Z|^{\frac{-2}{3}}Z + \frac{3e^{-\varsigma^2}\sin(\varsigma)}{2(1+|\varsigma|)}|Z|^{\frac{-1}{2}}Z,$$

$$|\omega(\varsigma, Z)| \leq \frac{2e^{-\varsigma^2}}{1+|\varsigma|}|Z|^{\frac{4}{3}}, \forall\, (\varsigma, Z) \in \mathbb{R} \times \mathbb{R}^N, |Z| \leq 1,$$

$$|\omega(\varsigma, Z)| \leq \frac{2e^{-\varsigma^2}}{1+|\varsigma|}|Z|^{\frac{3}{2}}, \forall\, (\varsigma, Z) \in \mathbb{R} \times \mathbb{R}^N, |Z| \geq 1,$$

$$|\nabla\omega(\varsigma, Z)| \leq \frac{2e^{-\varsigma^2}|Z|^{\frac{1}{3}} + 9|Z|^{\frac{1}{2}}}{6(1+|\varsigma|)}, \forall\, (\varsigma, Z) \in \mathbb{R} \times \mathbb{R}^N,$$

and

$$\omega(\varsigma, Z) \geq \frac{3e^{-\frac{\pi^2}{9}}|Z|^{\frac{4}{3}}}{2(3+\pi)}, \forall\, (\varsigma, Z) \in (0, \frac{\pi}{3}) \times \mathbb{R}^N, |Z| \leq 1.$$

Therefore, the conditions of Theorem 2 are satisfied, where

$$\frac{4}{3} = \gamma_1 = \gamma_3 < \gamma_2 = \frac{3}{2}, \; a_1(\varsigma) = a_2(\varsigma) = b(\varsigma) = \frac{2e^{-\varsigma^2}}{1+|\varsigma|}, \; \varphi(s) = \frac{8s^{\frac{1}{3}} + 9s^{\frac{1}{2}}}{12}.$$

Thus, by applying Theorem 2, we conclude that the system (2) has infinitely many nontrivial solutions.

Remark 5. *In light of the above example, one can easily figure out that Z and ω are not periodic in ς. Moreover, ω is of sub-quadratic. Therefore, System (2) with the above parameters can not be commented by the results obtained in [14]. In contrast to the outcome and conditions suggested in [15], our assumptions in the present paper are more effective. The resulting example supports the validity of the proposed hypotheses.*

5. Conclusions

We investigated in this research, the existence of infinitely many homoclinic solutions for fractional Hamiltonian systems (2). The present method is different from those considered in the literature in the sense that it provides less restrictive assumptions and assumes that $\mathcal{A}$ is coercive at infinity, ω is of sub-quadratic growth as $|Z| \to \infty$, and that Z and ω are not periodic in ς. The properties of the critical point theory have been employed to prove the main results. The findings in this paper not only generalize but also improve the recent results on fractional Hamiltonian systems (2). We provide a concrete example that demonstrates the advantage of our theorems over the previous results.

Author Contributions: A.M., H.B., J.A., F.K., and M.I. contributed to the design and implementation of the research, to the analysis of the results, and to the writing of the manuscript. All authors have read and agreed to the published version of the manuscript.

Funding: The deanship of Scientific Research at King Khalid University.

Data Availability Statement: Not available.

Acknowledgments: The authors extend their appreciation to the Deanship of Scientific Research at King Khalid University for funding this work through Small Groups (RGP.1/350/43). J. Alzabut is thankful to Prince Sultan University and Ostim Technical University for their endless support.

Conflicts of Interest: The authors declare no conflict of interest.

References

1. Abdellouahab, N.; Tellab, B.; Zennir, K. Existence and stability results of A nonlinear fractional integro-differential equation with integral boundary conditions. *Kragujev. J. Math.* **2022**, *46*, 685–699. [CrossRef]
2. Azzaoui, B.; Tellab, B.; Zennir, K. Positive solutions for a fractional configuration of the Riemann Liouville semilinear differential equation. *Math. Methods Appl. Sci.* **2022**. [CrossRef]
3. Bentrcia, T.; Mennouni, A. On the asymptotic stability of a Bresse system with two fractional damping terms: Theoretical and numerical analysis. *Discret. Contin. Dyn. Syst.—Ser. B* **2023**, *28*, 580–622. [CrossRef]
4. Mennouni, A.; Bougoffa, L.; Wazwaz, A.M. A new recursive scheme for solving a fractional differential equation of ray tracing through the crystalline lens. *Opt. Quantum Electron.* **2022**, *54*, 1–12 [CrossRef]
5. Nyamoradi, N.; Zhou, Y. Bifurcation results for a class of fractional Hamiltonian systems with Liouville-Wely fractional derivatives. *J. Vib. Control* **2014**, *5*, 1358–1368. [CrossRef]
6. Rajchakit, G.; Pratap, A.; Raja, R.; Cao, J.; Alzabut, J.; Huang, C. Hybrid control scheme for projective lag synchronization of Riemann Liouville sense fractional order memristive BAM neural networks with mixed delays. *Mathematics* **2019**, *7*, 759. [CrossRef]
7. Kilbas, A.; Bonilla, B.; Trujillo, J.J. Existence and uniqueness theorems for nonlinear fractional differential equations. *Demonstr. Math.* **2000**, *33*, 583–602. [CrossRef]
8. Omana, W.; Willem, M. Homoclinic orbits for a class of Hamiltonian systems. *Differ. Integral Equ.* **1992**, *114*, 1115–1120. [CrossRef]
9. Zhang, S.Q. Existence of a solution for the fractional differential equation with nonlinear boundary conditions. *Comput. Math. Appl.* **2011**, *61*, 1202–1208. [CrossRef]
10. Izydorek, M.; Janczewska, J. Homoclinic solutions for nonautonomous second order Hamiltonian systems with a coercive potential. *J. Math. Anal. Appl.* **2007**, *335*, 1119–1127. [CrossRef]
11. Baitiche, Z.; Derbazi, C.; Alzabut, J.; Samei, M.E.; Kaabar, M.K.A.; Siri, Z. Monotone Iterative Method for Langevin Equation in Terms of ψ−Caputo Fractional Derivative and Nonlinear Boundary Conditions. *Fractal Fract.* **2021**, *5*, 81. [CrossRef]
12. Boutiara, A.; Benbachir, M.; Alzabut, J.; Samei, M.E. Monotone iterative and upper–lower solutions techniques for solving nonlinear ψ−Caputo fractional boundary value problem. *Fractal Fract.* **2021**, *5*, 194. [CrossRef]
13. Mawhin, J.; Willem, M. *Critical Point Theory and Hamiltonian Systems*; Springer: New York, NY, USA, 1989.
14. Rabinowitz, P.H. *Minimax Methods in Critical Point Theory with Applications to Differential Equations*; CBMS Regional Conference Series in Mathematics; American Mathematical Society: Provodence, RI, USA, 1986; Volume 65.
15. Zhou, Y.; Lu, Z. Existence and multiplicity results of homoclinic solutions for fractional Hamiltonian systems. *Comput. Math. Appl.* **2017**, *73*, 1325–1345. [CrossRef]
16. Torres, C. Existence of solution for a class of fractional Hamiltonian systems. *Electron. J. Differ. Equ.* **2013**, *259*, 1–12.
17. Bartolo, P.; Benci, V.; Fortunato, D. Abstract critical point theorems and applications to some nonlinear problems with strong resonance at infinity. *Nonlinear Anal.* **1983**, *7*, 981–1012. [CrossRef]
18. Rabinowitz, P.H. Homoclinic orbits Some for a class of Hamiltonian systems. *Proceed. R. Soc. Edimburgh Sect. A* **1990**, *114*, 33–38. [CrossRef]
19. Ambrosetti, A.; Zelati, V.C. Multiple homoclinic orbits for a class of conservative systems. *Rend. Semin. Mat. Univ. Padova* **1993**, *89*, 177–194.
20. Ding, Y.H. Existence and multiplicity results for homoclinic solutions to a class of Hamiltonian systems. *Nonlinear Anal.* **1995**, *25*, 1095–1113.
21. Khelifi, F. Multiplicity of periodic solutions for a class of second order Hamiltonian systems. *Nonlinear Dyn. Syst. Theory* **2017**, *17*, 158–174.
22. Khachnaoui, K. Existence of even homoclinic solutions for a class of Dynamical Systems. *Nonlinear Dyn. Syst. Theory* **2015**, *15*, 287–301.
23. Timoumi, M. Periodic and subharmonic solutions for a class of noncoercive superquadratic Hamiltonian Systems. *Nonlinear Dyn. Syst.* **2011**, *11*, 319–336.
24. Xu, J.; O'Regan, D.; Zhang, K. Multiple solutions for a calss of fractional Hamiltonian systems. *Fract. Calc. Appl. Anal.* **2015**, *18*, 48–63. [CrossRef]

Disclaimer/Publisher's Note: The statements, opinions and data contained in all publications are solely those of the individual author(s) and contributor(s) and not of MDPI and/or the editor(s). MDPI and/or the editor(s) disclaim responsibility for any injury to people or property resulting from any ideas, methods, instructions or products referred to in the content.

Article

Soliton Solution of the Peyrard–Bishop–Dauxois Model of DNA Dynamics with M-Truncated and β-Fractional Derivatives Using Kudryashov's *R* Function Method

Xiaoming Wang [1], Ghazala Akram [2,*], Maasoomah Sadaf [2], Hajra Mariyam [2] and Muhammad Abbas [3,*]

[1] School of Mathematics & Computer Science, Shangrao Normal University, Shangrao 334001, China
[2] Department of Mathematics, University of the Punjab, Lahore 54590, Pakistan
[3] Department of Mathematics, University of Sargodha, Sargodha 40100, Pakistan
* Correspondence: ghazala.math@pu.edu.pk (G.A.); muhammad.abbas@uos.edu.pk (M.A.)

Abstract: In this paper, the Peyrard–Bishop–Dauxois model of DNA dynamics is discussed along with the fractional effects of the M-truncated derivative and β-derivative. The Kudryashov's *R* method was applied to the model in order to obtain a solitary wave solution. The obtained solution is explained graphically and the fractional effects of the β and M-truncated derivatives are also shown for a better understanding of the model.

Keywords: soliton solutions; fractional Peyrard–Bishop–Dauxois DNA model; M-truncated and β-fractional derivatives; Kudryashov's *R* function method

1. Introduction

The study of DNA structures is essential in various fields of science. The main purpose of this paper is to investigate the soliton oscillations for the fractional dynamical Peyrard–Bishop–Dauxois (PBD) model of DNA dynamics. The governing equation of the PBD model is a nonlinear evolution equation. The Peyrard–Bishop (PB) model for DNA denaturation was presented in 1989 [1]. DNA denaturation is the process of breaking down the DNA in such a way that the hydrogen bonds in the DNA break to unwind the double strands. The proposed model was a simple yet useful extension of the Ising models, which were previously being used to investigate DNA denaturation. Peyrard and Bishop further developed and improved the PB model along with Dauxois [2–5].

The Peyrard–Bishop–Dauxois model (PBD) model has been successfully used in many fruitful studies. Theodorakopoulos [6] used the PBD model in his study of bubble formation during the denaturation process. Hillebrand et al. [7] used numerical simulations to present a study on the bubbles' lifetime using the PBD model. Ares et al. [8] applied the same model to present a theoretical investigation of bubbles formed during DNA melting. They showed that the theoretical results matched with the previously reported experimental results. Some analytic results concerning the lengths of the thermal openings in the DNA structure were presented by Ares and Kalosakas in [9]. The simple yet effective PBD nonlinear model was found to be helpful in investigating the influence of heterogeneity on the DNA structure [10,11]. More results on the dynamical and statistical properties of the DNA structure were presented in [12–18].

The complex helical double-stranded structure of DNA molecules has been an interest of research for biologists, physicists and mathematicians for many years. In recent years, different useful extensions and modifications of the PBD dynamical model have been proposed, owing to its applicability and effectiveness in explaining many physical processes [19–21]. The thermal excitations in DNA molecules give rise to solitonic vibrations. The solitons for the nonlinear vibrations of the DNA molecules were computed in [22,23] in order to have a deeper insight into the dynamical properties. The PBD model

has also been explored using the ansatz technique [24], improved $\tan(\frac{\phi}{2})$-expansion technique, $\exp(-\phi(\eta))$-expansion technique, generalized $\left(\frac{G'}{G}\right)$-expansion technique and the exp-function technique [25].

At the same time, fractional calculus has become very popular during the last two decades. The fractional differential equations are the generalized form of the standard integer order differential equations. Over the years, different definitions of the fractional order derivatives have been proposed, which have been successfully utilized in several applications. The most widely used definitions include the definitions in Captuto's sense and Riemann–Liouville's sense. However, various studies have shown that the these previously well-accepted definitions have some limitations. The Caputo derivative is not able to deal with the problems with a singular kernel, whereas the Riemann–Liouville derivative has a seemingly more serious problem, i.e., it is unable to yield the derivative of a constant equal to zero. Such limitations have prompted researchers for more generalized definitions with a non-integer order.

Atangana et al. [26] introduced a fractional derivative that exhibits many useful mathematical properties. The definition is now commonly referred to as the β-derivative. Another recent attempt to define the fractional derivative was made by using the definition of the Mittag–Leffler function [27]. Both of these definitions have been proven to satisfy the basic mathematical laws of differential calculus, which encourages further explorations using these newly defined concepts. Recently, the fractional order PBD model was investigated [28] considering the definition of the β-derivative. The authors computed the traveling wave solutions of the considered model using different methods, keeping the fractional derivative as the β-derivative.

The M-truncated and β-fractional derivatives are recently developed definitions of fractional derivatives. Both proposed definitions are generalized forms of the classical integer order derivative and satisfy many useful mathematical properties exhibited by the classical integer order derivative. For example, the fractional derivative of a constant is zero according to these two definitions, which is in line with results of the classical calculus. The definition of the β-fractional derivative is simple and easily applicable. The M-truncated derivative involves the use of an extra parameter due to the involvement of Mittag–Leffler expansion, but it has been established as a good version of the fractional derivative because it unifies the fractional derivatives proposed by Katugampola, Khalil et al. and Sousa et al.

The aim of this work is to present a comparison of the solution of the fractional order PBD model for the M-truncated derivative and the β-derivative. The solution was computed using a recent effective technique, namely, the Kudryashov's R function method. The main objective of the work was then achieved by presenting a graphical comparison of the evolution in the shape of the constructed soliton for both definitions of the fractional derivative. It is observed that the conservations laws for the fractional PBD model have not been discussed in the literature to the best of our knowledge. Although this topic is beyond the scope of the current work, it will be useful to present theoretical investigations on the conservations laws of the considered model in future work.

The paper is organized as follows: in Section 2, the governing model is explained, while in Section 3, the definitions of the β-derivative and M-truncated derivative are given. Kudryashov's R function method is described in Section 4. The application of the method is presented in Section 5. The fractional effects on the obtained solution are graphically illustrated in Section 6. The whole work is concluded in Section 7.

2. Governing Model

The Hamiltonian for the PBD model is considered by using the Morse's potential, which can be expressed as

$$V_p(U_q - \mu_q) = r[\exp(-u(U_q - \mu_q)) - 1]^2. \tag{1}$$

The right side of Equation (1) is Morse's potential, where u and r denote the width and depth of Morse's potential, respectively. U_q, μ_q denote the nucleotides' displacements. The expression for the Hamiltonian for hydrogen links can be expressed [23] as

$$G(U) = \frac{1}{2n}u_q^2 + \frac{\psi_1}{2}\Delta^2 U_q + \frac{\psi_2}{4}\Delta^4 U_q + \tau(e^{-u\sqrt{2}U_q} - 1)^2, \qquad (2)$$

where ψ_1 is the strength of linear coupling, ψ_2 is the strength of nonlinear coupling and $u_q = n\frac{\partial U_q}{\partial t}$ denotes the momentum corresponding to the displacement U_q.

Equation (2) expresses the Hamiltonian for the description of the stretch in the hydrogen bonds of the DNA. This relation is essential for the derivation of a nonlinear evolution equation for the dynamical behavior of DNA. Initiating with Equation (2), the standard continuum approximation is used to derive an equation of motion, where the independent variable U denotes the displacement. As a result, the nonlinear evolution equation for DNA dynamics [23] can be written as

$$U_{tt} - (\Psi_1 + 3\Psi_2(U_x)^2)U_{xx} - 2pre^{-pU}(e^{-pU} - 1) = 0, \qquad (3)$$

where $\Psi_1 = \frac{\psi_1}{n}s^2$, $\Psi_2 = \frac{\psi_2}{n}s^4$, $r = \frac{\tau}{n}$, $p = \sqrt{2}u$ and $s =$ the inter-site nucleotide distance.

The fractional order model corresponding to Equation (3) is discussed in [28] using the β-derivative. In this research work, the following forms of the PBD model are to be studied. The PBD model with the β-derivative is considered as

$$D_t^{2\beta}(U) - (\Psi_1 + 3\Psi_2(D_x^\beta(U))^2)D_x^{2\beta}(U) - 2pre^{-pU}(e^{-pU} - 1) = 0. \qquad (4)$$

The PBD model with the M-truncated derivative is considered as

$$D_{M,t}^{2\beta,\alpha}(U) - (\Psi_1 + 3\Psi_2(D_{M,x}^{\beta,\alpha}(U))^2)D_{M,x}^{2\beta,\alpha}(U) - 2pre^{-pU}(e^{-pU} - 1) = 0. \qquad (5)$$

Both derivatives are explained in the next section.

3. Important Definitions

3.1. β-Derivative

The β-derivative [26] of a function l, where $l(t) : [a, \infty] \to R$, is given as

$$D_t^\beta(l(t)) = \lim_{\sigma \to 0} \frac{l(t + \sigma(t + \frac{1}{\Gamma(\beta)})^{1-\beta}) - l(t)}{\sigma}, \quad \beta \in (0,1]. \qquad (6)$$

The following properties are satisfied for β-differentiable functions $l(t)$ and $m(t)$, with $\beta \in (0,1]$ [26,29].

$$D_t^\beta(cl(t) + dm(t)) = c\, D_t^\beta(l(t)) + d\, D_t^\beta(m(t)), \ \forall\, c, d \in R, \qquad (7)$$

$$D_t^\beta(l(t) \times m(t)) = m(t)\, D_t^\beta(l(t)) + l(t)\, D_t^\beta(m(t)), \qquad (8)$$

$$D_t^\beta\left(\frac{l(t)}{m(t)}\right) = \frac{m(t)\, D_t^\beta(l(t)) - l(t)\, D_t^\beta(m(t))}{(m(t))^2}, \qquad (9)$$

$$D_t^\beta(l(t)) = \frac{d(l(t))}{dt}\left(t + \frac{1}{\Gamma(\beta)}\right)^{1-\beta}. \qquad (10)$$

The β-fractional integral can be expressed by the relation [26]

$$I_t^\beta h(t) = \int_0^t \left(y + \frac{1}{\Gamma(\beta)}\right)^{\beta-1} h(y)\, dy. \qquad (11)$$

3.2. M-Truncated Derivative

The M-truncated derivative [27] of a function l, where $l(t) : [0, \infty] \to R$, is given as

$$D_{M,t}^{\beta,\alpha}(l(t)) = \lim_{\sigma \to 0} \frac{l(t \, _jE_\alpha(\sigma t^{-\beta})) - l(t)}{\sigma}, \quad t > 0, \, \beta \in (0,1], \, \alpha > 0, \tag{12}$$

where $_jE_\alpha(.)$, $\alpha > 0$ is a truncated one-parameter Mittag–Leffler function.

The following properties are satisfied for functions $l(t)$ and $m(t)$, which are β-derivable, with $\beta \in (0,1]$ and $\alpha > 0$ [30].

$$D_{M,t}^{\beta,\alpha}(cl(t) + dm(t)) = c\, D_{M,t}^{\beta,\alpha}(l(t)) + d\, D_{M,t}^{\beta,\alpha}(m(t)), \quad \forall \, c, d \in R, \tag{13}$$

$$D_{M,t}^{\beta,\alpha}(l(t) \times m(t)) = m(t)\, D_{M,t}^{\beta,\alpha}(l(t)) + l(t) D_{M,t}^{\beta,\alpha}(m(t)), \tag{14}$$

$$D_{M,t}^{\beta,\alpha}\left(\frac{l}{m}\right)(t) = \frac{m(t)D_{M,t}^{\beta,\alpha}(l(t)) - l(t)D_{M,t}^{\beta,\alpha}(m(t))}{(m(t))^2}, \tag{15}$$

$$D_{M,t}^{\beta,\alpha}(l \circ m)(t) = l'(m(t))\, D_{M,t}^{\beta,\alpha} m(t), \tag{16}$$

$$D_{M,t}^{\beta,\alpha}(t^\psi) = \psi\, t^{\psi-\alpha}, \quad \psi \in R. \tag{17}$$

Let h be a function that is defined in $(c, \infty]$, where $c \geq 0$, and fix some $0 < \beta \leq 1$. The left M-truncated integral can be expressed by the relation [27]

$$_MI_c^{\beta,\alpha}h(t) = \int_c^t h(y) d_\gamma(y,c) = \Gamma(\alpha+1) \int_c^t h(y)(y-c)^{\beta-1} dy, \tag{18}$$

with $d_\gamma(y,c) = \Gamma(\alpha+1)(y-c)^{\beta-1}$.

The right M-truncated integral is expressed by the relation

$$_d^{\beta,\alpha}I_M h(t) = \int_t^d h(y) d_\gamma(d,y) = \Gamma(\alpha+1) \int_t^d h(y)(d-y)^{\beta-1} dy. \tag{19}$$

4. Description of Kudryashov's R Function Method [31]

Kudryashov's R function method [31] is a recently developed mathematical technique for the construction of traveling wave solutions of partial differential equations.

The R function can be written as

$$R(\xi) = \frac{1}{fe^{(\delta\xi)} + ge^{(-\delta\xi)}}, \tag{20}$$

which satisfies the differential equation

$$R_\xi^2 = \delta R^2(1 - \omega R^2), \quad \text{where } \omega = 4fg. \tag{21}$$

Here, f, g and δ are parameters of the R function. The value of ω depends on the parameters f and g in the definition of the R function. This definition of the R function allows us to express the nonlinear differential equation in terms of R and R_ξ, thus simplifying the equation to a great extent to obtain the exact solution. This is applicable to a large class of integrable nonlinear differential equations. Without losing generality, ω can be taken as 1.

In this study, this method is applied due to its novelty, generality and simplicity in solving the governing nonlinear model.

According to the Kudryashov's R function method [31], firstly, a suitable wave transformation is used to reduce a nonlinear partial differential of the form

$$P(U, U_x, U_{xt}, U_t, \ldots) = 0, \tag{22}$$

to an ODE as
$$D(v, v_\zeta, v_{\zeta\zeta}, v_{\zeta\zeta\zeta}, \dots) = 0. \quad (23)$$

The value of N is determined using the homogeneous balance, and then a solution is assumed in the form
$$v = \Sigma_{l=0}^{N} C_l R(\zeta)^l. \quad (24)$$

In order to obtain a polynomial in R or in R and R_ζ, Equation (24) and the derivatives of R are put into Equation (23).

When the polynomial involves R, the powers of R are collected, whereas, in the case of R and R_ζ, the collection of powers is carried out accordingly. The resulting system of equations can be solved to determine the values of the unknown parameters and C_l's parameter, which can be used to determine the solution of Equation (22).

5. Mathematical Analysis

The fractional model PBD model is considered, as described by Equations (1) and (4). In order to solve these nonlinear equations, the transformation $U(x, t) = v(\zeta)$ is considered, where

$$\zeta = \frac{1}{\beta}\left(x + \frac{1}{\Gamma(\beta)}\right)^\beta - \frac{\eta}{\beta}\left(t + \frac{1}{\Gamma(\beta)}\right)^\beta, \quad \text{(for } \beta\text{-derivative)}, \quad (25)$$

$$\zeta = \frac{\Gamma(\alpha+1)}{\beta}(x^\beta - \eta t^\beta), \quad \text{(for M-truncated derivative)}. \quad (26)$$

Using these transformations, Equations (1) and (4) are reduced to the following ODE.
$$\eta^2 v'' - (\Psi_1 + 3\Psi_2(v')^2)v'' - 2pre^{-pv}(e^{-pv} - 1) = 0. \quad (27)$$

Multiplication of Equation (27) with v' and then integration with regard to ζ gives
$$\frac{(\eta^2 - \Psi_1)}{2}(v')^2 - \frac{3}{4}\Psi_2(v')^4 + re^{-pv}(e^{-pv} - 2) + a = 0. \quad (28)$$

Here, a is an integration constant. Using the transformation
$$\Omega(\zeta) = e^{-pv(\zeta)}, \quad (29)$$

the following nonlinear ODE is retrieved.
$$\frac{(\eta^2 - \Psi_1)}{2p^2}\Omega^2(\Omega')^2 - \frac{3}{4p^4}\Psi_2(\Omega')^4 + r\Omega^5(\Omega - 2) + a\Omega^4 = 0. \quad (30)$$

The degree of nonlinear term is balanced with the degree of the highest order derivative in Equation (30) using the homogeneous balance principle described in [32], which provides the value $N = 2$. Hence, the proposed method suggests that the solution can be assumed in the form
$$\Omega(\zeta) = C_0 + C_1 R(\zeta) + C_2 R(\zeta)^2. \quad (31)$$

The function $\Omega(\zeta)$ is substituted from Equation (31) into Equation (30), and (21) is used for simplification. As a result, a polynomial is obtained in terms of R. This can be achieved with the help of Maple or Mathematica. Equating the coefficients of powers of R to 0 yields a system of algebraic equations.

The following values of the unknowns are obtained by solving the system of equations simultaneously.

$\eta = \eta$, $C_0 = 0$, $C_1 = 0$, $C_2 = \pm\frac{(\pm r + \sqrt{-ar + r^2})\omega}{r}$, $\Psi_1 = \mp(\pm r + \sqrt{-ar + r^2})p^2 + ap^2 + \eta^2$,
$\Psi_2 = \frac{1}{12}p^4(2r \pm 2\sqrt{-ar + r^2} - a)$.

Substituting these values into Equation (31) yields

$$\Omega(\xi) = \left(\frac{(r + \sqrt{-ar + r^2})\omega}{r}\right)\left(\frac{1}{fe^{\xi} + ge^{-\xi}}\right)^2, \qquad (32)$$

or

$$\Omega(\xi) = \left(\frac{(r + \sqrt{-ar + r^2})\omega}{r}\right)\left(\frac{4f}{4f^2 e^{\xi} + \omega e^{-\xi}}\right)^2, \qquad (33)$$

which is substituted into Equation (29).
Since

$$\Omega(\xi) = e^{-pv(\xi)},$$
$$\ln(\Omega(\xi)) = -pv(\xi),$$
$$v(\xi) = -\frac{1}{p}\ln(\Omega(\xi)),$$

therefore, $v(\xi)$ can be written as

$$v(\xi) = -\frac{1}{p}\ln\left(\left(\frac{(r + \sqrt{-ar + r^2})\omega}{r}\right)\left(\frac{4f}{4f^2 e^{\xi} + \omega e^{-\xi}}\right)^2\right). \qquad (34)$$

The resulting relation can be expressed as

$$U(x,t) = -\frac{1}{p}\ln\left(\left(\frac{(r + \sqrt{-ar + r^2})\omega}{r}\right)\left(\frac{4f}{4f^2 e^{\xi} + \omega e^{-\xi}}\right)^2\right), \qquad (35)$$

where $\omega = 4fg$ and $\delta = 1$ in the value of R.
Considering the β-derivative, the solution (35) can be written as

$$U(x,t) = -\frac{1}{p}\ln\left(\left(\frac{(r + \sqrt{-ar + r^2})\omega}{r}\right)\right.$$
$$\left.\left(\frac{4f}{4f^2 e^{\frac{1}{\beta}\left(x + \frac{1}{\Gamma(\beta)}\right)^{\beta} - \frac{\eta}{\beta}\left(t + \frac{1}{\Gamma(\beta)}\right)^{\beta}} + \omega e^{-\left(\frac{1}{\beta}\left(x + \frac{1}{\Gamma(\beta)}\right)^{\beta} - \frac{\eta}{\beta}\left(t + \frac{1}{\Gamma(\beta)}\right)^{\beta}\right)}}\right)^2\right), \qquad (36)$$

where $p = \sqrt{2}u$ and $\omega = 4fg$. The symbols u and r denote the width and depth of Morse's potential, whereas f and g are the parameters of the R function, respectively. Moreover, β is the fractional order of the derivative, η is the speed of the soliton and a is a constant of integration.

Considering the M-truncated derivative, solution (35) can be written as

$$U(x,t) = -\frac{1}{p}\ln\left(\left(\frac{(r + \sqrt{-ar + r^2})\omega}{r}\right)\right.$$
$$\left.\left(\frac{4f}{4f^2 e^{\frac{\Gamma(\alpha+1)}{\beta}(x^{\beta} - \eta t^{\beta})} + \omega e^{-(\frac{\Gamma(\alpha+1)}{\beta}(x^{\beta} - \eta t^{\beta}))}}\right)^2\right), \qquad (37)$$

where $p = \sqrt{2}u$ and $\omega = 4fg$. The symbols u and r denote the width and depth of Morse's potential, whereas f and g are the parameters of the R function, respectively. Moreover, β is the fractional order of the derivative, η is the speed of the soliton and a is a constant of integration. The parameter $\alpha > 0$ appears to be due to the truncated one-parameter Mittag–Leffler function in the definition of the M-truncated derivative.

6. Graphical Illustrations

The obtained solution for the β-derivative and M-truncated derivative is graphically plotted to compare the influence of the change in the fractional order of both kinds of derivatives. Figures 1–5 have been plotted to demonstrate the evolution of the wave profile corresponding to the obtained solution, as the fractional order is gradually increased by taking the values $\beta = 0.5$, $\beta = 0.75$, $\beta = 0.83$, $\beta = 0.9$ and $\beta = 1$, respectively. The graphs for Equation (36) are presented in Figures 1a–5a, which show the evolution of the wave profile using the definition of the β-derivative. For a better visualization of the physical structure of the soliton corresponding to the obtained solution, two-dimensional contour plots have been plotted as well. The contour plots corresponding to $\beta = 0.5$, $\beta = 0.75$, $\beta = 0.83$, $\beta = 0.9$ and $\beta = 1$ are shown in Figures 1c–5c respectively.

The graphs for Equation (37) are presented in Figures 1b–5b, which show the evolution of the wave profile using the definition of the M-truncated derivative. The corresponding contours are shown in Figures 1d–5d.

It is clear from the graphical demonstration that the shape of the wave appears as different for different values of the fractional order β using the β-derivative and M-truncated derivative. However, it is observed that the wave profile tends to become increasingly similar with an increase in the value of β. Ultimately, at $\beta = 1$, the soliton converges to the unique form, as depicted by Figure 5. Hence, it can be concluded that both definitions provide a solution that is in agreement with the usual Hamiltonian and the standard integer order equation of motion for the PBD model when β converges to unity.

Further confirmation of this observation is provided by the comparison of the line graphs of the obtained solution expressions for both definitions of the derivative. Figures 1e–5e show the comparison of 2D line graphs corresponding to the β-derivative and M-truncated derivative for different values of β at $x = 1$. It is evident from Figure 5e that the wave profiles for both definitions of the derivative become coincident with each other. A similar confirmation is provided by the 2D line graphs at $t = 1$, as depicted by Figures 1f–5f. For sake of convenience, the values of η, f and a are taken as unity.

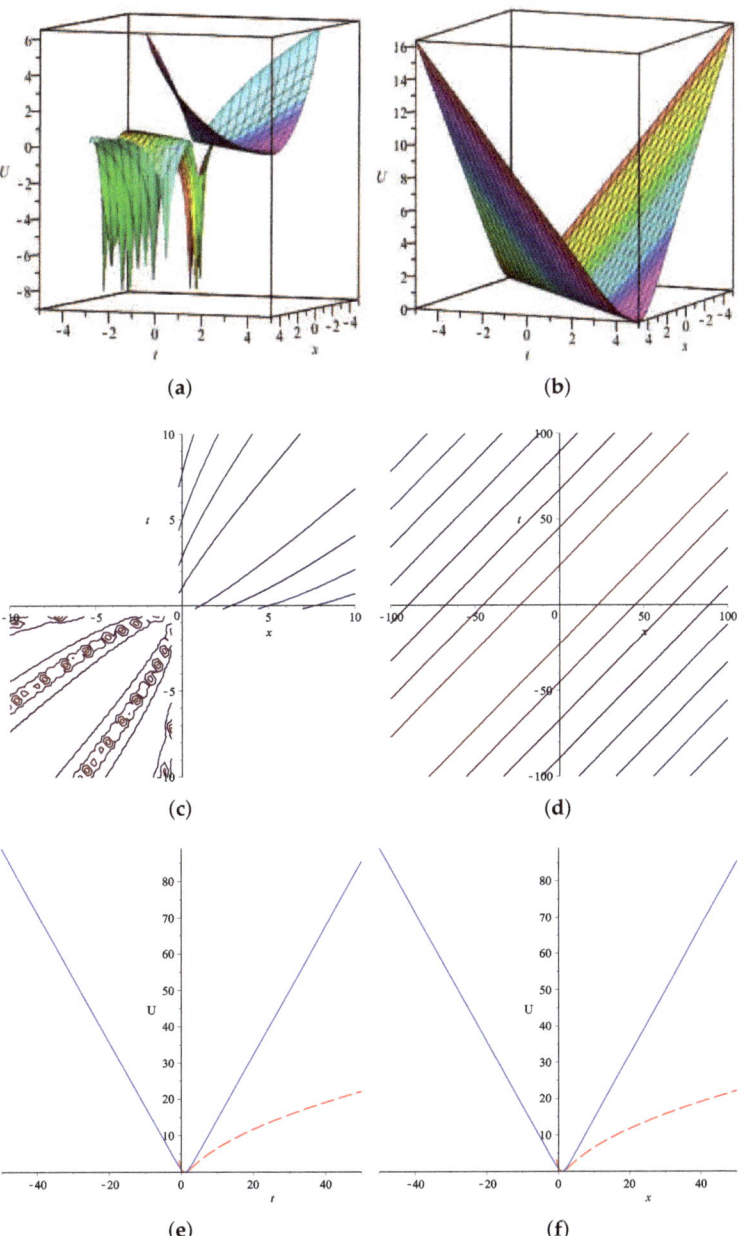

Figure 1. In (**a**), the graph of Equation (36) is given with $\beta = 0.5$, whereas, in (**b**), the graph of Equation (37) is given with $\beta = 0.5$ and $\alpha = 1$. In (**c**,**d**), the 2D contours corresponding to the graphs (**a**,**b**) are given. (**e**,**f**) show 2D comparison of both solutions for $x = 1$ and $t = 1$, respectively.

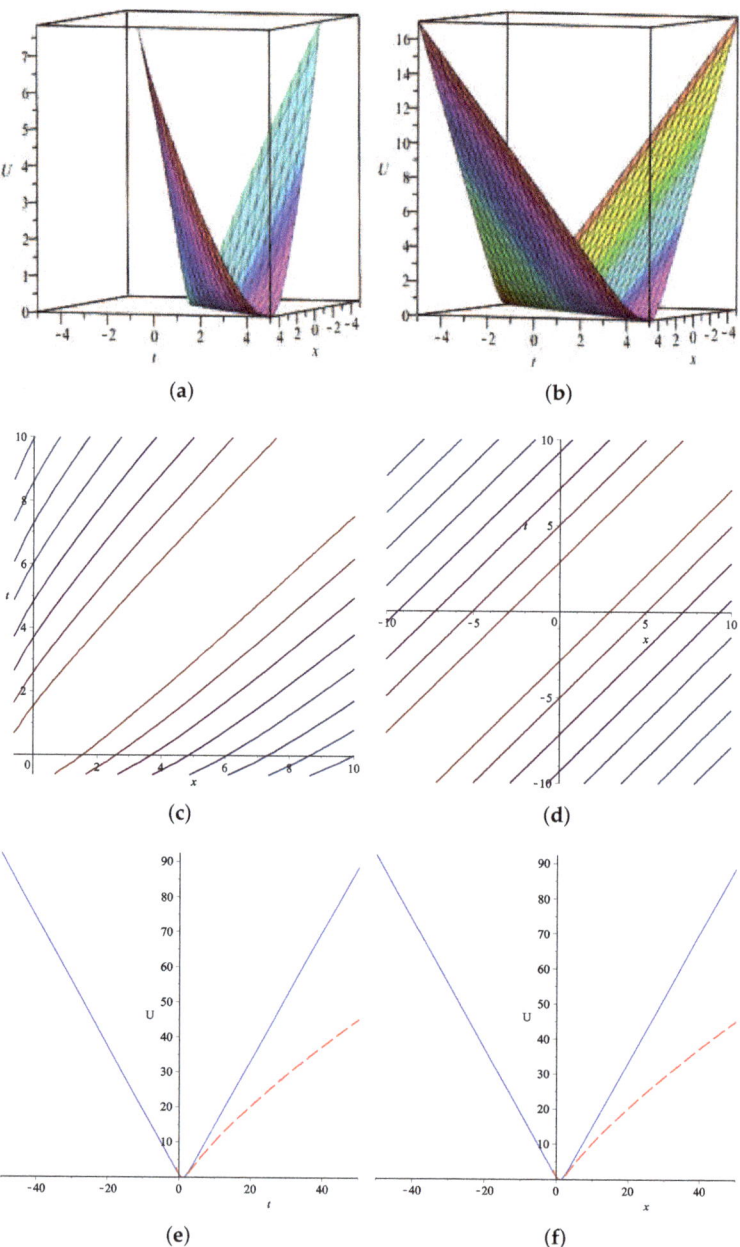

Figure 2. In (**a**), the graph of Equation (36) is given with $\beta = 0.75$, whereas, in (**b**), the graph of Equation (37) is given with $\beta = 0.75$ and $\alpha = 1$. In (**c**,**d**), the 2D contours corresponding to the graphs (**a**,**b**) are given. (**e**,**f**) show 2D comparison of both solutions for $x = 1$ and $t = 1$, respectively.

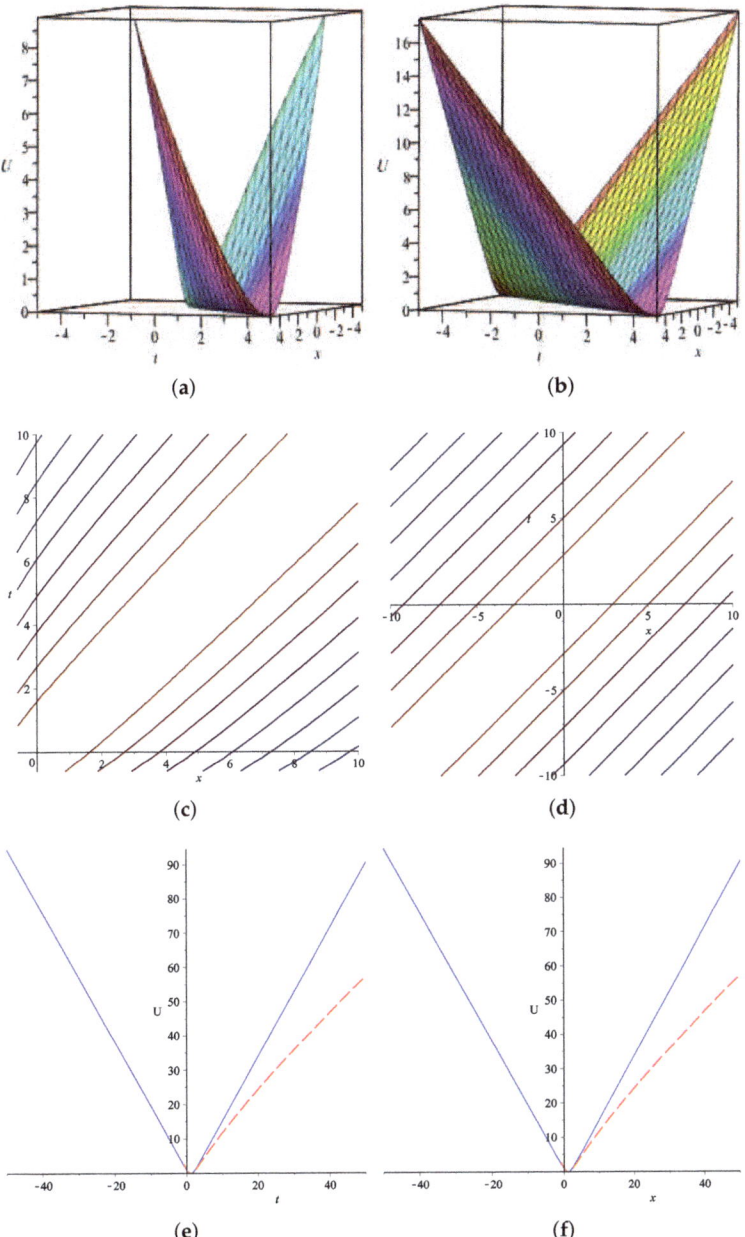

Figure 3. In (**a**), the graph of Equation (36) is given with $\beta = 0.83$ whereas in (**b**) graph of Equation (37) is given with $\beta = 0.83$ and $\alpha = 1$. In (**c**,**d**), the 2D contours corresponding to the graphs (**a**,**b**) are given. (**e**,**f**) show 2D comparison of both solutions for $x = 1$ and $t = 1$, respectively.

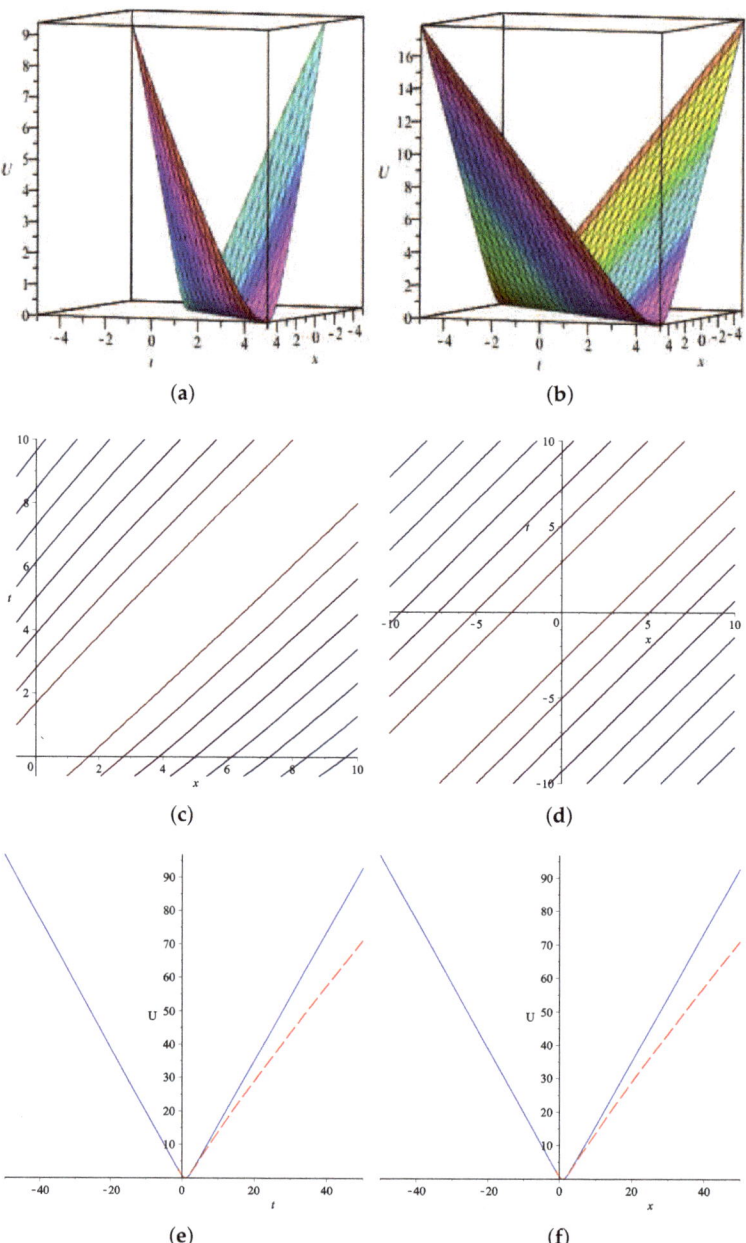

Figure 4. In (**a**), the graph of Equation (36) is given with $\beta = 0.9$, whereas, in (**b**), the graph of Equation (37) is given with $\beta = 0.9$ and $\alpha = 1$. In (**c**,**d**), the 2D contours corresponding to the graphs (**a**,**b**) are given. (**e**,**f**) show 2D comparison of both solutions for $x = 1$ and $t = 1$, respectively.

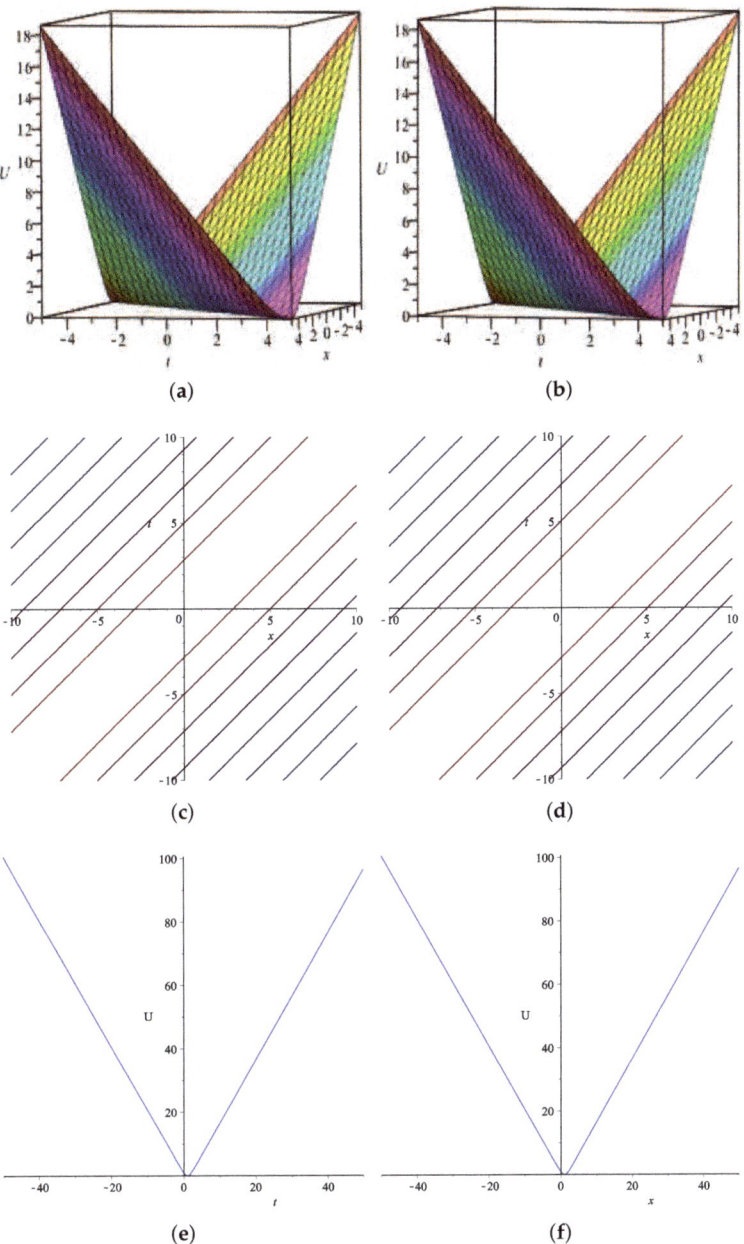

Figure 5. In (**a**), the graph of Equation (36) is given with $\beta = 1$, whereas, in (**b**), the graph of Equation (37) is given with $\beta = 1$ and $\alpha = 1$. In (**c,d**), the 2D contours corresponding to the graphs (**a,b**) are given. (**e,f**) show 2D comparison of both solutions for $x = 1$ and $t = 1$, respectively.

7. Conclusions

In this paper, the fractional PBD model was examined with the M-truncated derivative and β-derivative using Kudryashov's R technique. The obtained soliton solution was graphically illustrated to depict the effects of the fractional order of the derivative for both the M-truncated derivative and β-derivative, as shown in Figures 1–5. The obtained solution represents a dark soliton. It is evident that the wave profile has a localized decrease in the wave amplitude. The changes in the shape of the soliton solution have been observed by making variations in the value of fractional order β. The graphical interpretation of the obtained solution reveals that the graphs for both definitions are different for the same value of the fractional order β. However, as the value of β is increased, the wave profile corresponding to both definitions of the fractional derivative becomes increasingly similar. These observations show that both M-truncated and β derivatives provide results that are in good agreement if the fractional order is nearly one. Ultimately, the graphs related to the M-truncated derivative and the β-derivative tend to become the same as the value of β approaches unity. The reported results are novel and Kudryashov's R technique has been utilized to explore the considered model for the first time in this work to provide a comparison of the soliton solutions for β-fractional and M-truncated derivatives. The proposed research may be helpful for providing a deeper insight into fractional order nonlinear models and the related physical phenomena.

Author Contributions: Conceptualization, X.W., G.A., M.S., H.M. and M.A.; formal analysis, G.A., M.S. and H.M.; funding acquisition, X.W.; investigation, G.A., M.S. and H.M.; methodology, G.A., M.S., H.M. and M.A.; software, G.A., M.S., H.M. and M.A.; supervision, G.A. and M.A.; visualization, G.A., M.S., H.M. and M.A.; writing—original draft, X.W., G.A., M.S., H.M. and M.A.; writing—review and editing, G.A., M.S., H.M. and M.A. All authors equally contributed to this work. All authors have read and approved the final manuscript.

Funding: This research was funded/supported by the National Natural Science Foundation of China (Grant No. 11861053).

Acknowledgments: The authors are grateful to anonymous referees for their valuable suggestions, which significantly improved this manuscript.

Data Availability Statement: Not applicable.

Conflicts of Interest: The authors declare no conflict of interest.

References

1. Peyrard, M.; Bishop, A.R. Statistical mechanics of a nonlinear model for DNA denaturation. *Phys. Rev. Lett.* **1989**, *62*, 2755. [CrossRef]
2. Dauxois, T.; Peyrard, M.; Bishop, A.R. Entropy-driven DNA denaturation. *Phys. Rev. E* **1993**, *47*, R44–R47. [CrossRef] [PubMed]
3. Dauxois, T.; Peyrard, M.; Bishop, A.R. Dynamics and thermodynamics of a nonlinear model for DNA denaturation. *Phys. Rev. E* **1993**, *47*, 684–695. [CrossRef] [PubMed]
4. Dauxois, T.; Peyrard, M. Entropy-driven transition in a one-dimensional system. *Phys. Rev. E* **1995**, *51*, 4027–4040. [CrossRef] [PubMed]
5. Barré, J.; Dauxois, T. Lyapunov exponents as a dynamical indicator of a phase transition. *Europhys. Lett.* **2001**, *55*, 164. [CrossRef]
6. Theodorakopoulos, N. DNA denaturation bubbles at criticality. *Phys. Rev. E* **2008**, *E77*, 031919. [CrossRef] [PubMed]
7. Hillebrand, M.; Kalosakas, G.; Bishop, A.R.; Skokos, C. Bubble lifetimes in DNA gene promoters and their mutations affecting transcription. *J. Chem. Phys.* **2021**, *155*, 095101. [CrossRef] [PubMed]
8. Ares, S.; Voulgarakis, N.K.; Rasmussen, K.O.; Bishop, A.R. Bubble Nucleation and Cooperativity in DNA Melting. *Phys. Rev. Lett.* **2005**, *94*, 035504. [CrossRef] [PubMed]
9. Ares, S.; Kalosakas, G. Distribution of bubble lengths in DNA. *Nano Lett.* **2007**, *7*, 307–311. [CrossRef]
10. Cule, D.; Hwa, T. Denaturation of Heterogeneous DNA. *Phys. Rev. Lett.* **1997**, *79*, 2375–2378. [CrossRef]
11. Hillebrand, M.; Kalosakas, G.; Schwellnus, A.; Skokos, C. Heterogeneity and chaos in the Peyrard-Bishop-Dauxois DNA model. *Phys. Rev. E* **2019**, *E99*, 022213. [CrossRef] [PubMed]
12. Voulgarakis, N.K.; Kalosakas, G.; Rasmussen, R.O.; Bishop, A.R. Temperature-Dependent signatures of coherent vibrational openings in DNA. *Nano Lett.* **2004**, *4*, 629–632. [CrossRef]
13. Kalosakas, G.; Rasmussen, K.O.; Bishop, A.R. Non-exponential decay of base-pair opening fluctuations in DNA. *Chem. Phys. Lett.* **2006**, *432*, 291–295. [CrossRef]
14. Peyrard, M.; Farago, J. Nonlinear localization in thermalized lattices: Application to DNA. *Physcia A* **2000**, *288*, 199–217. [CrossRef]
15. Peyrard, M. Nonlinear dynamics and statistical physics of DNA. *Nonlinearity* **2004**, *17*, R1–R40. [CrossRef]

16. Weber, G.; Essex, J.W.; Neylon, C. Probing the microscopic flexibility of DNA from melting temperatures. *Nat. Phys.* **2009**, *5*, 769–773. [CrossRef]
17. Maniadis, P.; Alexandrov, B.S.; Bishop, A.R.; Rasmussen, K.O. Feigenbaum cascade of discrete breathers in a model of DNA. *Phys. Rev. Lett.* **2011**, *83*, 011904. [CrossRef] [PubMed]
18. Muniz, M.I.; Lackey, H.H.; Heemstra, J.M.; Weber, G. DNA/TNA mesoscopic modeling of melting temperatures suggests weaker hydrogen bonding of CG than in DNA/RNA. *Chem. Phys. Lett.* **2020**, *749*, 137413. [CrossRef]
19. Zoli, M. End-to-end distance and contour length distribution functions of DNA helices. *J. Chem. Phys.* **2018**, *148*, 214902. [CrossRef]
20. Hillebrand, M.; Kalosakas, G.; Skokos, C.; Bishop, A.R. Distributions of bubble lifetimes and bubble lengths in DNA. *Phys. Rev. E* **2020**, *102*, 062114. [CrossRef] [PubMed]
21. Zoli, M. Base pair fluctuations in helical models for nucleic acids. *J. Chem. Phys.* **2021**, *154*, 194102. [CrossRef]
22. Agüero, M.A.; Najera, M.D.; Carrilo, M. Nonclassic solitonic structures in DNA's vibrational dynamics. *Int. J. Mod. Phys.* **2008**, *22*, 2571–2582. [CrossRef]
23. Najera, L.; Carrillo, M.; Aguero, M.A. Non-classic solitons and the broken hydrogen bonds in DNA vibrational dynamics. *Adv. Stud. Theor. Phys.* **2010**, *4*, 495–510.
24. Ali, K.K.; Cattani, C.; Gómez-Aguilar, J.F.; Baleanu, D.; Osman, M.S. Analytical and numerical study of the DNA dynamics arising in oscillator-chain of Peyrard-Bishop model. *Chaos Solitons Fractals* **2020**, *139*, 110089. [CrossRef]
25. Manafian, J.; Ilhan, A.O.; Mohammed, A.S. Forming localized waves of the nonlinearity of the DNA dynamics arising in oscillator-chain of Peyrard–Bishop model. *AIMS Math.* **2020**, *5*, 2461–2483. [CrossRef]
26. Atangana, A.; Baleanu, D.; Alsaedi, A. Analysis of time-fractional Hunter-Saxton equation: A model of neumatic liquid crystal. *Open Phys.* **2016**, *14*, 145–149. [CrossRef]
27. Sousa, J.V.D.C.; de Oliveira, E.C. A new truncated M-fractional derivative type unifying some fractional derivative types with classical properties. *Int. J. Anal. Appl.* **2018**, *16*, 83–96.
28. Zafar, A.; Ali, K.K.; Raheel, M.; Jafar, N.; Nisar, K.S. Soliton solutions to the DNA Peyrard–Bishop equation with beta-derivative via three distinctive approaches. *Eur. Phys. J. Plus* **2020**, *135*, 726. [CrossRef]
29. Morales-Delgado, V.F.; Gómez-Aguilar, J.F.; Taneco-Hernandez, M.A. Analytical solutions of electrical circuits described by fractional conformable derivatives in Liouville-Caputo sense. *AEU-Int. J. Electron. Commun.* **2018**, *85*, 108–117. [CrossRef]
30. Salahshour, S.; Ahmadian, A.; Abbasbandy, S.; Baleanu, D. M-fractional derivative under interval uncertainty: Theory, properties and applications. *Chaos Solitons Fractals* **2018**, *117*, 84–93. [CrossRef]
31. Dan, J.; Sain, S.; Choudhury, A.G.; Garai, S. Solitary wave solutions of nonlinear PDEs using Kudryashov's R function method. *J. Mod. Opt.* **2020**, *67*, 1499–1507. [CrossRef]
32. Sirisubtawee, S.; Koonprasert, S. Exact traveling wave solutions of certain nonlinear partial differential equations using the (G'/G^2)-expansion method. *Adv. Math. Phys.* **2018**, *2018*, 7628651. [CrossRef]

Article

Collocation Method for Optimal Control of a Fractional Distributed System

Wen Cao [1,*] and Yufeng Xu [2]

[1] School of Mathematics and Statistics, Hunan University of Finance and Economics, 139 Fenglin 2nd Road, Changsha 410205, China
[2] School of Mathematics and Statistics, Central South University, 932 Lushan South Road, Changsha 410083, China
* Correspondence: wen0731@126.com

Abstract: In this paper, a collocation method based on the Jacobi polynomial is proposed for a class of optimal-control problems of a fractional distributed system. By using the Lagrange multiplier technique and fractional variational principle, the stated problem is reduced to a system of fractional partial differential equations about control and state functions. The uniqueness of this fractional coupled system is discussed. For spatial second-order derivatives, the proposed method takes advantage of Jacobi polynomials with different parameters to approximate solutions. For a temporal fractional derivative in the Caputo sense, choosing appropriate basis functions allows the collocation method to be implemented easily and efficiently. Exponential convergence is verified numerically under continuous initial conditions. As a particular example, the relation between the state function and the order of the fractional derivative is analyzed with a discontinuous initial condition. Moreover, the numerical results show that the integration of the state function will decay as the order of the fractional derivative decreases.

Keywords: collocation method; fractional optimal-control problem; fractional variational principle; exponential convergence

Citation: Cao, W.; Xu, Y. Collocation Method for Optimal Control of a Fractional Distributed System. *Fractal Fract.* **2022**, *6*, 594. https://doi.org/10.3390/fractalfract6100594

Academic Editor: Sameerah Jamal

Received: 7 September 2022
Accepted: 10 October 2022
Published: 14 October 2022

Publisher's Note: MDPI stays neutral with regard to jurisdictional claims in published maps and institutional affiliations.

Copyright: © 2022 by the authors. Licensee MDPI, Basel, Switzerland. This article is an open access article distributed under the terms and conditions of the Creative Commons Attribution (CC BY) license (https://creativecommons.org/licenses/by/4.0/).

1. Introduction

Optimal-control problems minimize a function (or a functional) with the states and control inputs of the system over a set of admissible control functions [1], which arises in many scientific and engineering problems, such as aeronautics [2] and economics [3]. In [4], by applying optimal control theory, the dynamics of a basic oncolytic virotherapy model was studied. The constrained dynamics of the optimal-control problem may be divided into two major classes: an ordinary differential equation (ODE) and a partial differential equation (PDE). The fractional differential equation usually came up by replacing the conventional derivatives in ODE/PDE with some sorts of fractional derivatives, whose order of derivative turns out to be some real numbers or even complex numbers. In recent years, with the development of fractional calculus, it has been verified that fractional differential equations model dynamical systems and physical processes more accurately than classic ODEs and PDEs do, and fractional controllers perform better than integer order controllers as well. In this paper, we shall investigate a class of fractional optimal-control problems. The dynamics of the system are described by a partial differential equation with a Caputo fractional derivative on a temporal variable and a second-order derivative on a spatial variable, comprising what is called a fractional optimal-control problem of a distributed system. Although integer-order optimal-control problems and fractional variational problems regarding a single variable have been extensively discussed [5–11], the optimal-control problems related to the fractional distributed system are not systematically developed yet. Therefore, it is meaningful to further study this topic.

As a matter of course, the above-mentioned optimal-control problems have to be solved to examine their further features. However, only few of them can be handled via analytical techniques. Therefore, tremendous efforts have been made regarding numerical methods. By means of a fractional variational principle and the Lagrange multiplier technique, the underlying fractional optimal-control problem can be converted to a system of partial differential equations with temporal fractional derivatives. As one of the pioneering works, two classes of the fractional variational problem with the Riemann–Liouville derivative are considered in [12], where the necessary condition (i.e., the Euler–Lagrange equation) for both cases are analytical deduced. In [13], a general formulation for a class of fractional optimal-control problems was derived by using techniques of calculus of variations, the Lagrange multiplier, and the formula for fractional integration by parts. Based on the foundations mentioned above, several numerical methods have been applied to solve fractional optimal-control problems. In [14], the dynamic system of fractional optimal-control problems are considered as fractional partial differential equations with a Caputo derivative, and numerical solutions of this problem are obtained by means of eigenfunctions. In [15], the modified Grünwald–Letnikov approach is employed to establish a central difference numerical scheme for both time-invariant and time-variant cases. In [16], the fractional optimal-control problem is converted into a general integer order problem by using Oustaloup's approximation for the fractional derivative operator. This method is allowed to solve a more complex problem of a fractional-free, final-time optimal-control problem. In [17,18], the considered fractional optimal-control problems are both reduced to a system of algebraic equations by using the normalized Legendre orthogonal basis. Nevertheless, in [17], the fractional integration and multiplication are approximated directly, while in [18], the fractional optimal-control problems are transformed into an equivalent variational problem. In [19], the fractional optimal-control problem of a distributed system is solved in cylindrical coordinates. Applying the method of separation of variables and eigenfunctions, an equivalent problem in terms of generalized state and control variables is defined, and it is computed by the Grünwald–Letnikov approach. Overall, numerical methods based on approximation by smooth polynomials are perfectly suitable for optimal-control problems defined on a bounded domain with regular boundary conditions. For instance, see [20–22]. A hybrid meshless method for fractional distributed optimal control was presented in [23].

Motivated by the above results, a collocation method with the Jacobi polynomial is established to solve the fractional optimal-control problem. It is well-known that the collocation method is a global numerical method with high accuracy, which was firstly applied by Slater and Kantorovic in 1934 [24]. The computation of this method at any given point depends on the information of the entire domain. Naturally, it has a great superiority in solving fractional problems since the fractional derivative we used here is defined in the Caputo sense and is non-local. In [25], a spectral Jacobi-collocation approximation for fractional integro-differential equations of the Volterra type is proposed, and the error of this method decaying exponentially is verified theoretically. In [26], the truncated Bessel series is used in a collocation scheme for solving a fractional optimal-control problem with a nonlinear fractional two-point boundary value problem. A local meshless collocation algorithm is applied to approximate the time fractional evolution model in [27]. In [28], by applying shifted Jacobi polynomials, the fractal-fractional derivative in the Atangana–Riemann–Liouville sense and the fractional derivatives in the Caputo and Atangan–Baleau–Caputo concepts have been used to study the optimal-control problem of the advection–diffusion–reaction equation.

In this paper, we will transform the fractional optimal-control problems into a system of fractional partial differential equations through the fractional variational principle, then solve the resulting system by the Jacobi collocation method. The numerical results under both continuous and discontinuous initial conditions will be provided. In the case of the continuous initial condition, the exponential convergence and high accuracy can be arrived with different Jacobi parameters. The influence of the fractional order on the state function will be analyzed in the case of the problem with a discontinuous initial condition. The remainder of this article is organized as follows: In Section 2, we will introduce some necessary preliminaries of fractional calculus to make this paper self-contained. In Section 3, the formulation of the fractional optimal-control problem is given and basic property is discussed. In Section 4, the derivation of the collocation method for solving the fractional optimal-control problem is performed. A numerical example is given in Section 5, and our conclusion is finally drawn in Section 6.

2. Mathematical Preparation

In this section, we introduce two frequently discussed fractional derivatives and their fundamental properties, which are useful in the analysis of the model and computation in what follows. We begin by recalling the Riemann–Liouville fractional integral.

Definition 1 ([29]). *Let $f(x) \in L^1([a,b])$, $s > 0$ be a finite and real number. Then,*

$$(_aI_x^s f)(x) = \frac{1}{\Gamma(s)} \int_a^x (x-t)^{s-1} f(t) dt, \tag{1}$$

and

$$(_xI_b^s f)(x) = \frac{1}{\Gamma(s)} \int_x^b (t-x)^{s-1} f(t) dt, \tag{2}$$

are named as left-sided Riemann–Liouville fractional integral and right-sided Riemann–Liouville fractional integral, respectively.

Definition 2 ([29]). *Let $f(x) \in AC([a,b])$ and $_aI_t^{n-s}f$, $_tI_b^{n-s}f \in C^n([a,b])$, $n-1 < s < n$, n is a natural number. Then,*

$$(_aD_x^s f)(x) = \frac{1}{\Gamma(n-s)} \frac{d^n}{dx^n} \int_a^x (x-t)^{n-s-1} f(t) dt, \tag{3}$$

and

$$(_xD_b^s f)(x) = \frac{(-1)^n}{\Gamma(n-s)} \frac{d^n}{dt^n} \int_x^b (t-x)^{n-s-1} f(t) dt, \tag{4}$$

are named as the left-sided Riemann–Liouville fractional derivative and right-sided Riemann–Liouville fractional derivative, respectively.

Definition 3 ([29]). *Let $f(x) \in AC([a,b])$, $n-1 < s < n$, n is a natural number. Then,*

$$(_a^C D_x^s f)(x) = \frac{1}{\Gamma(n-s)} \int_a^x (x-t)^{n-s-1} \left\{ \frac{d^n}{dt^n} f(t) \right\} dt, \tag{5}$$

and

$$(_x^C D_b^s f)(x) = \frac{(-1)^n}{\Gamma(n-s)} \int_x^b (t-x)^{n-s-1} \left\{ \frac{d^n}{dt^n} f(t) \right\} dt, \tag{6}$$

are named as the left-sided Caputo fractional derivative and right-sided Caputo fractional derivative, respectively.

Theorem 1 ([29]). *Let $0 < s < 1$. Then, Riemann–Liouville and Caputo fractional derivatives satisfy the following relation:*

$$(_xD_b^s f)(x) = (_x^C D_b^s f)(x) + f(b) \frac{(b-x)^{-s}}{\Gamma(1-s)}. \tag{7}$$

Based on Theorem 1, the Caputo fractional derivative is equivalent with the Riemann–Liouville fractional derivative for the continuously differentiable functions satisfying Dirichlet boundary condition $f(b) = 0$. More details on fractional derivatives and their properties can be found in monographes [29–31].

3. Analysis of Fractional Optimal-Control Problem

In this part, we focus on the formulation of a class of optimal problems with a distributed system involving the Caputo fractional derivative. The details are described as follows.

3.1. Formulation of Model

Let $0 \leq t \leq 1$, $0 \leq x \leq L$, and Q, R be two positive parameters of the system. Functions z and u depending on t and x (i.e., time and position) simultaneously represent some performance indices. Notice that the time domain may not necessary be $[0,1]$, and it can be generalized to $[0,T]$, $T > 0$. Our major task is: finding an optimal control input signal $u(x,t)$, which minimizes the cost functional

$$J = \int_0^1 \int_0^L Qz^2(x,t) + Ru^2(x,t) dx dt, \tag{8}$$

subject to the system dynamic constraints

$$^C_0D^s_t z(x,t) = \frac{\partial^2 z(x,t)}{\partial x^2} + u(x,t), \ 0 < s < 1, \tag{9}$$

the initial condition

$$z(x,0) = z_0(x), \ 0 \leq x \leq L, \tag{10}$$

and the boundary condition

$$\frac{\partial z(0,t)}{\partial x} = \frac{\partial z(L,t)}{\partial x} = 0, \ 0 < t < 1, \tag{11}$$

where s is the order of Caputo fractional derivative, $z(x,t)$ and $u(x,t)$ are the state and control functions, respectively. In [14], models (8)–(11) was discussed.

3.2. Fractional Variational Principle and Properties of Model

In order to deduce the necessary condition for problem (8)–(11), we impose a modified performance index by using the Lagrange multiplier λ as

$$\tilde{J} = \int_0^1 \int_0^L Qz^2(x,t) + Ru^2(x,t) + \lambda \left[^C_0D^s_t z(x,t) - \frac{\partial^2 z(x,t)}{\partial x^2} - u(x,t) \right] dx dt. \tag{12}$$

Assuming that $z^*(x,t)$ and $u^*(x,t)$ are the desired optimum solutions of (8)–(11), define

$$z(x,t) = z^*(x,t) + \varepsilon_1 \eta_1(x,t), \ \varepsilon_1 \in \mathbb{R}, \tag{13}$$
$$u(x,t) = u^*(x,t) + \varepsilon_2 \eta_2(x,t), \ \varepsilon_2 \in \mathbb{R}, \tag{14}$$

where $\varepsilon_1, \varepsilon_2$ are perturbation parameters, and $\eta_1(x,t)$ and $\eta_2(x,t)$ are arbitrary test functions satisfying $\eta_1(x,0) = \eta_{1x}(0,t) = \eta_{1x}(L,t) = 0$.

Substitute Equations (13) and (14) into functional (12), then $\tilde{J}$ becomes a scale function of ε_1 and ε_2. Obviously, $\tilde{J}$ has an extremum at $\varepsilon_1 = \varepsilon_2 = 0$. Differentiating $\tilde{J}$ with respect to $\varepsilon_1, \varepsilon_2$ and λ, respectively, we have

$$\frac{\partial \tilde{J}}{\partial \varepsilon_1} = \int_0^1 \int_0^L \left[2Qz(x,t)\eta_1(x,t) + \lambda\,{}_0^C D_t^s \eta_1(x,t) - \lambda \frac{\partial^2 \eta_1(x,t)}{\partial x^2} \right] dxdt, \qquad (15)$$

$$\frac{\partial \tilde{J}}{\partial \varepsilon_2} = \int_0^1 \int_0^L [2Ru(x,t)\eta_2(x,t) - \lambda \eta_2(x,t)]dxdt, \qquad (16)$$

$$\frac{\partial \tilde{J}}{\partial \lambda} = \int_0^1 \int_0^L \left[{}_0^C D_t^s z(x,t) - \frac{\partial^2 z(x,t)}{\partial x^2} - u(x,t) \right] dxdt. \qquad (17)$$

Applying fractional integration by parts formulae (see [29] (Page 76, Lemma 2.7)) to (15), we obtain

$$\int_0^1 \int_0^L \lambda \left[{}_0^C D_t^s \eta_1(x,t) - \frac{\partial^2 \eta_1(x,t)}{\partial x^2} \right] dxdt = \int_0^1 \int_0^L \eta_1(x,t) \left[{}_t D_1^s \lambda - \frac{\partial^2 \lambda(x,t)}{\partial x^2} \right] dxdt$$

$$+ \int_0^1 [\lambda_x(L,t)\eta_1(L,t) - \lambda_x(0,t)\eta_1(0,t)]dt + \int_0^L \eta_1(x,0)\,{}_t I_1^s \lambda(x,0)dx.$$

To minimize $\tilde{J}$ (the same as to minimize J), it is required that results of (15)–(17) are zeros when $\varepsilon_1 = \varepsilon_2 = 0$. Then, by the arbitrariness of λ, one could assume $\lambda_x(0,t) = \lambda_x(L,t) = 0$, $\lambda(x,1) = 0$ to have

$$\,{}_t^C D_1^s \lambda(x,t) = \frac{\partial^2 \lambda(x,t)}{\partial x^2} - 2Qz^*(x,t), \qquad (18)$$

$$\lambda(x,t) = 2Ru^*(x,t), \qquad (19)$$

$$\,{}_0^C D_t^s z^*(x,t) = \frac{\partial^2 z^*(x,t)}{\partial x^2} + u^*(x,t), \qquad (20)$$

since $\eta_1(x,t)$ and $\eta_2(x,t)$ are arbitrary.

Substituting (19) into (18), it is easy to find that the desired optimal solutions $u^*(x,t), z^*(x,t)$ satisfy the following coupled equations:

$$\,{}_t^C D_1^s u(x,t) = \frac{\partial^2 u(x,t)}{\partial x^2} - \frac{Q}{R} z(x,t), \qquad (21)$$

$$\,{}_0^C D_t^s z(x,t) = \frac{\partial^2 z(x,t)}{\partial x^2} + u(x,t), \qquad (22)$$

with the initial and boundary conditions

$$z(x,0) = z_0(x), \qquad u(x,1) = 0,$$

$$\frac{\partial z(0,t)}{\partial x} = \frac{\partial z(L,t)}{\partial x} = 0, \qquad \frac{\partial u(0,t)}{\partial x} = \frac{\partial u(L,t)}{\partial x} = 0.$$

Now, the problem (8)–(11) has been converted to a fractional coupled system (21) and (22).

Next, we discuss the uniqueness of system (21) and (22) because of the fact that existence result directly follows from the linearity of system itself (see [29] (Chapter 6)). Suppose that (u_1, z_1) and (u_2, z_2) are two pairs of solutions of (21) and (22); then, $\tilde{u} := u_1 - u_2$ and $\tilde{z} := z_1 - z_2$ must be the solutions of (21) and (22) by superposition principle. Therefore,

$$\,{}_t^C D_1^s \tilde{u}(x,t) = \frac{\partial^2 \tilde{u}(x,t)}{\partial x^2} - \frac{Q}{R} \tilde{z}(x,t), \qquad (23)$$

$$\,{}_0^C D_t^s \tilde{z}(x,t) = \frac{\partial^2 \tilde{z}(x,t)}{\partial x^2} + \tilde{u}(x,t). \qquad (24)$$

Multiplying $\tilde{u}$ and $\tilde{z}$ to (23) and (24), respectively, then subtracting one to another, then integrating from 0 to L with respect to x, we have

$$R\int_0^L \tilde{u}_t^c D_1^s \tilde{u}\, dx + Q\int_0^L \tilde{z}_0^c D_t^s \tilde{z}\, dx = Q\int_0^L \tilde{z}\tilde{z}_{xx}\, dx + R\int_0^L \tilde{u}\tilde{u}_{xx}\, dx. \tag{25}$$

In view of

$$\begin{aligned}
& Q\int_0^L \tilde{z}\tilde{z}_{xx}\, dx + R\int_0^L \tilde{u}\tilde{u}_{xx}\, dx \\
&= Q\left(\tilde{z}\tilde{z}_x\big|_0^L - \int_0^L \tilde{z}_x^2\, dx\right) + R\left(\tilde{u}\tilde{u}_x\big|_0^L - \int_0^L \tilde{u}_x^2\, dx\right) \\
&\leq 0,
\end{aligned}$$

we conclude that either one of the following inequalities hold:

$$R\int_0^L \tilde{u}\cdot({}_t^c D_1^s \tilde{u})\, dx \leq 0 \quad \text{or} \quad Q\int_0^L \tilde{z}\cdot({}_0^c D_t^s \tilde{z})\, dx \leq 0. \tag{26}$$

If the former case is true, we assume that $\tilde{u}$ is approximated by smooth polynomials $\varphi(x)$ and $\phi(t)$, which is $\tilde{u} = \varphi(x)\phi(t)$. Then,

$$\begin{aligned}
\int_0^L \tilde{u}\cdot({}_t^c D_1^s \tilde{u})\, dx &= \int_0^L \varphi(x)\phi(t)\cdot \varphi(x)({}_t^c D_1^s \phi(t))\, dx \\
&= \phi(t)\cdot({}_t^c D_1^s \phi(t))\int_0^L \varphi^2(x)\, dx.
\end{aligned} \tag{27}$$

Furthermore, notice that

$$\begin{aligned}
\int_0^1 \phi(t)\cdot({}_t^c D_1^s \phi(t))\int_0^L \varphi^2(x)\, dx\, dt &= \int_0^1 \phi(t)\cdot({}_t^c D_1^s \phi(t))\, dt \cdot \int_0^L \varphi^2(x)\, dx \\
&= \int_0^1 ({}_0 D_t^s \phi(t))\cdot \phi(t)\, dt \cdot \int_0^L \varphi^2(x)\, dx \\
&= \int_0^1 \left({}_0 D_t^{s/2}\phi(t)\right)^2 dt \cdot \int_0^L \varphi^2(x)\, dx \\
&\geq 0,
\end{aligned}$$

which implies that the right hand side of (27) is non-negative. Combining (26), one can immediately know that

$$\int_0^L \tilde{u}\cdot({}_t^c D_1^s \tilde{u})\, dx \equiv 0. \tag{28}$$

That is to say, $\tilde{u}$ is zero. The other argument for $\tilde{z}$ is similar. Thus, the pair of solutions of problem (21) and (22) is unique.

In order to observe the property of state function $z(x,t)$, we integrate both sides of (22) from 0 to L,

$$\int_0^L {}_0^c D_t^s z(x,t)\, dx = \int_0^L \frac{\partial^2 z(x,t)}{\partial x^2}\, dx + \int_0^L u(x,t)\, dx. \tag{29}$$

Obviously, the first term on the right side is zero according to boundary conditions. $u(x,t)$ is bounded because the problem is well-posed. That is, there exists a real number M satisfying $\zeta(t) = \int_0^L u(x,t)\, dx < M$ for any $t \in [0,1]$. Regarding the left hand side, it is easy to deduce that there exists $t_l^* \in [0,1]$, such that

$$\int_0^L {}_0^c D_t^s z(x,t)\, dx = \frac{t^{1-s}}{\Gamma(2-s)}\int_0^L z_t(x,t_l^*)\, dx. \tag{30}$$

Equations (29) and (30) lead to the relation between the change rate of energy of $z(x,t)$ and time t as

$$\int_0^L u(x,t)dx = \frac{t^{1-s}}{\Gamma(2-s)} \int_0^L z_t(x,t_l^*)dx. \tag{31}$$

On account of the fact that Equations (21) and (22) are coupled, it is easy to arrive at the following identity:

$$\int_0^L z(x,t)dx = -\frac{(1-t)^{1-s}}{\Gamma(2-s)} \int_0^L u_t(x,t_r^*)dx. \tag{32}$$

Combining (31) and (32), we obtain

$$\Phi(t,s) := \int_0^L z(x,t)dx = C \cdot \frac{(1-t)^{1-s}}{\Gamma(1-s)\Gamma(2-s)}, \quad 0 < s, t < 1, \tag{33}$$

where $C = -t_r^{*-s} \int_0^L z_t(x,t_l^*)dx \geq 0$. This indicates that the volume of $z(x,t)$ in the temporal direction will decay as the order s decreases, due to the non-negativity assumption of $z(x,0)$ and the diffusion property of the considered system. Conversely, if z_t is positive for each fixed x, then solution $z(x,t)$ will blow up eventually, which is physically impossible.

4. Numerical Algorithm

In this section, a collocation method is proposed to the solve fractional optimal control problem (8)–(11). Firstly, we recall the definition and properties of the Jacobi polynomials, occasionally called hypergeometric polynomials, which are used in our collocation method. From now on, we use symbols α and β to parameterize the Jacobi polynomials and let s, $0 < s < 1$ be the order of fractional derivative. Notice that when s approaches one, the corresponding fractional derivatives reduce to conventional integer-order derivatives.

Recently, Jacobi polynomial for solving differential equations has become increasingly popular because of the high accuracy of interpolation for ODE/PDE with certain regularity [32,33]. The well-known Jacobi polynomial $J_n^{\alpha,\beta}$ with indices $\alpha, \beta > -1$ of degree n are defined on interval $[-1,1]$ and can be expressed as

$$J_n^{\alpha,\beta}(\xi) = \frac{(-1)^n}{2^n \cdot n!}(1-\xi)^{-\alpha}(1+\xi)^{-\beta} \frac{d^n}{d\xi^n}\left[(1-\xi)^{\alpha+n}(1+\xi)^{\beta+n}\right], \quad -1 \leq \xi \leq 1, \tag{34}$$

which is a solution of the second order linear homogeneous differential equation

$$(1-\xi^2)\frac{d^2 Y(\xi)}{d\xi^2} + [\beta - \alpha - (\alpha+\beta+2)\xi]\frac{dY(\xi)}{d\xi} + n(n+\alpha+\beta+1)Y(\xi) = 0.$$

In order to use these polynomials on the interval $[0, L]$, we take the change of variable $x = \frac{L}{2}(\xi+1)$. Therefore, $0 \leq x \leq L$ is due to the range of ξ. The derivative of $J_n^{\alpha,\beta}$ on the interval $[0, L]$ can be represented by

$$\frac{d^m}{dt^m} J_n^{\alpha,\beta}\left(\frac{2x}{L}-1\right) = \frac{\Gamma(n+m+\alpha+\beta+1)}{\Gamma(n+\alpha+\beta+1)L^m} J_{n-m}^{\alpha+m,\beta+m}\left(\frac{2x}{L}-1\right), \tag{35}$$

where $m = 1, 2, 3, \cdots$.

One advantage of Jacobi polynomial is that its fractional derivatives still have a recurrence form. For special cases, the Riemann–Liouville fractional derivative of $J_n^{\alpha,\beta}$ can be presented in the form of the Jacobi polynomial. Let $0 < \alpha < 1$, $\beta = 0$; we have

$${}_0D_x^\alpha J_n^{-\alpha,0}\left(\frac{2x}{L}-1\right) = \frac{\Gamma(n+1)x^{-\alpha}}{\Gamma(n-\alpha+1)} J_n^{0,-\alpha}\left(\frac{2x}{L}-1\right), \tag{36}$$

and when $\alpha = 0, 0 < \beta < 1$, it reads that

$$_xD_1^\beta J_n^{0,-\beta}\left(\frac{2x}{L}-1\right) = \frac{\Gamma(n+1)(L-x)^{-\beta}}{\Gamma(n-\beta+1)}J_n^{-\beta,0}\left(\frac{2x}{L}-1\right). \quad (37)$$

Next, we present the basic idea of the collocation method with Jacobi polynomials. Denoting sets $\{x_j^{\alpha,\beta}\}, 0 \le j \le M$ and $\{t_j^s\}, 0 \le j \le N$ as the nodes of Jacobi–Gauss–Lobatto (JGL) quadratures on the interval $[-1,1]$, we set the JGL points $\{x_{L,j}^{\alpha,\beta}\}, 0 \le j \le M$ and $\{t_{1,j}^s\}, 0 \le j \le N$ on $[0,L] \times [0,1]$ as

$$x_{L,j}^{\alpha,\beta} = \frac{L}{2}\left(x_j^{\alpha,\beta}+1\right), \quad 0 \le j \le M,$$

$$t_{1,j}^s = \frac{1}{2}\left(t_j^s+1\right), \quad 0 \le j \le N.$$

Let $\{\psi_i(t), \phi_j(x)\}, \{\hat{\psi}_i(t), \phi_j(x)\}$ be the pairs of Jacobi basis polynomials; the approximations for solutions z_N and u_N can be expanded as

$$z_N(x,t) = \sum_{i=0}^{N}\sum_{j=0}^{M} a_{ij}\phi_j(x)\psi_i(t), \quad (38)$$

$$u_N(x,t) = \sum_{i=0}^{N}\sum_{j=0}^{M} b_{ij}\phi_j(x)\hat{\psi}_i(t), \quad (39)$$

by using the method of separation of variables. Here, $\{\psi_i(t), \phi_j(x)\}$ and $\{\hat{\psi}_i(t), \phi_j(x)\}$ are different Jacobi basis polynomials, as follows:

$$\phi_j(x) = J_j^{\alpha,\beta}\left(\frac{2x}{L}-1\right),$$

$$\psi_i(t) = J_i^{-s,0}(2t-1),$$

$$\hat{\psi}_i(t) = J_i^{0,-s}(2t-1).$$

Inserting (38) and (39) into (21) and (22) leads to

$$\sum_{i=0}^{N}\sum_{j=0}^{M} b_{ij}\phi_j(x) \cdot {}_tD_1^s\hat{\psi}_i(t) = \sum_{i=0}^{N}\sum_{j=0}^{M} b_{ij}\hat{\psi}_i(t)\frac{\partial^2\phi_j(x)}{\partial x^2} - \frac{Q}{R}\sum_{i=0}^{N}\sum_{j=0}^{M} a_{ij}\phi_j(x)\psi_i(t),$$

$$\sum_{i=0}^{N}\sum_{j=0}^{M} a_{ij}\phi_j(x) \cdot {}_0^CD_t^s\psi_i(t) = \sum_{i=0}^{N}\sum_{j=0}^{M} a_{ij}\psi_i(t)\frac{\partial^2\phi_j(x)}{\partial x^2} + \sum_{i=0}^{N}\sum_{j=0}^{M} b_{ij}\phi_j(x)\hat{\psi}_i(t).$$

Combining the relation (7) and the Riemann–Liouville fractional derivative (36) and (37), we obtain

$${}_0^CD_t^s J_i^{-s,0}(2t-1) = \frac{\Gamma(i+1)t^{-s}}{\Gamma(i-s+1)}J_i^{0,-s}(2t-1) - \frac{J_i^{-s,0}(-1)t^{-s}}{\Gamma(1-s)}, \quad (40)$$

and

$${}_t^CD_1^s J_i^{0,-s}(2t-1) = \frac{\Gamma(i+1)(1-t)^{-s}}{\Gamma(i-s+1)}J_i^{-s,0}(2t-1) - \frac{J_i^{0,-s}(1)(1-t)^{-s}}{\Gamma(1-s)}. \quad (41)$$

The second-order derivative of Jacobi polynomial can be expressed as

$$\frac{\partial^2\phi_j(x)}{\partial x^2} = \frac{\Gamma(j+3+\alpha+\beta)}{\Gamma(j+1+\alpha+\beta)L^2}J_{j-2}^{\alpha+2,\beta+2}\left(\frac{2x}{L}-1\right). \quad (42)$$

Eventually, a numerical scheme for solving (8)–(11) is established as follows:

$$\sum_{i=0}^{N}\sum_{j=0}^{M} b_{ij} \left[\frac{\Gamma(i+1)(1-t)^{-s}}{\Gamma(i-s+1)} J_i^{-s,0}(2t-1) - \frac{J_i^{0,-s}(1)(1-t)^{-s}}{\Gamma(1-\alpha)} \right] J_j^{\alpha,\beta}\left(\frac{2x}{L}-1\right)$$
$$= \sum_{i=0}^{N}\sum_{j=0}^{M} \left[b_{ij} \frac{\Gamma(j+3+\alpha+\beta)L^{-2}}{\Gamma(j+\alpha+\beta+1)} J_{j-2}^{2+\alpha,2+\beta}\left(\frac{2x}{L}-1\right) J_i^{0,-s}(2t-1) \right.$$
$$\left. -\frac{Q}{R} a_{ij} J_j^{\alpha,\beta}\left(\frac{2x}{L}-1\right) J_i^{-s,0}(2t-1) \right], \tag{43}$$

and

$$\sum_{i=0}^{N}\sum_{j=0}^{M} a_{ij} \left[\frac{\Gamma(i+1)t^{-s}}{\Gamma(i-s+1)} J_i^{0,-s}(2t-1) - \frac{J_i^{-s,0}(-1)t^{-s}}{\Gamma(1-\alpha)} \right] J_j^{\alpha,\beta}\left(\frac{2x}{L}-1\right)$$
$$= \sum_{i=0}^{N}\sum_{j=0}^{M} \left[a_{ij} \frac{\Gamma(j+3+\alpha+\beta)L^{-2}}{\Gamma(j+\alpha+\beta+1)} J_{j-2}^{2+\alpha,2+\beta}\left(\frac{2x}{L}-1\right) J_i^{-s,0}(2t-1) \right.$$
$$\left. + b_{ij} J_j^{\alpha,\beta}\left(\frac{2x}{L}-1\right) J_i^{0,-s}(2t-1) \right]. \tag{44}$$

Note that JGL points $\{x_{L,j}^{\alpha,\beta}\}, 0 \leq j \leq M$ and $\{t_{1,j}^s\}, 0 \leq j \leq N$ include $t_{1,0}^s = 0$, $t_{1,N}^s = 1, x_{L,0}^{\alpha,\beta} = 0, x_{L,M}^{\alpha,\beta} = L$, which are necessarily used to satisfy the initial and boundary conditions.

5. Numerical Experiment

In this section, we present two numerical examples to verify the efficiency of our algorithm. The same as the former part s is the order of fractional derivative, and α, β are Jacobi polynomials parameters. We first discuss an example with an exact solution to illustrate the implementation and efficiency of the proposed numerical method; then, a fractional optimal-control problem with noncontinuous initial input signal is considered. The MATLAB R2015b software is used for all computations in this section.

5.1. Numerical Solution for System with Smooth Initial Input Signal

As the first example, we assume that systems (21) and (22) have an analytical solution given by

$$u(x,t) = (t-1)\cos(x\pi),$$
$$z(x,t) = (1-t)\cos(x\pi).$$

Without loss of generality, we assume $R = Q = L = 1$ to simplify the computing procedures. In order to balance both sides of these equations, let

$$f_1(x,t) = \frac{1}{\Gamma(2-\alpha)}(1-t)^{1-s}\cos(x\pi) + \cos(x\pi)\left[\pi^2(1-t)+t-1\right], \tag{45}$$

and

$$f_2(x,t) = \frac{1}{\Gamma(2-\alpha)}t^{1-s}\cos(x\pi) + \cos(x\pi)\left[\pi^2(t-1)+t-1\right], \tag{46}$$

which are purposively added to the right hand side parts of Equations (21) and (22), respectively. Therefore, the initial input signal is governed by a cosine waveform

$$z_0(x) = -\cos(x\pi), \ 0 \leq x \leq 1. \tag{47}$$

One important advantage of the collocation method is the high accuracy. Firstly, we compare the exact and numerical solutions for $s = 0.7$, $\alpha = \beta = 3$. Figure 1a,b shows the exact and numerical solutions of state and control functions by severally fixing $x = 0.2$ and $t = 0.5$ and choosing $N = M = 10$ in collocation method. Note that the numerical solutions of both $z(x, t)$ and $u(x, t)$ are highly aligned with the exact solutions. Table 1 lists the maximum absolute errors (MAE) of the exact and numerical solution at $x = 0.2$ and $t = 0.5$ with four kinds of Jacobi polynomials parameters, which are

- $\alpha = \beta = -0.5$ (Chebyshev polynomials of the first kind),
- $\alpha = \beta = 0.5$ (Chebyshev polynomial of the second kind),
- $\alpha = \beta = 0$ (Legendre polynomials),
- $\alpha = 2, \beta = 3$ (non-specified Jacobi polynomials).

The result shows that the proposed algorithm provides high accuracy in cases of different Jacobi parameters. Figure 1c,d show that the relation between the degree M, N ($M = N$) of the polynomial and the logarithm of error (E) is almost linear, which indicates that the error decays exponentially.

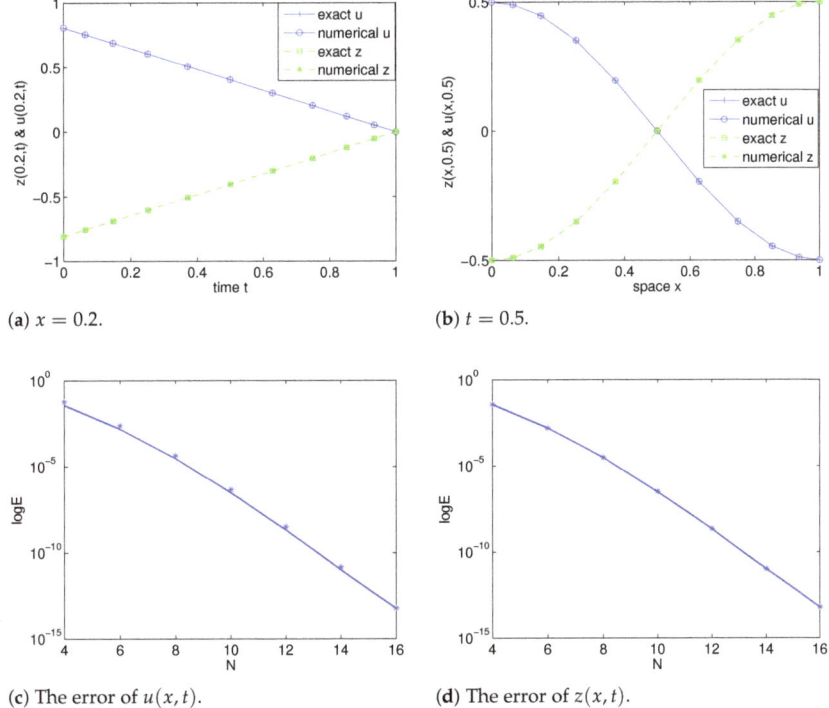

Figure 1. Numerical and analytical solution of system (21) and (22) (see (**a,b**)); the relation between N and error (E) with $s = 0.7$ and $\alpha = \beta = 3$ (see (**c,d**)).

Table 1. Maximum absolute errors (MAE).

M	α	β	MAE of z	MAE of u
5			1.05×10^{-3}	1.13×10^{-3}
10	-0.5	-0.5	3.36×10^{-8}	3.43×10^{-8}
15			2.89×10^{-15}	3.09×10^{-14}
5			2.78×10^{-3}	2.96×10^{-3}
10	0.5	0.5	1.82×10^{-7}	1.86×10^{-3}
15			4.51×10^{-14}	5.00×10^{-14}
5			1.98×10^{-3}	2.12×10^{-3}
10	0	0	9.45×10^{-8}	9.65×10^{-8}
15			2.62×10^{-14}	2.98×10^{-14}
5			5.95×10^{-3}	7.90×10^{-3}
10	2	3	1.80×10^{-6}	2.87×10^{-6}
15			2.87×10^{-13}	4.13×10^{-13}

5.2. Numerical Solution for System with Discontinuous Initial Input Signal

In this part, a kind of discontinuous initial condition is considered. Similarly, we take $R = Q = L = 1$, and we solve systems (21) and (22) with the initial condition expressed by a step-function signal

$$z_0(x) = \begin{cases} 10, & 0 \leq x < 0.5, \\ 0, & 0.5 \leq x \leq 1. \end{cases}$$

In computation, we select $N = M = 11$ and $\alpha = \beta = -0.5$. The numerical solution for $s = 0.9$ is displayed in Figure 2a. One can observe that the state function $z(x, t)$ becomes increasingly smooth after a short time because of the influences of diffusion and Neumann boundary conditions. Meanwhile, the state function will converge to a stable equilibrium that is not identical zero because the control input is not zero.

In Figure 2b–d, we sketched the curves of the control function with three different fractional orders ($s = 0.4$, $s = 0.6$ and $s = 0.9999$) as time goes by. In this case, we set $\alpha = \beta = 1$. This shows that when s is relatively small ($s = 0.4$), the state function $z(x, t)$ decays much faster than the case of relatively large s ($s = 0.6$). This coincides with the memory property of the fractional derivative, which is sometimes called the heavy tail feature. When s approaches 1, a comparatively slow and uniform decay phenomenon can be viewed, which matches our previous analysis.

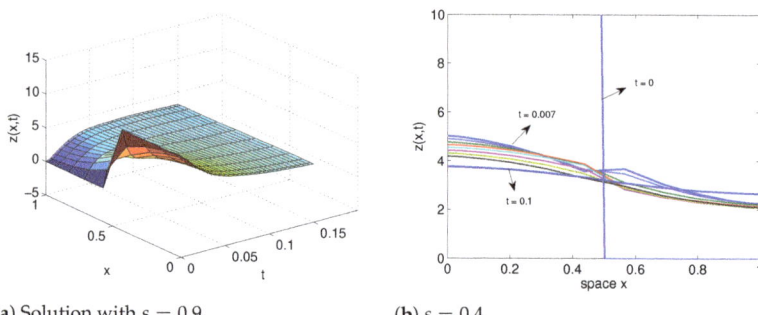

(**a**) Solution with $s = 0.9$. (**b**) $s = 0.4$.

Figure 2. *Cont.*

the smooth parameter is in the interval $0 < \alpha < 1$. The system has a quasi-zero stiffness property when $\alpha = 1$. Additionally, its stiffness is positive when $\alpha > 1$.

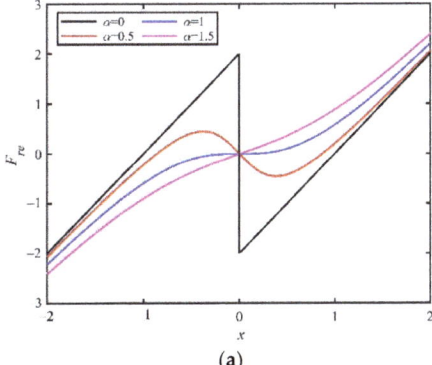 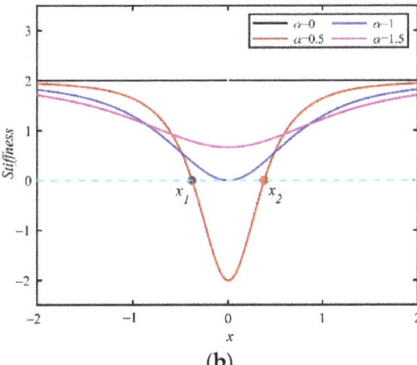

Figure 2. (a) The nonlinear restoring force F_{re}; (b) the stiffness of the SD oscillator; two points are $x_1 = -\alpha\sqrt{\alpha^{-2/3} - 1}$ and $x_2 = \alpha\sqrt{\alpha^{-2/3} - 1}$, respectively.

SD oscillators have been widely used in many fields due to their special nonlinear properties. Researchers have conducted many in-depth studies on SD oscillators. Avramov et al. [5] connected an SD-like truss with a spring–mass system and investigated snap-through and nonlinear vibration characteristics. Brennan et al. [6] used an SD-like model with snap-through characteristics to represent the wings of dipteran insects. Their results show that the snap-through phenomenon resulted in a velocity jump in the system. When the operating frequency was below the natural frequency, the system had a great advantage in flight. Ichiro et al. [7] studied the nonlinear characteristics of an elastic–plastic system using a multi-folding microstructure system composed of SD structures. Waite et al. [8] investigated the attractor coexistence and the competing resonance of a truss with the SD structure. Hao et al. [9,10] designed a quasi-zero-stiffness vibration isolator based on an SD oscillator. Currier et al. [11] designed a mechanical fish that had an SD-like spine structure. The structure provided sufficient acceleration for the fish to swim. SD oscillators are also widely applied in nonlinear energy sinks [12,13] and energy harvesting [14,15]. Myongwon et al. [16] demonstrated a 1D lattice of bistable elements. The lattices exhibited energy-harvesting capabilities from transition waves, and energy was transmitted in the form of waves. Tan et al. [17] designed a triboelectric nanogenerator constituted by a bow-type Teng with a snap-through phenomenon. The equipment converted low-frequency vibrations into electricity with a high efficiency.

In terms of nonlinear dynamics, the trilinear piecewise function method [18] and the elliptic function method [19] have been proposed for investigating the nonlinear dynamics characteristics of SD oscillators. Subsequently, Tian et al. [20] studied the codimension-two bifurcation and the Hopf bifurcation of an SD oscillator. Cao et al. [21] analyzed the limit case response of an SD oscillator. In this case, the SD oscillator lost hyperbolicity due to a discontinuous characteristic that was different from a standard double-well system. Shen et al. [22] studied the bifurcation characteristics of symmetric subharmonic orbits and asymmetric subharmonic orbits of a discontinuous SD oscillator. Han et al. [23] used singularity theory to obtain the transition set of a coupled SD oscillator. The chaos threshold was obtained using the Melnikov method. [24] The multiple buckling and the codimension-three bifurcation of an SD oscillator were analyzed [25,26]. Tian et al. [27] studied the chaos threshold of an asymmetric SD oscillator subjected to constant excitation with the topological equivalence method. Yue et al. [28] investigated the random bifurcation of an SD oscillator based on the generalized cell-mapping method. In terms of the frequency domain, Santhosh et al. [29] found a chaotic solution for an SD oscillator caused by the symmetry breaking. Chen et al. [30,31] studied the global bifurcation characteristics of a discontinuous SD oscillator that was equivalent to a Filippov system. Wang et al. [32] represented fractional damping using a Markov chain. The random P bifurcation of an SD oscillator with fractional damping was studied. Their results show that both the smooth parameter and the excitation amplitude induced a random P-bifurcation of the SD oscillator. Through experiments, Chang et al. [33] proved that the periodic motion of an SD oscillator is highly sensitive to the initial displacement and the smooth parameter.

The nonlinear dynamic behaviors of SD oscillators with integral damping have been thoroughly studied. However, two limitations exist in the current research. One limitation is that the Taylor series expansion method is used to mimic the nonlinear restoring force in SD oscillators. The calculation accuracy of the equivalence transformation is acceptable when displacement responses are small. However, this can produce large errors if displacement responses are large. The other limitation is that the integer-damping model is used to represent the energy dissipation. However, in terms of long-term dynamic behaviors, the memory properties and frequency dependence characteristics are not well revealed. It is proven that these properties can be more accurately revealed by the fractional damping model [34,35]. Caputo et al. [36] proposed a fractional-order model to describe the dissipation characteristics, which correlate well with the experimental results of many materials. Padovan et al. [37] investigated the nonlinear response characteristics of a Duffing system with fractional damping. Chang et al. [38] proposed a nonlinear fractional damping model based on the Caputo fractional model [39]. The nonlinear fractional damping model described the energy-dissipation propertoes of metal rubber damping, and the theoretical solution fit well with the results of dynamic load experiments. Their results show that the fractional term simultaneously influenced the frequency and the amplitude of the response. However, research on the vibration characteristics of SD oscillators with fractional damping is not sufficient.

Combined with the current research status, it is necessary to study the nonlinear characteristics of SD oscillators with fractional damping. Therefore, in this article, an equivalent piecewise function is proposed for accurately representing the nonlinear restoring force of an SD oscillator. Moreover, a nonlinear fractional damping model is introduced into the SD oscillator to represent the energy dissipation and viscoelastic properties of a metal rubber damping. This article mainly focuses on the nonlinear amplitude–frequency response and transition characteristics in the resonant region and snap-through phenomena in the non-resonant region of the system. In Section 1, an introduction to this paper is presented. In Section 2, the nonlinear piecewise function is used to approximate the nonlinear restoring force of the SD oscillator. The equivalent damping coefficient and the equivalent stiffness coefficient of fractional damping are derived using the energy equivalent method. The piecewise differential equation of the SD oscillator with nonlinear fractional damping is obtained. In Section 3, the amplitude–frequency response function, the stable criteria and the transition set of the SD oscillator are obtained through calculations. In Section 4, the influence of fractional damping parameters on the nonlinear dynamic characteristics is analyzed in detail. The conclusions are provided in Section 5.

2. The Model of an SD Oscillator with Nonlinear Fractional Damping

The differential equation of the SD oscillator with nonlinear fractional damping is:

$$m\left(\ddot{X}(t) + \ddot{\overline{A}}\right) + c\dot{X}(t) + 2k_0 X(t)\left(1 - \frac{L}{\sqrt{X(t)^2 + l^2}}\right) + k_1 X(t) + k_3 X(t)^3 + h D^p[X(t)] = 0 \qquad (3)$$

where $\overline{A} = A\cos(\omega t)$ is the external displacement excitation, A is the excitation amplitude, ω is the excitation frequency and $X(t)$ is the displacement. $F_{frac} = k_1 X(t) + k_3 X(t)^3 + h D^p[X(t)]$ is the damping force of a metal rubber damping [38]. k_1 is the linear stiffness coefficient, k_3 is the nonlinear stiffness coefficient, h is the fractional coefficient, p is the fractional order and $h D^p[X(t)]$ is the Caputo fractional model [39,40].

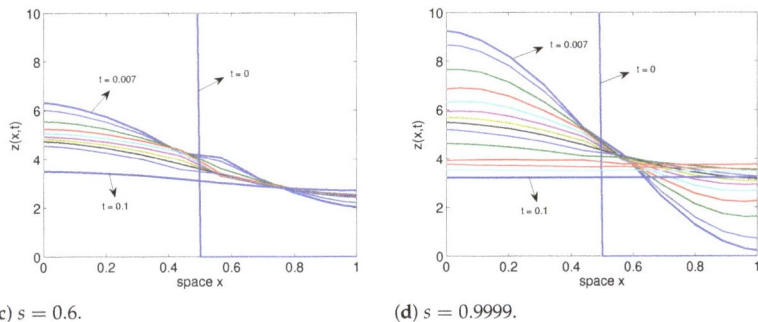

(c) $s = 0.6$. **(d)** $s = 0.9999$.

Figure 2. The state function at different moments with $\alpha = \beta = -0.5$ (see (**a**)) and $\alpha = \beta = 1$ (see (**b–d**)).

6. Conclusions

In this paper, a collocation method based on the Jacobi polynomial is presented for solving a class of optimal-control problems with a fractional distributed system. The problem is transformed into a system of fractional diffusion equations by using the fractional variational principle. The major feature of the resulting system is that both left-sided and right-sided fractional derivatives are involved, which makes it more difficult to handle. We approximate the numerical solutions in terms of the Jacobi polynomials in both temporal and spatial directions. The efficiency and exponential convergence are verified numerically. The numerical simulations show that the proposed method is validated for fractional optimal-control problem containing continuous or discontinuous initial conditions. In the case of discontinuous initial conditions, the results shows that the state function decays much faster when the order of fractional derivative s is relatively small, which coincides with the heavy tail feature of the fractional derivative.

Author Contributions: Conceptualization, W.C. and Y.X.; methodology, W.C.; validation, W.C. and Y.X.; formal analysis, W.C. and Y.X.; writing—original draft preparation, W.C; writing—review and editing, W.C.; and funding acquisition, W.C. All authors have read and agreed to the published version of the manuscript.

Funding: This research was funded by the Hunan Provincial Natural Science Foundation of China (grant number 2019JJ50019) and the Scientific Research Foundation of Hunan Provincial Education Department (grant number 18C0970).

Data Availability Statement: Not applicable.

Acknowledgments: The authors would like to thank the reviewers for their constructive comments to improve the manuscript.

Conflicts of Interest: The authors declare no conflict of interest.

References

1. Sage A.P.; White, C.C., III. *Optimal Systems Control*; Prentice-Hall: Englewood Cliffs, NJ, USA, 1977.
2. Betts, J.T.; Erb, S.O. Optimal low thrust trajectories to the moon. *SIAM J. Appl. Dyn. Syst.* **2003**, *2*, 144–170. [CrossRef]
3. Highfill, J.; McAsey, M. An optimal-control problem in economics. *Int. J. Mathemetics Math. Sci.* **1991**, *14*, 537–544. [CrossRef]
4. Abu-Rqayiqa, A.; Alayed, H.; Zannon, M. Optimal control of a basic model of oncolytic virotherapy. *J. Mathemetics Comput. Sci.* **2022**, *24*, 119–126. [CrossRef]
5. Bittner, L.; Bulirsch, R.; Heier, K.; Schmidt, W. (Eds.) Variational Calculus, Optimal Control and Applications. In Proceedings of the International Conference in Honour of L. Bittner and R. Klötzler, Trassenheide, Germany, 23–27 September 1996.
6. Hull, D.G. Variational calculus and approximate solution of optimal-control problems. *J. Optim. Theory Appl.* **2001**, *108*, 483–497. [CrossRef]
7. Biswas, R.K.; Sen, S. Free final time fractional optimal-control problems. *J. Frankl. Inst.-Eng. Appl. Math.* **2014**, *351*, 941–951. [CrossRef]

8. Kamocki, R. On the existence of optimal solutions to fractional optimal-control problems. *Appl. Math. Comput.* **2014**, *235*, 94–104. [CrossRef]
9. Almeida, R.; Torres, D.F.M. A discrete method to solve fractional optimal-control problems. *Nonlinear Dyn.* **2015**, *80*, 1811–1816. [CrossRef]
10. Xu, Y.; Agrawal, O.P. New fractional operators and application to fractional variational problem. *Comput. Math. Appl.* 2016, in Press. [CrossRef]
11. Paulen, R.; Kikar, M. *Optimal Operation of Batch Membrane Processes*; Springer: Berlin/Heidelberg, Germany, 2016.
12. Agrawal, O.P. Formulation of Euler-Lagrange equations for fractional variational problems. *J. Math. Anal. Appl.* **2002**, *272*, 368–379. [CrossRef]
13. Agrawal, O.P. A general formulation and solution scheme for fractional optimal-control problem. *Nonlinear Dyn.* **2004**, *38*, 323–337. [CrossRef]
14. Agrawal, O.P. Fractional optimal control of a distributed system using eigenfunctions. *ASME J. Comput. Nonlinear Dyn.* **2008**, *3*, 021204-1–021204-6. [CrossRef]
15. Baleanu, D.; Defterli, O.; Agrawal, O.P. A central difference numerical scheme for fractional optimal-control problems. *J. Vib. Control.* **2009**, *15*, 583–597. [CrossRef]
16. Tricaud, C.; Chen, Y.Q. An approximate method for numerically solving fractional order optimal control problems of general form. *Comput. Math. Appl.* **2010**, *59*, 1644–1655. [CrossRef]
17. Lotfi, A.; Dehghan, M.; Yousefi, S.A. A numerical technique for solving fractional optimal-control problems. *Comput. Math. Appl.* **2011**, *62*, 1055–1067. [CrossRef]
18. Lotfi, A.; Yousefi, S.A.; Dehghan, M. Numerical solution of a class of fractional optimal-control problems via the Legendre orthonormal basis combined with the operational matrix and the Gauss quadrature rule. *J. Comput. Appl. Math.* **2013**, *250*, 143–160. [CrossRef]
19. Özdemir, N.; Karadeniz, D.; İskender, B.B. Fractional optimal-control problem of a distributed system in cylindrical coordinates. *Phys. Lett. A* **2009**, *373*, 221–226. [CrossRef]
20. Safaie, E.; Farahi, M.H.; Ardehaie, M.F. An approximate method for numerically solving multi-dimensional delay fractional optimal-control problems by Bernstein polynomials. *Comput. Appl. Math.* **2015**, *34*, 831–846. [CrossRef]
21. Özdemir, N.; Agrawal, O.P.; İskender, B.B.; Karadeniz, D. Fractional optimal control of a 2-dimensional distributed system using eigenfunctions. *Nonlinear Dyn.* **2009**, *55*, 251–260. [CrossRef]
22. Bhrawy, A.H.; Doha, E.H.; Baleanu, D.; Ezz-Eldien, S.S.; Abdelkawy, M.A. An accurate numerical technique for solving fractional optimal-control problems. *Proc. Rom. Acad. Ser. A* **2015**, *16*, 47–54.
23. Darehmiraki, M.; Farahi, M.H.; Effati, S. Solution for the fractional distrubted optimal-control problem by hybrid meshless method. *J. Vib. Control* **2018**, *24*, 2149–64. [CrossRef]
24. Canuto, C.; Hussaini, M.Y.; Quarteroni, A.; Zang, T.A. *Spectral Methods: Fundamentals in Single Domains*' Springer: Berlin/Heidelberg, Germany, 2006.
25. Yang, Y.; Chen, Y.P.; Huang, Y.Q. Convergence analysis of the Jacobi spectral-collocation method for fractional integro-differential equations. *Acta Mathemetica Sci.* **2014**, *34B*, 673–690. [CrossRef]
26. Tohidi, E.; Nik, H.S. A Bessel collocation method for solving fractional optimal-control problems. *Appl. Math. Model.* **2015**, *39*, 455–465. [CrossRef]
27. Nikan, O.; Avazzadeh, Z. Numerical simulation of fractional evolution model arising in viscoelastic mechanics. *Appl. Numer. Math.* **2021**, *169*, 303–320. [CrossRef]
28. Shojaeizadeh, T.; Mahmoudi, M.; Darehmiraki, M. optimal-control problem of advection-diffusion-reaction equation of kind fractal-fractional applying shifted Jacobi polynomials. *Chaos Solitons Fractals* **2021**, *143*, 110568. [CrossRef]
29. Kilbas, A.A.; Srivastava, H.M.; Trujillo, J.J. *Theory and Applications of Fractional Differential Equations*; Elsevier: Amsterdam, The Netherlands, 2006.
30. Podlubny, I. *Fractional Differential Equations*; Academic Press: Cambridge, MA, USA, 1999.
31. Hilfer, R. *Fractional Calculus in Physics*; World Scientific Publishing: Singapore, 2000.
32. Bhrawy, A.H. A Jacobi-Gauss-Lobatto collocation method for solving generalized Fitzhugh-Nagumo equation with time-dependent coefficients. *Appl. Math. Comput.* **2013**, *222*, 255–264. [CrossRef]
33. Duan, B.P.; Zheng, Z.S.; Cao, W. Spectral approximation methods and error estimates for Caputo fractional derivative with applications to initial-value problems. *J. Comput. Phys.* **2016**, *3*, 108–128. [CrossRef]

Article

The Nonlinear Dynamics Characteristics and Snap-Through of an SD Oscillator with Nonlinear Fractional Damping

Minghao Wang [1], Enli Chen [1,*], Ruilan Tian [2] and Cuiyan Wang [1]

1 State Key Laboratory of Mechanical Behavior and System Safety of Traffic Engineering Structures, Shijiazhuang Tiedao University, Shijiazhuang 050043, China
2 Department of Engineering Mechanics, Shijiazhuang Tiedao University, Shijiazhuang 050043, China
* Correspondence: celstdu@163.com or chenenl@stdu.edu.cn; Tel.: +86-0311-879-35554

Abstract: A smooth and discontinuous (SD) oscillator is a typical multi-stable state system with strong nonlinear properties and has been widely used in many fields. The nonlinear dynamic characteristics of the system have not been thoroughly investigated because the nonlinear restoring force cannot be integrated. In this paper, the nonlinear restoring force is represented by a piecewise nonlinear function. The equivalent coefficients of fractional damping are obtained with an orthogonal function. The influence of fractional damping on the transition set, the amplitude–frequency response and the snap-through of the SD oscillator are analyzed. The conclusions are as follows: The nonlinear piecewise function accurately mimics the nonlinear restoring force and maintains a nonlinearity property. Fractional damping can significantly affect the stiffness and damping property simultaneously. The equivalent coefficients of the fractional damping are variable with regard to the fractional-order power of the excitation frequency. A hysteresis point, a bifurcation point, a frequency island, pitchfork bifurcations and transcritical bifurcations were discovered in the small-amplitude resonant region. In the non-resonant region, the increase in the fractional parameters leads to the probability of snap-through declining by increasing the symmetry of the attraction domain or reducing the number of stable states.

Keywords: SD oscillator; fractional damping; primary resonance; nonlinear dynamics

1. Introduction

Geometric nonlinearity is one of the three major nonlinear problems in engineering applications. Many engineering applications, such as vehicle suspension and gear driving systems, typically exhibit nonlinear characteristics. Nonlinear systems are made equivalent to linear systems to facilitate analytical calculations. In this process, the accurate nonlinear dynamics behavior of the nonlinear system cannot be obtained. If the system has been working at high intensity for a long time, the model errors caused by this equivalent linearization will accumulate. Therefore, establishing an accurate geometric nonlinear system model and analyzing the nonlinear dynamic behavior of the model can ensure the safe and stable operation of the system.

The smooth and discontinuous (SD) oscillator is a typical geometric nonlinear system. The system, which consists of one concentrated mass and two slanted springs, was simplified by a simply supported beam model [1]. The prototypical model of an SD oscillator is shown in Figure 1. This model has been widely used to study snap-through phenomena [2], energy-harvesting mechanisms [3], quasi-zero vibration isolators [4] and applications in many other fields.

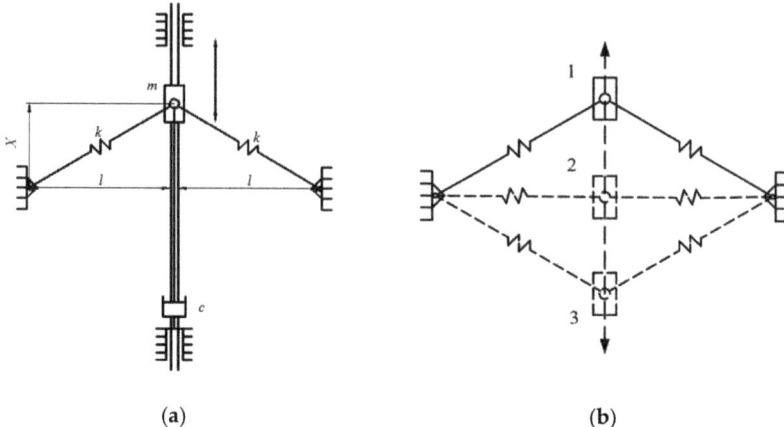

Figure 1. (a) The prototypical SD oscillator model; (b) the schematic diagram of stable positions of the SD oscillator.

In Figure 1, $X(t)$ is the displacement of the oscillator, m is the mass, c is the damping coefficient, k is the stiffness of the springs, l is the constant distance and L is the original length of the spring. The dynamics model of the prototypical SD oscillator is:

$$m\ddot{X}(t) + c\dot{X}(t) + 2kX(t)\left(1 - \frac{L}{\sqrt{X(t)^2 + l^2}}\right) = 0 \qquad (1)$$

This system (1) is made dimensionless by letting $\alpha = l/L$ (α is the smooth parameter) $\omega_0^2 = 2k/m$, $2\zeta = c/m$ and $x = X(t)/L$:

$$\ddot{x} + 2\zeta\dot{x} + \omega_0^2 x\left(1 - \frac{1}{\sqrt{x^2 + \alpha^2}}\right) = 0 \qquad (2)$$

where the nonlinear restoring force is $F_{re} = \omega_0^2 x\left(1 - 1/\sqrt{x^2 + \alpha^2}\right)$.

Notably, when the original length L is greater than the distance l ($0 < \alpha < 1$), the oscillator has two stable positions (position 1 and position 3, as shown in Figure 1b). When the displacement or the velocity of the oscillator is smaller than the threshold, the oscillator vibrates at a small amplitude in stable position 1 or 3. If the displacement or the velocity of the oscillator exceeds the threshold (the threshold is the boundary of the attract domain, which will be discussed in Section 4), the oscillator will quickly jump from stable position 1 to stable position 3, or from 3 to 1. These stable position changes are called "snap-through". However, when the original length L is smaller than the distance l ($\alpha > 1$), the oscillator has only one stable position (position 2). Thus, in this condition, the oscillator cannot change its stable position.

The dimensionless system parameters are selected as $\omega_0^2 = 2$, $\alpha = 0, 0.5, 1$ and 1.5. Diagrams of the nonlinear restoring force F_{re} and the stiffness of the SD oscillator are shown in Figure 2.

Figure 2a shows the nonlinear restoring force with different smooth parameters, and Figure 2b shows the stiffness of the SD oscillator. In Figure 2a, the nonlinear restoring force has a jump point at $x = 0$ when $\alpha = 0$. In Figure 2b, the stiffness is negative in the neighborhood of $x = 0$ ($x_1 < x < x_2$) when the smooth parameter is 0.5. The slope of F_{re}, i.e., the stiffness, approaches ω_0^2 when $|x|$ approaches infinity. These phenomena indicate that the system is discontinuous when $\alpha = 0$, and it has a negative stiffness property when the smooth parameter is in the interval $0 < \alpha < 1$. The system has a quasi-zero stiffness property when $\alpha = 1$. Additionally, its stiffness is positive when $\alpha > 1$.

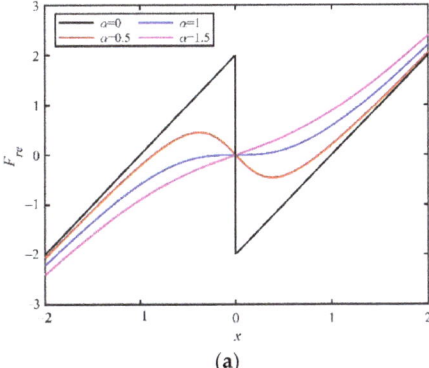
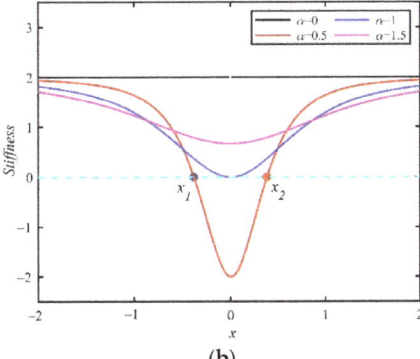

Figure 2. (a) The nonlinear restoring force F_{re}; (b) the stiffness of the SD oscillator; two points are $x_1 = -\alpha\sqrt{\alpha^{-2/3} - 1}$ and $x_2 = \alpha\sqrt{\alpha^{-2/3} - 1}$, respectively.

SD oscillators have been widely used in many fields due to their special nonlinear properties. Researchers have conducted many in-depth studies on SD oscillators. Avramov et al. [5] connected an SD-like truss with a spring–mass system and investigated snap-through and nonlinear vibration characteristics. Brennan et al. [6] used an SD-like model with snap-through characteristics to represent the wings of dipteran insects. Their results show that the snap-through phenomenon resulted in a velocity jump in the system. When the operating frequency was below the natural frequency, the system had a great advantage in flight. Ichiro et al. [7] studied the nonlinear characteristics of an elastic–plastic system using a multi-folding microstructure system composed of SD structures. Waite et al. [8] investigated the attractor coexistence and the competing resonance of a truss with the SD structure. Hao et al. [9,10] designed a quasi-zero-stiffness vibration isolator based on an SD oscillator. Currier et al. [11] designed a mechanical fish that had an SD-like spine structure. The structure provided sufficient acceleration for the fish to swim. SD oscillators are also widely applied in nonlinear energy sinks [12,13] and energy harvesting [14,15]. Myongwon et al. [16] demonstrated a 1D lattice of bistable elements. The lattices exhibited energy-harvesting capabilities from transition waves, and energy was transmitted in the form of waves. Tan et al. [17] designed a triboelectric nanogenerator constituted by a bow-type Teng with a snap-through phenomenon. The equipment converted low-frequency vibrations into electricity with a high efficiency.

In terms of nonlinear dynamics, the trilinear piecewise function method [18] and the elliptic function method [19] have been proposed for investigating the nonlinear dynamics characteristics of SD oscillators. Subsequently, Tian et al. [20] studied the codimension-two bifurcation and the Hopf bifurcation of an SD oscillator. Cao et al. [21] analyzed the limit case response of an SD oscillator. In this case, the SD oscillator lost hyperbolicity due to a discontinuous characteristic that was different from a standard double-well system. Shen et al. [22] studied the bifurcation characteristics of symmetric subharmonic orbits and asymmetric subharmonic orbits of a discontinuous SD oscillator. Han et al. [23] used singularity theory to obtain the transition set of a coupled SD oscillator. The chaos threshold was obtained using the Melnikov method. [24] The multiple buckling and the codimension-three bifurcation of an SD oscillator were analyzed [25,26]. Tian et al. [27] studied the chaos threshold of an asymmetric SD oscillator subjected to constant excitation with the topological equivalence method. Yue et al. [28] investigated the random bifurcation of an SD oscillator based on the generalized cell-mapping method. In terms of the frequency domain, Santhosh et al. [29] found a chaotic solution for an SD oscillator caused by the symmetry breaking. Chen et al. [30,31] studied the global bifurcation characteristics of a discontinuous SD oscillator that was equivalent to a Filippov system. Wang et al. [32] represented fractional damping using a Markov chain. The random P bifurcation of an SD oscillator with fractional damping was studied. Their results show that both the smooth parameter and the excitation amplitude induced a random P-bifurcation of the SD oscillator. Through experiments, Chang et al. [33] proved that the periodic motion of an SD oscillator is highly sensitive to the initial displacement and the smooth parameter.

The nonlinear dynamic behaviors of SD oscillators with integral damping have been thoroughly studied. However, two limitations exist in the current research. One limitation is that the Taylor series expansion method is used to mimic the nonlinear restoring force in SD oscillators. The calculation accuracy of the equivalence transformation is acceptable when displacement responses are small. However, this can produce large errors if displacement responses are large. The other limitation is that the integer-damping model is used to represent the energy dissipation. However, in terms of long-term dynamic behaviors, the memory properties and frequency dependence characteristics are not well revealed. It is proven that these properties can be more accurately revealed by the fractional damping model [34,35]. Caputo et al. [36] proposed a fractional-order model to describe the dissipation characteristics, which correlate well with the experimental results of many materials. Padovan et al. [37] investigated the nonlinear response characteristics of a Duffing system with fractional damping. Chang et al. [38] proposed a nonlinear fractional damping model based on the Caputo fractional model [39]. The nonlinear fractional damping model described the energy-dissipation propertoes of metal rubber damping, and the theoretical solution fit well with the results of dynamic load experiments. Their results show that the fractional term simultaneously influenced the frequency and the amplitude of the response. However, research on the vibration characteristics of SD oscillators with fractional damping is not sufficient.

Combined with the current research status, it is necessary to study the nonlinear characteristics of SD oscillators with fractional damping. Therefore, in this article, an equivalent piecewise function is proposed for accurately representing the nonlinear restoring force of an SD oscillator. Moreover, a nonlinear fractional damping model is introduced into the SD oscillator to represent the energy dissipation and viscoelastic properties of a metal rubber damping. This article mainly focuses on the nonlinear amplitude–frequency response and transition characteristics in the resonant region and snap-through phenomena in the non-resonant region of the system. In Section 1, an introduction to this paper is presented. In Section 2, the nonlinear piecewise function is used to approximate the nonlinear restoring force of the SD oscillator. The equivalent damping coefficient and the equivalent stiffness coefficient of fractional damping are derived using the energy equivalent method. The piecewise differential equation of the SD oscillator with nonlinear fractional damping is obtained. In Section 3, the amplitude–frequency response function, the stable criteria and the transition set of the SD oscillator are obtained through calculations. In Section 4, the influence of fractional damping parameters on the nonlinear dynamic characteristics is analyzed in detail. The conclusions are provided in Section 5.

2. The Model of an SD Oscillator with Nonlinear Fractional Damping

The differential equation of the SD oscillator with nonlinear fractional damping is:

$$m\left(\ddot{X}(t) + \ddot{\overline{A}}\right) + c\dot{X}(t) + 2k_0 X(t)\left(1 - \frac{L}{\sqrt{X(t)^2 + l^2}}\right) + k_1 X(t) + k_3 X(t)^3 + hD^p[X(t)] = 0 \quad (3)$$

where $\overline{A} = A\cos(\omega t)$ is the external displacement excitation, A is the excitation amplitude, ω is the excitation frequency and $X(t)$ is the displacement. $F_{frac} = k_1 X(t) + k_3 X(t)^3 + hD^p[X(t)]$ is the damping force of a metal rubber damping [38], k_1 is the linear stiffness coefficient, k_3 is the nonlinear stiffness coefficient, h is the fractional coefficient, p is the fractional order and $hD^p[X(t)]$ is the Caputo fractional model [39,40].

The reason the Caputo model is selected is because its initial condition is the same form as the integer-order differential equation. It is convenient for addressing the problem of initial value in dynamics [41].

The new length scale L_1 and new time scale t_1 are selected as:

$$L_1 = L, \; t_1 = \sqrt{\frac{m}{k_1}} \tag{4}$$

The following dimensionless transformances are determined:

$$x(\tau) = \frac{X(t)}{L}, \; \tau = \frac{t}{t_1}, \; 2\zeta = \frac{ct_1}{m}, \; K_0 = \frac{2k_0 t_1^2}{m}, \; K_1 = \frac{k_1 t_1^2}{m}, \; K_3 = \frac{k_3 t_1^2 L^2}{m},$$
$$H = \frac{h t_1^2}{m}, \; \alpha = \frac{l}{L}, \; \Omega = \omega t_1, \; F = \frac{A\Omega^2}{L}$$

By substituting the above dimensionless transformations into Equation (3), we can rewrite the equation as:

$$\ddot{x}(\tau) + 2\zeta \dot{x}(\tau) - K_0 F_n + K_1 x(\tau) + K_3 x(\tau)^3 + H D^p[x(\tau)] - F\cos(\Omega\tau) \tag{5}$$

The nonlinear restoring force of Equation (5) is defined as:

$$F_n = -x(\tau)\left(1 - \frac{1}{\sqrt{x(\tau)^2 + \alpha^2}}\right) \tag{6}$$

Equation (6) is nonintegral; therefore, the amplitude–frequency response function of the system cannot be obtained. The nonlinear piecewise function P_n is introduced to obtain the equivalent function of Equation (6):

$$P_n = \begin{cases} -x(\tau) + B_1, & x(\tau) < -x_0 \\ B_2 x(\tau)^3 + B_3 x(\tau)^2 + B_4 x(\tau), & -x_0 \leq x(\tau) < x_0 \\ -x(\tau) + B_5, & x(\tau) \geq x_0 \end{cases} \tag{7}$$

where $B_i (i = 1, 2, 3, 4, 5)$ is undetermined constants and $x_0 (x_0 > 0)$ is the piecewise point of Equation (7).

F_n' is the first derivative with respect to τ. Let $F_n' = 0$, and two extreme points $(\tilde{x}_{1,2}, \tilde{y}_{1,2})$ of Equation (6) can be obtained:

$$(\tilde{x}_{1,2}, \tilde{y}_{1,2}) = \left(\pm\sqrt{\alpha^{4/3} - \alpha^2}, \pm\sqrt{\alpha^{4/3} - \alpha^2}\left(1 - \frac{1}{\alpha^{2/3}}\right)\right) \tag{8}$$

Let the middle segment of Equation (7) satisfy Equation (8), and we can obtain:

$$\begin{cases} B_2 = \frac{\alpha^{4/3} - \alpha^{2/3}}{2(-1+\alpha^{2/3})\alpha^{8/3}} \\ B_3 = 0 \\ B_4 = \frac{3(-1+\alpha^{2/3})}{2\alpha^{2/3}} \end{cases} \tag{9}$$

Next, calculate the piecewise point x_0 and the corresponding function y_0 to obtain the constants B_1 and B_5. Obviously, $\lim_{x \to \infty} F_n' = -1$, and the following can be set:

$$P_n'(x_0) = -1 \tag{10}$$

When $x = x_0$, the piecewise point x_0 and the function y_0 of Equation (7) can be obtained:

$$x_0 = \frac{\sqrt{\frac{1}{3} - \frac{1}{\alpha^{2/3}}}}{\sqrt{\frac{-\alpha^{4/3} + \alpha^{2/3}}{(-1 + \alpha^{2/3})\alpha^{8/3}}}} \tag{11}$$

$$y_0 = \frac{\sqrt{1 - \frac{3}{\alpha^{2/3}}}\left(-4\alpha^{2/3} + 3\alpha^{2/3}\right)}{3\sqrt{3}\alpha^{10/3}\left(\frac{-\alpha^{4/3} + \alpha^{2/3}}{(-1 + \alpha^{2/3})\alpha^{8/3}}\right)^{3/2}} \tag{12}$$

Let the first and the third parts of Equation (7) satisfy the following conditions:

$$P_n(x_0) = y_0 \tag{13}$$

$$P_n(-x_0) = -y_0 \tag{14}$$

We can obtain B_1 and B_5:

$$\begin{cases} B_1 = \dfrac{\sqrt{1 - \frac{3}{\alpha^{2/3}}}\left(-4\alpha^{4/3} + \alpha^{2/3}(3 + \alpha^{4/3})\right)}{3\sqrt{3}(-1 + \alpha^{2/3})\alpha^{10/3}\left(\frac{-\alpha^{4/3} + \alpha^{2/3}}{(-1 + \alpha^{2/3})\alpha^{8/3}}\right)^{3/2}} \\ B_5 = \dfrac{\sqrt{1 - \frac{3}{\alpha^{2/3}}}\left(4\alpha^{4/3} - \alpha^{2/3}(3 + \alpha^{4/3})\right)}{3\sqrt{3}(-1 + \alpha^{2/3})\alpha^{10/3}\left(\frac{-\alpha^{4/3} + \alpha^{2/3}}{(-1 + \alpha^{2/3})\alpha^{8/3}}\right)^{3/2}} \end{cases} \tag{15}$$

By substituting Equations (9) and (15) into Equation (7), the nonlinear piecewise function is derived. By selecting $\alpha = 0.1, 0.5$ and 0.9, the results of F_n, P_n, a linear piecewise function and a three-order Taylor series-equivalent function, are depicted in Figure 3.

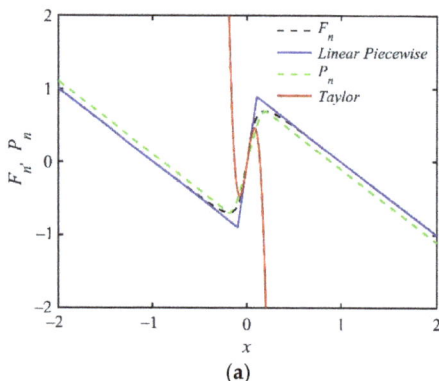
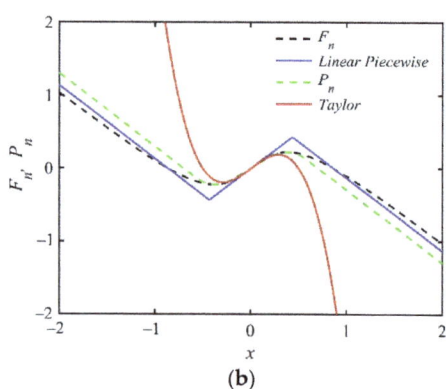

Figure 3. The results of F_n, P_n, a linear piecewise function, and a three-order Taylor series equivalent function (**a**) $\alpha = 0.1$; (**b**) $\alpha = 0.5$.

Figure 3 shows that using the three-order Taylor series-equivalent function to approach F_n is not effective because the deviation between curves for three-order Taylor series and F_n sharply increases. The linear piecewise function and P_n are in good agreement with F_n. However, a larger error is generated at the extreme points of F_n, and the nonlinear characteristics of the system are eliminated in the interval $-x_0 < x < x_0$, when the linear piecewise function is used to represent F_n. By analyzing the curve of P_n, it is found that P_n correlates well with F_n, and the nonlinear characteristics are maintained. Thus, many novel nonlinear phenomena have been discovered, such as the hysteresis point, the bifurcation point and transcritical bifurcation, which will be discussed in Section 4.

By substituting Equation (7) into Equation (5) to replace Equation (6), the differential equation of the SD oscillator with nonlinear fractional damping is written as:

$$\ddot{x}(\tau) + 2\zeta\dot{x}(\tau) - K_0 P_n + K_1 x(\tau) + K_3 x(\tau)^3 + HD^p[x(\tau)] = F\cos(\Omega\tau) \quad (16)$$

The Caputo model [39] is used to represent the viscoelastic characteristics of nonlinear fractional damping, i.e., the fractional term in Equation (16):

$$D^p[X] = \frac{1}{\Gamma(1-p)} \int_0^t \frac{X'(u)}{(t-u)^p} du \quad (17)$$

where $\Gamma(\cdot)$ is a gamma function.

When setting $HD^p[x(\tau)] = c_{eq}\dot{x}(\tau) + k_{eq}x(\tau)$, $\sin(\varphi)$ and $\cos(\varphi)$ are multiplied on both sides. Both sides of the equations are integrated in one vibration period because the sum of the energy dissipated by damping and the energy stored by springs is a constant.

$$\begin{cases} \frac{H}{\Gamma(1-p)} \lim_{T \to \infty} \frac{1}{T} \int_0^T \int_0^t \frac{-a\omega\sin(\omega u + \theta)}{(\tau-u)^p} du \sin(\omega\tau + \theta) dt = \oint c_{eq}(a\cos\varphi)\prime \times \sin\varphi dx \\ \frac{H}{\Gamma(1-p)} \lim_{T \to \infty} \frac{1}{T} \int_0^T \int_0^t \frac{-a\omega\sin(\omega u + \theta)}{(\tau-u)^p} du \cos(\omega\tau + \theta) dt = \oint k_{eq} a \cos\varphi \times \cos\varphi dx \end{cases} \quad (18)$$

where $x(\tau) = a\cos(\Omega\tau + \theta) = a\cos\varphi$.

Based on the orthogonality of trigonometric functions, the equivalent stiffness coefficient k_{eq} and the equivalent damping coefficient c_{eq} can be obtained as:

$$\begin{cases} k_{eq} = H\Omega^p \cos\left(\frac{p\pi}{2}\right) \\ c_{eq} = H\Omega^{p-1} \sin\left(\frac{p\pi}{2}\right) \end{cases} \quad (19)$$

It can be found that the fractional order p is the pth power or the $(p-1)$th power of the excitation frequency Ω in Equation (19). Thus, $c_{eq}\dot{x}(\tau) + k_{eq}x(\tau)$ is a variable coefficient function with different values of power Ω because the response frequency in $x(\tau)$ and $\dot{x}(\tau)$ is the same as the excitation frequency. Additionally, the fractional order p has different influences on k_{eq} and c_{eq} because of different values of the power. In terms of the vibration theory, fractional order p affects the stiffness property and the damping property of the system simultaneously.

Fractional order p is selected as 0, 0.3, 0.7 and 1. The results of the equivalent coefficients are depicted in Figure 4.

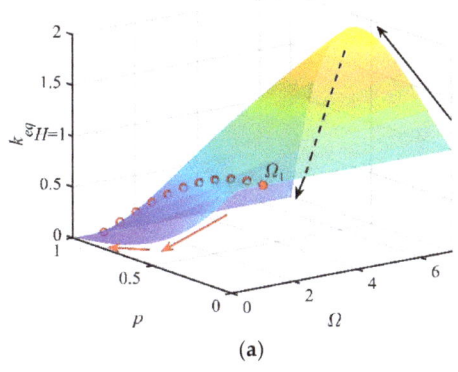

(a)

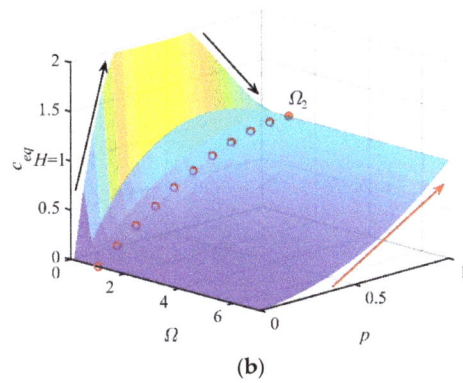

(b)

Figure 4. The results of (a) the equivalent stiffness coefficient k_{eq}; (b) the equivalent damping coefficient c_{eq}.

Figure 4a shows the results of the equivalent stiffness coefficient k_{eq}. Figure 4b shows the results of the equivalent damping coefficient c_{eq}. Figure 4 illustrates that k_{eq} increases with increases in Ω, while c_{eq} decreases. When Ω is above $\Omega_1 = e^{\pi \tan(p\pi/2)/2}$, k_{eq} first increases, then decreases as p increases (the variation tendency is marked by black arrows), while k_{eq} monotonically decreases when Ω is smaller than $\Omega_1 = e^{\pi \tan(p\pi/2)/2}$ (the variation tendency is marked by red arrows). When Ω is above $\Omega_2 = e^{-\pi \cot(p\pi/2)/2}$, c_{eq} monotonically increases as p increases (the variation tendency is marked by red arrows), while c_{eq} first increases, then decreases when Ω is smaller than $\Omega_2 = e^{-\pi \cot(p\pi/2)/2}$ (the variation tendency is marked by black arrows). When p equals 0, k_{eq} and c_{eq} equal H and 0, respectively. When p equals 1, k_{eq} and c_{eq} equal 0 and H, respectively. The above results illustrate that the fractional order and excitation frequency have a significant influence on the stiffness property and the damping property of the system simultaneously.

Substituting Equations (18) and (19) into Equation (16), the differential equation of the SD oscillator with a nonlinear fractional damping can be written as:

$$\ddot{x}(\tau) + \left(2\zeta + H\Omega^{p-1}\sin\left(\frac{p\pi}{2}\right)\right)\dot{x}(\tau) - K_0 P_n + \left(K_1 + H\Omega^p \cos\left(\frac{p\pi}{2}\right)\right)x(\tau) + K_3 x(\tau)^3 = F\cos(\Omega\tau) \quad (20)$$

3. The Bifurcation of the Amplitude–Frequency Response and the Stability Conditions of Steady-State Solutions

3.1. The Amplitude–Frequency Response Function of the Primary Resonance

The solution of Equation (20) is supposed as:

$$x(\tau) = a\cos(\Omega\tau + \theta) = a\cos\varphi \quad (21)$$

By substituting Equation (21) into Equation (20), and based on the average method, we can obtain:

$a < x_0$:

$$\begin{cases} \dot{a} = -\frac{1}{2\Omega}\left[2a\zeta\Omega + aH\Omega^p\sin\left(\frac{p\pi}{2}\right) + F\sin(\theta)\right] \\ a\dot{\theta} = \frac{1}{2\Omega}\left[\frac{a}{4}\left(3a^2(B_2 K_0 + K_3) + 4\left(B_4 K_0 + K_1 - \Omega^2\right)\right) \\ \quad + 4H\Omega^p\cos\left(\frac{p\pi}{2}\right)\right) - F\cos(\theta)\right] \end{cases} \quad (22)$$

$a > x_0$:

$$\begin{cases} \dot{a} = -\frac{1}{2\Omega}\left[2a\zeta\Omega + aH\Omega^p\sin\left(\frac{p\pi}{2}\right) + F\sin(\theta)\right] \\ a\dot{\theta} = \frac{1}{2\Omega}\left[\frac{K_0}{\pi}(-2B_1 + x_0)\sqrt{1-\left(\frac{x_0}{a}\right)^2} + \frac{K_0}{\pi}(2B_5 + x_0)\sqrt{1-\left(\frac{x_0}{a}\right)^2}\right. \\ \quad -\frac{K_0 x_0}{2\pi}\sqrt{1-\left(\frac{x_0}{a}\right)^2}(3a^2 B_2 + 4B_4 + 2B_2 x_0^2) + \frac{2}{\pi}aK_0 \mathrm{acos}\left(\frac{x_0}{a}\right) \\ \quad +\frac{a}{2\pi}K_0 \mathrm{asin}\left(\frac{x_0}{a}\right)(3a^2 B_2 + 4B_4) + aK_1 + \frac{3}{4}a^3 K_3 - a\Omega^2 \\ \quad \left. +aH\Omega^p\cos\left(\frac{p\pi}{2}\right) - F\cos(\theta)\right] \end{cases} \quad (23)$$

By eliminating θ, the amplitude–frequency response functions can be obtained as:

$a < x_0$:

$$\left(2a\zeta\Omega + aH\Omega^p\sin\left(\tfrac{p\pi}{2}\right)\right)^2 + \left(\tfrac{a}{4}\left(3a^2(B_2 K_0 + K_3)\right.\right. \\ \left.\left.+4\left(B_4 K_0 + K_1 - \Omega^2\right)\right) + 4H\Omega^p\cos\left(\tfrac{p\pi}{2}\right)\right)^2 = F^2 \quad (24)$$

$a > x_0$:

$$\left(2a\zeta\Omega + aH\Omega^p\sin\left(\tfrac{p\pi}{2}\right)\right)^2 + \left(\tfrac{K_0}{\pi}(-2B_1 + x_0)\sqrt{1-\left(\tfrac{x_0}{a}\right)^2}\right. \\ +\tfrac{K_0}{\pi}(2B_5 + x_0)\sqrt{1-\left(\tfrac{x_0}{a}\right)^2} - \tfrac{K_0 x_0}{2\pi}\sqrt{1-\left(\tfrac{x_0}{a}\right)^2}(3a^2 B_2 + 4B_4 + 2B_2 x_0^2) \\ +\tfrac{2}{\pi}aK_0\mathrm{acos}\left(\tfrac{x_0}{a}\right) + \tfrac{a}{2\pi}K_0\mathrm{asin}\left(\tfrac{x_0}{a}\right)(3a^2 B_2 + 4B_4) + aK_1 + \tfrac{3}{4}a^3 K_3 \\ \left. -a\Omega^2 + aH\Omega^p\cos\left(\tfrac{p\pi}{2}\right)\right)^2 = F^2 \quad (25)$$

3.2. The Stability Conditions of the Steady-State Solution

$a = \bar{a} + \Delta a$ and $\theta = \bar{\theta} + \Delta \theta$ are substituted into Equations (22) and (23). $\bar{a}$ and $\bar{\theta}$ are the singular points of Equations (22) and (23). Δa and $\Delta \theta$ are small disturbances. By eliminating $\bar{\theta}$, the following can be obtained:

$a < x_0$:

$$\begin{cases} \frac{d\Delta a}{dt} = -R_{11}\Delta a - R_{12}\Delta \theta \\ \frac{d\Delta \theta}{dt} = R_{13}\Delta a - R_{14}\Delta \theta \end{cases} \tag{26}$$

$a > x_0$:

$$\begin{cases} \frac{d\Delta a}{dt} = -R_{11}\Delta a - R_{21}\Delta \theta \\ \frac{d\Delta \theta}{dt} = R_{22}\Delta a - R_{14}\Delta \theta \end{cases} \tag{27}$$

The detail of $R_{i,j}(i = 1, 2; j = 1, 2, 3, 4)$ is written in Appendix A.

Based on the Lyapunov theory, calculate the eigenvalues of the determinant, and the stability conditions of the steady-state solutions are:

$a < x_0$:

$$(R_{11} + R_{14} > 0) \wedge (R_{12}R_{13} + R_{11}R_{14} > 0) \tag{28}$$

$a > x_0$:

$$(R_{11} + R_{14} > 0) \wedge (R_{21}R_{22} + R_{11}R_{14} > 0) \tag{29}$$

3.3. The Transition Set of the Amplitude–Frequency Response Function

The unfolding functions are constructed by Equations (24) and (25).

$a < x_0$:

$$G(a, \Omega, A, \alpha) = \left(2a\zeta\Omega + aH\Omega^p \sin\left(\frac{p\pi}{2}\right)\right)^2 + \left(\frac{a}{4}(3a^2(B_2K_0 + K_3)\right. \\ \left. + 4\left(B_4K_0 + K_1 - \Omega^2\right) + 4H\Omega^p \cos\left(\frac{p\pi}{2}\right)\right)\right)^2 - F^2 \tag{30}$$

$a > x_0$:

$$G(a, \Omega, A, \alpha) = \left(2a\zeta\Omega + aH\Omega^p \sin\left(\frac{p\pi}{2}\right)\right)^2 + \left(\frac{K_0}{\pi}(-2B_1 + x_0)\sqrt{1 - \left(\frac{x_0}{a}\right)^2}\right. \\ + \frac{K_0}{\pi}(2B_5 + x_0)\sqrt{1 - \left(\frac{x_0}{a}\right)^2} - \frac{K_0 x_0}{2\pi}\sqrt{1 - \left(\frac{x_0}{a}\right)^2}(3a^2B_2 + 4B_4 + 2B_2x_0^2) \\ + \frac{2}{\pi}aK_0 a\cos\left(\frac{x_0}{a}\right) + \frac{a}{2\pi}K_0 a\sin\left(\frac{x_0}{a}\right)(3a^2B_2 + 4B_4) + aK_1 + \frac{3}{4}a^3K_3 \\ \left. - a\Omega^2 + aH\Omega^p \cos\left(\frac{p\pi}{2}\right) - F\cos(\theta)\right)^2 - F^2 \tag{31}$$

The excitation frequency Ω and the excitation amplitude A are defined as bifurcation parameters. Based on the singularity theory, the bifurcation plane of the amplitude–frequency response is derived. It is too complex to obtain the explicit formulation of the transition set. Therefore, the transition set obtained is

$$\sum = Bif \cup Hys \tag{32}$$

where Bif is the bifurcation set and Hys is the hysteresis set.

$$Bif = \left\{(f, \alpha) \in \mathbb{R}^2 | \exists (a, \Omega), \exists G = G_a = G_\Omega = 0\right\} \tag{33}$$

$$Hys = \left\{(f, \alpha) \in \mathbb{R}^2 | \exists (a, \Omega), \exists G = G_a = G_{aa} = 0\right\} \tag{34}$$

The specific formulations of Equations (33) and (34) are written in Appendix B.

4. The Nonlinear Characteristics Analysis of the SD Oscillator with Nonlinear Fractional Damping

4.1. The Nonlinear Characteristics in the Resonant Region

First, the correctness of Equations (24) and (25) should be verified. The ODE45 method is used to calculate the numerical solutions to obtain the amplitude–frequency response of the system. The calculation step $t_{step} = 0.0025$. Only forced vibration phenomena are concerned, so that the initial displacement and the initial velocity are zero to exclude the influence of transient resonance. Thus, the results of the numerical solution, Equations (24) and (25) are shown in Figure 5.

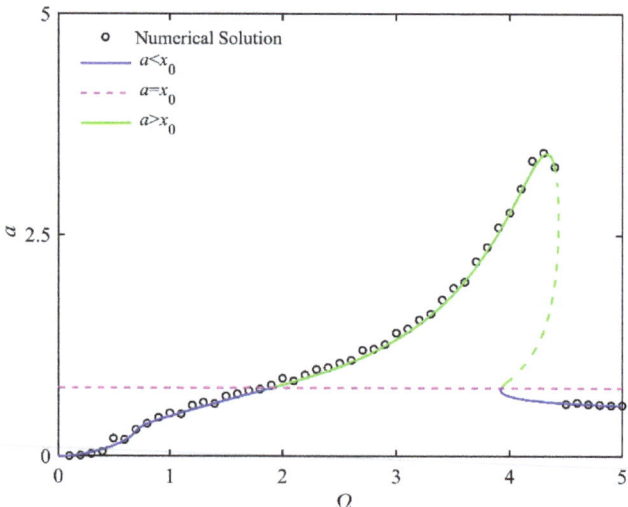

Figure 5. The results of the amplitude-frequency response function and the numerical solution with $\zeta = 0.1443$, $K_0 = 20$, $K_1 = 1$, $K_3 = 0.0256$, $H = 1$, $p = 0.5$, $\alpha = 0.9$, $A = 0.08$.

Figure 5 displays the results of the amplitude–frequency response of Equations (24) and (25), and the numerical solution. The pink dashed line represents the vibration amplitude $a = x_0$. The blue and green solid lines represent the stable solutions calculated by Equations (24) and (25), respectively, while the unstable solution is drawn as a green dashed line. Circles are the numerical solution. The numerical solution is in good agreement with the theoretical solution. The correctness of Equations (24) and (25) is verified.

4.1.1. The Influence of the Smooth Parameter in the Transition Set of the System

Based on Equation (32), the influence of the smooth parameter and excitation parameters in the amplitude–frequency response is studied. The parameters selected are $\zeta = 0.1443$, $K_0 = 20$, $K_1 = 1$, $K_3 = 0.0128$, $H = 1$, and $\alpha \in [0.89, 0.99]$. The transition set, the amplitude–frequency response curves and the distribution of the attractors in the frequency island are depicted in Figure 6.

Figure 6a,b show the results of the bifurcation set and the hysteresis set of Equations (33) and (34), respectively. The explicit function of the bifurcation set and the hysteresis set cannot be directly obtained because the expressions of Equations (33) and (34) are too complex. Thus, in Figure 6a, three surfaces, $G = 0$ (the red surface), $G_a = 0$ (the green surface) and $G_\Omega = 0$ (the blue surface), are drawn in the three-dimension space (Ω, A, a), and their intersection $Bif_1 = (1.6606, 0.051901, 0.38956)$ is obtained as the numerical solution of the bifurcation set. Using the same numerical method, in Figure 6b, the result of the hysteresis set $Hys_1 = (1.0149, 0.06301, 0.34944)$ can be obtained, and the red surface is $G = 0$, the green surface is $G_a = 0$, and the blue surface is $G_{aa} = 0$. After obtaining the transition set, all of the bifurcation conditions of the amplitude–frequency response of the SD oscillator can be calculated.

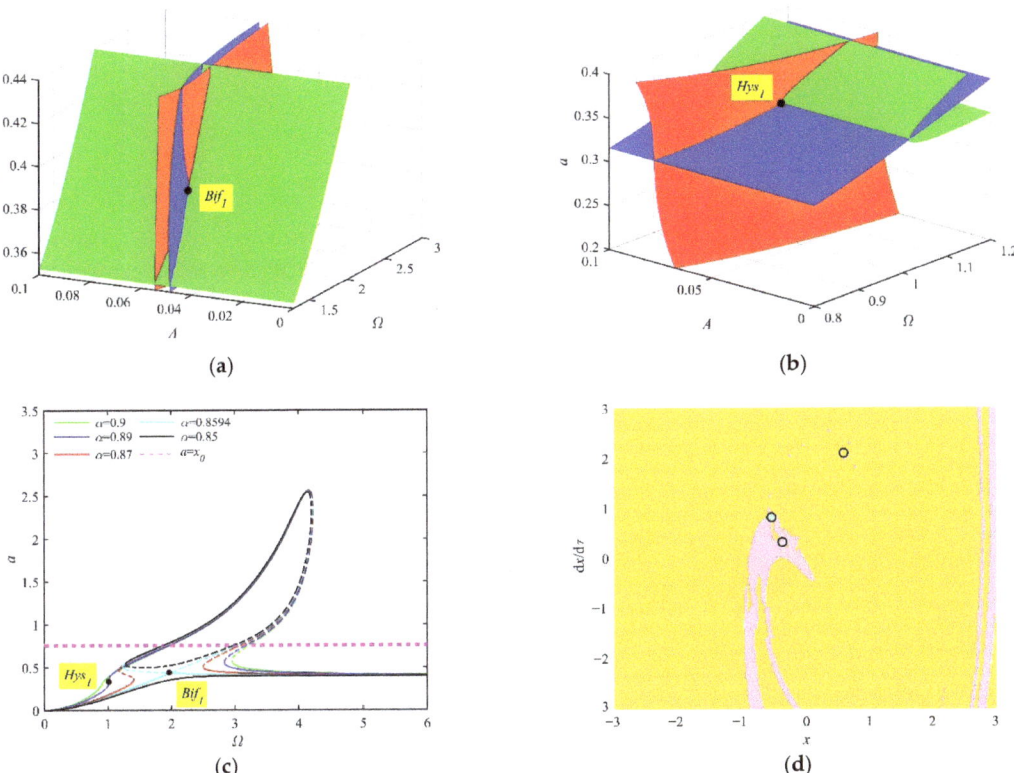

Figure 6. (a) The bifurcation set Bif_1; (b) the hysteresis set Hys_1; (c) the amplitude–frequency response curves; (d) the attractors and the attraction domain with $\alpha = 0.85$ and $\Omega = 2.5$.

As shown in Figure 6c, a hysteresis point is generated, as the smooth parameter α equals 0.89. The hysteresis phenomenon leads to the appearance of pitchfork bifurcation. Comparing the green curve and the red curve in Figure 6c, the number of the results of a increases from 1 to 3 in the interval $0.5 < \Omega < 1.5$, so that a new multi-solution coexistence region is generated. When $\alpha = 0.8594$, a bifurcation point is generated. The bifurcation phenomenon leads to the appearance of transcritical bifurcation. Subsequently, a frequency island, which is depicted by closed black curves, occurs in the resonant region. There are three coexistent attractors in the entire region of the frequency island. The three attractors are depicted in Figure 6d by orange, purple and cyan circles, respectively. The attraction domains are drawn in the same colors as the attractors. The orange attractor is a stable attractor with the largest amplitude and the widest attraction domain, corresponding to the top black branch of the frequency island; the purple attractor is a stable attractor with the smallest amplitude and a narrow attraction domain corresponding to the bottom black solid line; and the other unstable attractor corresponds to the black dashed line in Figure 6c.

The above novel nonlinear phenomena in the small amplitude region are disclosed due to the fact that the nonlinear piecewise function P_n maintains the nonlinear property of the system in the interval $-x_0 < x < x_0$. Because of the frequency island, the vibration amplitude of the SD oscillator can be adjusted by imposing a disturbance to change the displacement or the velocity in order to make them exceed the boundary of the attraction domain.

Next, the frequency island is further analyzed in terms of the distributions of the attractors and the time history of vibration. Thus, the distribution of attractors in the frequency island, the time history of vibration of stable attractors and those without the frequency island are drawn in Figures 7 and 8. To highlight the differences, the parameters in Figures 7 and 8 are selected as $\Omega = 2$, $\alpha = 0.85$ and $\Omega = 2$, $\alpha = 0.9$, respectively.

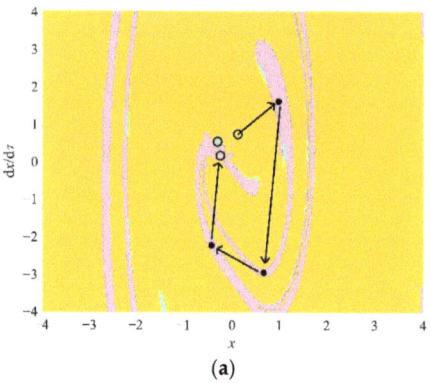
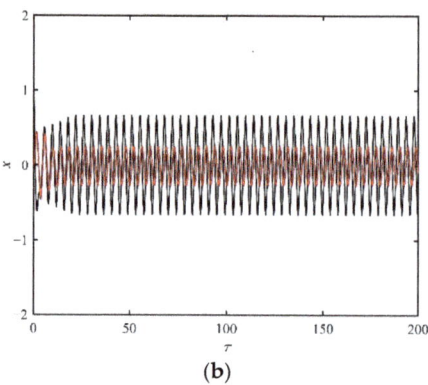

Figure 7. (a) The distribution of attractors in the frequency island; (b) the time history of vibration, the initial conditions of black line are selected as $(0.5, 0)$, the initial conditions of red line are selected as $(-0.5, 0.5)$.

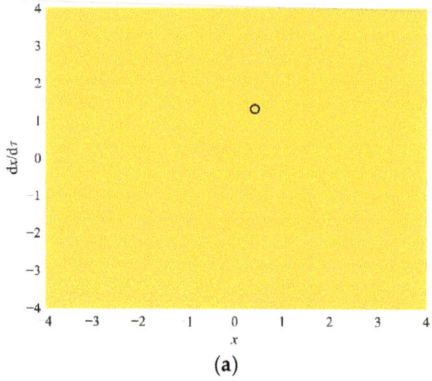
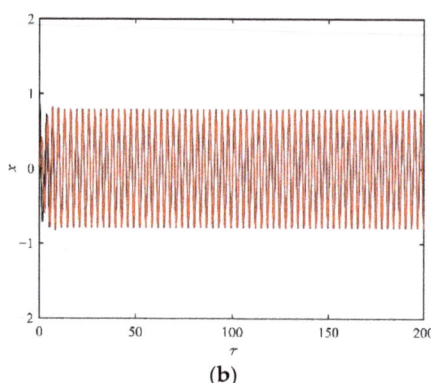

Figure 8. (a) The distribution of attractors without the frequency island; (b) the time history of vibration, the initial conditions of black line, are selected as $(1, 0)$, the initial conditions of red line are selected as $(0, 0)$.

Figure 7a shows that two stable attractors (the orange circle and the purple circle) with different amplitudes coexist with an unstable attractor (the cyan circle) in the frequency island. Figure 7b shows the time history of vibration. The stable motion in the black line corresponds to the orange attractor in Figure 7a, and the stable motion in the red line corresponds to the purple attractor in Figure 7a. In Figure 7a, the black arrows and black dots are schematic representations of the attractor-switching phenomenon, supposing a disturbance is imposed in the system, which is in the stable state of the orange attractor. The displacement and the velocity of the system are changed to the first black dot, which marks that the system has entered the purple attraction domain. After a period of time, the system goes through several unstable states (the other black dots) before finally returning to a stable state (the purple circle). The vibration characteristic also changes from the black line to the red line in Figure 7b, and the vibration amplitude significantly decreases. However, without the frequency island, this phenomenon cannot be generated because there is only one attractor, as shown in Figure 8.

In Figure 8a, there is only one stable attractor, and the attraction domain is full of the entire state space. Thus, no matter what the initial conditions are, for example $(1,0)$ or $(0,0)$, the stable state of the system can always be represented by the red line in Figure 8b. For most nonlinear systems, a narrow hysteresis region where the attractor-switching phenomenon can be generated, such as $2.5 < \Omega < 4.1$ in Figure 6c, is found in the resonant region. It is rare that the frequency island results in the entire resonant region generating the attractor-switching phenomenon.

4.1.2. The Influence of the Fractional Damping Parameters in the Transition Set of the System

From the above investigations, when the smooth parameter α decreases and nonlinearity increases, a transition process is disclosed: a hysteresis point followed by a bifurcation point and a frequency island. Further, with the frequency island, the fractional SD oscillator has a novel attractor-switching phenomenon among the entire resonant region. Thus, it is worth investigating the influence of the fractional damping parameters on the transition set. The results of the transition sets with different fractional damping parameters are shown in Figure 9.

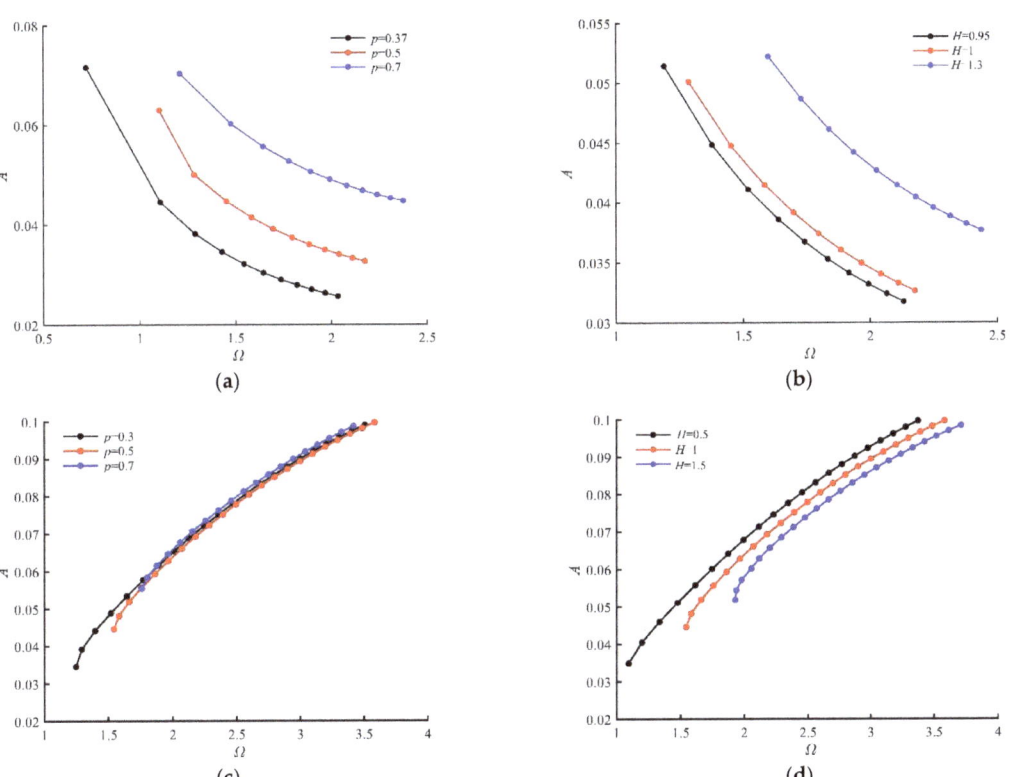

Figure 9. The results of transition set with $\alpha = 0.89$; (**a**) the hysteresis set with $p = 0.37, 0.5, 0.7$ and $H = 1$; (**b**) the hysteresis set of Equation (20) with $H = 0.95, 1, 1.3$ and $p = 0.5$; (**c**) the bifurcation set with $p = 0.3, 0.5, 0.7$ and $H = 1$; (**d**) the bifurcation set with $H = 0.5, 1, 1.5$ and $p = 0.5$.

Figure 9a,b show the influence of the fractional damping parameters on the hysteresis set of the system. As the fractional parameters increase, the hysteresis point requires the generation of a larger excitation amplitude and higher excitation frequency. In other words, the hysteresis point moves to the high-frequency and large-amplitude region. Figure 9b,c exhibit the influence of the fractional damping parameters in the bifurcation set. As the fractional damping order p increases, the bifurcation point moves to the high-frequency region, but the excitation amplitude has little change. As the fractional damping coefficient H increases, the bifurcation point moves to the high-frequency and small-amplitude region. In other words, the system needs a small excitation amplitude to generate a bifurcation point.

After analyzing the influence of the fractional damping on the hysteresis set and the bifurcation set, the influence of these parameters in the frequency island is investigated. The smooth parameter is selected as $\alpha = 0.7$. The amplitude–frequency response curves with different fractional damping parameters are drawn in Figure 10.

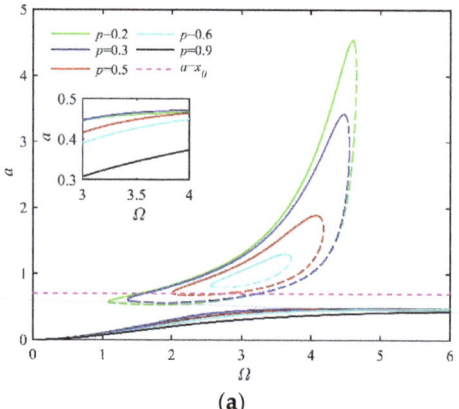
(a)

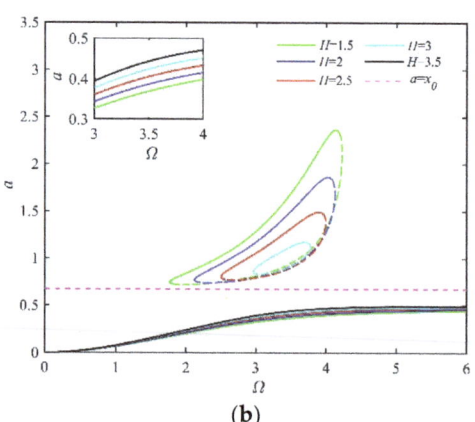
(b)

Figure 10. The amplitude frequency response curves with (a) $H = 1$, $p = 0.2, 0.3, 0.5, 0.6$ and 0.9; (b) $p = 0.5$, $H = 1.5, 2, 2.5, 3$ and 3.5.

Figure 10 shows the amplitude–frequency response curves with differential fractional damping parameters. With the increase in the fractional parameters, both the frequency interval and amplitude of the stable solution in the frequency island decrease. When $p = 0.9$ in Figure 10a and $H = 3.5$ in Figure 10b, the frequency island disappears, while the stable solution with a small amplitude remains. The amplitude of the existing attractor decreases as the fractional order increases, while the amplitude increases as the fractional coefficient increases. The results correlate well with Figure 4, because with the fractional order equals 1 and $\Omega > \Omega_2 = e^{-\pi \cot(p\pi/2)/2}$, the fractional damping has the equivalent of linear damping and is the strongest damping effect, causing the amplitude to decrease. As the fractional coefficient increases and $\Omega > \Omega_1 = e^{\pi \tan(p\pi/2)/2}$, the fractional damping has a stiffness property and a damping property, but the stiffness property is dominated, causing the amplitude to slightly increase.

To further investigate the reason why the frequency island disappears, the distribution of attractors in the frequency island is depicted in Figures 11 and 12.

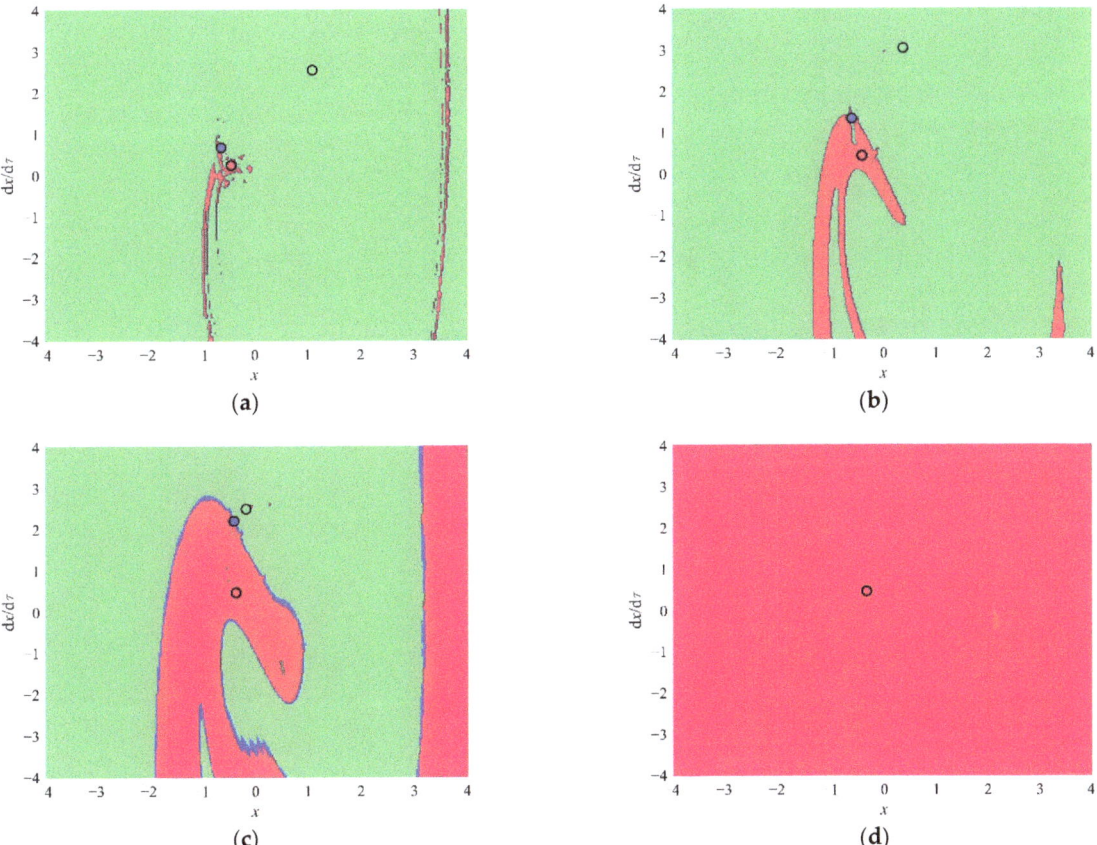

Figure 11. The distribution of attractors in the frequency island with parameters are set as $\Omega = 3$, $H = 2$ (**a**) $p = 0.2$, (**b**) $p = 0.5$, (**c**) $p = 0.625$ and (**d**) $p = 0.7$.

In Figures 11 and 12, the stable attractor with a large amplitude is drawn in green, the stable attractor with a small amplitude is drawn in red and the unstable attractor is drawn in dark blue. These figures show the influence of the fractional parameters on the attractors in the frequency island. Figure 11 shows that as the fractional order increases, the green attractor moves closer to the blue attractor; meanwhile, the red attraction domain expands. Then, the green attractor collides with the blue attractor and disappears, while the red attraction domain fills the entire state space since $p = 0.7$. This is the reason why the frequency island disappears as the fractional order increases.

Figure 12 shows that as the fractional coefficient increases, the green attractor collides with the blue attractor and becomes a new chaotic attractor (the chaotic attraction domain and the chaotic attractor are multicolored in Figure 12c). Subsequently, the chaotic attractor disappears; meanwhile, the red attraction domain expands until it fills the entire state space as shown in Figure 12d. This is the reason why the frequency island disappears as the fractional coefficient increases.

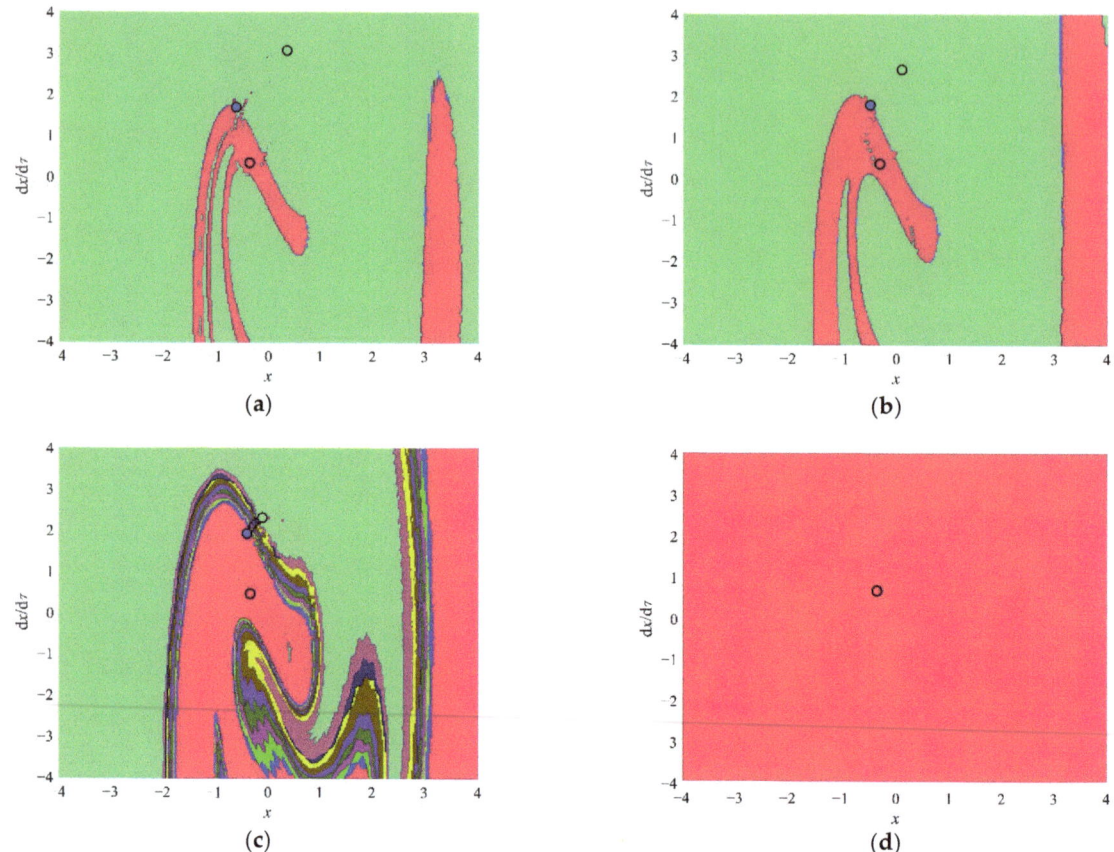

Figure 12. The distribution of attractors in the frequency island with parameters are set as $\Omega = 3$, $p = 0.7$ (**a**) $H = 1.5$, (**b**) $H = 2.5$, (**c**) $H = 3$ and (**d**) $H = 3.5$.

4.2. Analysis of the Snap-Through Phenomenon in the Non-Resonant Region

In the non-resonant region, this article mainly focuses on the snap-through phenomenon that is commonly discovered in multi-well dynamics systems. A multi-well system which generates snap-through phenomena has been analyzed in terms of the nonlinear energy and the competing resonance. When the energy is sufficient to exceed the energy threshold of the potential well, two types of transition phenomena are generated: one is inner-well motion → inter-well motion → inner-well motion (it is a different potential well from the initial well), and the other is inner-well motion → inter-well motion [8,12].

In this section, the influence of the fractional parameters on the snap-through phenomenon in the non-resonant region is analyzed in terms of the global dynamics. The distribution of attractors is obtained when $\Omega = 1$ (the frequency is lower than the natural frequency) and 8.5 (the frequency is higher than the natural frequency). The initial displacement x_s and the initial velocity $\dot{x}_s$ are selected as $(x_s, \dot{x}_s) = (-0.7, 0)$ to keep the steady-state motion of the system corresponding to the same initial attractor. The random impulse disturbance, which has an amplitude of $x_{im} \in [-1, 4]$, is applied 100 times, and the experiment is repeated 100 times. The probabilities that the system generates snap-through due to the random disturbance and the distribution of attractors in the non-resonant region are shown in Figures 13–16.

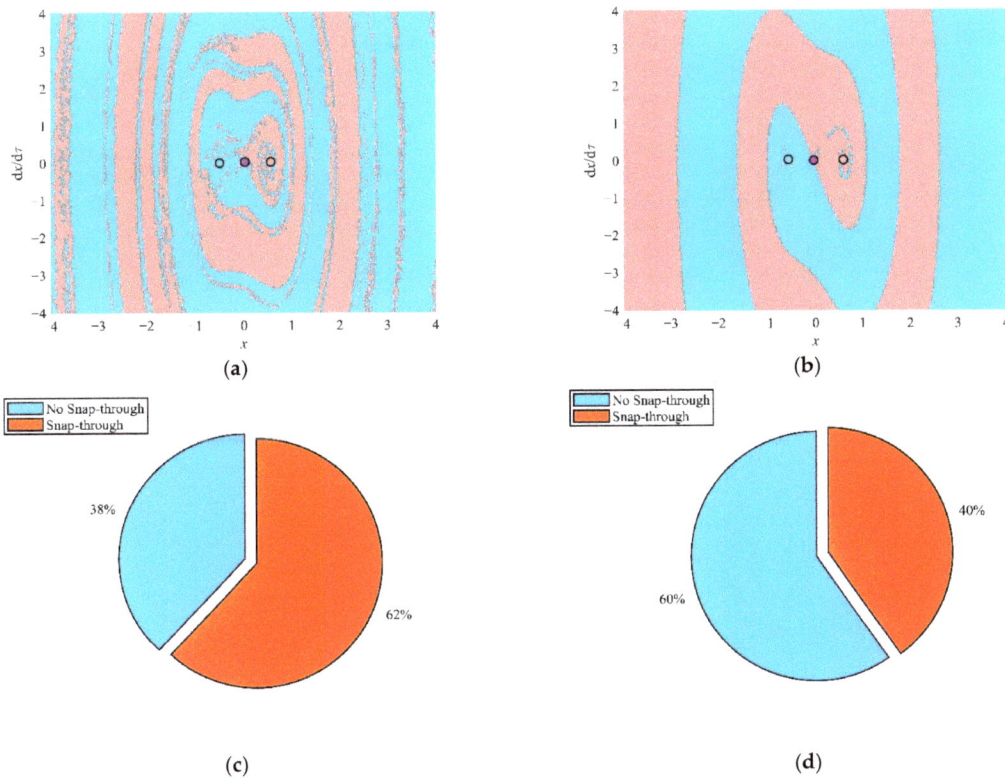
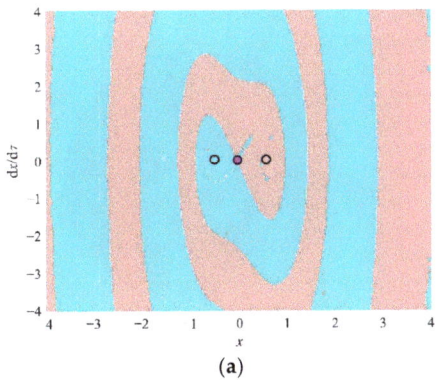
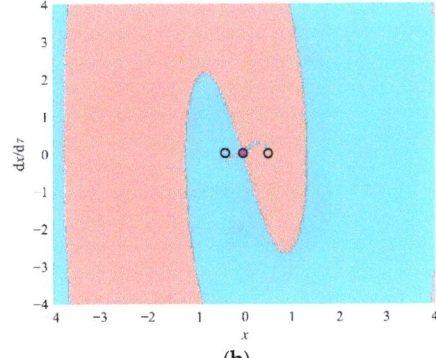

Figure 13. The distribution of attractors with the parameters are set as $\Omega = 1$, $H = 1$ (**a**) $p = 0$, and (**b**) $p = 0.99$, and the probability of the snap-through with (**c**) $p = 0$ and (**d**) $p = 0.99$.

Figure 14. *Cont.*

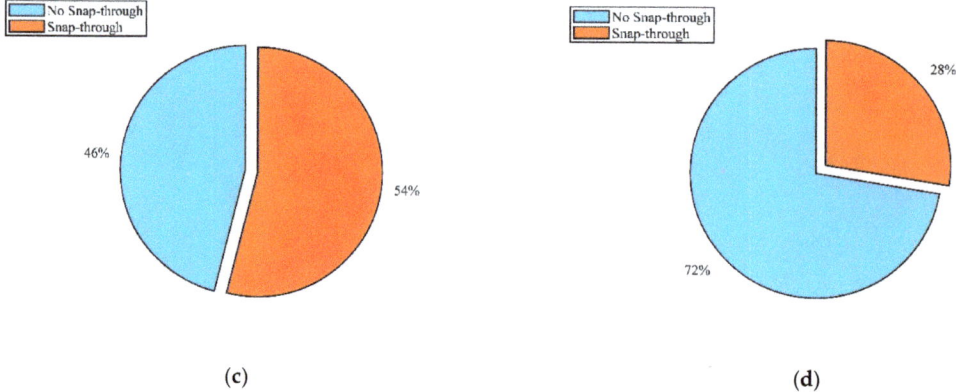

(c)　　　　　　　　　　　　　　　　　(d)

Figure 14. The distribution of attractors with the parameters are set as $\Omega =1$, $p = 0.5$ (**a**) $H = 1$, (**b**) $H = 4$, and the probability of the snap-through with (**c**) $H = 1$ and (**d**) $H = 4$.

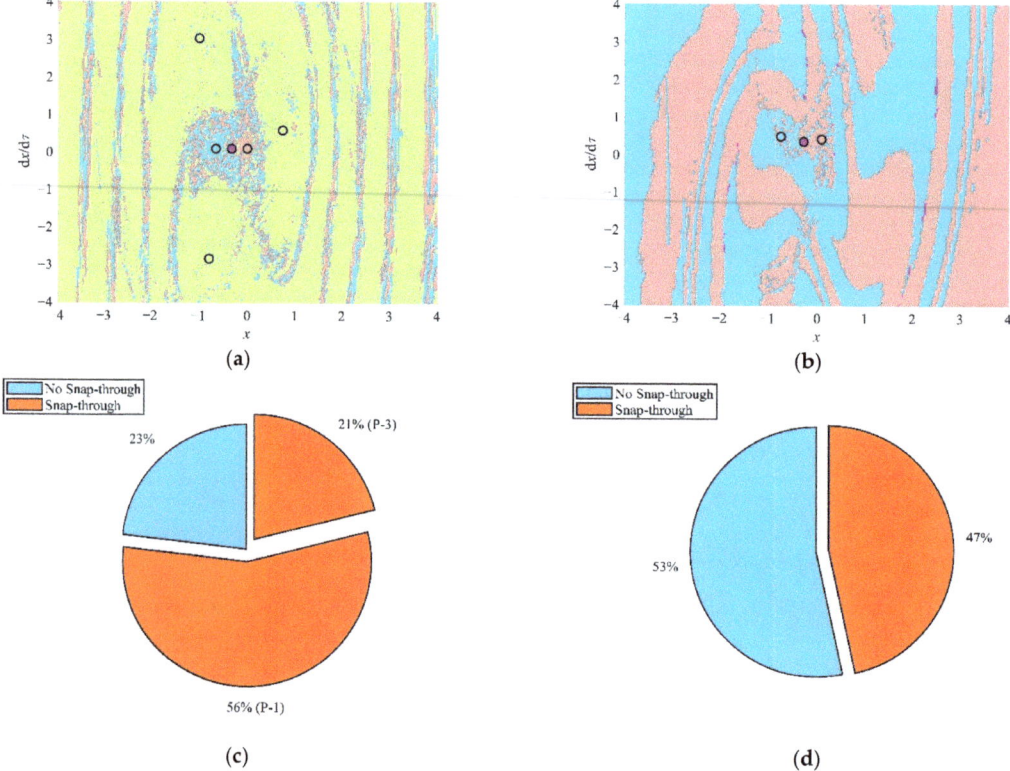

Figure 15. The distribution of attractors with the parameters are set as $\Omega = 8.5$, $H = 1$ (**a**) $p = 0.1$, (**b**) $p = 0.99$, and the probability of the snap-through with (**c**) $p = 0.1$ and (**d**) $p = 0.99$.

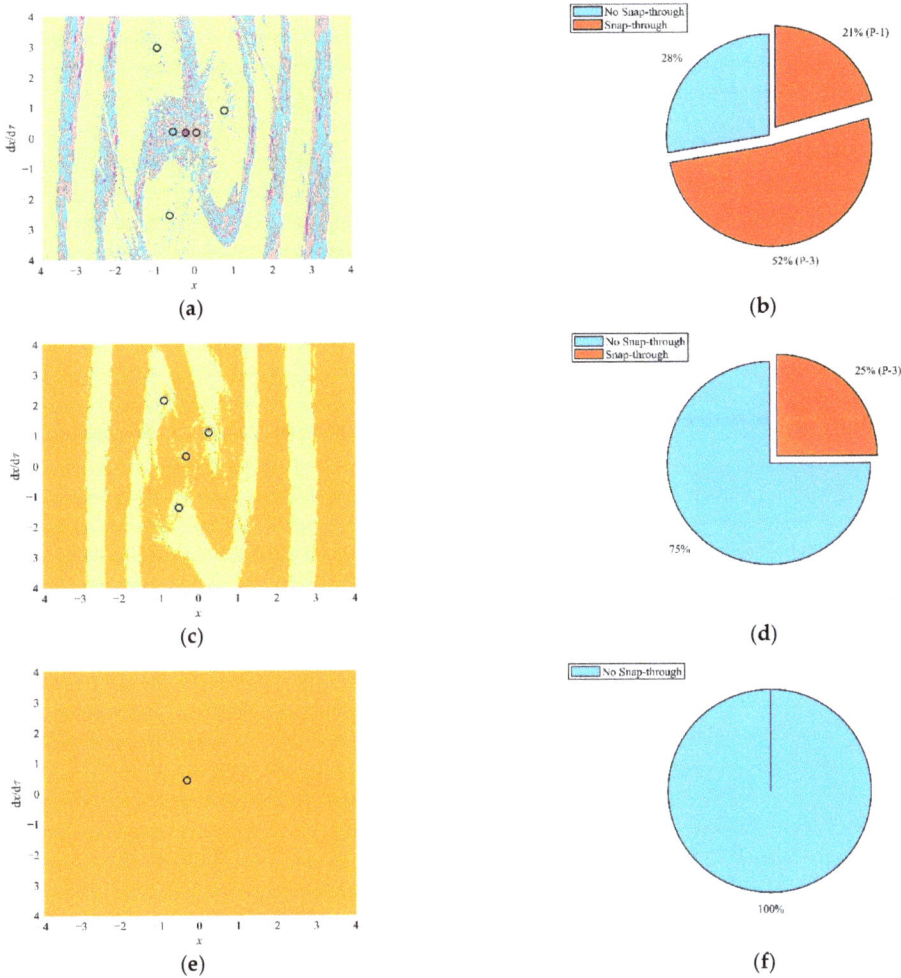

Figure 16. The distribution of attractors with the parameters are set as $\Omega = 8.5$, $p = 0.5$ (**a**) $H = 1$, (**c**) $H = 3$, (**e**) $H = 4$; (**b,d,f**) are the diagrams of the probability of the snap-through with $H = 1, 3$ and 4, respectively.

Figure 13a,b show that the distribution of the attraction domain is helicoid. Two stable attractors (the cyan circle and the pink circle) and one unstable attractor (the purple circle) coexist. By increasing the fractional order, the continuity of the attraction domain increases, and the symmetry enhances. Thus, as shown in Figure 13c,d, the probability of the snap-through decreases from 62% to 40%, which means that the asymptotic stability of the steady-state solution increases.

Figure 14a,b show that by increasing the fractional coefficient, the continuity of the attraction domain of the stable solutions increases, and the symmetry enhances. The probability of the snap-through decreases from 54% to 28% in Figure 14c,d. The asymptotic stability of the steady-state solution increases.

When the excitation frequency is smaller than the natural frequency, the increase in the fractional parameters leads to the continuity and symmetry of the attraction domain of the stable solution increasing. Meanwhile, the asymptotic stability of the steady-state solution increases.

Figure 15a shows that when the excitation frequency is larger than the natural frequency, one stable period-three attractor (the green circles) and three period-one attractors coexist. The attraction domain of the period-one attractors is discontinuous and narrow, which means that the asymptotic stability of the period-one motion is weak. The probability of the snap-through is 77%, which is shown in Figure 15c. By increasing the fractional order, the continuity of the period-one attraction domain increases, and the period-three attractor disappears (the existence conditions of the period-three are broken), as shown in Figure 15b. The probability of the snap-through decreases from 77% to 47%. Note that the two period-one attraction domains are still asymmetric; therefore, the probability of the snap-through in Figure 15d is higher than that in Figure 13d.

Figure 16a,c,e show that by increasing the fractional coefficient, three period-one attractors merge and evolve to a period-one attractor, and the period-one attraction domain expands. The asymptotic stability of the period-one motion increases. Meanwhile, the period-three attractor disappears because the existence condition of the period-three motion is broken. As the fractional coefficient equals 4, the period-three attractor disappears, while the period-one attraction domain fills the entire state space, as shown in Figure 16e. The system evolves from a tristable state to a bistable state and finally to a monostable state. Figure 16b,d,f illustrate that as the continuity of the attraction domain increases, the probability of the snap-through decreases from 73% to 0%. No snap-through occurs when the system is monostable, as shown in Figure 16f.

When the frequency is greater than the natural frequency, caused by an increase in the fractional coefficient, the asymptotic stability of the steady-state solution increases, and the number of the coexisting attractors changes. Thus, the probability of the snap-through decreases. This influence is different from the increase in the fractional order.

5. Conclusions

A new nonlinear piecewise function is proposed to establish the differential equation of the SD oscillator with fractional damping. The Caputo fractional model was used to represent the fractional damping, and the equivalent stiffness coefficient and the equivalent damping coefficient were calculated. The nonlinear dynamics characteristics and snap-through phenomena were studied. The influence of fractional damping on nonlinear dynamic characteristics was analyzed, and some novel and interesting nonlinear phenomena were disclosed. The conclusions from the investigation are as follows:

1. The nonlinear restoring force is accurately represented by the piecewise nonlinear function. The nonlinear characteristics of the restoring force in the interval $-x_0 < x < x_0$ are retained, so that some novel nonlinear phenomena are found.
2. The orthogonal function is used to calculate the equivalent fractional coefficients. The equivalent stiffness coefficient and the equivalent damping coefficient are variable with respect to the pth and the $(p-1)$th power of the excitation frequency. In the high-frequency region, the stiffness characteristic of the fractional model is dominant. The stiffness characteristic increases first and then decreases as the fractional order increases. In the low-frequency region, the damping characteristic of the fractional model is dominant. The damping characteristic increases first and then decreases as the fractional order increases. The fractional model affects the stiffness property and the damping property, simultaneously.
3. Based on the amplitude–frequency response functions, a novel transition process is found. With the decrease in the smooth parameter, the nonlinearity of the system increases. A hysteresis point appears first, followed by a bifurcation point and a frequency island. There are three attractors (two stable attractors and one unstable attractor) in the frequency island. In addition, the variation in the number and the stable state of attractors means that pitchfork bifurcation and transcritical bifurcation are found. It is rare that the vibration amplitude of the system can be changed in the entire resonant region because of the frequency island.

4. As the fractional parameters increase, the hysteresis point moves to the high-frequency and large-amplitude region, and the bifurcation point moves to the high-frequency and small-amplitude region. The frequency interval of the frequency island shortens. Finally, the frequency island disappears because the stable attractor and the unstable attractor collide.
5. In the non-resonant region, the increase in the fractional parameters leads to the probability of the snap-through decreasing and the asymptotic stability of the steady-state solution increasing. When the excitation frequency is smaller than the natural frequency, the symmetry of the attraction domain enhances and the continuity increases. When the excitation frequency is larger than the natural frequency, the number of stable states of the system decreases. When the system is in a monostable state, no snap-through occurs.

Based on the above investigations, some novel nonlinear phenomena, such as a frequency island, of the SD oscillator with nonlinear fractional damping are revealed. This investigation may provide a theoretical basis for applying SD oscillators in energy harvesting, vibration isolation, and many other fields. In the future, some vibration isolation experiments and theoretical investigations for fractional SD oscillators utilizing the novel frequency island phenomenon may be useful for ultra-low-frequency vibration isolators.

Author Contributions: Conceptualization, M.W. and E.C.; methodology, M.W.; software, M.W.; validation, E.C., R.T. and C.W.; formal analysis, M.W.; investigation, M.W.; resources, E.C.; data curation, E.C.; writing—original draft preparation, M.W.; writing—review and editing, E.C. and R.T.; visualization, M.W.; supervision, E.C.; project administration, E.C.; funding acquisition, E.C. All authors have read and agreed to the published version of the manuscript.

Funding: This research was funded by the National Natural Science Foundation of China, grant number 12072205 and the Natural Science Foundation of Hebei Province, grant number A2022210024.

Institutional Review Board Statement: Not applicable.

Informed Consent Statement: Not applicable.

Data Availability Statement: Not applicable.

Acknowledgments: Thanks to the State Key Laboratory of Mechanical Behavior and System Safety of Traffic Engineering Structures.

Conflicts of Interest: The authors declare no conflict of interest.

Appendix A

$$R_{11} = \left(2\zeta\Omega + H\Omega^p \sin\left(\frac{p\pi}{2}\right)\right)/2\Omega$$

$$R_{12} = \left(\frac{\bar{a}}{4}\left(3\bar{a}^2(B_2K_0 + K_3) + 4\left(B_4K_0 + K_1 - \Omega^2\right) + 4H\Omega^p \cos\left(\frac{p\pi}{2}\right)\right)\right)/2\Omega$$

$$R_{13} = \left(9\bar{a}^2(B_2K_0 + K_3) + 4\left(B_4K_0 + K_1 - \Omega^2\right) + 4H\Omega^p \cos\left(\frac{p\pi}{2}\right)\right)/8\pi$$

$$R_{14} = \bar{a}\left(2\zeta\Omega + H\Omega^p \sin\left(\frac{p\pi}{2}\right)\right)/2\pi$$

$$R_{21} = \frac{1}{2\Omega}\left(\frac{K_0}{\pi}(-2B_1 + x_0)\sqrt{1-\left(\frac{x_0}{\bar{a}}\right)^2} + \frac{K_0}{\pi}(2B_5 + x_0)\sqrt{1-\left(\frac{x_0}{\bar{a}}\right)^2} - \frac{K_0 x_0}{2\pi}\sqrt{1-\left(\frac{x_0}{\bar{a}}\right)^2}\left(3\bar{a}^2 B_2 + 4B_4 2B_2 x_0^2\right)\right.$$

$$\left. + \frac{\bar{a}^2}{2\pi}K_0 a\cos\left(\frac{x_0}{\bar{a}}\right) + \frac{\bar{a}}{2\pi}\left(3\bar{a}^2 B_2 + 4B_4\right)K_0 a\sin\left(\frac{x_0}{\bar{a}}\right) + \bar{a}K_1 + \frac{3}{4}\bar{a}^3 K_3 - \bar{a}\Omega^2 + \bar{a}H\Omega^p \cos\left(\frac{p\pi}{2}\right)\right)$$

$$R_{22} = (2\bar{a}^2 K_0 x_0 - 18\bar{a}^4 B_2 K_0 x_0 - 8\bar{a}^2 B_4 K_0 x_0 - 8B_1 K_0 x_0^2 + 8B_5 K_0 x_0^2 + 8K_0 x_0^3 + 6\bar{a}^2 B_2 K_0 x_0^3 - 8B_4 K_0 x_0^3$$

$$- 4B_2 K_0 x_0^5 + 4\bar{a}^3 K_1 \pi \sqrt{1 - \left(\frac{x_0}{\bar{a}}\right)^2} + 9\bar{a}^5 K_3 \pi \sqrt{1 - \left(\frac{x_0}{\bar{a}}\right)^2} - 4\bar{a}^3 \pi \sqrt{1 - \left(\frac{x_0}{\bar{a}}\right)^2} \Omega^2 + 2\bar{a}^3 K_0 \sqrt{1 - \left(\frac{x_0}{\bar{a}}\right)^2} \mathrm{acos}\left(\frac{x_0}{\bar{a}}\right)$$

$$+ 2\bar{a}^3 \left(9\bar{a}^2 B_2 + 4B_4\right) K_0 \sqrt{1 - \left(\frac{x_0}{\bar{a}}\right)^2} \mathrm{asin}\left(\frac{x_0}{\bar{a}}\right) + 4\bar{a}^3 H \pi \sqrt{1 - \left(\frac{x_0}{\bar{a}}\right)^2} \Omega^p \cos\left(\frac{p\pi}{2}\right) \Big/ \left(8\bar{a}^3 \pi^2 \sqrt{1 - \left(\frac{x_0}{\bar{a}}\right)^2}\right)$$

Appendix B

$$\widetilde{G}_a = \left(4K_1 + 3a^2 K_3 + K_0\left(6 - 6/\alpha^{2/3} + 3a^2\left(\alpha^{4/3} - \alpha^{2/3}\right)\Big/\left(2\left(-1 + \alpha^{2/3}\right)\alpha^{8/3}\right)\right) - 4\Omega^2 + 4H\Omega^p \cos(p\pi/2)\right)$$

$$G_\Omega = -\frac{4f^2 \Omega^3}{L^2} + 2a\left(2a\zeta + aHp\Omega^{p-1}\sin\left(\frac{p\pi}{2}\right)\right)\left(2\zeta\Omega + H\Omega^p \sin\left(\frac{p\pi}{2}\right)\right) + \frac{a^2}{8}\left(-8\Omega + 4Hp\Omega^{p-1}\cos\left(\frac{p\pi}{2}\right)\right)\widetilde{G}_a$$

$a < x_0$:

$$G = -\frac{f^2 \Omega^4}{L^2} + \frac{1}{16}a^2 \left(3a^2\left(K_3 + \frac{K_0\left(\alpha^{4/3} - \alpha^{2/3}\right)}{2\left(-1 + \alpha^{2/3}\right)\alpha^{8/3}}\right) + 4\left(K_1 + \frac{3K_0\left(-1 + \alpha^{2/3}\right)}{2\alpha^{2/3}} - \Omega^2\right) + 4H\Omega^p \cos\left(\frac{p\pi}{2}\right)\right)^2$$
$$+ \left(2a\zeta\Omega + aH\Omega^p \sin\left(\frac{p\pi}{2}\right)\right)^2$$

$$G_a = \frac{a}{8}\left(6a^2\left(K_3 + \frac{K_0\left(\alpha^{4/3} - \alpha^{2/3}\right)}{2\left(-1 + \alpha^{2/3}\right)\alpha^{8/3}}\right)\widetilde{G}_a + 16\left(2\zeta\Omega + H\Omega^p \sin\left(\frac{p\pi}{2}\right)\right)^2 \widetilde{G}_a^2\right)$$

$$G_{aa} = \frac{1}{8}\left(\left(3a^2\left(-2K_3\left(-1 + \alpha^{2/3}\right)\alpha^{8/3} + K_0\left(-\alpha^{4/3} + \alpha^{2/3}\right)\right) 8\left(3K_0\left(\alpha^{4/3} + \left(-2 + \alpha^{2/3}\right)\alpha^2\right)\right.\right.\right.$$
$$+ 2\left(-1 + \alpha^{2/3}\right)\alpha^2\left(K_1 - \Omega^2\right)\right)\left(-9a^2\left(2K_3\alpha^{2/3}\left(-\alpha^{4/3} + \alpha^2\right) + K_0\left(-1 + \alpha^{2/3}\right)\right)$$
$$- 8\left(3K_0\left(\alpha^{4/3} + \left(-2 + \alpha^{2/3}\right)\alpha^2\right) + 2\left(-1 + \alpha^{2/3}\right)\alpha^2\left(K_1 - \Omega^2\right)\right) - 16H\left(-1 + \alpha^{2/3}\right)\alpha^2 \Omega^p \cos\left(\frac{p\pi}{2}\right)\right)$$
$$\Big/\left(\left(-1 + \alpha^{2/3}\right)^2 a^{14/3}\right) + 16\left(2\zeta\Omega + H\Omega^p \sin\left(\frac{p\pi}{2}\right)\right)^2 + 6a^2\left(K_3 + \frac{K_0\left(\alpha^{4/3} - \alpha^{2/3}\right)}{2\left(-1 + \alpha^{2/3}\right)\alpha^{8/3}}\right)\widetilde{G}_a + \widetilde{G}_a^2\right)$$

$$G_\Omega = -\frac{4f^2 \Omega^3}{L^2} + 2a\left(2a\zeta + aHp\Omega^{p-1}\sin\left(\frac{p\pi}{2}\right)\right)\left(2\zeta\Omega + H\Omega^p \sin\left(\frac{p\pi}{2}\right)\right) + \frac{a^2}{8}\left(-8\Omega + 4Hp\Omega^{p-1}\cos\left(\frac{p\pi}{2}\right)\right)\widetilde{G}_a$$

$a > x_0$:

$$G = -\frac{f^2 \Omega^4}{L^2} + \frac{1}{16}a^2 \left(3a^2\left(K_3 + \frac{K_0\left(\alpha^{4/3} - \alpha^{2/3}\right)}{2\left(-1 + \alpha^{2/3}\right)\alpha^{8/3}}\right) + 4\left(K_1 + \frac{3K_0\left(-1 + \alpha^{2/3}\right)}{2\alpha^{2/3}} - \Omega^2\right) + 4H\Omega^p \cos\left(\frac{p\pi}{2}\right)\right)^2$$
$$+ \left(2a\zeta\Omega + aH\Omega^p \sin\left(\frac{p\pi}{2}\right)\right)^2$$

$$G_a = -\left(\left(\left(4K_0(2B_1 - x_0)\sqrt{1 - \left(\frac{x_0}{a}\right)^2} - 4K_0(2B_5 + x_0)\sqrt{1 - \left(\frac{x_0}{a}\right)^2} + 2K_0 x_0 \sqrt{1 - \left(\frac{x_0}{a}\right)^2}\left(3a^2 B_2 + 4B_4 + 2B_2 x_0^2\right)\right.\right.\right.$$
$$- 8aK_0 \mathrm{acos}\left(\frac{x_0}{a}\right) - 2a\left(3a^2 B_2 + 4B_4\right)K_0 \mathrm{asin}\left(\frac{x_0}{a}\right) - a\pi\left(4K_1 + 3a^2 K_3 - 4\Omega^2 + 4H\Omega^p \cos\left(\frac{p\pi}{2}\right)\right)\right)$$
$$\times \left(8a^2 K_0 x_0 - 2a^2\left(3a^2 B_2 + 4B_4\right)K_0 x_0 - 4K_0(2B_1 - x_0)x_0^2 + 4K_0 x_0^2(2B_5 + x_0) - 12a^2 B_2 K_0 x_0\left(a^2 - x_0^2\right)\right.$$
$$- 2K_0 x_0^3\left(3a^2 B_2 + 4B_4 + 2B_2 x_0^2\right) + 8a^3 K_0 \sqrt{1 - \left(\frac{x_0}{a}\right)^2}\mathrm{acos}\left(\frac{x_0}{a}\right) + 12a^5 B_2 K_0 \sqrt{1 - \left(\frac{x_0}{a}\right)^2}\mathrm{asin}\left(\frac{x_0}{a}\right)$$
$$+ 2a^3\left(3a^2 B_2 + 4B_4\right)K_0 \sqrt{1 - \left(\frac{x_0}{a}\right)^2}\mathrm{asin}\left(\frac{x_0}{a}\right) + a^3 \pi \sqrt{1 - \left(\frac{x_0}{a}\right)^2}\left(4K_1 + 9a^2 K_3 - 4\Omega^2 + 4H\Omega^p \cos\left(\frac{p\pi}{2}\right)\right)\right)\right)$$
$$\Big/\left(8a^3 \pi^2 \sqrt{1 - \left(\frac{x_0}{a}\right)^2}\right)\right) + 2a\left(2\zeta\Omega + H\Omega^p \sin\left(\frac{p\pi}{2}\right)\right)^2$$

$$G_{aa} = \left(\sqrt{1-\left(\frac{x_0}{a}\right)^2}(8a^2K_0x_0 - 18a^4B_2K_0x_0 - 8a^2B_4K_0x_0 - 8B_1K_0x_0^2 + 8B_5K_0x_0^2\right.$$

$$+8K_0x_0^3 + 6a^2B_2K_0x_0^3 - 8B_4K_0x_0^3 - 4B_2K_0x_0^5 + 4a^3K_1\pi\sqrt{1-\left(\frac{x_0}{a}\right)^2} + 9a^5K_3\pi\sqrt{1-\left(\frac{x_0}{a}\right)^2}$$

$$-4a^3\pi\sqrt{1-\left(\frac{x_0}{a}\right)^2}\Omega^2 + 8a^3K_0\sqrt{1-\left(\frac{x_0}{a}\right)^2}\mathrm{acos}\left(\frac{x_0}{a}\right) + 2a^3\left(9a^2B_2 + 4B_4\right)K_0\sqrt{1-\left(\frac{x_0}{a}\right)^2}\mathrm{asin}\left(\frac{x_0}{a}\right)$$

$$+4a^3H\pi\sqrt{1-\left(\frac{x_0}{a}\right)^2}\Omega^p\cos\left(\frac{p\pi}{2}\right)\right)^2 - 4a^3\pi\sqrt{1-\left(\frac{x_0}{a}\right)^2}\Omega^2 + 8a^3K_0\sqrt{1-\left(\frac{x_0}{a}\right)^2}\mathrm{acos}\left(\frac{x_0}{a}\right)$$

$$+2a^3\left(9a^2B_2 + 4B_4\right)K_0\sqrt{1-\left(\frac{x_0}{a}\right)^2}\mathrm{asin}\left(\frac{x_0}{a}\right) + 4a^3H\pi\sqrt{1-\left(\frac{x_0}{a}\right)^2}\Omega^p\cos\left(\frac{p\pi}{2}\right)\right)^2$$

$$-a^3\sqrt{1-\left(\frac{x_0}{a}\right)^2}\left(12a^2K_1\pi + 45a^4K_3\pi - 8K_1\pi x_0^2 - 36a^2K_3\pi x_0^2 + 24aK_0x_0\sqrt{1-\left(\frac{x_0}{a}\right)^2}\right.$$

$$-90a^3B_2K_0x_0\sqrt{1-\left(\frac{x_0}{a}\right)^2} - 24aB_4K_0x_0\sqrt{1-\left(\frac{x_0}{a}\right)^2} + 12aB_2K_0x_0^3\sqrt{1-\left(\frac{x_0}{a}\right)^2} - 12a^2\pi\Omega^2$$

$$+8\pi x_0^2\Omega^2 + 8K_0\left(3a^2 - 2x_0^2\right)\mathrm{acos}\left(\frac{x_0}{a}\right) + 2K_0\left(45a^4B_2 - 8B_4x_0^2 + 12a^2\left(B_4 - 3B_2x_0^2\right)\right)\mathrm{asin}\left(\frac{x_0}{a}\right)$$

$$+12a^2H\pi\Omega^p\cos\left(\frac{p\pi}{2}\right) - 8H\pi x_0^2\Omega^p\cos\left(\frac{p\pi}{2}\right)\right)\left(4K_0(2B_1 - x_0)\sqrt{1-\left(\frac{x_0}{a}\right)^2}\right.$$

$$-4K_0(2B_5 + x_0)\sqrt{1-\left(\frac{x_0}{a}\right)^2} + 2K_0x_0\sqrt{1-\left(\frac{x_0}{a}\right)^2}\left(3a^2B_2 + 4B_4 + 2B_2x_0^2\right) - 8aK_0\mathrm{acos}\left(\frac{x_0}{a}\right)$$

$$-2a\left(3a^2B_2 + 4B_4\right)K_0\mathrm{asin}\left(\frac{x_0}{a}\right) - a\pi\left(4K_1 + 3a^2K_3 - 4\Omega^2 + 4H\Omega^p\cos\left(\frac{p\pi}{2}\right)\right)\right)$$

$$+x_0^2\left(4K_0(2B_1 - x_0)\sqrt{1-\left(\frac{x_0}{a}\right)^2} - 4K_0(2B_5 + x_0)\sqrt{1-\left(\frac{x_0}{a}\right)^2} + 2K_0x_0\sqrt{1-\left(\frac{x_0}{a}\right)^2}\left(3a^2B_2 + 4B_4 + 2B_2x_0^2\right)\right.$$

$$-8aK_0\mathrm{acos}\left(\frac{x_0}{a}\right) - 2a\left(3a^2B_2 + 4B_4\right)K_0\mathrm{asin}\left(\frac{x_0}{a}\right)$$

$$-a\pi\left(4K_1 + 3a^2K_3 - 4\Omega^2 + 4H\Omega^p\cos\left(\frac{p\pi}{2}\right)\right)\right)\left(8a^2K_0x_0 - 2a^2\left(3a^2B_2 + 4B_4\right)K_0x_0\right.$$

$$-4K_0(2B_1 - x_0)x_0^2 + 4K_0x_0^2(2B_5 + x_0) - 12a^2B_2K_0x_0(a^2 - x_0^2) - 2K_0x_0^3\left(3a^2B_2 + 4B_4 + 2B_2x_0^2\right)$$

$$+8a^3K_0\sqrt{1-\left(\frac{x_0}{a}\right)^2}\mathrm{acos}\left(\frac{x_0}{a}\right) + 12a^5B_2K_0\sqrt{1-\left(\frac{x_0}{a}\right)^2}\mathrm{asin}\left(\frac{x_0}{a}\right) + 2a^3\left(3a^2B_2 + 4B_4\right)$$

$$\times K_0\sqrt{1-\left(\frac{x_0}{a}\right)^2}\mathrm{asin}\left(\frac{x_0}{a}\right) + a^3\pi\sqrt{1-\left(\frac{x_0}{a}\right)^2}\left(4K_1 + 9a^2K_3 - 4\Omega^2 + 4H\Omega^p\cos\left(\frac{p\pi}{2}\right)\right)\right)$$

$$+3\left(a^2 - x_0^2\right)\left(4K_0(2B_1 - x_0)\sqrt{1-\left(\frac{x_0}{a}\right)^2} - 4K_0(2B_5 + x_0)\sqrt{1-\left(\frac{x_0}{a}\right)^2}\right.$$

$$+2K_0x_0\sqrt{1-\left(\frac{x_0}{a}\right)^2}\left(3a^2B_2 + 4B_4 + 2B_2x_0^2\right) - 8aK_0\mathrm{acos}\left(\frac{x_0}{a}\right) - 2a\left(3a^2B_2 + 4B_4\right)K_0\mathrm{asin}\left(\frac{x_0}{a}\right)$$

$$-a\pi\left(4K_1 + 3a^2K_3 - 4\Omega^2 + 4H\Omega^p\cos\left(\frac{p\pi}{2}\right)\right)\right)\left(8a^2K_0x_0 - 2a^2\left(3a^2B_2 + 4B_4\right)K_0x_0\right.$$

$$-4K_0(2B_1 - x_0)x_0^2 + 4K_0x_0^2(2B_5 + x_0) - 12a^2B_2K_0x_0(a^2 - x_0^2) - 2K_0x_0^3\left(3a^2B_2 + 4B_4 + 2B_2x_0^2\right)$$

$$+8a^3K_0\sqrt{1-\left(\frac{x_0}{a}\right)^2}\mathrm{acos}\left(\frac{x_0}{a}\right) + 12a^5B_2K_0\sqrt{1-\left(\frac{x_0}{a}\right)^2}\mathrm{asin}\left(\frac{x_0}{a}\right) + 2a^3\left(3a^2B_2 + 4B_4\right)$$

$$\times K_0\sqrt{1-\left(\frac{x_0}{a}\right)^2}\mathrm{asin}\left(\frac{x_0}{a}\right) + a^3\pi\sqrt{1-\left(\frac{x_0}{a}\right)^2}\left(4K_1 + 9a^2K_3 - 4\Omega^2 + 4H\Omega^p\cos\left(\frac{p\pi}{2}\right)\right)\right)$$

$$+ 16a^6\pi^2\left(1 - \left(\frac{x_0}{a}\right)^2\right)^{3/2}\left(2\zeta\Omega + H\Omega^p\sin\left(\frac{p\pi}{2}\right)\right)^2\right) / \left(8a^6\pi^2\left(1 - \left(\frac{x_0}{a}\right)^2\right)^{3/2}\right)$$

References

1. Cao, Q.J.; Wiercigroch, M.; Pavlovskaia, E.E.; Grebogi, C.; Thompson, J.M.T. Archetypal oscillator for smooth and discontinuous dynamics. *Phys. Rev. E* **2006**, *74*, 046218. [CrossRef]
2. Ashwani, K.P.; Nalin, A.C.; Dennis, S.B.; Sanjay, P.B.; Anthony, M.W. Feedback stabilization of snap-through buckling in a preloaded two-bar linkage with hysteresis. *Int. J. Nonlinear Mech.* **2007**, *43*, 277–291.
3. Yang, T.; Liu, J.Y.; Cao, Q.J. Response analysis of the archetypal smooth and discontinuous oscillator for vibration energy harvesting. *Phys. A Stat. Mech. Its Appl.* **2018**, *507*, 358–373. [CrossRef]
4. Hao, Z.F.; Cao, Q.J.; Wiercigroch, M. Two-sided damping constraint control for high-performance vibration isolation and end-stop impact protection. *Nonlinear Dyn.* **2016**, *86*, 2129–2144. [CrossRef]
5. Avramov, K.V.; Mikhlin, Y.V. Snap-through truss as a vibration absorber. *J. Vib. Control* **2004**, *10*, 291–308. [CrossRef]
6. Brennan, M.J.; Elliott, S.J.; Bonello, P.; Vincent, J.F.V. The "click" mechanism in dipteran flight: If it exists, then what effect does it have? *J. Theor. Biol.* **2003**, *224*, 205–213. [CrossRef]
7. Ichiro, A.; Nakazawa, M. Non-linear dynamic behavior of multi-folding microstructure systems based on origami skill. *Int. J. Non-Linear Mech.* **2010**, *45*, 337–347.

8. Waite, J.J.; Virgin, L.N.; Wiebe, R. Competing responses in a discrete mechanical system. *Int. J. Bifurc. Chaos* **2014**, *24*, 1430003. [CrossRef]
9. Hao, Z.F.; Cao, Q.J. The isolation characteristics of an archetypal dynamical model with stable-quasi-zero-stiffness. *J. Sound Vib.* **2015**, *340*, 61–79. [CrossRef]
10. Hao, Z.F.; Cao, Q.J. A novel dynamical model for GVT nonlinear supporting system with stable-quasi-zero-stiffness. *J. Theor. Appl. Mech.* **2014**, *52*, 199–213.
11. Currier, T.M.; Lheron, S.; Modarres-Sadeghi, Y. A bio-inspired robotic fish utilizes the snap-through buckling of its spine to generate accelerations of more than 20 g. *Bioinspir. Biomim.* **2020**, *15*, 055006. [CrossRef]
12. Ding, H.; Chen, L.Q. Designs, analysis, and applications of nonlinear energy sinks. *Nonlinear Dyn.* **2020**, *100*, 3061–3107. [CrossRef]
13. Geng, X.F.; Ding, H.; Mao, X.Y.; Chen, L.Q. Nonlinear energy sink with limited vibration amplitude. *Mech. Syst. Signal Process.* **2021**, *156*, 107625. [CrossRef]
14. Jiang, W.A.; Chen, L.Q. Snap-through piezoelectric energy harvesting. *J. Sound Vib.* **2014**, *333*, 4314–4325. [CrossRef]
15. Speciale, A.; Ardito, R.; Marco, B.; Ferrari, M.; Ferrari, V.; Frangi, A.A. Snap-through buckling mechanism for frequency-up conversion in piezoelectric energy harvesting. *Appl. Sci.* **2020**, *10*, 3614. [CrossRef]
16. Myongwon, H.; Andres, F. Topological wave energy harvesting in bistable lattices. *Smart Mater. Struct.* **2022**, *31*, 015021.
17. Tan, D.G.; Zhou, J.X.; Wang, K.; Zhao, X.; Wang, Q.; Xu, D. Bow-type bistable triboelectric nanogenerator for harvesting energy from low-frequency vibration. *Nano Energy* **2022**, *92*, 106746. [CrossRef]
18. Cao, Q.J.; Wiercigroch, M.; Pavlovskaia, E.E.; Thompson, J.M.T.; Grebogi, C. Piecewise linear approach to an archetypal oscillator for smooth and discontinuous dynamics. *Philos. Trans. R. Soc. A Math. Phys. Eng. Sci.* **2008**, *366*, 635–652. [CrossRef]
19. Tian, R.L.; Cao, Q.J.; Li, Z.X. Hopf bifurcations for the recently proposed smooth-and-discontinuous oscillator. *Chin. Phys. Lett.* **2010**, *27*, 074701.
20. Tian, R.L.; Cao, Q.J.; Yang, S.P. The codimension-two bifurcation for the recent proposed SD oscillator. *Nonlinear Dyn.* **2010**, *59*, 19–27. [CrossRef]
21. Cao, Q.J.; Wiercigroch, M.; Pavlovskaia, E.E.; Grebogi, C.; Thompson, J.M.T. The limit case response of the archetypal oscillator for smooth and discontinuous dynamics. *Int. J. Non-Linear Mech.* **2008**, *43*, 462–473. [CrossRef]
22. Shen, J.; Li, Y.; Du, Z. Subharmonic and grazing bifurcations for a simple bilinear oscillator. *Int. J. Non-Linear Mech.* **2014**, *60*, 70–82. [CrossRef]
23. Han, Y.W.; Cao, Q.J.; Chen, Y.S.; Wiercigroch, M. A novel smooth and discontinuous oscillator with strong irrational nonlinearities. *Sci. China Phys. Mech. Astron.* **2012**, *55*, 1832–1843. [CrossRef]
24. Cao, Q.J.; Han, Y.W.; Liang, T.W.; Wiercigroch, M.; Piskarev, S. Multiple buckling and codimension-three bifurcation phenomena of a nonlinear oscillator. *Int. J. Bifurc. Chaos* **2014**, *24*, 1430005. [CrossRef]
25. Han, Y.W.; Cao, Q.; Chen, Y.S.; Wiercigroch, M. Chaotic thresholds for the piecewise linear discontinuous system with multiple well potentials. *Int. J. Non-Linear Mech.* **2015**, *70*, 145–152. [CrossRef]
26. Han, Y.W.; Cao, Q.J.; Ji, J. Nonlinear dynamics of a smooth and discontinuous oscillator with multiple stability. *Int. J. Bifurc. Chaos* **2015**, *25*, 1530038. [CrossRef]
27. Tian, R.L.; Wu, Q.L.; Yang, X.W.; Si, C.D. Chaotic threshold for the smooth-and-discontinuous oscillator under constant excitations. *Eur. Phys. J. Plus* **2013**, *128*, 80–91. [CrossRef]
28. Yue, X.L.; Xu, W.; Wang, L. Stochastic bifurcations in the SD (smooth and discontinuous) oscillator under bounded noise excitation. *Sci. China Phys.* **2013**, *56*, 1010–1016. [CrossRef]
29. Santhosh, B.; Padmanabhan, C.; Narayanan, S. Numeric-analytic solutions of the smooth and discontinuous oscillator. *Int. J. Mech. Sci.* **2014**, *84*, 102–119. [CrossRef]
30. Chen, H. Global analysis on the discontinuous limit case of a smooth oscillator. *Int. J. Bifurc. Chaos* **2016**, *26*, 1650061. [CrossRef]
31. Chen, H.B.; Jaume, L.; Tang, Y.L. Global dynamics of a SD oscillator. *Nonlinear Dyn.* **2018**, *91*, 1755–1777. [CrossRef]
32. Wang, L.; Xue, L.; Xu, W.; Yue, X. Stochastic P-bifurcation analysis of a fractional smooth and discontinuous oscillator via the generalized cell mapping method. *Int. J. Non-Linear Mech.* **2017**, *96*, 56–63. [CrossRef]
33. Chang, Y.J.; Chen, E.L.; Feng, M. Experimental study of the nonlinear dynamics of a smooth and discontinuous oscillator with different smoothness parameters and initial values. *J. Theor. Appl. Mech.* **2019**, *57*, 935–946. [CrossRef]
34. Mainardi, F. Fractional relaxation-oscillation and fractional diffusion-wave phenomena. *Chaos Solitons Fractals* **1996**, *7*, 1461–1477. [CrossRef]
35. Koeller, R.C. Applications of fractional calculus to the theory of viscoelasticity. *J. Appl. Mech.* **1984**, *51*, 299–307. [CrossRef]
36. Caputo, M.; Mainardi, F. A new dissipation model based on memory mechanism. *Pure Appl. Geophys.* **1971**, *91*, 134–147. [CrossRef]
37. Padovan, J.; Sawicki, J.T. Nonlinear vibrations of fractionally damped systems. *Nonlinear Dyn.* **1998**, *16*, 321–336. [CrossRef]
38. Chang, Y.J.; Tian, W.W.; Chen, E.L.; Shen, Y.J.; Xing, W.C. Dynamic model for the nonlinear hysteresis of metal rubber based on the fractional-order derivative. *J. Vib. Shock* **2020**, *39*, 233–241.
39. Caputo, M. Linear models of dissipation whose Q is almost frequency independent. *Ann. Geophys.* **1966**, *19*, 383–393. [CrossRef]
40. Caputo, M. Linear model of dissipation whose Q is almost frequency independent-II. *Geophys. J. Int.* **2007**, *13*, 239–529. [CrossRef]
41. Tarasov, V.E.; Zaslavsky, G.M. Dynamics with low-level fractionality. *Phys. A Stat. Mech. Its Appl.* **2006**, *368*, 399–415. [CrossRef]

Article

Symmetry Analysis and PT-Symmetric Extension of the Fifth-Order Korteweg-de Vries-Like Equation

Gangwei Wang *,†, Bo Shen, Mengyue He †, Fei Guan and Lihua Zhang †

School of Mathematics and Statistics, Hebei University of Economics and Business, Shijiazhuang 050061, China
* Correspondence: wanggangwei@heuet.edu.cn
† These authors contributed equally to this work.

Abstract: In the present paper, PT-symmetric extension of the fifth-order Korteweg-de Vries-like equation are investigated. Several special equations with PT symmetry are obtained by choosing different values, for which their symmetries are obtained simultaneously. In particular, for the particular equation, its conservation laws are obtained, including conservation of momentum and conservation of energy. Reciprocal Bäcklund transformations of conservation laws of momentum and energy are presented for the first time. The important thing is that for the special case of $\epsilon = 3$, the corresponding time fractional case are studied by Lie group method. And what is interesting is that the symmetry of the time fractional equation is obtained, and based on the symmetry, this equation is reduced to a fractional ordinary differential equation. Finally, for the general case, the symmetry of this equation is obtained, and based on the symmetry, the reduced equation is presented. Through the results obtained in this paper, it can be found that the Lie group method is a very effective method, which can be used to deal with many models in natural phenomena.

Keywords: PT-symmetric; fifth-order Korteweg-de vries-like equation; symmetry analysis; conservation laws

1. Introduction

The authors [1] considered the complex PT-symmetric extension of the classical Korteweg-de Vries (KdV) equation

$$u_t - iu(iu_x)^\epsilon + u_{xxx} = 0, \quad (1)$$

where i is the imaginary unit, they discussed the features of these equations for $\epsilon = 0, 1, 3, 2n + 1$. Indeed, the classical KdV equation is PT symmetric, however is not symmetric under P or T. PT symmetric quantum mechanics is related to many integrable models [1–3]. If $\epsilon = 1$, this situation is the classical KdV equation, which has been studied in a large amount of papers. For more description on the classical KdV equation, see [1] and references therein.

Based on the results of [1], the following fifth-order KdV-like equation will be considered in the present paper

$$u_t - iu(iu_x)^\epsilon + \alpha u_{xxx} + \beta u_{xxxxx} = 0, \quad (2)$$

it is clear that this equation is also PT symmetric. This equation includes fifth order nonlinear dispersion term. If $\beta = 0$, it reduced to Equation (3) [1]. While $\alpha = 0$, this equation becomes the fifth-order KdV equation. In general, objectively speaking, higher order equations are more difficult to handle than lower order equations. This is because we know that the higher the order of the equation, the more difficult it will be to calculate and the longer it will take to process. Indeed, there are many nonlinear natural phenomena that might be more reasonably described using higher order nonlinear evolution equations (NLEEs).

Because of the importance of NLEEs, there are many approaches there to deal with them, some of which include but are not limited to, for example, the Hirota bilinear method [4], the inverse scattering transformation method [5], Darboux transformations [6], the structure-preserving method [7–9], the Lie symmetry method [10–18], and so on.

If $\epsilon = 1$ for Equation (2), it is the general Kawahara equation. There have been many papers have investigated Kawahara type equations, including exact solutions, symmetry, etc. Kawahara [19] derived this equation. The author [20] studied solitary wave solution for the generalized Kawahara equation. New solitons solutions and periodic solutions are derived in [21]. Nonlinear self-adjointness of a generalized fifth-order KdV equation are studied in [22]. The author [23] considered symmetry analysis and exact solutions to the fifth-order KdV types of equations. Homotopy analysis method is used to study the Kawahara equation [24]. New analytical cnoidal and solitary wave solutions of the Extended Kawahara equation are presented in [25].

From the known literature, for the PT-symmetric extension of the higher-order fifth-order KdV equation, so far, there is no corresponding references to study this equation. In view of this, this paper uses the symmetry method to systematically study this equation. For different parameters of ϵ, the symmetry of these equations are investigated separately, and especially for $\epsilon = 1$, the conservation law of this equation are derived. The interesting thing is that the reciprocal Bäcklund transformations of the conservation of momentum and energy are presented for this equation.

In Section 2, symmetry analysis and conservation laws of this Equation (2) for $\epsilon = 1$ are presented. In Section 3, symmetry analysis and travelling wave solutions for $\epsilon = 0$ are displayed. Symmetry analysis for $\epsilon = 3$ are derived, and the time fractional form of this equation is studied in Section 4. Symmetry analysis and reductions for $\epsilon = 2n + 1$ are given in Section 5. In the last Section 6, the conclusion of this paper is obtained.

2. Symmetry Analysis and Conservation Laws for $\epsilon = 1$

2.1. Symmetry Analysis

If $\epsilon = 1$, one can get

$$u_t + u(u_x) + \alpha u_{xxx} + \beta u_{xxxxx} = 0, \tag{3}$$

this is the general Kawahara equation [22,23,26–29], the Lie algebra is spanned by the following vector fields

$$V_1 = t\frac{\partial}{\partial x} + \frac{\partial}{\partial u}, V_2 = \frac{\partial}{\partial t}, V_3 = \frac{\partial}{\partial x}. \tag{4}$$

Additionally, one can get the high order Lie-Bäcklund symmetries as follows

$$\eta_u = c_2 t u_x + c_3 u u_x + c_1 u_x + c_3 u_{xxx} + c_3 u_{xxxxx} - c_2. \tag{5}$$

2.2. Conservation Laws

For the one-dimensional case, the conservation law can be written in the following form

$$T^t + T^x = 0, \tag{6}$$

using the method proposed in [11], the following multiplier can be obtained

$$\Lambda = c_1 u_t - c_1 x + c_2 u_{xxxx} + c_2 \frac{\alpha}{\beta} u_{xx} + c_2 \frac{u^2}{2\beta} + c_3 u + c_4, \tag{7}$$

for this multiplier, one can get the following conservation laws:
Conservation of momentum P:

$$\partial_t(u) + \partial_x\left(\frac{1}{2}u^2 + \alpha u_{xx} + \beta u_{xxxx}\right) = 0, \tag{8}$$

thus,
$$\frac{d}{dt}P = 0, P = \int_{-\infty}^{\infty} u\, dx. \tag{9}$$

Conservation of Energy E:
$$\partial_t\left(\frac{1}{2}u^2\right) + \partial_x\left(\frac{1}{3}u^3 + \alpha u u_{xx} + \beta u u_{xxxx} - \frac{1}{2}\alpha u_x^2 + \frac{1}{2}\beta u_{xx}^2 - \beta u_x u_{xxx}\right) = 0, \tag{10}$$

thus,
$$\frac{d}{dt}E = 0, E = \int_{-\infty}^{\infty} u^2\, dx. \tag{11}$$

In addition, the other two conservation laws are
$$\begin{aligned}
T^t &= \frac{1}{2}u^2 t - ux, \\
T^x &= \frac{1}{3}u^3 t - \frac{1}{2}u^2 x + \alpha u t u_{xx} + \beta u t u_{xxxx} - \frac{1}{2}\alpha t u_x^2 - \beta t u_x u_{xxx} \\
&\quad + \frac{1}{2}\beta t u_{xx}^2 + \alpha u_x - \alpha x u_{xx} + \beta u_{xxx} - x\beta u_{xxxx},
\end{aligned} \tag{12}$$

and
$$\begin{aligned}
T^t &= \frac{1}{6\beta} u\left(3\alpha u_{xx} + 3\beta u_{xxxx} + u^2\right), \\
T^x &= \frac{1}{8\beta}\left(4\alpha^2 u_{xx}^2 + 8\alpha\beta u_{xx} u_{xxxx} + 4\alpha u^2 u_{xx} + 4\beta^2 u_{xxxx}^2 + 4\beta u^2 u_{xxxx} + u^4 - 4\alpha u u_{tx}\right. \\
&\quad \left. + 4\alpha u_t u_x - 4\beta u u_{txxx} + 4\beta u_t u_{xxx} - 4\beta u_{tx} u_{xx} + 4\beta u_{txx} u_x\right).
\end{aligned} \tag{13}$$

2.3. Reciprocal Bäcklund Transformations to Conservation of Momentum and Energy

In order to get reciprocal Bäcklund transformations to conservation of Momentum and Energy, we consider the following results [30]

$$\begin{aligned}
(T^t)'_{t'} + (T^x)'_{x'} &= 0, \\
\frac{\partial}{\partial t'} &= \frac{F}{T}\frac{\partial}{\partial x} + \frac{\partial}{\partial t}, \frac{\partial}{\partial x'} = \frac{1}{T}\frac{\partial}{\partial x}.
\end{aligned} \tag{14}$$

From this transformation, it should be possible to obtain the following statement:

Corollary 1. *Reciprocal Bäcklund transformations to conservation of Momentum*

$$\begin{cases} (T^t)' = \frac{1}{u}, \\ (T^x)' = -\frac{\left(\frac{1}{2}u^2 + \alpha u_{xx} + \beta u_{xxxx}\right)}{u}. \end{cases} \tag{15}$$

Proof. First, one has

$$\begin{aligned}
(T^t)'_{t'} &= \frac{\left(\frac{1}{2}u^2 + \alpha u_{xx} + \beta u_{xxxx}\right)}{u}\frac{-u_x}{u^2} + \frac{-u_t}{u^2} \\
&= \frac{-\left(\frac{1}{2}u^2 + \alpha u_{xx} + \beta u_{xxxx}\right)u_x - u u_t}{u^3}, \\
(T^x)'_{x'} &= \frac{1}{u}\left(-\frac{\left(\frac{1}{2}u^2 + \alpha u_{xx} + \beta u_{xxxx}\right)}{u}\right)_x = \\
&\quad \frac{-\left(\frac{1}{2}u^2 + \alpha u_{xx} + \beta u_{xxxx}\right)_x u + u_x\left(\frac{1}{2}u^2 + \alpha u_{xx} + \beta u_{xxxx}\right)}{u^3}.
\end{aligned} \tag{16}$$

Thus,

$$(T^t)'_{t'} + (T^x)'_{x'} = \frac{-\left(\frac{1}{2}u^2 + \alpha u_{xx} + \beta u_{xxxx}\right)u_x - uu_t}{u^3}$$
$$+ \frac{-\left(\frac{1}{2}u^2 + \alpha u_{xx} + \beta u_{xxxx}\right)_x u + u_x\left(\frac{1}{2}u^2 + \alpha u_{xx} + \beta u_{xxxx}\right)}{u^3} \quad (17)$$
$$= \frac{-uu_t - \left(\frac{1}{2}u^2 + \alpha u_{xx} + \beta u_{xxxx}\right)_x u}{u^3} = 0.$$

In the same proof process, one can get

Corollary 2. *Reciprocal Bäcklund transformations to conservation of energy:*

$$\begin{cases} (T^t)' = \frac{2}{u^2}, \\ (T^x)' = -\frac{2\left(\frac{1}{3}u^3 + \alpha u u_{xx} + \beta u u_{xxxx} - \frac{1}{2}\alpha u_x^2 + \frac{1}{2}\beta u_{xx}^2 - \beta u_x u_{xxx}\right)}{u^2}. \end{cases} \quad (18)$$

□

3. Symmetry Analysis and Travelling Wave Solutions for $\epsilon = 0$
3.1. Symmetry Analysis

While $\epsilon = 0$, one has

$$u_t - iu + \alpha u_{xxx} + \beta u_{xxxxx} = 0, \quad (19)$$

using the transformation

$$u(x,t) = e^{it}v(x,t), \quad (20)$$

one obtains the following linear partial differential equation (PDE):

$$v_t + \alpha v_{xxx} + \beta v_{xxxxx} = 0, \quad (21)$$

as it is a linear equation, it contains an infinite number of conservation laws.
The corresponding vector field can be obtained as follows

$$V_1 = v\frac{\partial}{\partial v}, V_2 = \frac{\partial}{\partial t}, V_3 = \frac{\partial}{\partial x}, V_4 = F\frac{\partial}{\partial v}, \quad (22)$$

where F satisfy the following PDE:

$$F_t + \alpha F_{xxx} + \beta F_{xxxxx} = 0. \quad (23)$$

3.2. Travelling Wave Solutions

For the travelling wave transformation $V_2 + \lambda V_3$, the invariant and invariant functions are

$$\xi = x - \lambda t, v = v(\xi), \quad (24)$$

substituting Equation (24) into Equation (21), one has

$$-\lambda v' + \alpha v''' + \beta v^{(5)} = 0, \quad (25)$$

solving this equation, one can get

$$v(\xi) = c_1 e^{-\frac{1}{2}\frac{\sqrt{-2\beta\left(\alpha + \sqrt{\alpha^2 + 4\beta\lambda}\right)}\xi}{\beta}} + c_2 e^{\frac{1}{2}\frac{\sqrt{-2\beta\left(\alpha + \sqrt{\alpha^2 + 4\beta\lambda}\right)}\xi}{\beta}}$$
$$+ c_3 e^{-\frac{1}{2}\frac{\sqrt{2}\sqrt{\beta\left(-\alpha + \sqrt{\alpha^2 + 4\beta\lambda}\right)}\xi}{\beta}} + c_4 e^{\frac{1}{2}\frac{\sqrt{2}\sqrt{\beta\left(-\alpha + \sqrt{\alpha^2 + 4\beta\lambda}\right)}\xi}{\beta}}, \quad (26)$$

where c_1, c_2, c_3, c_4 are constants. Putting (26) into (20), one can get

$$u(x,t) = e^{it}\left(c_1 e^{-\frac{1}{2}\sqrt{\frac{-2\beta\left(\alpha+\sqrt{\alpha^2+4\beta\lambda}\right)}{\beta}}(x-\lambda t)} + c_2 e^{\frac{1}{2}\sqrt{\frac{-2\beta\left(\alpha+\sqrt{\alpha^2+4\beta\lambda}\right)}{\beta}}(x-\lambda t)} \right. \tag{27}$$

$$\left. + c_3 e^{-\frac{1}{2}\frac{\sqrt{2}\sqrt{\beta\left(-\alpha+\sqrt{\alpha^2+4\beta\lambda}\right)}(x-\lambda t)}{\beta}} + c_4 e^{\frac{1}{2}\frac{\sqrt{2}\sqrt{\beta\left(-\alpha+\sqrt{\alpha^2+4\beta\lambda}\right)}(x-\lambda t)}{\beta}}\right).$$

4. Symmetry Analysis for $\epsilon = 3$

When $\epsilon = 3$, from Equation (2), one should obtain the following PDE

$$u_t - u(u_x)^3 + \alpha u_{xxx} + \beta u_{xxxxx} = 0, \tag{28}$$

unfortunately, we cannot write this equation in the form of a conservation law. However, it is still possible to study this equation using the symmetry method.

If $\alpha \neq 0, \beta = 0$, this equation reduces approximately to Equation (10) in [1]

$$u_t - u(u_x)^3 + \alpha u_{xxx} = 0. \tag{29}$$

After tedious calculations, one can obtain

$$V_1 = x\frac{\partial}{\partial x} + 3t\frac{\partial}{\partial t}, V_2 = \frac{\partial}{\partial t}, V_3 = \frac{\partial}{\partial x}. \tag{30}$$

When $\alpha = 0, \beta \neq 0$, the following vector fields are derived

$$V_1 = 3x\frac{\partial}{\partial x} + 15t\frac{\partial}{\partial t} - 2u\frac{\partial}{\partial u}, V_2 = \frac{\partial}{\partial t}, V_3 = \frac{\partial}{\partial x}. \tag{31}$$

While $\alpha \neq 0, \beta \neq 0$, one gets the vector fields are as follows:

$$V_1 = \frac{\partial}{\partial t}, V_2 = \frac{\partial}{\partial x}. \tag{32}$$

Symmetry Analysis for Time Fractional form of Equation (28)

For this case, one can have

$$u_t^\gamma - u(u_x)^3 + \alpha u_{xxx} + \beta u_{xxxxx} = 0, \tag{33}$$

where $0 < \gamma \leq 1$, it is clear that this equation is a new PDE. If $\gamma = 1$, in the discussion above, this equation has PT symmetry. To study the more general case, we again use Lie symmetry to study this equation. Generally speaking, because this is a fractional differential equation, due to the nature of fractional differential equations, if the Lie symmetry method is used to study it, it is slightly different from the ordinary Lie symmetry method.

Firstly, considering the following one parameter Lie group of point transformations [31,32]

$$\begin{aligned}
t^* &= t + \epsilon\tau(x,t,u) + O(\epsilon^2),\\
x^* &= x + \epsilon\xi(x,t,u) + O(\epsilon^2),\\
u^* &= u + \epsilon\eta(x,t,u) + O(\epsilon^2),\\
\frac{\partial^\gamma \bar{u}}{\partial \bar{t}^\gamma} &= \frac{\partial^\gamma u}{\partial t^\gamma} + \epsilon\eta_\gamma^0(x,t,u) + O(\epsilon^2),\\
\frac{\partial^3 \bar{u}}{\partial \bar{x}^3} &= \frac{\partial^3 u}{\partial x^3} + \epsilon\eta^{xxx}(x,t,u) + O(\epsilon^2),\\
\frac{\partial^5 \bar{u}}{\partial \bar{x}^5} &= \frac{\partial^5 u}{\partial x^5} + \epsilon\eta^{xxxxx}(x,t,u) + O(\epsilon^2),
\end{aligned} \tag{34}$$

where

$$\begin{aligned}
\eta^x &= D_x(\eta) - u_x D_x(\xi) - u_t D_x(\tau), \\
\eta^{xx} &= D_x(\eta^x) - u_{xt} D_x(\tau) - u_{xx} D_x(\xi), \\
\eta^{xxx} &= D_x(\eta^{xx}) - u_{xxt} D_x(\tau) - u_{xxx} D_x(\xi), \\
\eta^{xxxx} &= D_x(\eta^{xxx}) - u_{xxxt} D_x(\tau) - u_{xxxx} D_x(\xi), \\
\eta^{xxxxx} &= D_x(\eta^{xxxx}) - u_{xxxxt} D_x(\tau) - u_{xxxxx} D_x(\xi),
\end{aligned} \tag{35}$$

where D_x is given by the following results

$$D_x = \frac{\partial}{\partial x} + u_x \frac{\partial}{\partial u} + u_{xx} \frac{\partial}{\partial u_x} + u_{xxx} \frac{\partial}{\partial u_{xx}} + u_{xxxx} \frac{\partial}{\partial u_{xxx}} + u_{xxxxx} \frac{\partial}{\partial u_{xxxx}} + \cdots, \tag{36}$$

the infinitesimal generator is given by

$$V = \tau(x,t,u)\frac{\partial}{\partial t} + \xi(x,t,u)\frac{\partial}{\partial x} + \eta(x,t,u)\frac{\partial}{\partial u}. \tag{37}$$

From [31,32], one has

$$\eta_\gamma^0 = D_t^\gamma(\eta) - \gamma D_t(\tau)\frac{\partial^\gamma u}{\partial t^\gamma} - \sum_{n=1}^\infty \binom{\gamma}{n} D_t^n(\xi) D_t^{\gamma-n}(u_x) - \sum_{n=1}^\infty \binom{\gamma}{n+1} D_t^{n+1}(\tau) D_t^{\gamma-n}(u), \tag{38}$$

and

$$D_t^\gamma(\eta) = \frac{\partial^\gamma \eta}{\partial t^\gamma} + \eta_u \frac{\partial^\gamma u}{\partial t^\gamma} - u\frac{\partial^\gamma \eta_u}{\partial t^\gamma} + \sum_{n=1}^\infty \binom{\gamma}{n} \frac{\partial^n \eta_u}{\partial t^n} D_t^{\gamma-n}(u) + \mu, \tag{39}$$

where

$$\mu = \sum_{n=2}^\infty \sum_{m=2}^n \sum_{k=2}^m \sum_{r=0}^{k-1} \binom{\gamma}{n}\binom{n}{m}\binom{k}{r}\frac{1}{k!}\frac{t^{n-\gamma}}{\Gamma(n+1-\gamma)}[-u]^r \frac{\partial^m}{\partial t^m}[u^{k-r}]\frac{\partial^{n-m+k}\eta}{\partial t^{n-m}\partial u^k}, \tag{40}$$

and

$$\begin{aligned}
\eta_\gamma^0 &= \frac{\partial^\gamma \eta}{\partial t^\gamma} + (\eta_u - \gamma D_t(\tau))\frac{\partial^\gamma u}{\partial t^\gamma} - u\frac{\partial^\gamma \eta_u}{\partial t^\gamma} + \mu \\
&+ \sum_{n=1}^\infty \left[\binom{\gamma}{n}\frac{\partial^\gamma \eta_u}{\partial t^\gamma} - \binom{\gamma}{n+1}D_t^{n+1}(\tau)\right]D_t^{\gamma-n}(u) \\
&- \sum_{n=1}^\infty \binom{\gamma}{n}D_t^n(\xi)D_t^{\gamma-n}(u_x).
\end{aligned} \tag{41}$$

From the above analysis, it can be seen that, if $\alpha \neq 0, \beta \neq 0$, for this general case, the vector fields are shown by:

$$V_1 = \frac{\partial}{\partial x}. \tag{42}$$

When $\alpha \neq 0, \beta = 0$, one can obtain the following equation

$$u_t^\gamma - u(u_x)^3 + \alpha u_{xxx} = 0, \tag{43}$$

if $\gamma = 1$, it is can be found in paper [1]. Based on the above analysis, one can get

$$V_1 = x\frac{\partial}{\partial x} + 3t\frac{\partial}{\partial t}, V_2 = \frac{\partial}{\partial x}. \tag{44}$$

While $\alpha = 0, \beta \neq 0$, one has

$$u_t^\gamma - u(u_x)^3 + \beta u_{xxxxx} = 0, \tag{45}$$

vector fields are presented as follows

$$V_1 = 3x\gamma \frac{\partial}{\partial x} + 15t\frac{\partial}{\partial t} - 2\gamma u\frac{\partial}{\partial u}, V_2 = \frac{\partial}{\partial x}. \tag{46}$$

Now for the operator V_1, one has the corresponding characteristic equations as follows

$$\frac{dx}{3x} = \frac{\gamma dt}{15t} = \frac{-du}{2u}, \tag{47}$$

solving this equation generates the following similarity variable and functions

$$\xi = xt^{-\frac{\gamma}{5}}, \quad u = t^{-\frac{2\gamma}{15}}f(\xi), \tag{48}$$

using the Erdelyi-Kober fractional differential operator $P_\beta^{\tau,\alpha}$ of order [31,32]

$$(P_\beta^{\tau,\alpha} g) := \prod_{j=0}^{n-1}\left(\tau + j - \frac{1}{\beta}\xi\frac{d}{d\xi}\right)(K_\beta^{\tau+\alpha,n-\alpha}g)(\xi), \tag{49}$$

$$n = \begin{cases} [\alpha] + 1, & \alpha \notin \mathbb{N}, \\ \alpha, & \alpha \in \mathbb{N}, \end{cases} \tag{50}$$

and the Erdélyi-Kober fractional integral operator [31,32]

$$(K_\beta^{\tau,\alpha}g)(\xi) := \begin{cases} \frac{1}{\Gamma(\alpha)}\int_1^\infty (u-1)^{\alpha-1}u^{-(\tau+\alpha)}g(\xi u^{\frac{1}{\beta}})du, & \alpha > 0, \\ g(\xi), & \alpha = 0 \end{cases} \tag{51}$$

one can reduce Equation (2) into an ordinary differential equation of fractional order as follows

$$\left(P_{\frac{5}{\gamma}}^{1-\frac{2\gamma}{15}-\gamma,\gamma}f\right)(\xi) = uu_\xi^3 - \beta f_{\xi\xi\xi\xi\xi}. \tag{52}$$

5. Symmetry Analysis and Reductions for $\epsilon = 2n+1$

5.1. Symmetry Analysis

When $\epsilon = 2n+1$ is an odd integer, for this case, one has

$$u_t + (-1)^n u(u_x)^{2n+1} + \alpha u_{xxx} + \beta u_{xxxxx} = 0, \tag{53}$$

for the general case, one can derive the following vector fields

$$V_1 = \frac{\partial}{\partial t}, V_2 = \frac{\partial}{\partial x}. \tag{54}$$

5.2. Reductions

Case 1: V_2

For this case, invariant and invariant functions are

$$\xi = x, u = u(\xi), \tag{55}$$

substituting Equation (55) into Equation (53), one can get

$$(-1)^n u(u_\xi)^{2n+1} + \alpha u_{\xi\xi\xi} + \beta u_{\xi\xi\xi\xi\xi} = 0. \tag{56}$$

Case 2: V_1

In this case, one has invariant and invariant functions

$$\tau = t, u = u(\tau), \tag{57}$$

putting Equation (57) into Equation (53), one obtains

$$u_\tau = 0,\tag{58}$$

from Equation (58) only a trivial solution can be obtained.

Case 3: $V_2 + \lambda V_3$

It is clear that this is travelling wave transformation, one can get the invariant and invariant functions are

$$\zeta = x - \lambda t, u = u(\zeta),\tag{59}$$

substituting Equation (59) into Equation (53), one has

$$-\lambda u_\zeta + (-1)^n u(u_\zeta)^{2n+1} + \alpha u_{\zeta\zeta\zeta} + \beta u_{\zeta\zeta\zeta\zeta\zeta} = 0.\tag{60}$$

6. Conclusions

In this paper, symmetries and PT-symmetric extension of the fifth-order KdV-like equation are considered. Taking different values for ϵ, several different equations with PT symmetry properties are obtained. And using the symmetry method, the symmetries of these equations are obtained. In particular, for ϵ equal to 1, this equation was systematically studied and its symmetry as well as conservation laws are obtained. It should be emphasized that the reciprocal Bäcklund transformations of conservation laws of momentum and energy are derived. For the special case of $\epsilon = 3$, the corresponding integer order and fractional order symmetry are discussed, and for the time fractional order form, the equation is simplified into a fractional order ordinary differential equation on the basis of symmetry. Finally, the general case is considered, for which two symmetries are obtained.

In conclusion, this paper has shown the following two results, the first one is to preserve the PT symmetry, and the second one is how to extend symmetry analysis to fifth-order KdV-like equations. However for other cases such as variable coefficients, they will be investigated in future work.

Author Contributions: Validation, F.G.; Formal analysis, M.H.; Investigation, B.S.; Writing—original draft, G.W.; Writing—review and editing, L.Z. All authors have read and agreed to the published version of the manuscript.

Funding: This research was funded by "333 Talent Project" of Hebei Province (C20221021), Key Program of Hebei University of Economics and Business (2020ZD11), Youth Team Support Program of Hebei University of Economics and Business, Study on system dynamics of sci- entific and technological innovation promoting the expansion and quality of residents' consumption in Hebei Province (20556201D), Youth Top-notch Talent Support Program of Higher Education of Hebei Province of China (BJ2020011), Science and Technology Program of Colleges and Universities in Hebei Province (QN2020144), Scientific Research and Development Program Fund Project of Hebei University of Economics and Business (2020YB15), National Natural Science Foundation of China (12105073).

Institutional Review Board Statement: Not applicable.

Informed Consent Statement: Not applicable.

Data Availability Statement: Not applicable.

Acknowledgments: The authors are very grateful to the Editors and anonymous referees for their valuable comments and suggestions.

Conflicts of Interest: The authors declare no conflict of interest.

References

1. Bender, C.M.; Brody, D.C.; Chen, J.H.; Furlan, E. PT-symmetric extension of the Korteweg-de Vries equation. *J. Phys. A Math. Theor.* **2007**, *40*, F153–F160. [CrossRef]
2. Bender, C.M.; Boettcher, S. Real spectra in non-Hermitian Hamiltonians having PT symmetry. *Phys. Rev. Lett.* **1997**, *80*, 5243–5246. [CrossRef]

3. Zhou, Q.; Biswas, A. Optical solitons in parity-time-symmetric mixed linear and nonlinear lattice with non-Kerr law nonlinearity. *Superlatt. Microstruc.* **2017**, *109*, 588–598. [CrossRef]
4. Hirota, R. Exact solution of the Korteweg-deVries equation for multiple colli- sions of solitons. *Phys. Rev. Lett.* **1971**, *27*, 1192–1194. [CrossRef]
5. Ablowitz, M.J.; Segur, H. *Solitons and the Inverse Scattering Transformation*; SIAM: Philadelphia, PA, USA, 1981.
6. Guo, B.L.; Ling, L.M.; Liu, Q.P. High-order solutions and generalized Darboux Transformations of derivative nonlinear Schrödinger equations. *Stud. Appl. Math.* **2013**, *130*, 317–344. [CrossRef]
7. Hu, W.; Wang, Z.; Zhao, Y.; Deng, Z. Symmetry breaking of infinite-dimensional dynamic system. *Appl. Math. Lett.* **2020**, *103*, 106207. [CrossRef]
8. Hu, W.; Xu, M.; Song, J.; Gao, Q.; Deng, Z. Coupling dynamic behaviors of flexible stretching Hub-Beam system. *Mech. Syst. Sign. Proc.* **2021**, *151*, 107389. [CrossRef]
9. Hu, W.; Yu, L.; Deng, Z. Minimum control energy of spatial beam with assumed attitude adjustment target. *Acta Mech. Soli. Sini.* **2020**, *33*, 51–60. [CrossRef]
10. Olver, P.J. *Application of Lie Group to Differential Equation*; Springer: New York, NY, USA, 1986.
11. Bluman, G.W.; Cheviakov, A.F.; Anco, S.C. *Applications of Symmetry Methods to Partial Differential Equations*; Springer: New York, NY, USA, 2010.
12. Vu, K.T.; Butcher, J.; Carminati, J. Similarity solutions of partial differential equations using DESOLV. *Comp. Phys. Comm.* **2007**, *176*, 682–693. [CrossRef]
13. Dimas, S.; Tsoubelis, D. SYM: A new symmetry-finding package for Mathematica. In *The 10 th International Conference in Modern Group Analysis*; Ibragimov, N.H., Sophocleous, C., Damianou, P.A., Eds.; University of Cyprus: Nicosia, Cyprus, 2005; pp. 64–70.
14. Zhao, Z.L.; He, L.; Lie, L. Symmetry, nonlocal symmetry analysis, and interaction of solutions of a (2 + 1)-dimensional KdV-mKdV equation. *Theor. Math. Phys.* **2021**, *206*, 142–162. [CrossRef]
15. Wang, G.; Wazwaz, A.M. A new (3 + 1)-dimensional KdV equation and mKdV equation with their corresponding fractional forms. *Fractals* **2022**, *30*, 2250081. [CrossRef]
16. Wang, G.; Wazwaz, A.M. On the modified Gardner type equation and its time fractional form. *Chaos Solitons Fractals* **2022**, *123*, 127768. [CrossRef]
17. Wang, G. A new (3 + 1)-dimensional Schrödinger equation: derivation, soliton solutions and conservation laws. *Nonlinear Dyn.* **2021**, *104*, 1595–1602. [CrossRef]
18. Wang, G. A novel (3 + 1)-dimensional sine-Gorden and a sinh-Gorden equation: Derivation, symmetries and conservation laws. *Appl. Math. Lett.* **2021**, *113*, 106768. [CrossRef]
19. Kawahara, T. Oscillatory solitary waves in dispersive media. *J. Phys. Soc. Japan* **1972**, *33*, 260–264. [CrossRef]
20. Biswas, A. Solitary wave solution for the generalized Kawahara equation. *Appl. Math. Lett.* **2009**, *22*, 208–210. [CrossRef]
21. Wazwaz, A.M. New solitary wave solutions to the modified Kawahara equation. *Phys. Lett. A* **2007**, *360*, 588–592. [CrossRef]
22. Freire, I.L.; Sampaio, J.C.S. Nonlinear self-adjointness of a generalized fifth-order KdV equation. *J. Phys. A Math. Theor.* **2012**, *45*, 032001. [CrossRef]
23. Liu, H.; Li, J.; Liu, L. Lie symmetry analysis, optimal systems and exact solutions to the fifth-order KdV types of equations. *J. Math. Anal. Appl.* **2010**, *368*, 551–558. [CrossRef]
24. Abbasbandy, S. Homotopy analysis method for the Kawahara equation. *Nonlinear Anal. Real.* **2010**, *11*, 307–312. [CrossRef]
25. El-Tantawy, S.A.; Salas, A.H.; Alharthi, M.R. Novel analytical cnoidal and solitary wave solutions of the Extended Kawahara equation. *Chaos. Soliton. Fract.* **2021**, *147*, 110965. [CrossRef]
26. El-Tantawy, S.A.; Salas, A.H.; Alyousef, H.A.; Alharthi, M.R. Novel exact and approximate solutions to the family of the forced damped Kawahara equation and modeling strong nonlinear waves in a plasma. *Chin. J. Phys.* **2022**, *77*, 2454–2471. [CrossRef]
27. Aljahdaly, N.H.; El-Tantawy, S.A. Novel anlytical solution to the damped Kawahara equation and its application for modeling the dissipative nonlinear structures in a fluid medium. *J. Ocean. Eng. Sci.* **2021**. [CrossRef]
28. El-Tantawy, S.A.; Salas, A.H.; Alharthi, M.R. On the dissipative extended Kawahara solitons and cnoidal waves in a collisional plasma: Novel analytical and numerical solutions. *Phys. Fluids* **2021**, *33*, 106101. [CrossRef]
29. Gandarias, M.L.; Rosa, M.; Recio, E.; Anco, S. Conservation laws and symmetries of a generalized Kawahara equation. *AIP Conf. Proc.* **2017**, *1836*, 020072. [CrossRef]
30. Kingston, J.G.; Rogers, C. Reciprocal Bäcklund transformations of conservation laws. *Phys. Lett. A* **1982**, *92*, 261–264.
31. Sahadevan, R.; Bakkyaraj, T. Invariant analysis of time fractional generalized Burgers and Korteweg-de Vries equations. *J. Math. Anal. Appl.* **2012**, *393*, 341–347. [CrossRef]
32. Wang, G.W.; Liu, X.Q.; Zhang, Y.Y. Lie symmetry analysis to the time fractional generalized fifth-order KdV equation. *Commun. Nonlinear Sci. Numer. Simul.* **2013**, *18*, 2321–2326. [CrossRef]

Article

A New Perspective on the Exact Solutions of the Local Fractional Modified Benjamin–Bona–Mahony Equation on Cantor Sets

Kang-Jia Wang * and Feng Shi

School of Physics and Electronic Information Engineering, Henan Polytechnic University, Jiaozuo 454003, China
* Correspondence: kangjiaw@hpu.edu.cn

Abstract: A new local fractional modified Benjamin–Bona–Mahony equation is proposed within the local fractional derivative in this study for the first time. By defining some elementary functions via the Mittag–Leffler function (MLF) on the Cantor sets (CSs), a set of nonlinear local fractional ordinary differential equations (NLFODEs) is constructed. Then, a fast algorithm namely Yang's special function method is employed to find the non-differentiable (ND) exact solutions. By this method, we can extract abundant exact solutions in just one step. Finally, the obtained solutions on the CS are outlined in the form of the 3-D plot. The whole calculation process clearly shows that Yang's special function method is simple and effective, and can be applied to investigate the exact ND solutions of the other local fractional PDEs.

Keywords: local fractional derivative; Mittag–Leffler function; Yang's special function method; cantor sets

Citation: Wang, K.-J.; Shi, F. A New Perspective on the Exact Solutions of the Local Fractional Modified Benjamin–Bona–Mahony Equation on Cantor Sets. *Fractal Fract.* **2023**, *7*, 72. https://doi.org/10.3390/fractalfract7010072

Academic Editors: Sameerah Jamal and Ricardo Almeida

Received: 30 November 2022
Revised: 28 December 2022
Accepted: 5 January 2023
Published: 9 January 2023

Copyright: © 2023 by the authors. Licensee MDPI, Basel, Switzerland. This article is an open access article distributed under the terms and conditions of the Creative Commons Attribution (CC BY) license (https://creativecommons.org/licenses/by/4.0/).

1. Introduction

As is known to all, many complex phenomena occurring in nature involving in optics [1–5], vibration [6,7], social and economic [8], thermal science [9,10], and others [11–13] can be modeled by the partial differential equations (PDEs). In recent years, the fractional derivative has been adopted to PDEs to describe many phenomena arising in scientific and engineering fields, such as physics [14–18], biology [19–21], chemistry [22–24], mechanics [25–27], communication engineering [28–31], and so on [32,33]. Finding the exact solution of the fractional partial differential equation is helpful to further understand and analyze the dynamic behavior of the fractional partial differential equation. Compared with the mathematical model with an integer derivative, the fractional derivative mathematical model can more accurately describe the complex phenomena. Recently, the local fractional derivative (LFD) has attracted wide attention in various fields and some outstanding research results have emerged. In [34], the q-homotopy analysis transform method is applied to study the local fractional Poisson equation. In [35], the local fractional Fokker Planck equation is proposed and the reduced differential transform method and local fractional series expansion method are considered. In [36], the factorization technique is derived to investigate some local fractional PDEs. In [37], the Sumudu transform method, alongside the Adomian decomposition method, is used to employ the local fractional PDEs. In [38], the Mittag–Leffler function-based method is adopted to find the non-differentiable exact solutions of the (2 + 1)-dimensional local fractional breaking soliton equation. In [39], the local fractional variational iteration method is presented to investigate the local fractional heat conduction equation. In [40], the extended rational fractal sine–cosine method is used and six sets of the exact solutions are obtained. In [41], the Local fractional Fourier series method is utilized to study the wave equations. Many other studies can be seen in [42–46]. On the inspiration of the latest research results about the LFD, we present a new local fractional modified Benjamin–Bona–Mahony equation (LFMBBME) below:

$$\frac{\partial^\vartheta \aleph_\vartheta}{\partial t^\vartheta} + \frac{\partial^\vartheta \aleph_\vartheta}{\partial x^\vartheta} + k\aleph_\vartheta^2 \frac{\partial^\vartheta \aleph_\vartheta}{\partial x^\vartheta} + \frac{\partial^{2\vartheta}}{x^{2\vartheta}}\left(\frac{\partial^\vartheta \aleph_\vartheta}{\partial t^\vartheta}\right) = 0, \qquad (1)$$

where $\vartheta(0 < \vartheta \leq 1)$ is the fractional order, $\frac{\partial^\vartheta \aleph_\vartheta}{\partial t^\vartheta}$ and $\frac{\partial^\vartheta \aleph_\vartheta}{\partial x^\vartheta}$ are the local fractional derivatives. The definitions are presented in Section 2. In this work, we aim to investigate the exact ND solutions of the LFMBBME via a fast algorithm known as Yang's special function method, which can avoid the complicated calculation process and obtain abundant exact solutions in one step. The ideas within work are expected to open up some new horizons in the study of local fractional PDEs. The rest of this article is structured as follows. In Section 2, the properties of the LFD and some special functions are presented. In Section 3, a set of nonlinear local fractional ODEs is constructed. In Section 4, Yang's special function method is used to find the exact ND solutions, and the behaviors of the solutions on the CS are presented. Finally, a conclusion is reached in Section 5.

2. Basic Theory

In this section, some basic theory that is used to study the problem is presented.

Definition 1. *The LFD of* $\Xi(x)$ *with order* ϑ *is defined as* [47]:

$$\frac{d^\vartheta \Xi(x)}{dx^\vartheta}\bigg|x = x_0 = \lim_{x \to x_0} \frac{\Delta^\vartheta[\Xi(x) - \Xi(x_0)]}{(x - x_0)^\vartheta}, \qquad (2)$$

where $\Delta^\vartheta[\Xi(x) - \Xi(x_0)] \cong \Gamma(1 + \vartheta)[\Xi(x) - \Xi(x_0)]$ with Euler's gamma function.

$$\Gamma(1 + \vartheta) =: \int_0^\infty x^{\vartheta - 1} \exp(-x) dx.$$

For the LFD, there is the following rule chain [47]:

$$\frac{d^{k\vartheta} \Xi(x)}{dx^{k\vartheta}} = \underbrace{\frac{d^\vartheta}{dx^\vartheta} \cdots \frac{d^\vartheta}{dx^\vartheta}}_{k \text{ times}} \Xi(x).$$

Definition 2. *The local fractional integral (LFI) of* $\Xi(x)$ *with the fractional order* ϑ $(0 < \vartheta \leq 1)$ *is defined by* [47]:

$$_aI_b^\vartheta \Xi(x) = \frac{1}{\Gamma(1+\vartheta)} \int_a^b \Xi(x)(dx)^\vartheta = \frac{1}{\Gamma(1+\vartheta)} \lim_{\Delta x_k \to 0} \sum_{k=0}^{N-1} \Xi(x_k)(\Delta x_k)^\vartheta \qquad (3)$$

Here, $\Delta x_k = x_{k+1} - x_k$ and $x_0 = a < x_1 < \ldots < x_{N-1} < x_N = b$.

Property 1. *The properties of the LFD are listed as follows* [47]:

(1) $\dfrac{d^\vartheta}{dt^\vartheta}[p(t) \pm q(t)] = \dfrac{d^\vartheta}{dt^\vartheta} p(t) \pm \dfrac{d^\vartheta}{dt^\vartheta} q(t),$ \hfill (4)

(2) $\dfrac{d^\vartheta}{dt^\vartheta}[p(t)q(t)] = q(t)\dfrac{d^\vartheta}{dt^\vartheta} p(t) + p(t)\dfrac{d^\vartheta}{dt^\vartheta} q(t),$ \hfill (5)

(3) $\dfrac{d^\vartheta}{dt^\vartheta}[p(t)/q(t)] = \dfrac{\left[q(t)\dfrac{d^\vartheta}{dt^\vartheta} p(t) - p(t)\dfrac{d^\vartheta}{dt^\vartheta} q(t)\right]}{q(t)^2},$ \hfill (6)

Definition 3. The MLF on the CS with fractional order ϑ is defined as [47]:

$$\text{MI}_\vartheta(\wp^\gamma) = \sum_{\Im=0}^{\infty} \frac{\wp^{\Im\vartheta}}{\Gamma(1+\Im\vartheta)}. \tag{7}$$

Definition 4. Based on the MLF, we can derive four special functions, namely the SE function, the CH function, the SE function, and the CS function, as [47]:

$$\text{SH}_\vartheta\left(\wp^\vartheta\right) = \frac{2}{\text{MI}_\vartheta\left(\wp^\vartheta\right) + \text{MI}_\vartheta\left(-\wp^\vartheta\right)}, \tag{8}$$

$$\text{CH}_\vartheta\left(\wp^\vartheta\right) = \frac{2}{\text{MI}_\vartheta\left(\wp^\vartheta\right) - \text{MI}_\vartheta\left(-\wp^\vartheta\right)}, \tag{9}$$

$$\text{SE}_\vartheta\left(\wp^\vartheta\right) = \frac{2}{\text{MI}_\vartheta\left(i^\vartheta \wp^\vartheta\right) + \text{MI}_\vartheta\left(-i^\vartheta \wp^\vartheta\right)}, \tag{10}$$

$$\text{CS}_\vartheta\left(\wp^\vartheta\right) = \frac{2i^\vartheta}{\text{MI}_\vartheta\left(i^\vartheta \wp^\vartheta\right) - \text{MI}_\vartheta\left(-i^\vartheta \wp^\vartheta\right)}. \tag{11}$$

The behaviors of the four special functions on the CS using $\vartheta = \ln 2 / \ln 3$ are displayed in Figure 1.

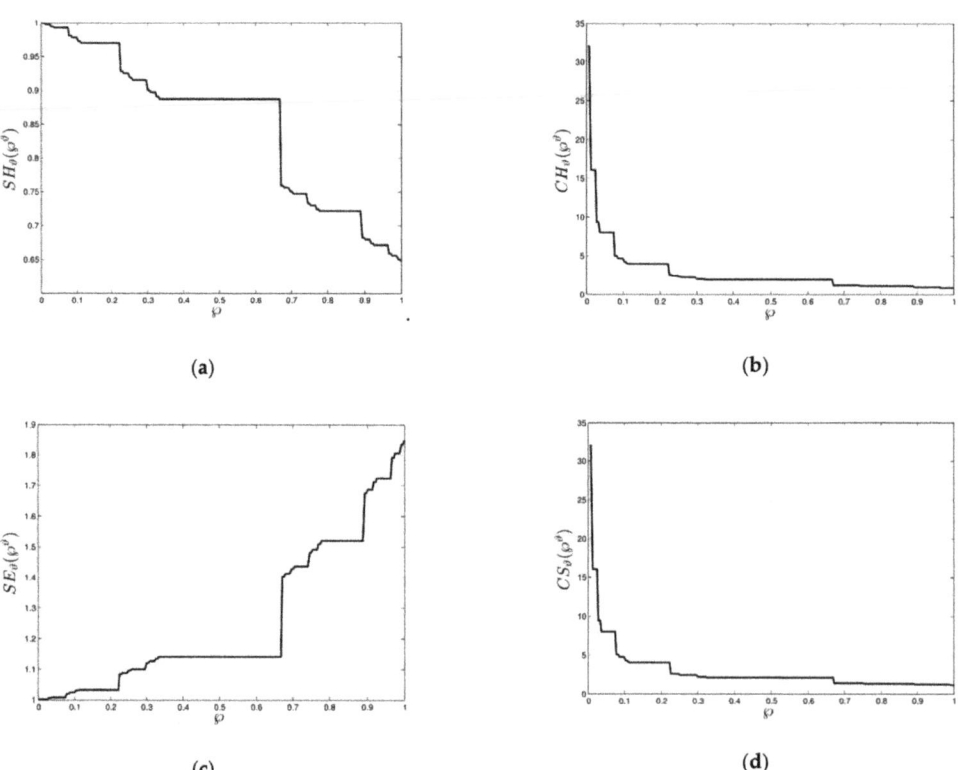

Figure 1. The outline of the special functions on the CS: (**a**) for the SE function, (**b**) for the CH function, (**c**) for the SE function, (**d**) and for the CS function.

Property 2. *The properties of the MLF are given as [47]:*

$$(1) \quad D^{(\vartheta)} \mathrm{MI}_\theta\left(\Delta \xi^\vartheta\right) = \Delta \mathrm{MI}_\theta\left(\xi^\vartheta\right), \tag{12}$$

$$(2) \quad \mathrm{MI}_\theta\left(\xi^\vartheta\right) \mathrm{MI}_\theta\left(\zeta^\vartheta\right) = \mathrm{MI}_\theta\left(\xi^\vartheta + \zeta^\vartheta\right), \tag{13}$$

$$(3) \quad \mathrm{MI}_\theta\left(\xi^\vartheta\right) \mathrm{MI}_\theta\left(-\zeta^\vartheta\right) = \mathrm{MI}_\theta\left(\xi^\vartheta - \zeta^\vartheta\right) \tag{14}$$

$$(4) \quad \mathrm{MI}_\theta\left(\xi^\vartheta\right) \mathrm{MI}_\theta\left(i^\vartheta \zeta^\vartheta\right) = \mathrm{MI}_\theta\left(\xi^\vartheta + i^\vartheta \zeta^\vartheta\right) \tag{15}$$

$$(5) \quad \mathrm{MI}_\theta\left(i^\vartheta \xi^\vartheta\right) \mathrm{MI}_\theta\left(i^\vartheta \zeta^\vartheta\right) = \mathrm{MI}_\theta\left(i^\vartheta \xi^\vartheta + i^\vartheta \zeta^\vartheta\right) \tag{16}$$

3. Construct of the NLFODEs

In the view of Equation (8), we define the following NLFODE [48]:

$$\varphi_\theta\left(\wp^\vartheta\right) = \chi_1 \mathrm{SH}_\theta\left(\chi_2 \wp^\vartheta\right), \tag{17}$$

Taking the LFD of Equation (17), we have:

$$D^{(\vartheta)} \varphi_\theta\left(\wp^\vartheta\right) = D^{(\vartheta)} \left[\chi_1 \mathrm{SH}_\theta\left(\chi_2 \wp^\vartheta\right)\right] = D^{(\vartheta)} \left[\frac{2\chi_1}{\mathrm{MI}_\theta\left(\chi_2 \wp^\vartheta\right) + \mathrm{MI}_\theta\left(-\chi_2 \wp^\vartheta\right)}\right]$$
$$= -\frac{2\chi_1 \chi_2 \left[\mathrm{MI}_\theta\left(\chi_2 \wp^\vartheta\right) - \mathrm{MI}_\theta\left(-\chi_2 \wp^\vartheta\right)\right]}{\left[\mathrm{MI}_\theta\left(\chi_2 \wp^\vartheta\right) + \mathrm{MI}_\theta\left(-\chi_2 \wp^\vartheta\right)\right]^2} \tag{18}$$

which gives:

$$\left[D^{(\vartheta)} \varphi\left(\wp^\vartheta\right)\right]^2$$
$$= \left\{-\frac{2\chi_1 \chi_2 \left[\mathrm{MI}_\theta\left(\chi_2 \wp^\vartheta\right) - \mathrm{MI}_\theta\left(-\chi_2 \wp^\vartheta\right)\right]}{\left[\mathrm{MI}_\theta\left(\chi_2 \wp^\vartheta\right) + \mathrm{MI}_\theta\left(-\chi_2 \wp^\vartheta\right)\right]^2}\right\}^2 = 4\chi_1^2 \chi_2^2 \frac{\left[\mathrm{MI}_\theta\left(2\chi_2 \wp^\vartheta\right) + \mathrm{MI}_\theta\left(-2\chi_2 \wp^\vartheta\right) - 2\right]}{\left[\mathrm{MI}_\theta\left(\chi_2 \wp^\vartheta\right) + \mathrm{MI}_\theta\left(-\chi_2 \wp^\vartheta\right)\right]^4}$$
$$= 4\chi_1^2 \chi_2^2 \frac{\left[\mathrm{MI}_\theta\left(\chi_2 \wp^\vartheta\right) + \mathrm{MI}_\theta\left(-\chi_2 \wp^\vartheta\right)\right]^2 - 4}{\left[\mathrm{MI}_\theta\left(\chi_2 \wp^\vartheta\right) + \mathrm{MI}_\theta\left(-\chi_2 \wp^\vartheta\right)\right]^4} = \chi_1^2 \chi_2^2 \left(\frac{4}{\left[\mathrm{MI}_\theta\left(\chi_2 \wp^\vartheta\right) + \mathrm{MI}_\theta\left(-\chi_2 \wp^\vartheta\right)\right]^2}, -, \frac{16}{\left[\mathrm{MI}_\theta\left(\chi_2 \wp^\vartheta\right) + \mathrm{MI}_\theta\left(-\chi_2 \wp^\vartheta\right)\right]^4}\right) \tag{19}$$
$$= \chi_2^2 \chi_1^2 \left[\mathrm{SH}_\theta^2\left(\wp^\vartheta\right) - \mathrm{SH}_\theta^4\left(\wp^\vartheta\right)\right] = \chi_2^2 \varphi_\theta^2\left(\wp^\vartheta\right) \left[1 - \frac{1}{\chi_1^2} \varphi_\theta^2\left(\wp^\vartheta\right)\right]$$
$$= \chi_2^2 \varphi_\theta^2\left(\wp^\vartheta\right) - \frac{\chi_2^2}{\chi_1^2} \varphi_\theta^4\left(\wp^\vartheta\right)$$

Based on Equation (9), we can construct the following NLFODE [48]:

$$\varphi_\theta\left(\wp^\vartheta\right) = \chi_1 \mathrm{CH}_\theta\left(\chi_2 \wp^\vartheta\right), \tag{20}$$

Taking the LFD of the above equation as:

$$D^{(\vartheta)} \varphi_\theta\left(\wp^\vartheta\right) = D^{(\vartheta)} \left[\chi_1 \mathrm{CH}_\theta\left(\chi_2 \wp^\vartheta\right)\right] = D^{(\vartheta)} \left[\frac{2\chi_1}{\mathrm{MI}_\theta\left(\chi_2 \wp^\vartheta\right) - \mathrm{MI}_\theta\left(-\chi_2 \wp^\vartheta\right)}\right]$$
$$= -\frac{2\chi_1 \chi_2 \left[\mathrm{MI}_\theta\left(\chi_2 \wp^\vartheta\right) + \mathrm{MI}_\theta\left(-\chi_2 \wp^\vartheta\right)\right]}{\left[\mathrm{MI}_\theta\left(\chi_2 \wp^\vartheta\right) - \mathrm{MI}_\theta\left(-\chi_2 \wp^\vartheta\right)\right]^2} \tag{21}$$

Then, we have:

$$\begin{aligned}
&\left[D^{(\vartheta)}\varphi\left(\wp^\vartheta\right)\right]^2 \\
&= \left\{-\frac{2\chi_1\chi_2\left[\mathrm{MI}_\vartheta\left(\chi_2\wp^\vartheta\right)+\mathrm{MI}_\vartheta\left(-\chi_2\wp^\vartheta\right)\right]}{\left[\mathrm{MI}_\vartheta\left(\chi_2\wp^\vartheta\right)-\mathrm{MI}_\vartheta\left(-\chi_2\wp^\vartheta\right)\right]^2}\right\}^2 = 4\chi_1^2\chi_2^2\frac{\left[\mathrm{MI}_\vartheta\left(2\chi_2\wp^\vartheta\right)+\mathrm{MI}_\vartheta\left(-2\chi_2\wp^\vartheta\right)+2\right]}{\left[\mathrm{MI}_\vartheta\left(\chi_2\wp^\vartheta\right)-\mathrm{MI}_\vartheta\left(-\chi_2\wp^\vartheta\right)\right]^4} \\
&= 4\chi_1^2\chi_2^2\frac{\left[\mathrm{MI}_\vartheta\left(\chi_2\wp^\vartheta\right)-\mathrm{MI}_\vartheta\left(-\chi_2\wp^\vartheta\right)\right]^2+4}{\left[\mathrm{MI}_\vartheta\left(\chi_2\wp^\vartheta\right)-\mathrm{MI}_\vartheta\left(-\chi_2\wp^\vartheta\right)\right]^4} = \chi_1^2\chi_2^2\left(\frac{4}{\left[\mathrm{MI}_\vartheta\left(\chi_2\wp^\vartheta\right)-\mathrm{MI}_\vartheta\left(-\chi_2\wp^\vartheta\right)\right]^2}+\frac{16}{\left[\mathrm{MI}_\vartheta\left(\chi_2\wp^\vartheta\right)-\mathrm{MI}_\vartheta\left(-\chi_2\wp^\vartheta\right)\right]^4}\right) \\
&= \chi_2^2\chi_1^2\left[\mathrm{CH}_\vartheta^2\left(\wp^\vartheta\right)+\mathrm{CH}_\vartheta^4\left(\wp^\vartheta\right)\right] \\
&= \chi_2^2\varphi_\vartheta^2\left(\wp^\vartheta\right)+\frac{\chi_2^2}{\chi_1^2}\varphi_\vartheta^4\left(\wp^\vartheta\right)
\end{aligned} \quad (22)$$

We can also consider the following NLFODE [48]:

$$\varphi_\vartheta\left(\wp^\vartheta\right) = \chi_1\mathrm{SE}_\vartheta\left(\chi_2\wp^\vartheta\right), \quad (23)$$

Similarly, its LFD is given by:

$$\begin{aligned}
D^{(\vartheta)}\varphi_\vartheta\left(\wp^\vartheta\right) &= D^{(\vartheta)}\left[\chi_1\mathrm{SE}_\vartheta\left(\chi_2\wp^\vartheta\right)\right] = D^{(\vartheta)}\left[\frac{2\chi_1}{\mathrm{MI}_\vartheta\left(\chi_2 i^\vartheta\wp^\vartheta\right)+\mathrm{MI}_\vartheta\left(-\chi_2 i^\vartheta\wp^\vartheta\right)}\right] \\
&= -\frac{2\chi_1\chi_2\left[i^\vartheta\mathrm{MI}_\vartheta\left(\chi_2 i^\vartheta\wp^\vartheta\right)-i^\vartheta\mathrm{MI}_\vartheta\left(-\chi_2 i^\vartheta\wp^\vartheta\right)\right]}{\left[\mathrm{MI}_\vartheta\left(\chi_2 i^\vartheta\wp^\vartheta\right)+\mathrm{MI}_\vartheta\left(-\chi_2 i^\vartheta\wp^\vartheta\right)\right]^2}
\end{aligned} \quad (24)$$

Such that

$$\begin{aligned}
&\left[D^{(\vartheta)}\varphi_\vartheta\left(\wp^\vartheta\right)\right]^2 \\
&= \left\{-\frac{2\chi_1\chi_2\left[i^\vartheta\mathrm{MI}_\vartheta\left(\chi_2 i^\vartheta\wp^\vartheta\right)-i^\vartheta\mathrm{MI}_\vartheta\left(-\chi_2 i^\vartheta\wp^\vartheta\right)\right]}{\left[\mathrm{MI}_\vartheta\left(\chi_2 i^\vartheta\wp^\vartheta\right)+\mathrm{MI}_\vartheta\left(-\chi_2 i^\vartheta\wp^\vartheta\right)\right]^2}\right\}^2 = -4\chi_1^2\chi_2^2\frac{\left[\mathrm{MI}_\vartheta\left(2\chi_2 i^\vartheta\wp^\vartheta\right)+\mathrm{MI}_\vartheta\left(-2\chi_2 i^\vartheta\wp^\vartheta\right)-2\right]}{\left[\mathrm{MI}_\vartheta\left(\chi_2 i^\vartheta\wp^\vartheta\right)+\mathrm{MI}_\vartheta\left(-\chi_2 i^\vartheta\wp^\vartheta\right)\right]^4} \\
&= -4\chi_1^2\chi_2^2\frac{\left[\mathrm{MI}_\vartheta\left(\chi_2 i^\vartheta\wp^\vartheta\right)+\mathrm{MI}_\vartheta\left(-\chi_2 i^\vartheta\wp^\vartheta\right)\right]^2-4}{\left[\mathrm{MI}_\vartheta\left(\chi_2 i^\vartheta\wp^\vartheta\right)+\mathrm{MI}_\vartheta\left(-\chi_2 i^\vartheta\wp^\vartheta\right)\right]^4} = \chi_1^2\chi_2^2\left(\begin{array}{c}-\frac{4}{\left[\mathrm{MI}_\vartheta\left(\chi_2 i^\vartheta\wp^\vartheta\right)+\mathrm{MI}_\vartheta\left(-\chi_2 i^\vartheta\wp^\vartheta\right)\right]^2} \\ +\frac{16}{\left[\mathrm{MI}_\vartheta\left(\chi_2 i^\vartheta\wp^\vartheta\right)+\mathrm{MI}_\vartheta\left(-\chi_2 i^\vartheta\wp^\vartheta\right)\right]^4}\end{array}\right) \\
&= \chi_1^2\chi_2^2\left[-\mathrm{SE}_\vartheta^2\left(\wp^\vartheta\right)+\mathrm{SE}_\vartheta^4\left(\wp^\vartheta\right)\right] = \chi_2^2\varphi_\vartheta^2\left(\wp^\vartheta\right)\left[-1+\frac{1}{\chi_1^2}\varphi_\vartheta^2\left(\wp^\vartheta\right)\right] \\
&= -\chi_2^2\varphi_\vartheta^2\left(\wp^\vartheta\right)+\frac{\chi_2^2}{\chi_1^2}\varphi_\vartheta^4\left(\wp^\vartheta\right)
\end{aligned} \quad (25)$$

In the light of Equation (11), we construct another NLFODE as [48]:

$$\varphi_\vartheta\left(\wp^\vartheta\right) = \chi_1\mathrm{CS}_\vartheta\left(\chi_2\wp^\vartheta\right), \quad (26)$$

Applying the LFD for Equation (26) as:

$$\begin{aligned}
D^{(\vartheta)}\varphi_\vartheta\left(\wp^\vartheta\right) &= D^{(\vartheta)}\left[\chi_1\mathrm{CS}_\vartheta\left(\chi_2\wp^\vartheta\right)\right] = D^{(\vartheta)}\left[\frac{2\chi_1 i^\vartheta}{\mathrm{MI}_\vartheta\left(\chi_2 i^\vartheta\wp^\vartheta\right)-\mathrm{MI}_\vartheta\left(-\chi_2 i^\vartheta\wp^\vartheta\right)}\right] \\
&= \frac{2\chi_1\chi_2\left[\mathrm{MI}_\vartheta\left(\chi_2 i^\vartheta\wp^\vartheta\right)+\mathrm{MI}_\vartheta\left(-\chi_2 i^\vartheta\wp^\vartheta\right)\right]}{\left[\mathrm{MI}_\vartheta\left(\chi_2 i^\vartheta\wp^\vartheta\right)-\mathrm{MI}_\vartheta\left(-\chi_2 i^\vartheta\wp^\vartheta\right)\right]^2}
\end{aligned} \quad (27)$$

Thus, we have:

$$
\begin{aligned}
&\left[D^{(\vartheta)}\varphi\left(\wp^\vartheta\right)\right]^2 \\
&= \left\{\frac{2\chi_1\chi_2\left[\mathrm{MI}_\vartheta\left(\chi_2 i^\vartheta \wp^\vartheta\right)+\mathrm{MI}_\vartheta\left(-\chi_2 i^\vartheta \wp^\vartheta\right)\right]}{\left[\mathrm{MI}_\vartheta\left(\chi_2 i^\vartheta \wp^\vartheta\right)-\mathrm{MI}_\vartheta\left(-\chi_2 i^\vartheta \wp^\vartheta\right)\right]^2}\right\}^2 = 4\chi_1^2\chi_2^2\frac{\left[\mathrm{MI}_\vartheta\left(2\chi_2 i^\vartheta \wp^\vartheta\right)+\mathrm{MI}_\vartheta\left(-2\chi_2 i^\vartheta \wp^\vartheta\right)+2\right]}{\left[\mathrm{MI}_\vartheta\left(\chi_2 i^\vartheta \wp^\vartheta\right)-\mathrm{MI}_\vartheta\left(-\chi_2 i^\vartheta \wp^\vartheta\right)\right]^4} \\
&= 4\chi_1^2\chi_2^2\frac{\left[\mathrm{MI}_\vartheta\left(\chi_2 i^\vartheta \wp^\vartheta\right)-\mathrm{MI}_\vartheta\left(-\chi_2 i^\vartheta \wp^\vartheta\right)\right]^2+4}{\left[\mathrm{MI}_\vartheta\left(\chi_2 i^\vartheta \wp^\vartheta\right)-\mathrm{MI}_\vartheta\left(-\chi_2 i^\vartheta \wp^\vartheta\right)\right]^4} = \chi_1^2\chi_2^2\left(\frac{-4}{\left[\mathrm{MI}_\vartheta\left(\chi_2 i^\vartheta \wp^\vartheta\right)-\mathrm{MI}_\vartheta\left(-\chi_2 i^\vartheta \wp^\vartheta\right)\right]^2}+\frac{16}{\left[\mathrm{MI}_\vartheta\left(\chi_2 i^\vartheta \wp^\vartheta\right)-\mathrm{MI}_\vartheta\left(-\chi_2 i^\vartheta \wp^\vartheta\right)\right]^4}\right) \quad (28) \\
&= \chi_1^2\chi_2^2\left[-\mathrm{CS}_\vartheta^2(\wp^\vartheta)+\mathrm{CS}_\vartheta^4(\wp^\vartheta)\right] = \chi_2^2\varphi_\vartheta^2(\wp^\vartheta)\left[-1+\frac{1}{\chi_1^2}\varphi_\vartheta^2(\wp^\vartheta)\right] \\
&= -\chi_2^2\varphi_\vartheta^2(\wp^\vartheta)+\frac{\chi_2^2}{\chi_1^2}\varphi_\vartheta^4(\wp^\vartheta)
\end{aligned}
$$

From Equations (19), (22), (25), and (28), we can conclude the general NLFODE as the following form by introducing two parameters p and q:

$$\left[D^{(\vartheta)}\varphi_\vartheta\left(\wp^\vartheta\right)\right]^2 = p\chi_2^2\varphi_\vartheta^2\left(\wp^\vartheta\right)+q\frac{\chi_2^2}{\chi_1^2}\varphi_\vartheta^4\left(\wp^\vartheta\right), \quad (29)$$

Obviously, its exact ND solutions are given as:

$$\varphi_\vartheta\left(\wp^\vartheta\right) = \begin{cases} \chi_1\mathrm{SH}_\vartheta(\chi_2\wp^\vartheta), & \text{for } p=1, q=-1 \\ \chi_1\mathrm{CH}_\vartheta(\chi_2\wp^\vartheta), & \text{for } p=1, q=1 \\ \chi_1\mathrm{SE}_\vartheta(\chi_2\wp^\vartheta), & \text{for } p=-1, q=1 \\ \chi_1\mathrm{CS}_\vartheta(\chi_2\wp^\vartheta), & \text{for } p=-1, q=1 \end{cases}. \quad (30)$$

4. Yang's Special Function Method

In this section, Yang's special function method will be adopted to search for the exact ND solutions. For this goal, the following ND transformation is considered [49–51]:

$$\aleph_\vartheta\left(x^\vartheta, t^\vartheta\right) = \aleph_\vartheta\left(\wp^\vartheta\right), \quad \wp^\vartheta = \rho^\vartheta x^\vartheta - \omega^\vartheta t^\vartheta, \quad (31)$$

Additionally, there is:

$$\lim_{\vartheta\to 1}\wp^\vartheta = \rho x - \omega t, \quad (32)$$

Putting Equation (31) into Equation (1) gives:

$$\frac{\partial^\vartheta \aleph}{\partial t^\vartheta} = -\omega^\vartheta\frac{d^\vartheta \aleph}{d\wp^\vartheta}, \quad (33)$$

$$\frac{\partial^\vartheta \aleph_\vartheta}{\partial x^\vartheta} = \rho^\vartheta\frac{d^\vartheta \aleph_\vartheta}{d\wp^\vartheta}, \quad (34)$$

$$\frac{\partial^{2\vartheta}}{x^{2\vartheta}}\left(\frac{\partial^\vartheta \aleph_\vartheta}{\partial t^\vartheta}\right) = -\rho^{2\vartheta}\omega^\vartheta\frac{d^{3\vartheta}\aleph_\vartheta}{d\zeta^{3\vartheta}}, \quad (35)$$

Taking them into Equation (1) yields:

$$\left(\rho^\vartheta - \omega^\vartheta\right)\frac{d^\vartheta \aleph}{d\wp^\vartheta} + k\rho^\vartheta \aleph^2\frac{d^\vartheta \aleph}{d\wp^\vartheta} - \rho^{2\vartheta}\omega^\gamma\frac{d^{3\vartheta}\aleph}{d\wp^{3\vartheta}} = 0, \quad (36)$$

where $\rho^\vartheta - \omega^\vartheta \neq 0$.

Applying the LFI to Equation (36) and ignoring the integral constant yields:

$$\left(\rho^\vartheta - \omega^\vartheta\right)\aleph_\vartheta + \frac{1}{3}k\rho^\vartheta \aleph_\vartheta^3 - \rho^{2\vartheta}\omega^\gamma\frac{d^{2\vartheta}\aleph_\vartheta}{d\wp^{2\vartheta}} = 0, \quad (37)$$

By multiplying both sides of above equation by $\frac{d^\vartheta \aleph_\vartheta}{d\wp^\vartheta}$, we have:

$$\left(\rho^\vartheta - \omega^\vartheta\right)\aleph_\vartheta \frac{d^\vartheta \aleph_\vartheta}{d\wp^\vartheta} + \frac{1}{3}k\rho^\vartheta \aleph_\vartheta^3 \frac{d^\vartheta \aleph_\vartheta}{d\wp^\vartheta} - \rho^{2\vartheta}\omega^\gamma \frac{d^{2\vartheta}\aleph_\vartheta}{d\wp^{2\vartheta}} \frac{d^\vartheta \aleph_\vartheta}{d\wp^\vartheta} = 0, \tag{38}$$

Taking the LFI of the above equation leads to:

$$\frac{1}{2}\left(\rho^\vartheta - \omega^\vartheta\right)\aleph_\vartheta^2 + \frac{1}{12}k\rho^\vartheta \aleph_\vartheta^4 - \frac{1}{2}\rho^{2\vartheta}\omega^\gamma \left(\frac{d^\vartheta \aleph_\vartheta}{d\wp^\vartheta}\right)^2 = \Delta, \tag{39}$$

Here, Δ is the integral constant. Letting Δ to be zero, we have:

$$\frac{1}{2}\left(\rho^\vartheta - \omega^\vartheta\right)\aleph_\vartheta^2 + \frac{1}{12}k\rho^\vartheta \aleph_\vartheta^4 - \frac{1}{2}\rho^{2\vartheta}\omega^\gamma \left(\frac{d^\vartheta \aleph_\vartheta}{d\wp^\vartheta}\right)^2 = 0. \tag{40}$$

Such that:

$$\left(\frac{d^\vartheta \aleph_\vartheta}{d\wp^\vartheta}\right)^2 = \frac{\rho^\vartheta - \omega^\vartheta}{\rho^{2\vartheta}\omega^\vartheta}\aleph_\vartheta^2 + \frac{k}{6\rho^\vartheta \omega^\vartheta}\aleph_\vartheta^4. \tag{41}$$

By comparing Equation (41) and Equation (29), we have:
Set 1: For $p = 1$, $q = -1$, there is:

$$\frac{\rho^\vartheta - \omega^\vartheta}{\rho^{2\vartheta}\omega^\vartheta} = \chi_2^2, \tag{42}$$

$$\frac{k}{6\rho^\vartheta \omega^\vartheta} = -\frac{\chi_2^2}{\chi_1^2}, \tag{43}$$

According to Equations (42) and (43), we have:

$$\chi_1 = \sqrt{\frac{6(\omega^\vartheta - \rho^\vartheta)}{k\rho^\vartheta}}, \quad \chi_2 = \sqrt{\frac{\rho^\vartheta - \omega^\vartheta}{\rho^{2\vartheta}\omega^\vartheta}}, \tag{44}$$

Thus, we can obtain the exact solution of Equation (1) as:

$$\aleph_\vartheta(x,t) = \sqrt{\frac{6(\omega^\vartheta - \rho^\vartheta)}{k\rho^\vartheta}}\,\mathrm{SH}_\vartheta\left(\sqrt{\frac{\rho^\vartheta - \omega^\vartheta}{\rho^{2\vartheta}\omega^\vartheta}}\left(\rho^\vartheta x^\vartheta - \omega^\vartheta t^\vartheta\right)\right). \tag{45}$$

For $\omega^\vartheta = 1$, $\rho^\vartheta = 2$, $k = -1$, we display the profile of the exact ND solution given by Equation (45) on the CS in Figure 2. Here, the t and x are both selected on the CS range 0 to 1, and the fractional order is used as $\vartheta = \ln 2/\ln 3$. It can be found that the value of the solution is between 1 and 1.8. In addition, the figure is the blocky structure which conforms to the CS characteristics.

Set 2: For $p = 1$, $q = 1$, there is:

$$\frac{\rho^\vartheta - \omega^\vartheta}{\rho^{2\vartheta}\omega^\vartheta} = \chi_2^2, \tag{46}$$

$$\frac{k}{6\rho^\vartheta \omega^\vartheta} = \frac{\chi_2^2}{\chi_1^2}, \tag{47}$$

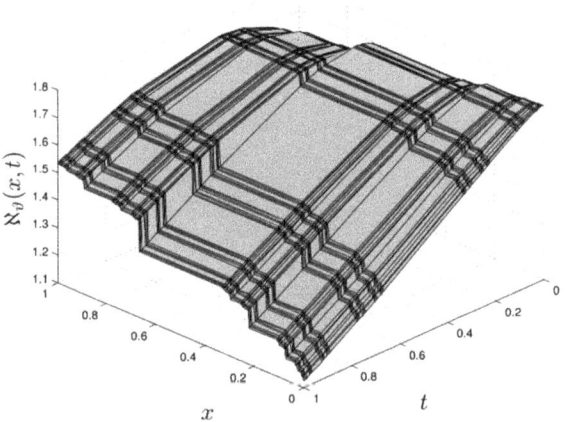

Figure 2. The profile of Equation (45) on CS with $\omega^\vartheta = 1$, $\rho^\vartheta = 2$, and $k = -1$ for $\vartheta = \ln 2/\ln 3$.

We have:
$$\chi_1 = \sqrt{\frac{6(\rho^\vartheta - \omega^\vartheta)}{k\rho^\vartheta}}, \quad \chi_2 = \sqrt{\frac{\rho^\vartheta - \omega^\vartheta}{\rho^{2\vartheta}\omega^\vartheta}}, \tag{48}$$

Then, the second exact ND solution of Equation (1) is attained as:

$$\aleph_\vartheta(x,t) = \sqrt{\frac{6(\rho^\vartheta - \omega^\vartheta)}{k\rho^\vartheta}} \mathrm{CH}_\vartheta\left(\sqrt{\frac{\rho^\vartheta - \omega^\vartheta}{\rho^{2\vartheta}\omega^\vartheta}}\left(\rho^\vartheta x^\vartheta - \omega^\vartheta t^\vartheta\right)\right). \tag{49}$$

For using $\omega^\vartheta = 1$, $\rho^\vartheta = 2$, $k = 1$, we display the solution Equation (49) on the CS for $\vartheta = \ln 2/\ln 3$ in Figure 3. The values of t and x are all selected on the CS from 0 to 1. It can be found that the profile of Equation (49) is the blocky structure, and when the coordinate (x, t) is close to $(0, 0)$, the value of the solution increases rapidly.

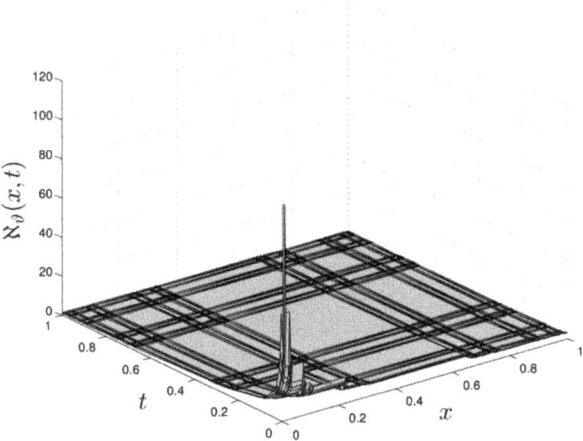

Figure 3. The profile of Equation (49) on CS with $\omega^\vartheta = 1$, $\rho^\vartheta = 2$, $k = 1$ for $\vartheta = \ln 2/\ln 3$.

Set 3: For $p = -1, q = 1$, there is:

$$\frac{\rho^\vartheta - \omega^\vartheta}{\rho^{2\vartheta}\omega^\vartheta} = -\chi_2^2, \tag{50}$$

$$\frac{k}{6\rho^\vartheta \omega^\vartheta} = \frac{\chi_2^2}{\chi_1^2}, \tag{51}$$

There is:

$$\chi_1 = \sqrt{\frac{6(\omega^\vartheta - \rho^\vartheta)}{k\rho^\vartheta}}, \quad \chi_2 = \sqrt{\frac{\omega^\vartheta - \rho^\vartheta}{\rho^{2\vartheta}\omega^\vartheta}}, \tag{52}$$

Correspondingly, we can find the exact ND solutions of Equation (1) as:

$$\aleph_\vartheta(x,t) = \sqrt{\frac{6(\omega^\vartheta - \rho^\vartheta)}{k\rho^\vartheta}} \mathrm{SE}_\vartheta \left(\sqrt{\frac{\omega^\vartheta - \rho^\vartheta}{\rho^{2\vartheta}\omega^\vartheta}} \left(\rho^\vartheta x^\vartheta - \omega^\vartheta t^\vartheta\right) \right), \tag{53}$$

By choosing the parameters as $\omega^\vartheta = 2$, $\rho^\vartheta = 1$, $k = 1$, we display the outline of Equation (53) on CS for $\vartheta = \ln 2/\ln 3$ in Figure 4. Here, the outline of the solution is also the blocky structure which corresponds to the characteristics of the CS. Additionally, the value of the solution increases rapidly when (x, t) is close to (1, 0).

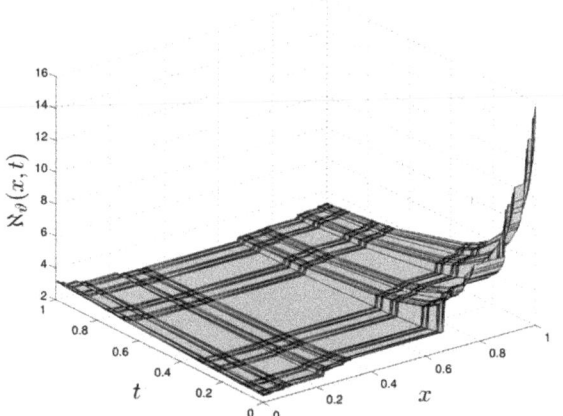

Figure 4. The profile of Equation (53) on CS with $\omega^\vartheta = 2$, $\rho^\vartheta = 1$, $k = 1$ for $\vartheta = \ln 2/\ln 3$.

Set 4: For $p = -1, q = 1$, there is:

$$\frac{\rho^\vartheta - \omega^\vartheta}{\rho^{2\vartheta}\omega^\vartheta} = -\chi_2^2, \tag{54}$$

$$\frac{k}{6\rho^\vartheta \omega^\vartheta} = \frac{\chi_2^2}{\chi_1^2}, \tag{55}$$

There is:

$$\chi_1 = \sqrt{\frac{6(\omega^\vartheta - \rho^\vartheta)}{k\rho^\vartheta}}, \quad \chi_2 = \sqrt{\frac{\omega^\vartheta - \rho^\vartheta}{\rho^{2\vartheta}\omega^\vartheta}}, \tag{56}$$

Correspondingly, we can find the exact ND solutions of Equation (1) as:

$$\aleph_\vartheta(x,t) = \sqrt{\frac{6(\omega^\vartheta - \rho^\vartheta)}{k\rho^\vartheta}} \text{CS}_\vartheta\left(\sqrt{\frac{\omega^\vartheta - \rho^\vartheta}{\rho^{2\vartheta}\omega^\vartheta}}\left(\rho^\vartheta x^\vartheta - \omega^\vartheta t^\vartheta\right)\right). \tag{57}$$

For using $\omega^\vartheta = -1$, $\rho^\vartheta = 1$, $k = -1$, we display the profile of the Equation (57) solution on the CS with $\vartheta = \ln 2/\ln 3$ in Figure 5. Similar to Equation (49), the blocky structure increases rapidly when (x, t) is close to $(0, 0)$.

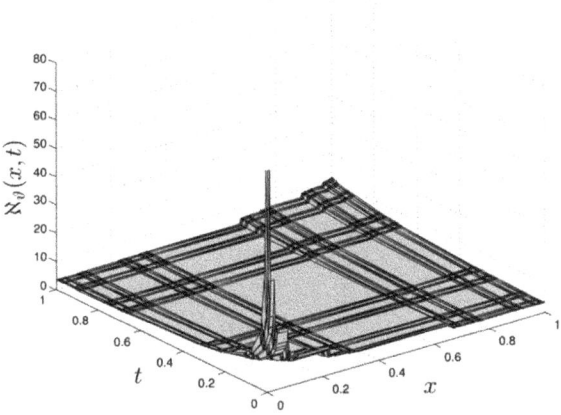

Figure 5. The profile of Equation (57) on CS with $\omega^\vartheta = -1$, $\rho^\vartheta = 1$, $k = -1$ for $\vartheta = \ln 2/\ln 3$.

It should be noted that the correctness of the exact obtained ND solutions provided by Equations (45), (49), (53), and (57) are verified by substituting them into Equation (41).

5. Conclusions

This paper proposes a new local fractional modified Benjamin–Bona–Mahony equation based on the local fractional derivative. A group of nonlinear local fractional ordinary differential equations is constructed by defining some elementary functions via the Mittag–Leffler function on the Cantor set. A simple and effective approach, called Yang's special function method, is suggested for the first time to solve this problem. By using this method, we can obtain four different exact solutions in just one step. Furthermore, the obtained solutions on the Cantor set are outlined in the form of a 3-D plot. It is revealed that the one-step method is effective and can be utilized to study the other local fractional PDEs.

Author Contributions: Conceptualization, K.-J.W.; methodology, K.-J.W.; writing—original draft preparation, K.-J.W.; software, F.S.; validation, F.S. All authors have read and agreed to the published version of the manuscript.

Funding: This work is supported by the Key Programs of Universities in Henan Province of China (22A140006), the Fundamental Research Funds for the Universities of Henan Province (NSFRF210324), the Program of Henan Polytechnic University (B2018-40), and the Innovative Scientists and Technicians Team of Henan Provincial High Education (21IRTSTHN016).

Data Availability Statement: The data that support the findings of this study are available from the corresponding author upon reasonable request.

Conflicts of Interest: The authors declare no conflict of interest.

References

1. Biswas, A.; Milovic, D.; Koh, R. Optical soliton perturbation in a log-law medium with full nonlinearity by He's semi-inverse variational principle. *Inverse Probl. Sci. Eng.* **2021**, *20*, 227–232. [CrossRef]
2. Wang, K.J.; Liu, J.-H. Diverse optical soliton solutions to the Kundu-Mukherjee-Naskar equation via two novel techniques. *Optik* **2023**, *273*, 170403. [CrossRef]
3. Muniyappan, A.; Sahasraari, L.N.; Anitha, S.; Ilakiya, S.; Biswas, A.; Yıldırım, Y.; Triki, H.; Alshehri, H.M.; Belic, M.R. Family of optical solitons for perturbed Fokas–Lenells equation. *Optik* **2022**, *249*, 168224. [CrossRef]
4. Wang, K.J. Diverse soliton solutions to the Fokas system via the Cole-Hopf transformation. *Optik* **2023**, *272*, 170250. [CrossRef]
5. Lü, X.; Chen, S.-J. New general interaction solutions to the KPI equation via an optional decoupling condition approach. *Commun. Nonlinear Sci. Numer. Simul.* **2021**, *103*, 105939. [CrossRef]
6. Qie, N.; Houa, W.F.; He, J.H. The fastest insight into the large amplitude vibration of a string. *Rep. Mech. Eng.* **2021**, *2*, 1–5. [CrossRef]
7. He, C.H.; Tian, D.; Salman, H.F.; Zekry, M.H. Hybrid Rayleigh-Van der Pol-Duffing Oscillator (HRVD): Stability Analysis and Controller. *J. Low Freq. Noise Vib. Act. Control.* **2022**, *41*, 244–268. [CrossRef]
8. Guo, A.; Ding, X.; Zhong, F.; Cheng, Q.; Huang, C. Predicting the future chinese population using shared socioeconomic pathways, the sixth national population census, and a PDE model. *Sustainability* **2019**, *11*, 3686. [CrossRef]
9. Sohail, M.; Naz, R.; Shah, Z.; Kumam, P.; Thounthong, P. Exploration of temperature dependent thermophysical characteristics of yield exhibiting non-Newtonian fluid flow under gyrotactic microorganisms. *AIP Adv.* **2019**, *9*, 125016. [CrossRef]
10. Abdelsalam, S.I.; Sohail, M. Numerical approach of variable thermophysical features of dissipated viscous nanofluid comprising gyrotactic micro-organisms. *Pramana* **2020**, *94*, 1–12. [CrossRef]
11. Dashraath, P.; Wong, J.L.; Lim, M.X.; Lim, L.M.; Li, S.; Biswas, A.; Choolani, M.; Mattar, C.; Su, L.L. Coronavirus disease 2019 (COVID-19) pandemic and pregnancy. *Am. J. Obstet. Gynecol.* **2020**, *222*, 521–531. [CrossRef]
12. Wang, K.J. Variational principle and diverse wave structures of the modified Benjamin-Bona-Mahony equation arising in the optical illusions field. *Axioms* **2022**, *11*, 445. [CrossRef]
13. Singh, A.P.; Biswas, A.; Shukla, A.; Maiti, P. Targeted therapy in chronic diseases using nanomaterial-based drug delivery vehicles. *Signal Transduct. Target. Ther.* **2019**, *4*, 1–21. [CrossRef]
14. Liu, J.-G.; Yang, X.-J.; Geng, L.-L.; Yu, X.-J. On fractional symmetry group scheme to the higher dimensional space and time fractional dissipative Burgers equation. *Int. J. Geom. Methods Mod. Phys.* **2022**, *19*, 2250173. [CrossRef]
15. Wang, K.J. Bäcklund transformation and diverse exact explicit solutions of the fractal combined KdV-mKdV equation. *Fractals* **2022**, *30*, 2250189. [CrossRef]
16. Muhammad, S.; Mohyud-Din, S.T. Reduced differential transform method for time-fractional heat equations. *Int. J. Mark. Trade Policy* **2012**, *1*, 13–22.
17. Wang, K.L. New perspective to the fractal Konopelchenko-Dubrovsky equations with M-truncated fractional derivative. *Int. J. Geom. Methods Mod. Phys.* **2023**, *2023*, 2350072. [CrossRef]
18. Xiao, B.; Huang, Q.; Chen, H.; Chen, X.; Long, G. A fractal model for capillary flow through a single tortuous capillary with roughened surfaces in fibrous porous media. *Fractals* **2021**, *29*, 2150017. [CrossRef]
19. Baleanu, D.; Abadi, M.H.; Jajarmi, A.; Vahid, K.Z.; Nieto, J.J. A new comparative study on the general fractional model of COVID-19 with isolation and quarantine effects. *Alex. Eng. J.* **2022**, *61*, 4779–4791. [CrossRef]
20. Zhang, Y.; Yu, X.; Sun, H.; Tick, G.R.; Wei, W.; Jin, B. Applicability of time fractional derivative models for simulating the dynamics and mitigation scenarios of COVID-19. *Chaos Solitons Fractals* **2020**, *138*, 109959. [CrossRef]
21. Ghanbari, B.; Kumar, S.; Kumar, R. A study of behaviour for immune and tumor cells in immunogenetic tumour model with non-singular fractional derivative. *Chaos Solitons Fractals* **2020**, *133*, 109619. [CrossRef]
22. He, J.H. A simple approach to one-dimensional convection-diffusion equation and its fractional modification for E reaction arising in rotating disk electrodes. *J. Electroanal. Chem.* **2019**, *854*, 113565. [CrossRef]
23. Singh, H.; Srivastava, H.M. Numerical simulation for fractional-order Bloch equation arising in nuclear magnetic resonance by using the Jacobi polynomials. *Appl. Sci.* **2020**, *10*, 2850. [CrossRef]
24. Kumar, S.; Kumar, A.; Momani, S.; Aldhaifallah, M.; Nisar, K.S. Numerical solutions of nonlinear fractional model arising in the appearance of the strip patterns in two-dimensional systems. *Adv. Differ. Equ.* **2019**, *2019*, 1–19. [CrossRef]
25. Patnaik, S.; Sidhardh, S.; Semperlotti, F. Towards a unified approach to nonlocal elasticity via fractional-order mechanics. *Int. J. Mech. Sci.* **2021**, *189*, 105992. [CrossRef]
26. Wang, G.; Liu, Y.; Wu, Y.; Su, X. Symmetry analysis for a seventh-order generalized KdV equation and its fractional version in fluid mechanics. *Fractals* **2020**, *28*, 2050044. [CrossRef]
27. Raja, M.A.; Manzar, M.A.; Shah, S.M.; Chen, Y. Integrated intelligence of fractional neural networks and sequential quadratic programming for Bagley-Torvik systems arising in fluid mechanics. *J. Comput. Nonlinear Dyn.* **2020**, *15*, 051003. [CrossRef]
28. Kiani-B, A.; Fallahi, K.; Pariz, N.; Leung, H. A chaotic secure communication scheme using fractional chaotic systems based on an extended fractional Kalman filter. *Commun. Nonlinear Sci. Numer. Simul.* **2009**, *14*, 863–879. [CrossRef]

29. Tian, X.; Sun, X.; Yu, X.; Li, X. Modulation pattern recognition of communication signals based on fractional low-order Choi-Williams distribution and convolutional neural network in impulsive noise environment. In Proceedings of the 2019 IEEE 19th International Conference on Communication Technology (ICCT), Xi'an, China, 16–19 October 2019; IEEE: New York, NY, USA, 2019; pp. 188–192.
30. Kalikulov, N.; Zhussip, D.; Zhexenov, N.; Kizilirmak, R.C. Multipath diversity for OFDM based visible light communication systems Through fractional sampling. *Wirel. Pers. Commun.* **2020**, *112*, 2715–2724. [CrossRef]
31. Dimitrov, D.; Abdo, H. Tight independent set neighborhood union condition for fractional critical deleted graphs and ID deleted graphs. *Discret. Contin. Dyn. Syst. S* **2019**, *12*, 711. [CrossRef]
32. Xiao, B.; Wang, W.; Zhang, X.; Long, G.; Fan, J.; Chen, H.; Deng, L. A novel fractal solution for permeability and Kozeny-Carman constant of fibrous porous media made up of solid particles and porous fibers. *Powder Technol.* **2019**, *349*, 92–98. [CrossRef]
33. Stojiljković, V.; Ramaswamy, R.; Abdelnaby, O.A.A.; Radenović, S. Some Novel Inequalities for LR-(k,h-m)-p Convex Interval Valued Functions by Means of Pseudo Order Relation. *Fractal Fract.* **2022**, *6*, 726. [CrossRef]
34. Singh, J.; Ahmadian, A.; Rathore, S.; Kumar, D.; Baleanu, D.; Salimi, M.; Salahshour, S. An efficient computational approach for local fractional Poisson equation in fractal media. *Numer. Methods Part. Differ. Equ.* **2021**, *37*, 1439–1448. [CrossRef]
35. Singh, J.; Jassim, H.K.; Kumar, D. An efficient computational technique for local fractional Fokker Planck equation. *Phys. A: Stat. Mech. Its Appl.* **2020**, *555*, 124525. [CrossRef]
36. Yang, X.J.; Gao, F.; Srivastava, H.M. A new computational approach for solving nonlinear local fractional PDEs. *J. Comput. Appl. Math.* **2018**, *339*, 285–296. [CrossRef]
37. Ziane, D.; Baleanu, D.; Belghaba, K.; Cherif, M.H. Local fractional Sumudu decomposition method for linear partial differential equations with local fractional derivative. *J. King Saud Univ. Sci.* **2019**, *31*, 83–88. [CrossRef]
38. Wang, K.J.; Si, J. On the non-differentiable exact solutions of the (2+1)-dimensional local fractional breaking soliton equation on Cantor sets. *Math. Methods Appl. Sci.* **2023**, *46*, 1456–1465. [CrossRef]
39. Yang, X.J.; Baleanu, D. Fractal heat conduction problem solved by local fractional variation iteration method. *Therm. Sci.* **2013**, *17*, 625–628. [CrossRef]
40. Wang, K.J. Investigation to the local fractional Fokas system on Cantor set by a novel technology. *Fractals* **2022**, *30*, 2250112. [CrossRef]
41. Yang, Y.J.; Baleanu, D.; Yang, X.J. Analysis of fractal wave equations by local fractional Fourier series method. *Adv. Math. Phys.* **2013**, *2013*, 632309. [CrossRef]
42. Wang, K.L. A novel perspective to the local fractional bidirectional wave model on Cantor sets. *Fractals* **2022**, *30*, 2250107. [CrossRef]
43. Wang, K.L. A novel perspective to the local fractional Zakharov-Kuznetsov-modified equal width dynamical model on Cantor sets. *Math. Methods Appl. Sci.* **2022**, *46*, 622–630. [CrossRef]
44. Dubey, V.P.; Singh, J.; Alshehri, A.M.; Dubey, S.; Kumar, D. A comparative analysis of two computational schemes for solving local fractional Laplace equations. *Math. Methods Appl. Sci.* **2021**, *44*, 13540–13559. [CrossRef]
45. Su, W.H.; Yang, X.J.; Jafari, H.; Baleanu, D. Fractional complex transform method for wave equations on Cantor sets within local fractional differential operator. *Adv. Differ. Equ.* **2013**, *2013*, 1–8. [CrossRef]
46. Sang, X.; Zhang, Z.; Yang, H.; Han, X. Exact Traveling Wave Solutions of the Local Fractional Bidirectional Propagation System Equations. *Fractal Fract.* **2022**, *6*, 653. [CrossRef]
47. Yang, X.J.; Baleanu, D.; Srivastava, H.M. *Local Fractional Integral Transforms and Their Applications*; Academic Press: Cambridge, MA, USA, 2015.
48. Yang, X.J.; Gao, F.; Srivastava, H.M. Non-differentiable exact solutions for the nonlinear ODEs defined on fractal sets. *Fractals* **2017**, *25*, 1740002. [CrossRef]
49. Ghanbari, B. Abundant exact solutions to a generalized nonlinear Schrödinger equation with local fractional derivative. *Math. Methods Appl. Sci.* **2021**, *44*, 8759–8774. [CrossRef]
50. Yang, X.J.; Gasimov, Y.S.; Gao, F.; Allahverdiyeva, N. Travelling-wave solutions for Klein-Gordon and Helmholtz equations on cantor sets. *Proc. Inst. Math. Mechanics.* **2017**, *43*, 123–131.
51. Ghanbari, B. On novel nondifferentiable exact solutions to local fractional Gardner's equation using an effective technique. *Math. Methods Appl. Sci.* **2021**, *44*, 4673–4685. [CrossRef]

Disclaimer/Publisher's Note: The statements, opinions and data contained in all publications are solely those of the individual author(s) and contributor(s) and not of MDPI and/or the editor(s). MDPI and/or the editor(s) disclaim responsibility for any injury to people or property resulting from any ideas, methods, instructions or products referred to in the content.

MDPI
St. Alban-Anlage 66
4052 Basel
Switzerland
www.mdpi.com

Fractal and Fractional Editorial Office
E-mail: fractalfract@mdpi.com
www.mdpi.com/journal/fractalfract

Disclaimer/Publisher's Note: The statements, opinions and data contained in all publications are solely those of the individual author(s) and contributor(s) and not of MDPI and/or the editor(s). MDPI and/or the editor(s) disclaim responsibility for any injury to people or property resulting from any ideas, methods, instructions or products referred to in the content.

www.ingramcontent.com/pod-product-compliance
Lightning Source LLC
LaVergne TN
LVHW070405100526
838202LV00014B/1398